# Mapping Human Rights and Subalterns in Modern India

ISBN: 978-93-5128-151-1

Price: ₹ 990

*Published by*

Kalpaz Publications
C-30, Satyawati Nagar,
Delhi – 110052
E-mail: kalpaz@hotmail.com
Ph.: 9212142040
*Printed at:* G. Print Process, Delhi

**Cataloging in Publication Data—DK**
Courtesy: D.K. Agencies (P) Ltd. <docinfo@dkagencies.com>

**Mapping human rights and subalterns in modern India /**
Jagannatham Begari.
pages cm
Includes bibliographical references.
ISBN 9789351281511

1. Human rights—India. 2. Dalits—Civil rights—India. 3. People with social disabilities—Civil rights—India. I. Begari, Jagannatham, editor.

DDC 323.0954 23

# Mapping Human Rights and Subalterns in Modern India

Jagannatham Begari

KALPAZ

*Dedicate to*
*Medhansh and Saniksha*

# Contents

*Foreword* ... 9
*Preface and Acknowledgements* ... 13
*List of Contributors* ... 15
*Introduction and Theoretical Framework* ... 17

1. Dr Ambedkar and the Future of Indian Democracy ... 39
   —*Jean Dreze*

2. Globalisation, the State and Dalits ... 47
   —*Anand Teltumbde*

3. The Politics of Human Rights in India ... 89
   —*Ajay Gudavarty*

4. Language Rights: Implementing Worldwide Language Rights and Promoting Social Justice ... 105
   —*Tania Hossain*

5. 'We are not what we were': The Nicobarese Socio-cultural Milieu Post the Tsunami, 2004 ... 117
   —*Ajay Saini*

6. Gender and Educational Policy: A study of dropout girls from rural Andhra Pradesh and Telangana state ... 133
   —*Nagaraju Gundimeda*

7. Right to Language in the context of Globalisation and Democracy ... 155
   —*Dr Avinash Pandey*

8. Dalit fiction and the Urban Problematic: Reading Manu Joseph's 'Serious Men' ... 167
   —*Abhishek Das*

9. Dalit Movement in Gujarat: Response of the Society and the State- An Overview ... 175
   —*Rajesh Lakum and Jagannatham Begari*

10. Globalised Rights and Localised Violations: The Case of Palamur Labour in Telangana ........ 205
*—Dr Venkatesh Nayak*

11. Development for Whom? Displacing People, Destroying Identity and Suppressing the Voices of the Tribals: A Human Rights Perspective ........ 225
*—Sheikh RafiqUllah*

12. Understanding Humiliation from Double Victimisation Perspective: A Case Study of a Female Divorcee ........ 239
*—Bijaya Kumar Mohanty*

13. Women and Right to Food: A Special Focus on the Tribal Belt of Odisha ........ 249
*—Rajadarshini Patra*

14. Caste and Class: Trends and Challenges for 'Dalits' with in the compass of Indian Writing ........ 259
*—Patel Heena L and Yogesh N Vansiya*

15. Trajectory of Tribal Life: Cases of Missing Human Rights ........ 271
*—Deba Ranjan Hota*

16. Unveiling the Plight of Domestic Workers in Delhi: A Hidden Workforce ........ 279
*—Vibha Singh*

17. Political Economy of Tribal Development in Madhya Pradesh: The Case of Korku Tribe ........ 287
*—Janmejaya Mishra*

*Index* ........ 297

# Foreword

Human Rights is both an area of academic enquiry and an everyday life activity. This is one domain where there is convergence of knowledge and action. It is this convergence where theory or concepts guide human actions and in turn it is these actions which define and redefine the concepts and the theoretical constructs. Since it is a dynamic process that is in constant motion, any meaningful debate is rendered relevant to the academic for enriching the concepts and to the activists for creative involvement in the emancipatory project. It is the direct social relevance of the discourse that does complicate the human rights concepts and practices for a simple reason that in a conflict ridden hierarchical society action cannot be unilinear. Every act of human rights produces multiple reactions, disadvantaged groups extending support and the privileged opposing the actions. This tension extends or engulfs even the academic enquiry.

Human Rights essentially deal with the project of freedom, that all human rights activities implicitly or explicitly attempt to enlarge the boundaries of freedom. In the process they confront institutionalized power which tends to be assymmetrical. In a way power defines the limits of freedom and freedom the limits of power. Thus there is a constant and intense contestation between power and freedom. Theoretically the logical limit of freedom is anarchy and logical limit of power is tyranny and despotism. Every society attempts in its own way to strike a balance but no society ever succeeded in arriving at a satisfactory equilibrium.

This volume "Mapping Human Rights and Subalterns in Modern India" edited by B. Jagannatham has to be located in these larger ongoing debates and changes in contemporary Indian Society. The subalterns are gradually growing conscious of their rights and the privileged and powerful are opposed to any attempt at foundational changes of a social structure. Unwilling to concede any new right nor enforce already guaranteed rights, there has been confrontation between different social groups and economic classes. Rights question got caught in this Quagmire. How to retrieve the central concerns of human rights remains one of the formidable challenges of human rights movement at one level and rights discourse at another level. There have been some serious attempts to negotiate with this complex context.

Indian Constitution a product of freedom struggle attempted to arrive at a legal and political equilibrium through balancing of power and emerging democratic aspirations. In the process there are intrinsic tensions in the Constitutional arrangement of power. Dr. Ambedkar who took upon this responsibility as Chairman of Drafting Committee saw a way out by charging the Indian State with the task of resolving not only the tensions but play a proactive role in the democratic transformation of the Indian society. He had a clear vision; he postulated that political equality guaranteed through one person, one vote, one value, would or should lead to social and economic democracy, failing which he cautioned that people of India will blow up the structure of political democracy so laboriously built by the Constituent Assembly.

The six to seven decades of Indian democracy not only realized what the Constitution envisioned but the very future of Indian democracy is endangered. For the confrontation between the subalterns and the exploiting classes has been growing sharper and sharper. The Indian state that has been mandated to negotiate and change the balance of power in favour of the disadvantaged has been hijacked by the conservative and reactionary forces. The transformative state has been turned upside down and it is increasingly used against the struggling masses and metamorphosing itself into a brutal state. The democratic space is shrinking and the future of human rights appear hazy.

The Constitutional scheme of things has come under terrific strain as feared by Dr. Ambedkar. If one has to trace the factors or causes that landed the Nation-State in such a state, it would be undoubtedly the unfolding nexus between reactionary ideology, corporate capital and imperialist interests. The locus of powers shifted from Nation-State to global economic agencies in such a way that maneuverability of the State is hard it. It is now playing more a role of an agent of global capital than Indian people's fulcrum of power. With the result it is employing its coercive power against its own people subverting the rights of the people more so of the subaltern groups. The place of rights in this scenario is one of displacement. This is not only Indian experience but experience all over the world. It is a paradox of our times that while human rights practices are fast degenerating, the standards of rights both at the international and national levels are raised to new heights.

In India there are these two powerful trends; one, serious subversion of rights; two, equally forceful resistance from people. There is the resistance to safeguard the rights themselves at one end and use the available rights to fight for self-respect and dignity as far as Dalits are concerned and to protect nature and its resources in the case of Tribals. The women are demanding for equity and equal opportunities. In fact, the underlying aspiration of all political struggles and social movements signify the urge for greater freedom. It looks that people want freedom to fight for Justice and demand right to resistance for enlargement of freedom. The papers included in this volume bring out strikingly this interface between human rights and subaltern groups of Indian society.

This volume is an attempt to capture the unfolding contradictions on the ground and perplexing ambiguities that concepts are inflicted with. The running theme of almost all the papers is to grasp the adversities and people's resistance. The range of groups that are hard hit include Dalits, adivasis, women, girl child, migrant labour, domestic workers so on. The papers also covered issues that are at stake. These relate to development, democracy, displacement of tribals, right to food, language rights and missing human rights and so on. These analyses, narrations and probings are rich and insightful. This is a valuable contribution to understanding nature of democracy at this stage of India's developmental transition or transitional development.

**Professor G. Haragopal**
*Former Dean, Social of Social Sciences*
*University of Hyderabad, Hyderabad &*
*ICSSR National fellow, TISS, Hyderabad*

# Preface and Acknowledgements

This volume encompasses the papers that were presented and deliberated in the ICSSR National Conference on 'Human Rights in India: Dalits, Tribals and Minorities', held In Gandhinagar on 21-22 November 2013, organised by Centre for Gandhian Thought and Peace Studies, School of Social Sciences, Central University of Gujarat. A few papers of the volume had contributed by the scholar-cum-activists on the human rights and the rights of subalterns in India. The themes which are debated in the conference predominantly on theory and practice of human rights: rights of Dalits, Tribals and Minorities; justice, social transformation, human rights, democracy and movements, the response of the State, women and human rights and development. In the light of this, the book is an attempt to explicate, explore and illuminate the rights of subalterns in modern India. The book interrogates the notion of human rights of subalterns and evaluates the domain of exclusion and marginality of dalits, tribals and women. Thus, the book examines the present model of development in India and its impact on the subaltern sections of modern India. The emphasis of book on the rights of Dalits, tribals and social justice. It focuses upon the language rights and writings from subaltern writers and singers who creates consciousness among the people. The discourse on human rights and subalterns is however not a new domain in the social sciences. The scholars had conceptualised and interrogated these discourses in depth. However, it is fact that still there is an adequate scope to interrogate and theorise human rights, subalterns and development in the era of globalisation. This volume primarily emphasises on those areas.

This work, undoubtedly, would not have been possible without the support of my supervisor and mentor Professor G. Haragopal. He has been a constant source of motivation and inspirationas a mentor and he has always taken a keen interest and inquisitiveness in my research and facilitated me in developing the interest in academics in general and research in particular. I express my deep felt sincere gratitude to Professor R.K. Kale, Former Vice-Chancellor, Central University of Gujarat, Gandhinagar for hisastute guidance, constructive and sagacious support and motivational suggestions and encouragement. I thank Professor S.A. Bari, Vice Chancellor and Professor S.L. Heremath, Registrar of the Central University of Gujarat for their support and encouragement.

I wish to thank Professor G. Sudarshanam, Dr Vanamala ma'am, Professor B. Chandrasekhar Rao, Professor M. Kodandaram, Professor G. Krishna Reddy, Dr K.Y. Ratnam and Dr R. Ramdas Dr G. Nagaraju (Sociology) University of Hyderabad. I wish to express my thanks to N. Sukumar (DU), Ajay Gudavarthy (JNU) and G. Vijay (HCU) whose astute advice provided me to enquire the domain of knowledge critically. My heartfelt thanks to Professor Manoranjaan Mohanty and Professor Ghanshyam Shah). I thank Professor N. Rajaram, Dean, School of Social Sciences, Central University of Gujarat. I wish to express my thanks to my colleagues: Beryl Anand, Dhananjay Rai, Smruthi Ranjan Dhal and Priya Ranjan Kumar for their support and encouragement. I also acknowledge adoration and fondness of my students and scholars from the Centre for Gandhian Thought and Peace Studies. I thank all the authors of the book for their contribution to the edited book. Special thanks to Dr Jean Dreze, Dr Anand Teltumbde, Professor E.V. Ramakrishnan, (Emeritus Professor), Dr Martin Makwan (NavsarjanTrust, Ahmedabad, Gujarat), Dr Tania Husian (Wasida University, Tokyo, Japan.

I express my gratitude to my family members: sister Gangamma, brother Sanjeev and sister-in- law Manjula. I acknowledge the love and affection of my family members: Krishna Veni, Shivaleela, Ravishanker, Uday Kumar and Kiran Kumar. It is glad to record the support, love and affection of my life-partner: Shailaja as it would not have been possible to publish this book without her support. My loving and affectionate son Medhansh and daughter Saniksha are always there and whose smiling and kindling faces provides me stimulation to carry out all my academic activities. Lastly, without the support of my late parents: Shivamma and Mallaiah, it would not have been possible for me to come up to this level and achieve whatever that I have achieved. It is a great occasion for me to recall once again their adversities and hitches that they had to undergo for the progress of me and my family members. I humbly bow my head and thank them. I know they are always with me with their showering of blessings on each of my activity.

However, the onus of errors and omissions, if any, is purely that of mine.

# List of Contributors

**Abhishek Das,** Research Scholar, Department of English, University of Delhi, Delhi

**Ajay Gudavarthy,** Assistant Professor, Centre for Political Studies, Jawaharlal Nehru University, New Delhi

**Ajay Saini,** Doctoral Research Fellow (School of Social Work) and Teaching Associate (Research and Development) at the Tata Institute of Social Sciences, Mumbai.

**Anand Teltumbde,** is a writer and civil rights activist of the Committee for the Protection of Democratic Rights, Maharashtra

**Avinash Pandey,** Assistant-Professor, Department of Linguistics, University of Mumbai, Mumbai

**Bijaya Kumar Mohanty,** Assistant Professor, Ramjas College, University of Delhi

**Debranjan Hota,** Visiting Faculty, School of Social Sciences, Central University of Gujarat, Gandhinagar

**Jagannatham Begari,** Assistant Professor, Centre for Studies in Gandhian Thought and Peace Studies, Central University of Gujarat, Gándhinagar

***Janmejaya Mishra,*** *Aga Khan Rural Support Pragramme (India), presently based at Ahmedabad, Gujarat.*

**Jean Dreze,** is Visiting Professor at the Department of Economics, Ranchi University, Ranchi Uttarakand

**Nagaraju Gundimeda,** Associate Professor, Department of Sociology, School of Social Sciences, Hyderabad Central University-Hyderabad-500046

**Praveen Kachhap,** Programme Officer, Ojus Medical Institute, Mumbai

**Priya Namrata Topno,** Research Scholar, Tata Institute of Social Sciences, Mumbai

**Rajadarshini Patra,** PhD. Scholar, School of Women's Studies, Utkal University, Vanivihar, Bhubaneswar, Odisha

**Rajesh Lakum,** Ph.D. Scholar, Centre for Studies in Society and Development, Central University of Gujarat, Gandhinagar

**Rohidas Munde,** Assistant Professor, Department of Civics and Politics, University of Mumbai

**Sheikh RafiqUllah,** Ph.D. Scholar, Department of Political Science, University of Hyderabad, Hyderabad

**Tania Hossain,** Associate Professor, Faculty of Letters, Arts and Sciences, Waseda University, Tokyo, Japan

**VenkateshNayak,** Assistant Professor,Department of Social Exclusion Studies, School of Inter-Disciplinary Studies, The English and Foreign Languages University, Hyderabad

**Vibha Singh,** Research scholar, Tata Institute of Social Sciences, Mumbai

# Introduction and Theoretical Framework

—*Jagannatham Begari*

The world, today, has moved towards modernity and globalisation and is being considered as a global village. In spite of these, the world also has been witnessing discrimination based on race, class, caste, region, ethnicity, religion, and so on in the modern era. There are international organisations, Commissions, Committees and Agreements at the international level to protect and promote human rights and strive for egalitarian values like equality, liberty and fraternity. In spite of constitutional provisions and protective measures in India, the subalterns, particularly the Dalits, tribals and religious minorities continue to face discrimination and continuous violence against them. This disturbing trend has led to a spurt in people's movements. There are numerous instances of minorities and weaker sections not being allowed to: eat which they like, wear clothes of their choice, or live where they want to live. The marginalised sections are being forced to do work against their will. Even today, one hears about instances of Dalits being burnt alive and women being raped. The lives of intellectuals, writers, singers and other voices of subalterns are under constant threat. The writings and literary responses are generally considered by ruling class as threat to the established socio-political order. Thus, in spite of constitutional provisions and protective measures, institutional and structural discrimination is very much in evidence in modern India. Today, many educational institutions have become hubs of the social discrimination. It is to note that most of the so-called theorists and thinkers speak about egalitarian values, but, in practice, discriminate lower social class or caste than theirs. These forms of discrimination are sometimes visible and many times invisible. Intellectual arrogance seems to have become a trend among intellectuals. Dalits, tribals and religious minorities are the worst victims of this kind of discrimination which can be found in all types of educational establishments–be it higher educational institutes or even primary educational institutions not with standing these. In the name of development, both major and minor projects are being established. Tribals, Dalits and other weaker sections are generally the victims of such ventures since they risk being displaced without any substantial rehabilitation and resettlement.

The scholars from the school of subalterns and human rights argues that the hostility towards the subalterns, particularly the Dalits and those belonging to the minority communities, is most strongly manifested in the opposition to the reservation policy by many academicians and policy makers. Such persons conveniently forget that the reservation policy which is considered as one of the important support bases for the marginalised sections to develop socially, economically and enter the mainstream and contribute more towards nation building. Their specious argument is that the service, health and education sectors are largely in private hands who are not bound by the reservation policy. It is high time that the reservation policy is extended to the private sector also. The lawmakers and law implementers are supposed to be the protectors of the Constitution and weaker sections of the society. However, on many occasions, they themselvesare the forefront in violation of the human rights of weaker sections. This trend is indeed a sad state of affairs in modern India. Thus, understanding and interpreting the philosophy of B.R. Ambedkar, Karl Marx, Phule, Periyar and other thinkers who believes in egalitarianism is essential in fighting against the socio-economic and political inequalities and discrimination. In this light of this scenario, this book tries to understand the evolution of human rights and the paradigm shift.

The debates on human rights suggest that natural rights were the earliest form of rights. The right to life was the earliest right to be recognised and came to be considered as an inalienable right. These are the rights which are owed to a man. Over a period of time, these inalienable rights acquired a deeper meaning and larger dimension.[1] The consciousness of freedom and, therefore, of rights stems from the ability of the human being to confront the nature. For none of the other species is endowed with the ability to comprehend the laws of the nature, nor can take advantage of these laws of the nature as human beings do. The inalienable rights, called natural rights, came into existence when human life was vulnerable and there was no protection whatsoever. Survival of life itself was problematic at this stage. The problems leading to the solutions, resolutions throwing up the problems got linked with the nature of production.[2] Rights existed in a limited form in the early Greek and Roman civilisations, or even in the ancient Asiatic civilisations, but the beginning of the rights, as understood in the modern sense, could be traced to Magna Carta of the early therteenth century. The human history witnessed the modern revolutions that were fought by the people to assert their rights and liberties. In the process, they had to oppose the then existing order and achieve their rights. The Puritan Revolution gave the Magna Carta for the humanity in the year 1613. The English Revolution in the seventeenth century had shown how constitutional liberties were achieved through the Bill of Rights, and that levying of taxes and raising the army could be done only with the consent of Parliament. This Revolution naturally influenced other revolutions all over the world. The American War of Independence gave the Declaration of Rights. It proclaimed that all men are created equal and emphasised inalienable rights, popular sovereignty and the right to revolution. The French Revolution can be considered as a significant step towards the establishment of individual liberties. This Revolution was against the feudal oppression by the French aristocracy. It gave rise to universal values like the doctrine of equality and the right of the people to govern by themselves. The two World Wars further strengthened the rights discourse. All these revolutions and wars played an important role in the emergence of human rights. The Industrial Revolution gave a new momentum to human history. It led to renaissance and reformation of the then contemporary society.[3]

The United Nations Organisation came into existence in the year 1945 for the purpose of safeguarding world peace. The Universal Declaration of Human Rights had provided the foundation for the modern concepts of human rights. It further strengthened universal values like freedom, equality and dignity of the human being, right to life, liberty and security of a person, annihilation of all forms of slavery and strict prohibition on arbitrary interference by the State into the privacy of family, freedom of movement and equality of rights of men and women. Apart from all, there are freedom of opinion, freedom of expression, peaceful assembly, right to social security and right to work. In the changed world political economy, it was necessary to enact the international Covenant on Civil and Political rights (1976), international Covenant on Economic, Social and Cultural Rights (1976) and Developmental Rights (1986). The Vienna Declaration, adopted at the World Conference on Human Rights in 1993, further expanded the notion of human rights.[4] This philosophical and historical scenario explains that all the revolutions and wars aimed at the promotion of rights and upholding the dignity of the general masses against feudalism and monarchy. These encouraged other nations and individuals and institutions to fight, protect and promote the rights.[5] Against this backdrop, it is it essential to explore the evolution of human rights in India.

It is to note that the history of movements is not a new phenomenon; it had roots in ancient, medieval and modern times. The transition from the medieval to modern period resulted in an exceptional change in the Indian history. With the advent of British rule in India, a new era started. This created ripples in the political and legal spheres, leading to the imposition of British political and legal culture in India. There had been a long history of struggles in India against the exploitation, colonial rule and cultural backwardness. With such an experience, along with the impact of International human rights discourse, India became a major partner in human rights organisations, Covenants and Conventions. The framers of Indian Constitution incorporated the human rights values in the Constitution. The British government in India had not only deprived the freedom of Indian people, but also exploited the masses and ruined India economically, politically, culturally and spiritually. As a result, there was a strong resistance demanding fundamental freedoms –

both civil and political. It is proved that the British rulers discriminated against Indians in matters of their political and civil liberties and rights. They resorted to arbitrary acts such as brutal assaults, deportation etc., against Indians fighting for national independence, equal justice and economic equality.[6] The British rulers also enacted some laws against injustices. The British government in India enacted several laws.[7] After witnessing the colonial rule, it became essential for every Indian to recognise, protect and strive for the implementation of human rights as these are not only basic issues and freedoms, but also inalienable for them to lead dignified lives.[8] After independence, India adopted its Constitution. The major focus of the Constitution was on protection of human rights, which found expression in the Preamble, Fundamental Rights, Directive Principles of state policy, reservations for the Scheduled Castes and the Scheduled Tribes and special provisions for Anglo-Indians and OBCs.[9] In spite of Indian Constitution and protective measures, marginalised sections in India continue tend to face socio-economic and political discrimination. In the light of this, it is pertinent to interrogate the notion of exclusion and human rights.

## Mapping Social Exclusion and Marginality: Interrogating Human Rights

The terms social exclusion, marginality and humiliation may appear to be diverse concepts, yet, these are interrelated and interdependent and their meanings are similar. The notion of exclusion could be understood on the basis of race, religion, ethnicity, nation and social origin. India has been no exception to this trend. Exclusion seen at the policy level is primarily because of its consequences on underdevelopment, inequality and deprivation that it particularly brings to the excluded and discriminated groups. Social exclusion has been defined as 'the process through which individuals or groups are wholly or partially excluded from full participation in the society in which they live." These definitions on exclusion are particularly emphasised on the societal relations or institutions that cause exclusion and its consequences in terms of deprivation in multiple spheres, mainly through denial of equal rights. The concept, thus, focuses attention on social relations, the processes that exclude some groups and the institutions that underlie this process and the adverse consequences in multiple spheres on the excluded groups.[10] The notion of exclusion revolves around the societal inter-relations and institutions that exclude, discriminate, isolate and deprive some groups on the basis of group's identities like caste and ethnicity or religion. It is the caste-based exclusion, which has formed the basis for various anti-discriminatory politics in India. Historically, the caste system has regulated the social and economic life of the people in India. Theoretical formulations of Ambedkar recognised that its essential form, caste as a system of social and economic governance or organisation, is governed by certain customary rules and norms, which are unique and distinct.

The organisational scheme of the caste system is based on the division of people into social groups (castes) in which the civil, political, cultural, and economic rights of each individual caste are predetermined or ascribed by birth and made hereditary. The civil, cultural, and economic rights are therefore, unequal and hierarchal. The most important feature of the caste system is that it provides for a regulatory mechanism to enforce the social and economic organisation through the instruments of social ostracism (social and economic penalties). It is further reinforced with the justification and support from the philosophical elements in the Hindu religion. The fundamental characteristic of caste system is to have fixed civil, cultural, and economic rights for each caste, with restrictions for change implies forced exclusion" of one caste from the rights of other caste.[11] It is to note that the exclusion and the denial of equal opportunity in economic spheres would operate through markets and non-market transactions. Discrimination can occur through 'unfavourable inclusion,' namely, through differential treatment in terms and condition of contract, one of them would reflect in discrimination in the prices charged and received by discriminated groups. The notion of exclusion and discrimination can occur in terms of access to social needs supplied by the government. Exclusion can be found in the civil, political and cultural spheres. S. K. Thorat has pointed out that economic discrimination clearly had an adverse impact on profits, wages and efficiency in the allocation of labour. Economic theory implies that the economic discrimination would slow down economic growth by reducing efficiency due to less than optimal allocation of labour among firms and economy by reducing job commitments and efforts of workers who perceive themselves to be victims of discrimination. In case of income distribution, it is clear that in so far as exclusion and discrimination refers to the denial of access to resources, employment and common facilities that can certainly impoverishes the lives of individuals belongs to excluded groups is very much prevalent.[12] In this regard, it is essential to conceptualise the notion of humiliation.

Gopal Guru has said that the notion of humiliation is almost endemic to social life that it is active basically through asymmetrics of intersecting sets of attitudes-arrogance and obeisance, self-respect and servility, reverence and repulsion. He asserts that it continues to survive in different forms, depending upon the specific social context. This endemic character of the concept of humiliation can be explained in terms of the social paradox produced by the socially dominant elite from different societies. As Gopal Guru states, this paradox involves the dynamics of social life with contradictory responses offered by the modern elite. Thus, on the one hand, the dynamics of social life shakes the social elite from the humiliating social protocols that regulate feudal society, on the other, these so-called modern elites tend to reproduce structures, both institutional (state) and moral (friendship) that underlie and renew the phenomenon of humiliation. Those social elites, who were the object of humiliation at the hands of the estate and caste lords, or the colonial masters, somehow become the source of humiliation/degradation of something of which they were victims in the first instance.[13] The reorganisation of modern society based on the division between the private and public spheres was accompanied by the possibility of misrecognition, degradation, and humiliation. Transgression of the boundaries between the private and public was considered as the context for humiliation. The philosophers/thinkers in the west seem to have made sustained attempts to philosophise and theorise the experience of humiliation and suggest its elimination in favour of respect, recognition and dignity.[14] In India too, there are attempts are made to theorise the notion of discrimination, and resist it.

It is posited that, at one level, the idea of the public sphere based on the language of rights does help the slave and the untouchable to successfully overcome the element of fear and fate. At another level, the reorganisation of society on modern lines also creates the condition for the production of humiliation. The ideological spell can arrest the growth of assertion against humiliation. These are two conditions that provide a formative context for the definition of humiliation. First, an element of comparison generates within a person the capacity for self-reflectivity necessary for gaining insights into oneself and others. Second, the emergence and the articulation of the language of rights make the assertion against humiliation possible. The language of rights helps the previously servile classes to achieve self-definition through detecting /resisting humiliation. Modernity plays an important role in generating among the servile a critical consciousness about actual and possible forms of humiliation, emanating from local configuration of power.[15] Valerian Rodrigues suggests that the public domain, which could be called the bourgeoisie social order, at the theoretical level, promises people a sense of respect and dignity. This is mainly because this 'modern sphere' assigns equal status to people. Rodrigues reaffirms the concern that the biggest challenge for the Constitution of the public domain in India was to include the Indian untouchableswithin it.[16]

## Marginalisation of Dalits from the Mainstream

It is to note that the term 'marginality' refers to location of a person, group, or a community practically 'outside' the mainstream, though ideally, the orientation may be towards it. It has also been used in the sense of duality where member of an 'in-group' are also member of an "out-group," but not fully accepted in the either groups. At the individual level, marginality leads to a "dual personality", or to a "double consciousness" where a person, maintaining a double personality, lives with two cultures and, thus, remains a "cultural hybrid," sharing intimately cultural traditions of two distinct peoples or groups of people.[17] The term marginal or marginality has also been used in terms of "marginal culture" and marginal area." While marginal culture refers to a distant or border culture, the marginal area is conceived as a region where two cultures overlap and where the occupying group partakes of the traits of both cultures". Marginality may further be viewed in terms of the relations between the centre and periphery where a marginal man, group, or community, located at the periphery, is practically deprived of all resources and opportunities, including the prestige esteem, though he or it may be part of a total system consisting both of the centre and the periphery.[18] In the light of this discussion, it is intend to evaluate the marginalisation of Dalits in India from the Mainstream.

All countries in the world have been witnessing inequalities of various kinds. India, however, has a unique cocktail of lethal divisions and disparities. few countries have to contend with such extreme inequalities in so many dimensions, including large economic inequalities, as well as major disparities of caste, class and gender. Caste and gender inequality is exceptionally high in India, particularly, in large parts of the northern and western regions, where the subjugation of women is fairly comprehensive.[19] It is the mutual reinforcement of different inequalities that creates such enormous disparities in Indian society.[20] Educational inequalities are also is equally prevalent in India. Educational inequalities are partly a reflection of class, caste and gender inequalities. These have an influence of their own, reflecting differences in access to schooling, learning abilities, parental education, and so on. There are often significant differences in educational achievements between siblings, even of the same caste and class.[21]

Indian society is highly stratified, with many glaring inequalities among different socio-economic groups. The worst positioning among them are the Dalits and Tribals. The caste system segregated the Dalits from the rest of the society to such as an extent that they were denied even the basic human rights that one must enjoy in order to ensure one's bare existence. Denial of the right to drink water from any public well and to walk on the road in broad daylight were some of the notable examples of social persecution of the Dalits at the hands of the upper caste Hindus.[22] The unique feature of the caste system was that it assigned an occupation not to an individual, but to a group of individuals. A particular individual was ordained to undertake a particular occupation, just because he or she belonged to a particular group, i.e., caste. This led Ambedkar to argue that the caste system did not result only in division of labour, but it culminated in the division of labourers. The former is the result of preference, choice and aptitude of an individual and the latter is independent of the individual will. The former is voluntary, while the latter is not only obligatory, but also coercive. Thus, like in the social sphere, in the economic sphere too, the caste system amounted to a travesty of individual freedom.[23] But the effects of the birth-based occupational distribution on different castes were entirely opposite in nature. It came to be regarded as a divine privilege to the upper castes enjoying the virtual monopoly of education, industry, trade commerce, and so on; and onthe other hand, it spelt disaster for the lower castes. This is because the latter were assigned tasks involving only manual labour. They were, thus, prevented from earning/accumulating wealth, which restricted their needs to bare existence. What was even more deplorable was that menial labour was stigmatised. Thus, the absence of freedom of occupation, low earnings, implicit restriction on needs, and stigma on menial labour destroyed the economy of the lower castes. They came to be wholly dependent on the upper castes for their survival.[24] The dominant sections and subalterns are two varied sections in the society.

## The Notion of Civil Society and Political Society: Debating Marginality

The notion of Political society, which is a potentially radical concept that is purportedly 'constitutive outside' of civil society was developed by Partha Chatterjee. He asserts that civil society is a sphere of modern civil institutions governed by rationality, legality and contractual relations of entry and exit of individual rights and citizenship, sovereignty and property relations. These principles and institutions of modernity in post-colonial societies such as India not only represent very limited elite sections of the society, but also enter into an irreconcilable conflict with democracy. He therefore, states: 'civil society would appear as the closed association of modern elite groups, sequestered from the wider popular life of the communities. The rest, in fact, the majority of the subaltern sections of the society, are thereby recognised as political society. They cannot be accommodated in the elite dominated civil society, not as rights-bearing citizens, but as 'populations'.[25] He further says that the idea of political society is potentially radical in identifying that the population that constitute an alternative site, are neither agents of the state, nor the civil society. They are constitutively outside the process of political participation. For the sake of survival and livelihood, they have to negotiate with both the state and civil society or public sphere led by the middle-class bourgeois subjects and social elites. Chatterjee asserts that not only State, but also the civil society uses the power blocks and dominate the subaltern classes for preserving their own interests. In fact, the associations in civil society are not only not accessible, but also strong actors against the interests of those who reside in the political society. Therefore, the modes of protest of the political society are not consistent with the principles and institutional norms of (liberal) civil society.[26]

## State Modernity and Development: Critical Interrogation

After independence, the conditions of the Dalits slightly changed because of modernity which advocated the ideology of progress and development. However, in the post-modern era, the power of nation state has become quite limited. Post-modernity has now displaced modernity, leading to the process of globalisation. There is general understanding among people that the discourse on globalisation announces the end of the nation-state. In fact, the decline of the nation-state is responsible for the marginalisation of development programmes. The state has withdrawn from the areas of social, cultural, and economic welfare of the society. It has had an adversely impact on the marginalised sections further. The modernisation project of India was exogenously initiated, with colonialism as its launched pad.[27] It is to be notedthat the principal sources of modernity in India are colonialism, planned economic development and the promised equality and social justice. The planned economic development endorsed large scale industrial production and modernisation of agriculture as progressive measures. The process of industrialisation was sought to be achieved through gigantic factories, high-rise dams and high tech firms. The overall tempo was one of the cultivating the scientific temper, associated with western science and technology. Modernisation of agriculture had two dimensions-getting rid of feudal elements through agrarian reforms and developing agriculture through the green revolution. The examples of discontents of Indian modernity are displacement of labour by technology resulting in an army of unemployed youth, submerging of farm lands because of big dams resulting in uprooting millions of peasants; sapping farm lands of their natural fertility because of over use of modern fertilizers, and so on. The responses to these discontents are: youth and student protests, anti-dam mobilisations, environmental and ecological movements, articulations against the violence of Green Revolution, and so on. The other source of Indian modernity is inclusion of the values of equality and social justice in the Indian Constitution to eradicate the hierarchical social order. The Constitutional promise could not be realised in the first few decades of independence because of the deep entrenchment of traditional vested interests and because of the inaudibility of the voices of protests from the traditionally under privileged and gradually the situation changed and Adivasis, Dalits and OBCs started demanding their due share in the polity and economy - proportionate to their population.[28] More than one fifth of India's population is illiterate; nearly two thirds our population lacks basic sanitation; nearly 40 per cent of population lives in poverty. Moreover, daily wage earners and rural migrant labourers have lost their livelihood permanently. It has affected the interests of the landless labourers, marginalised farmers, backward classes, the Dalits the marginalised and women. These sections have faced various kinds of exploitation at the hands of their masters or rulers.[29] Thus, it is necessary evaluate the rights of subalterns in this regard.

## Debating the Rights of Dalits, Tribals and Minorities in Modern India

The discourse on the human rights has not received its due attention in the curriculum in social science research. Sometimes, the debate on human rights is confined to academic and conventional necessities and there is no meaningful discussion on the issues at stake. The marginalised sections have started asserting for their rights. Starting from the Silent Revolution, Reform Movement and Bhakti Movement, the people of the country had questioned and resisted the caste discrimination. In spite of UDHR and the presence of other international organisations which protect and promote human rights, however, they did not change the society substantially as far as India is concerned. However, it is to be accepted that human rights are considered merely as guiding principles. In spite of India's Constitution, the marginalised sections are still excluded from the mainstream as India is moving towards technocratic governance. This has become a great challenge for the human rights discourse and movements as well. Many writers and poets, like the Tamil poet, Tiruvalvur, advocated equality, social justice and liberty through their writings and created consciousness among the people. According to B.K. Nagla, "In India, we are not able to theorise human rights properly. There is an absence of discussions and deliberations on human rights discourse". He further says that theliterature from grassroots plays a major role in protection and promotion of human rights in India. This creative literature need to be promoted and to resist the violation of rights, and conventional scholars have to learn from such literature. The literature on human rights, Dalit rights, tribals and women has contributed substantially in understanding and theorising human rights and social justice. Therefore, he is convinced that indigenous narratives of human rights in fighting the domination is essential for theorising the plight of subalterns in modern India.[30] With this backdrop, it is necessary to comprehend the philosophical and theoretical quest of scholars in the area of human rights and dalit studies.

## Indian Constitution and Protective Measures

This is evidence that the provisions laid down in the Indian Constitution for the tribals are provisions of statutory recognition, proportionate representation in the legislatures, right of using own language for education and other purposes, profess their own faith and development according to their own genius. The Constitution had also enjoined upon the state to promote the educational and economic interests of the weaker sections of the society, including Tribals. Besides these, there are provisions that empower the state to bring areas inhabited by Tribes under the 5th or the 6th Schedules for purpose of special treatment in respect of administration of the Tribals. The provisions laid down in the Constitution of India thus aimed at safeguarding, protecting and promoting the interests of the Tribals. At the heart of the problems of Tribal development lies the discrepancy between theory and practice (316- xaxa).[31] The Fundamental Rights embodied in the Indian Constitution guarantee all Indian citizens the right to life and dignity and ensure that they will lead their lives in peace, enjoy civil liberties, such as equality before the law, freedom of expression, freedom of association and peaceful assembly, freedom of religion, and the right to constitutional remedies. The Directive Principles of State Policy lay down that it is the moral obligation of the state to "strive to promote the welfare of the people by securing and protecting as effectively as it may a social order in which justice, social, economic and political, shall inform all the institutions of the national life.It is also stated that the state shall, in particular, direct its policy towards securing equality among citizens, adequate means of livelihood, equal pay for equal work, health, and strength of workers, protection against exploitation and against moral and material abandonment. The Constitution has adopted the policy of protective discrimination to promote the social and economic interests of the Scheduled castes, Scheduled Tribes and other weaker sections of the society. [32] In the light of this, it is necessary to comprehend the rights of subalterns in the era of globalisation.

## Interrogating the Rights of Subalterns in the Era of Globalisation

Ghansham Shah asserts that it is necessary to study the discourse on human rights and reassess the emerging dimensions of human rights starting from the 14th Century to the present times. He further points out that the assertion of rights had been witnessed during the Bhakti movement, reform movement, and radical reform movements and followed by identity movements, feminist movements and tribal movements. He further says that the people had learnt philosophy of Buddha to question the injustice and the culture of questioning, resistance has been continuing in India in spite of the state's suppressive approach. He has further pointed out that it is the right time to redefine and conceptualise human rights further as Dalits are experiencing humiliation, tribals are facing alienation, continuously losing their resources and livelihood and the security of Muslim minorities isin danger in the era of globalisation. According to Mohanty, the people are witnessing equity - but not equality. The people need not merely in a notional equality before the law, but need an equalitarian and a just society. Therefore, he asserts that one has to differentiate between equity and equality. The term 'equity' is defined by the elites. Ghanshyam Shah points out that subalterns sections deserve not only political equality, but also socio-economic equality. He further highlights that people want *samata* (equality) not *samrasta* as it is dominant culture and got mixed with the elite class. Ambedkar frequently remindedthe people that nothing is static, everything is changing. Therefore, Shah posits that it is an essential to question the injustice and domination in any form. He further asserts thatit is the time to redefine human rights discourse as Dalits, tribals, minorities, of course, women, are coming up with new demands and asserting their rights. Therefore, he mentions that the scholars have to specify and theorise their problems and rights independently. He also makes a point that the state is supposed to protect the rights of the marginalised sections, however, it violates their rights, implicitly, legitimises the discrimination and the domination that the marginalised sections have been facingin India since centuries. Therefore, the human rights movement needs to redefine the rights discourse, strategies and approaches towards the marginalised sections (from bottom-down approach). Shah goes on to state: "We have to sensitise ourselves, rethink our experiences and ask why the discrimination and deprivation taking place and redefine human rights discourse and movements accordingly."[33]

Manoranjan Mohanty has pointed out that the terms 'Dalit' and 'Adivasis' are empowering and liberating concepts in contemporary times. The conventional movements had ignored subalterns' movements. The generation of scholars did not merely confine themselves to the domain of academics, but have been active in human rights movement and their substantial contribution is rooted in the social movements'and they work with commitment. He argues that human rights movements are democratic in nature, however, these movements must have an alliance with Dalit, women, Adivasi and environment movements. He further argued that the human rights movement must be viewed from the perspective of the subaltern movements. There is a paradigm shift from the human rights to people's rights and democratic rights. The meanings of these concepts have further expanded. The question here is, how are the oppressed people going to achieve their demands and goals? Mohanty also points out there are celebrations of events, speeches, human rights days, but there are no substantial debates on human rights in the realm of electoral politics. However, the debates that are taking place are generally about good governance,a corruption free government, and so on. He said that this kind of trend is a sorry state of affairs. He is convinced that the human rights discourse is alive at the ground level. Even though the debate is alive among the poor, Dalit, women and other subaltern sections, Mohanty does not find a similar spirit among the rich political elites and dominant sections of the society. While the elites want economic growth, the subalterns want human rights, democratic rights and civil rights. Mohanty laments that the voices of human rights are not heard by the state, but cautions that the people are watching and witnessing this negative response of the state. He also asserts that the obligation of the state is to provide free education and work. He says that the rights are political affirmations of denial of human conditions pursuit through struggles. The human rights discourse or human rights movement want to restructure the power relations of caste, class and gender in the country.[34]

Mohanty has further mentioned that Indians fought for the freedom and justice. Therefore, it was expected that the first Union Government of India could have been focused on free primary education, welfare policies, employment opportunities and implementing the provisions of Constitution rigorously in its first Five Year Plan. However, the government did not act in this direction for a long time. On the other hand, it started thinking of economic growth and formulating policies which would benefit the rich propertied classes. As a result of anti-people's policies, the resistance movements surfaced all over the country. Therefore, to overcome the people's movements, the government started using the language of human rights by launching policies like Right to Food Security Act, Right to Information Act, Right to Employment Guarantee Act and formulating inclusive policies. It suppressed the people's movement. Manoranjan Mohanty also mentions that the governments believe that through welfare policies and populist policies, they can address the problems of Dalits. However, the people do not want mere material benefits which are temporary relief for their problems, but are demanding land distribution, land reforms, equal opportunities, free education, employment opportunities and permanent solution to their problems and to live with the self-respect, dignity and decent life and enjoy socio-economic and political rights which are enshrined in the Indian Constitution. The rights based programmes and policies and development are merely intended to satisfy international agencies and organisations. However, the people and movement from the below say that this is not what they fought for. Instead, they fought for education and equal opportunities through which their creative potentialities can be are realised.

Martin Makwan has said that when Ambedkar first presented the Constitution to India's stalwarts, he had said that we were entering the age of contradictions. Martin laments that though all are equal according to the Constitution, inequalities still exist in the society. Unless and until the consciousness of the people increases, there would be no substantial meaning to the Constitution. Even after more than six decades of independence in India, there is a contradiction between the people's expectations and desires and what actually they have actually gained. To justify his propositions, Martin gives substantial realities from the state of Gujarat which is considered as a relatively developed state. He says that discrimination still exists in different forms in a sophisticated way. He has pointed out that there are 1500 children studying in the government primary schools from the Saurashtra region of Gujarat state are forced to clean the bathrooms in schools. The study reveals that in 90 per cent of the villages, Dalits are denied entry into hotels, the 'two glass system' is still in vogue, 55 per cent of Dalit children are seated separately in the schools and in 64 per cent of village panchayats, the members from the Dalit community are not allowed to sit on the chairs along with upper caste members. There is an open discrimination against Dalits in Gujarat despite its slogan of speed development and vibrant Gujarat. He further said that though the government is willing to give loans to the private industries like Nano Company, but does not give the loans to the poor marginalised sections. He further argues that the government of Gujarat huge amounts of loans to the rich propertied classes at 0.1 per cent interest. In contrast, manual scavengers are given loans at 7 per cent interest and in many cases, no loans were given to them. Based on these, Martin Makwan has said that there is the structural discrimination being done by the State itself against marginalised sections.[35]

## Globalisation, State and Exclusion of Marginalised sections and the Gap between India's Formal and Substantial Democracy

The Dalit challenge to the state is a part of new stirring of consciousness among the marginalised sections that reject the patronising attitude of the upper castes and the state and insists on their rightful share in the power structure of society. This has led to the construction of a new view of history and the Indian nation, which apart from highlighting oppression by the upper and middle castes, points out that Dalits have been marginalised and excluded from the mainstream. [36] It is apparent that India lives in a paradoxical syndrome. The contemporary social and economic transition in India has furthered those paradoxes. While with fast economic development, it has emerged to be the world hub of trained manpower and prosperity, it has also remained backward with the highest burden of poverty, illiteracy and unemployment. The mismatch between economic growth and social development has contributed to emerging social instability and perversion in many areas of social and economic lives. These are reflected in the paradoxical social momentum of fluidity, flux and deformities on one hand and consolidation on the other.[37] The dismal state of social development, persisting injustice and inequality has largely resulted from the state's failure to adhere to the broad guidelines of the United Nations. Such scenario has persisted due to organised apathy of the power elite to implement the social welfare and reform policies, on the one hand, and ignorance of the marginalised sections about their rights and entitlements, on the other[38] Therefore, India has remained a land of social discontent which is widely reflected in the form of organised protests, collective mobilisation and social movements. Notwithstanding the decline of conventional class-oriented social movements, India continues to experience the proliferation of social movements of peasants, farmers, tribals, ethnic minorities, women, displaced persons, Dalits, workers, and so on. Significantly, most of these movements have emerged and sustained in India due to poor economic conditions, deprivation, social exclusion and political subordination.[39]

Manoranjan Mohanty advocated a decentralised, responsive, and participatory state. Rajni Kothari posits that the path of development which the state in India has adopted is deeply flawed and it is focused on market efficiency, profitability, development and national security which has made the Indian state unresponsive, if not hostile, to the basic rights of the common man. The practice of neo-liberalism has, however, evolved in such a way as to depart significantly from the template that theory provides. The somewhat chaotic evolution and uneven geographical development of state institutions, powers, and functions over the last thirty years suggests, furthermore, that the neo-liberal state may be an unstable and contradictory political form.[40] Thus, in essence, the NEP aims at progressive reduction in the role of the 'state' in the economic management of the country and securing a transition of the 'centrally planned' Indian economy to a free market economy. It argues that this transition is going to erodethe welfare role of the state. The movements, based on identity, inevitably address their claims of recognition to the state, they challenge particular regimes, but do not ordinarily look beyond the institution of the state for the resolution of their problems. The process of economic reform, on the other hand, seeks to effect the withdrawal, or at least the retreat, of the state, especially in the productive and distributive aspects of the social order, and asserts the importance of extra-state spheres like the market. Simultaneously, a variety of social movements and new institutional experiments have sought consciously to challenge the state.[41] Despite the advocacy of a more broad based view of governance, the state remains, for the present, central to the developmental experiences and futures of countries like India. For a decade–and- a-half, the Indian debate on the state remained trapped within the either/or discourse of state vs. market, such that the 'retreat of the state' was seen as a euphemism for a greater role for the market. These developments pose a threat to many of the institutions-including modern nation state – that are accustomed to treat as somehow eternal, and the conceptual categories and assumptions that underpin them. The process of globalisation, which contributes to the increasing municipalisation of the nation-state, begins with the underpinning of at least one essential feature of the state-its sovereignty.[42] Along with globalisation, there has also, since the late 1980s, been a resurgence of assertions based on ethnic identities, of language, tribe, and religion or, as in the Indian context, caste. These assertions are today questioning the concept of a homogeneous nation state based upon a common national sentiment. In India, in recent years, Dalit movements/parties have questioned the legitimacy of the state and demanding the representation of all segments of the population. [43]

Jean Dreze's paper focuses on Ambedkar's understanding of democracy. He has brought out that the future of Indian democracy depends a great deal on a revival of Dr. Ambedkar's visionof democracy. According to him, Ambedkar'sunderstanding of democracy is based on morality, rationality, equality, liberty and fraternity. Ambedkar had a vision of democracy, which needs to be rediscovered today. Besides these, he argues that one must also enlarge the vision of Ambedkar in the light of recent developments. Anand Teltumbde in his paper has highlighted that the acute economic crisis forced the then central government to adopt deregulation and liberalisation. Subsequently, Rajiv Gandhi gave a major push to these policies. He posits that globalisation has been pushing scores of poor people to the margin, while rapidly transforming the country into something the elites always dreamt of. He further says that the Indian state is a constitutional state which is supposed to inherit its values and ideology and conduct itself as ordained by it. The Indian Constitution can be taken as the epitome of virtue within the liberal tradition. However, the Indian state has miserably failed in meeting the constitutional expectations. He has pointed out that personal empowerment, socio-economic empowerment, socio-political empowerment and socio-cultural empowerment are most essential for the overall development of Dalits.

Anand Teltumbde has argues that the Indian state is a constitutional state which is supposed to inherit its values and ideology and conduct itself as ordained by it. The Indian Constitution can be taken as the epitome of virtue within the liberal tradition. However, the Indian state has miserably failed in meeting the constitutional expectations. He has contended in his paper that globalisation has been pushing scores of poor people to the margin, while rapidly transforming the country into something the elites always dreamt of. Teltumbde also has highlighted that the acute economic crisis forced the Central government to adopt deregulation and liberalisation. Subsequently, governments gave a major push to these policies. Globalization, an agenda of capitalism in crisis, driven by imperialist institutions like IMF, World Bank, and WTO along the ideology of neo-liberalism has essentially a pro-rich bias. Wherever they were implemented, they have worsened the situation of masses of poor people in absolute as well as in relative terms.The implications of globalisation on Dalits are two fold in higher education: One, they will be deprived of reservation in these private institutions and two, the expensive higher education will go beyond their reach. His paper also argues that in India too all the ill effects of the globalization were experienced by the poor people in terms of inflation, de-industrialization, casualization of labour, unemployment, worsening food security, gnawing inequality, de-peasantization, destruction of environment and agriculture, suppression of democratic rights, pollution of culture and most importantly its indigenous fall out in terms of fascist, fundamentalist, communalist and obscurantist programme of Hindutva. Since, the impact of all these is to be borne in direct proportion of the poverty and deprivation, the Dalits are naturally hit by globalization the hardest.Teltumbde argues that in the era of globalisation, there is an adversary impact on Dalits as a being disadvantaged socially oppressed group and being a part of the poor, they are continued to deny education, employment and health facilities.He has further pointed out that personal empowerment, socio-economic empowerment, socio-political empowerment and socio-cultural empowerment are most essential for the overall development of Dalits. However, he has argues, in the era of globalisation, it is difficult for the empowerment of dalits as the state became the facilitator.

Ajay's paper focuses on the evolution of human rights, Conventions, Covenants and other Agreements at the international level. However, he mentions that the rights have relied on the more specific historical, social and cultural context and depends on across and within particular societies. The interface between global and domestic human rights continue to raise political and philosophical significant questions regarding the Eurocentric character of the global human rights. In the light of this, Ajay's paper focuses on three significant issues which are relevant to the emerging discourse and politics of human rights in India. These are: (a) The debate on the centrality of the legal (concrete) dimension of the human rights, as against the moral (abstract) dimension that translates into preeminence for civil-political rights; (b) the debate on universal human rights versus cultural relativism espoused by many states in the non-European part of the world and (c) the debate on the 'third generation' human rights as articulated in the 'Right to Development' foregrounds the original idea of *indivisibility* that is constitutive of human rights. The paper evaluates that the discourse, politics and practices of human rights emerge from a complex and continuous exchange between political movements, and institutions both at the national and international levels by drawing continuities between the discourse around 'Right to Development' and taking the instance of the anti-liquor movement led by women in Andhra Pradesh.

Avinash's paper reflects on the future of languages in the era of globalisation. This engagement has been more prominent inrecent times. He posits that the forces of globalisation create a hierarchical order of languages where the international languages, mainly English, rapidly grow in their communicative potential and, in the process, they impoverish regional or domestic languages like Marathi and bring 90 per cent of vernacular languages to the verge of extinction. Thus, the accumulation of the linguistic capital of English is taking place by the deflation and dispossession of the linguistic capital of other languages. He brings out that this trend is threat to national and vernacular languages.Tania Hussain posits that there is a difference between the languages used in the schools and the language spoken outside the schools. She differentiates between the rights to get education in English language and the right to education through the mother tongue(s). These two rights are essential for linguistic minorities to participate in the mainstream society, as well as retain connection with their home or community language. Her paper carries the debate based on two proponents: Brutt-Griffler and Skutnabb-Kangas. Sheasserts that it is necessary for children to learn both the languages: home language and the dominant (English) language.

Nagaraju focuses on the dropout girls from the rural Andhra Pradesh and Telangana states. He states that in order to realize the universalisation of primary and secondary education for girls, the government of India introduced a new scheme named after *Kasturba, Gandhi* wife of Mahatma Gandhi. He states that based on an in-depth analysis of the functioning of KGBV schools across the Andhra and Telangana states, one can find a wide gap between the policy proclamation and implementation. Gundemeda has pointed out that multiple factors determine the continuity of girls' dropouts. The primary factors of dropouts were family economic and socio-cultural conditions. More than 40 per cent girl children dropout due to economic vulnerability and the family size which pushes the parents to stop the girls' education at an early stage.

Girl children are the first victims of any major crisis in family. He further brings out issues like death of a family member, child caring and parent's migration to other villages affects the educational opportunities of rural girls. The paper recommends that the proper infrastructure facility and tools of learning for the holistic development of children need to be provided and improved. Although the constitutional framers recognised the important role of education, however, lack of political will and structural inequities in policy framing tend to reflect on the function and performance of the government schemes.

Ajay Saini's paper deals with the post-tsunami socio-cultural milieu of the Nicobarese and the changes brought in the socio-cultural domains of the community after the governmental humanitarian interventions undertaken in the islands in the aftermath of the natural calamity. This paper evaluates the pre- and the post-tsunami spatial location, subsistence, housing, economy, social structure and political organisation of the community in the Nicobar Islands since 2011. He has pointed out that the Indian Ocean tsunami of 26, December 2004 virtually destabilized the entire Nicobarese society by destroying human lives, houses, live-stock, fertile lands and vegetation. The geography of the islands has been altered due to the submergence of land areas. All these changes posed solemn threats to the Nicobarese and their continuity in the islands. He states that the post-tsunami phase has replaced the traditional authority of the elderly with that of the bureaucracy. The change ushered into the economic structure of the Nicobarese has adversely impacted the social stratification causing the erosion of various traditions and social norms. Vibha Singh emphasises on the practice of paid domestic workers in Delhi and the treatment meted out to migrant tribal domestic workers by the employers, local agents in the villages and placement agencies in the city. Based on the study, he contends that the migrated domestic workers, mostly young girls hired from rural and tribal belts of Jharkhand, Odisha, Assam and other eastern states, face discrimination in Delhi. Vibha Singh also brings out thatinadequate food and water, hardlyany facility of proper accommodation, less salary, long hours of work, no time for rest, inhuman conditions for work, physical and sexual exploitation are some of the issues which the full time tribal domestic workers in Delhi have to face.

Abhishek interrogates the potential of the urban space as a neutralising entity to unravel the insidious manner in which the caste system operates. The Ambedkarite discourse of progress premised upon a'right based' understanding of the caste problematic and which depended substantially on the success of the secular state as a guarantee for mitigating caste from the national consciousness. Das highlights that an acutely casteist nation organises all its spaces-rural and urban, isolated and cosmopolitan in a manner that replicates the 'asymmetrical relations', the access to social, cultural and national resources are manipulated in a covert and overt manner, bypassing the constitutional safeguards assured by the state executive. The paper asserts that both the urban and rural spheres respective idiosyncratic functioning are united in their redundant association with casteist values. Urban media is not exempt from it. Even in the era of globalisation, a new hostility has been systematically ingrained in the social matrix against the Dalits who sought material accomplishments. Venkatesh Nayak states that the cost of such projection could be undermining the second generation socio-economic and cultural rights. The promotion and prioritisation of rights could prove incapable in establishing a regime of genuine global human rights. Such projection helps in offering legitimacy to the 'state withdrawal' syndrome in a welfare economy. In such a situation, people from a backward socio-economic region like Telangana, having the experience of colonial and post-colonial uneven development trajectories might become the victims of such human rights violations. Nayak's paper attempts to fill the gap between universal claims of human rights (de jure rights) and localised violations of Palamur labour rights (de facto rights) at the structural and at the agency levels.

Bijaya Kumar Mohanty's paper evaluates the humiliation of women from a double victimisation perspective and asserts that human nature is a multi-layered affair and people do acknowledge or respond to events at many levels. Multi-layered understanding of human nature is the focusof hispaper. He further emphasises on certain socio-cultural or socio-psychological practices within the domain or through which a person largely lives his/her everyday life, or subjected to certain kind of humiliating practices. To pursue these lines of contentions, he evaluates the notion of humiliation based on the case study of divorced women. Rajesh and Jagannatham examine the notion of caste violence and atrocities on Dalits and the response of the state and society in the state of Gujarat. This paper argues that the Dalits face humiliation and discrimination based on their social status which raises the question of violations of human rights. It also deals with the notion of identity, movement, political mobilisation, institutional inequalities, caste discrimination, deprivation and violence. M.B. Gaijan posits that for centuries, India has been a multi-lingual and multi-cultural nation and points out that since ancient times, the powerful class/caste dominates all the domains in the country such as trade, technology, social, political and economy. Subaltern sections resisted these dominations through songs and writings.

Priya Namrata Topno & Praveen Kachhap's paper conceptualised the issue of displacement with reference to mining activities in Jharkhand and its impact on the socio-economic conditions of the tribals of that state. They assert that miningactivities have displaced and threatened thousands of tribals in Jharkhand. On one hand, it is argued that mines are the backbone of a country as they play a vital role in economic growth and development of a country but, on the other, more so in the context of Jharkhand, it has been found that mining has turned into monsters to displace the majority of the tribal population. Debranjan Hotaexamines the rights of tribals in India and their aspirations after independence based on the case studies from the state of Gujarat in India. He posits that the paradigm of neo-liberal development has ignored the aspirations of Tribals. The rich resources from the tribal regions are used as source of raw materials for the interests of dominant sections. This contradiction has got intensified further in the era of globalisation in India. Raoof Ahmad Lone critically evaluates the development-induced displacement based on case studies and suggests certain recommendations for sustainable development and welfare oriented development. He agrees that projects, dams, irrigation canals and other infrastructuraldevelopment projects are necessary,however, there should not be violation of Acts and forced displacement of poor in the name of development.The only possible way to mitigate the negative impacts and reduce the sufferings for the government isfor thestate to be responsive and proper compensation and rehabilitation mechanismsput in place for the displaced people. Janmejaya Mishra has examined the nature of poverty and marginalisation of the Korku tribe in Khandwa district of Madhya Pradesh. He provides analytical insights into the contributing factors for the poverty and the processes of marginalisation of tribes, while alongside discussing the politics of tribal development through the anatomy of a development project in the *Khalwa* block based on the ethnographic research approach. Mishra brings out that widespread poverty, food insecurity, malnutrition, mass scale exploitation by money lenders, traders and political leaders and gross violation of human rights in the region are the main woes of the marginalised Korku tribe in recent times.

In other words, the book is an attempt to trace the dynamics of human rights discourses and the rights of subalterns of modern India. It is an attempt to understand the notion of exclusion of subalterns in India from the domain of mainstream not merely in the name of development but also India's social system which is hierarchical and iniquitous. The book argues that it is due to the globalisation and current development model, dalits, tribals, minorities and other weaker sections are deprived of their rights. Therefore, the rights of marginalised sections which are enumerated in the India's Constitution are in greater threat. The book focuses further on the plight of the slum dwellers in metropolitan cities and migration of the poor people from the backward regions to metropolitan cities which explains the violation of fundamental rights of subalterns. It also emphasises on the importance of vernacular literature and writings from the grassroots in resisting against the social inequalities and neo liberal development model as well. There are papers which deals with the decline of the vitality of vernacular languages in India in the era of globalisation and consequences. A few papers in the volume explicitly or implicitly deals with the politics of human rights in India and trends and challenges. This volume raises very fundamental questions that either present development model meant for whom? Either is it meant for the rich and elite castes/classes or poor and marginalised sections? State either giving priority to equity or equality.

## Notes

1. Haragopal G. Political Economy of Human Rights: Emerging Dimensions, Himalaya Publications: Bombay, 1992, p. 4.
2. *Ibid.* p. 4.
3. Hobsbawm, Eric. The Age of Revolution- 1789-1848, Vintage Books, New York, 1996.
4. Charvet , John and Kaczynska-Nay , Elisa. The Liberal Project and Human Rights: The Theory and Practice of a New World Order, Cambridge University Press: Cambridge, 2008, pp. 83-93.
5. *Ibid.* pp.83-93.
6. Sastry T.S.N. Indian and Human Rights Reflections, Concept Publications: New Delhi, 2005, pp. 41-43.
7. Murali, K. Civil Liberties Movement During Freedom Struggle, PGDHR: Hyderabad, 2005, pp. 7-10.
8. Sastry, T.S.N. op.cit. pp. 41-43.
9. *Ibid.* pp. 41-43.
10. Thorat, Sukhdeo, Caste, Social Exclusion and Poverty Linkages- Concept, Measurement and Empirical Evidence, Concept Paper for PACS, New Delhi, October, 2005, p. 3.
11. *Ibid.* Penguin Books, New Delhi, pp. 241-242.
12. Thorat, Sukhdeo, Caste, social exclusion and poverty linkages- Concept, Measurement and Empirical Evidence, Concept paper for PACS, New Delhi, October, 2005, p. 3.
13. Guru, Gopal, Humiliation: Claims and Context, Oxford University Press, New Delhi, 2009, p. 1.
14. *Ibid.* New Delhi, 2009. p. 2.
15. *Ibid.* New Delhi, 2009. p. 5.
16. *Ibid.* New Delhi, 2009, p. 13.
17. Ram, Nandu, Beyond Ambedkar, Essays on Dalits in India, Har-Anand Publications, New Delhi, 2009, p. 201.
18. *Ibid.* New Delhi, 2009, p. 202.
19. Dreze, Jean & Sen, Amartya, An Uncertain Glory: India and Its Contradictions, Allen Lane, Penguin Books, 2013, p. 213.
20. *Ibid.* New Delhi, 2013, p. 214.
21. *Ibid.* 2013, p. 217.
22. State, Market and The Dalits: Analytics of the New Economic Policy (in edit) Michal, SM, 'Dalits in Modern India: Vision and Values' Vistaar Publications, New Delhi, 1999, p. 289.
23. *Ibid.* New Delhi, 1999, p. 289.
24. *Ibid.* New Delhi, 1999, p. 290.
25. Gudavarthy, Ajay (2013)Politics of Post-Civil Society: Contemporary History of Political Movements in India, Sage Publications, New Delhi, pp. 180.
26. *Ibid.* New Delhi, p. 181.

27. *Ibid.* New Delhi, p. 19.
28. T.K. Oomen, 'Multiple Modernities and the Rise of New Social Movements: The Case of India', (in edit) "Nation, Civil Society and Social Movements", Sage publications, New Delhi, p. 245.
29. B.K. Nagla, Social Exclusion, Globalisation and marginalised groups (in edit), Paramjit S. Judge, Mapping Social Exclusion in India: Caste, Religion and Borderlands, Cambridge University Press, 2014, p. 48.
30. UGC Emeritus Professor, Central University of Gujarat, delivered Inaugural lecture, at the National Conference on Human Rights in India: Dalits, Tribals and Minorities; held on 21-22 November 2013.
31. *Ibid.* Jaipur, pp.285-287.
32. *Ibid*, p. 290.
33. Former Director, Centre for Social Studies, Surat, delivered Inaugural lecture, at the National Conference on Human Rights in India: Dalits, Tribals and Minorities; held on 21-22 November 2013.
34. Honorary Professor, CSDS, New Delhi, delivered Key Note Address, at the National Conference on Human Rights in India: Dalits, Tribals and Minorities; held on 21-22 November 2013.
35. Former Director, NAVASARG Trust, Ahmedabad, delivered Inaugural lecture, at the National Conference on Human Rights in India: Dalits, Tribals and Minorities; held on 21-22 November 2013.
36. Jayal, Niraja Kumar, pp. 24-25.
37. *Ibid.*p. 300.
38. *Ibid.* (in edit) Ghosh, Biswajit (2012): "Interrogating Development: Discourse on Development in India", Rawat Publications, Jaipur, pp. 285-287.
39. *Ibid.* (in edit) Ghosh, Biswajit (2012): "Interrogating Development: Discourse on Development in India", Rawat Publications, Jaipur, pp. 285-287.
40. David Harwey (2005), Neoliberalism, Oxford University Press, Oxford, pp. 63-65.
41. Jayal, Niraja Gopal and Pai, Sudha, Introduction (in edit) Democratic Governance in India: Challenges of Poverty, Development, and Identity, Sage Publications, New Delhi, 2001, p.11.
42. *Ibid.* New Delhi, 2001, p.19.
43. *Ibid.* Jayal, Niraja Gopal and Pai, Sudha, p. 25.

# 1

# Dr Ambedkar and the Future of Indian Democracy*

*—Jean Dreze*

A few years ago, when a student from Delhi University asked Noam Chomsky what he thought about Indian democracy, Chomsky replied (echoing Gandhi's view of western civilisation) that "it would be a good idea". Had Dr Ambedkar been present, I am sure that he would have agreed. Indeed, Indian democracy today is a faint shadow of the hopes he had for it. He was well aware, of course, that his hopes might be dashed. The future of Indian democracy depends a great deal on the revival of Dr Ambedkar's visionary conception of democracy. This vision, I believe, also needs to be enlarged and updated in the light of recent experience.

## Revolutionary Democracy

Dr Ambedkar's vision of democracy was closely related to his ideal of a "good society". He was clear about this ideal. On many occasions, he stated that he envisaged a good society as one based on "liberty, equality and fraternity". Democracy, as he saw it, was both the end and the means of this ideal. It was the end because he Ultimately Considered Democracy as coterminous with the realisation of liberty, equality and fraternity. At the same time, democracy was also the means through which this ideal was to be attained. Dr Ambedkar's notion of "democratic government" went back to the fundamental idea of "government of the people, by the people and for the people", but "democracy" meant much more to him than democratic government. It was a way of life: "Democracy," he said, "is not merely a form of government. It is primarily a mode of associated living, of conjoint communicated experience. It is essentially an attitude of respect and reverence towards fellowmen."

Another crucial feature of Dr Ambedkar's conception of democracy is that it was geared to social transformation and human progress. Conservative notions of democracy, such as the idea that it is mainly a device to prevent bad people from seising power, did not satisfy him.

---

* An earlier version of this paper was Published in Indian Journal of Human Rights, 9, Jan-Dec 2005.

In an inspiring definition of the term, he described democracy as "a form and a method of government whereby revolutionary changes in the economic and social life of the people are brought about without bloodshed".

For this to happen, it was essential to link political democracy with economic and social democracy. Indeed, Dr Ambedkar's vision of democracy was inseparable from his commitment to socialism. Sometimes he referred to this combined ideal as "social democracy", in a much wider sense than that in which the term is understood today. The neglect of economic democracy was, in his view, one of the chief causes of "the failure of democracy in Western Europe". As he put it: "The second wrong ideology that has vitiated parliamentary democracy is the failure to realise that political democracy cannot succeed where there is no social or economic democracy. Social and economic democracy is the tissues and the fibre of a political democracy. The tougher the tissue and the fibre, the greater the strength of the body. Democracy is another name for equality. Parliamentary democracy developed a passion for liberty. It never made a nodding acquaintance with equality. It failed to realise the significance of equality and did not even endeavour to strike a balance between liberty and equality, with the result that liberty swallowed equality and has made democracy a name and a farce." In this and other respects, his analysis of the fate of democracy in Western Europe largely applies to India today.

## Rationality and Liberation

Dr Ambedkar's passion for democracy was closely related to his commitment to rationality and the scientific outlook. At an obvious level, rationality is necessary for democratic government since public debate (an essential aspect of democratic practice) is impossible in the absence of a shared adherence to common sense, logical argument and critical enquiry. Rational thinking is even more relevant if we adopt Dr Ambedkar's broad view of democracy as a state of "liberty, equality and fraternity". Indeed, rationality is conducive, if not indispensable to the realisation of these ideals. A person who is not free can afford to be irrational, since he or she is not in command in any case, but if we are to take control of our lives, rationality and a scientific outlook are essential.

There is also a close affinity between rationality and equality. For one thing, propaganda and manipulation are common tools of subjugation. The caste system, for instance, has been propped over the centuries by an elaborate edifice of irrational dogmas. The scientific outlook is essential to liberate and protect oneself from ideological manipulation. For another, the scientific spirit has a strong anti-authoritarian dimension. Authority rests on the notion that one person's view or wish counts more than another's. In scientific argument, this is not the case. What counts is that the coherence of the argument and the strength of the evidence. In that sense, the scientific outlook is a protection against the arbitrary exercise of power.

Even fraternity (perhaps better called solidarity or friendship) has something to do with rationality. Indeed, rational enquiry can be of great help in dispelling the prejudices that divide and oppose human beings. Science can also have a unifying influence in human affairs: the delights of scientific enquiry can be universally shared, irrespective of race, nationality, religion or other identities. As Bertrand Russell observed, "In the welter of conflicting fanaticisms, one of the few unifying forces is scientific truthfulness".

There is a view that reason and science are "western" notions, alien to the people of India, who have their own "modes of knowledge". This view is bound to astonish anyone who has cared to read the Buddha's teachings. Many centuries before Descartes, Buddha urged his followers to use their reason and not to believe anything without proof. In "*Buddha or Karl Marx*", one of his last speeches, Dr Ambedkar includes the following in his summary of the essential teachings of the Buddha: "Everyone has a right to learn. Learning is as necessary for man to live as food is. Nothing is infallible. Nothing is binding forever. Everything is subject to inquiry and examination."

This is not to deny that there are other modes of knowledge than rational argument and scientific discourse. That is the case not only in India, but all over the world. For instance, no amount of rational argument can convey what a jasmine flower smells like. Direct experience is indispensable. Similarly, if you hold the hand of an Iraqi child who has been wounded by American bombs, you may learn something about the nature of war that no amount of scientific information on "collateral damage" is likely to convey. In *The Buddha and His Dharma*, Dr Ambedkar gives a fine account of the distinction between *Vidya* (knowledge) and *Praja* (insight). In the step from *Vidya* to *Praja*, non-scientific modes of learning often play an important role.But this does not detract from the fundamental importance of rationality in individual enlightenment and social living.

One reason for bringing this up is that recent threats to Indian democracy include a concerted attack on rationality and the scientific spirit. I am thinking particularly of the Hindutva movement. As various scholars have noted, this movement can be interpreted as a sort of "revolt of the higher castes": an attempt to reassert the traditional authority of the upper castes, threatened as it is by the expansion of political democracy in independent India. This reassertion of Brahminical authority, in the garb of Hindu unity or even national unity, involves a suppression of rational thinking and critical enquiry. That is the real significance of the seemingly irrational statements and actions of many political leaders of the saffron variety: the call for teaching astrology in universities, the substitution of myths for history, the search for Lord Ram's "authentic" birthplace, the handover of research institutions to certified obscurantists, among other examples. I doubt that Mr Murli Manohar Joshi really cared for the inclusion of astrology in the university curriculum when he was in charge of the "Ministry of Human Resource Development", but what he possibly did care for was the nurturing of a spirit of submission to Brahminical obscurantism. Resisting this and other attacks on rationality is an important requirement of the defence of democracy in India today.

## Morality and Social Order

One of the most interesting features of Dr Ambedkar's political philosophy is his stress on the ethical dimension of democracy, or what he called "morality". One aspect of this is the importance of "constitutional morality", that is, of abiding by the spirit of the constitution and not just its legal provisions. Going beyond this, Dr Ambedkar felt that "morality", in the sense of social ethics, was indispensable for the realisation of liberty and equality. In the absence of morality, he thought, there were only two alternatives: "anarchy" or "the police".

One of Dr Ambedkar's many criticisms of the caste system was that it undermines social ethics and morality. In *Annihilation of Caste*, he thundered: "The effects of caste on the ethics of the Hindus are simply deplorable. Caste has killed public spirit. Caste has destroyed the sense of public charity. Caste has made public opinion impossible. A Hindu's public is his caste. "Virtue has become caste-ridden and morality has become caste-bound." He ultimately identified morality with "fraternity"-"a sentiment which leads an individual to identify himself with the good of others".

Dr Ambedkar's emphasis on morality was well integrated with his commitment to rationality and the scientific spirit. In particular, he considered that morality was always subject to rational scrutiny. His attraction to Buddhism has to be seen in the light of his twin commitment to morality and reason. Not only did he regard the Buddha's Dharma as compatible with (indeed committed to) reason, he also saw it as an expression of the ideal of "liberty, equality and fraternity". At one point, he stated that this ideal of his derived directly "from the teachings of my master, the Buddha". Towards the end of his life, he even seems to have nurtured the hope that the Dharma would become a universal code of social ethics.

In retrospect, Dr Ambedkar's vision of the Dharma as a universal code of ethics was perhaps a little naïve. I would even suggest that his devotion to the Buddha's teachings occasionally jarred with his commitment to critical enquiry and independence of mind. Having said this, his recognition of social ethics as an essential ingredient of democracy has not lost its relevance. If democracy is just political competition between self-interested individuals (as in, say, the median voter model), it will never succeed in bringing about liberty, equality and fraternity. In particular, it will never do justice to minority interests.

To illustrate, consider the problem of urban destitution in India – the plight of wandering beggars, street children, leprosy patients, the homeless, and others. These people constitute a small minority and they have no political power whatsoever (most of them do not even vote). Nor are they likely to have any in the foreseeable future. This is the main reason why the problem remains almost entirely unaddressed. If this problem is to come within the ambit of democratic politics (and there are signs that this is beginning to happen), it can only be on the basis of ethical concern. This illustration pertains to a relatively confined aspect of India's social problems, but the potential reach of ethical concerns in democratic politics is very wide. If social ethics acquire a central role in democratic politics, a new world may come into view.

## Democracy and Socialism

As mentioned earlier, Dr Ambedkar's vision of democracy encompassed "political, social and economic democracy". As he saw it, political democracy alone could not be expected to go very far, if glaring economic and social inequalities remained. A well-known expression of this concern was his parting speech to the Constituent Assembly: "On the 26th January 1950, we are going to enter into a life of contradictions. In politics we will have equality and in social and economic life we will have inequality. How long shall we continue to live this life of contra-dictions? How long shall we continue to deny equality in our social and economic life? If we continue to deny it for long, we will do so only by putting our political democracy in peril."

Dr Ambedkar's diagnosis raised the question of how the "contra-diction" was to be removed. Since he had distanced himself in the same speech from extra-constitutional methods (including not only violence, but also *satyagraha*), the answer presumably lay in democratic practice. However, Dr Ambedkar himself warned that the whole process of democratic practice in an unequal society was vulnerable to being derailed by vested interests. There is a hint of a chicken-and-egg problem here: what comes first, democracy or socialism?

At one stage, it seems, Dr Ambedkar envisaged that both would be enshrined in the Indian Constitution. A socialist constitution, as he saw it, was the key to reconciling democracy and socialism. Without constitutional protection for socialist principles such as state ownership of land and key industries, democracy would not be able to prevent the growth of economic disparities that would undermine socialism and ultimately democracy itself.

Dr Ambedkar's blueprint for a socialist constitution was presented in *States and Minorities*, an early memorandum submitted to the Constituent Assembly.

In retrospect, this memorandum looks a little simplistic in some important respects. For instance, one would hesitate to advocate "collective farming" with the same confidence today, in the light of recent evidence. However, this does not lessen the value of the larger idea of a socialist constitution, helping to reconcile socialism with democracy. And some aspects of Dr Ambedkar's blueprint are still relevant today.

Whatever its merits, Dr Ambedkar's proposal of a socialist constitution was a political non-starter. It had little chance of being accepted by the Constituent Assembly, where privileged interests were well represented. However, Dr Ambedkar did not abandon the idea of constitutional safeguards for socialist ideals and economic democracy. Ultimately, these were embodied in the "Directive Principles" of the Indian Constitution, which deal with a wide range of economic and social rights. The Directive Principles are indeed far-reaching, if one takes these seriously:

"In my judgment, the Directive Principles have a great value, for they lay down that our ideal is economic democracy. [Our] object in framing this Constitution is really twofold: (1) to lay down the form of political democracy, and (2) to lay down that our ideal is economic democracy and also to prescribe that every Government shall strive to bring about economic democracy."

As it turned out, however, the Directive Principles were not taken seriously in independent India. These were not enforceable in a court of law, and nor did electoral politics succeed in holding the state accountable to their realisation, as Dr Ambedkar had envisaged. We are left with a lopsided democracy, where reasonably sound democratic institutions coexist with social conditions that threaten to make parliamentary democracy "a name and a farce". Contrary to Dr Ambedkar's expectations, democracy in independent India has neither flourished nor perished. Instead, it has limped along, burdened by the "contradiction" he had identified, which is still with us today.

## The Future of Indian Democracy

How would Dr Ambedkar feel about Indian democracy today, if he were to be able to take a look at it? Quite likely, he would be very disappointed. He would certainly be appalled to find that the caste system, with all its horrors, is still alive. He would be equally dismayed by the continued subjugation of women in Indian society, and by other social inequalities that undermine democracy as he understood it. Political democracy did survive in some fashion, but social and economic democracy is still a distant goal. In fact, even political democracy is not in the pink of health. Further, Indian democracy is facing new challenges, including extreme economic inequality, growing militarism, rampant corruption, the expansion of corporate power, and the resurgence of Hindu majoritarianism (the biggest threat to democracy in India, according to Dr Ambedkar).

Having said this, there are also counter-trends, in the form of a growth of democratic space and democratic spirit. A startling variety of social movements have flourished in India, and creative initiatives strive to expand the boundaries of political democracy year after year. The quality of Indian democracy is also gradually enhanced by a better representation of women in politics, wider opportunities for people's involvement in local governance, and the spread of education among disadvantaged groups. The most powerful and promising trend is the growing participation of the underprivileged in democratic processes.

As discussed earlier, Dr Ambedkar had a visionary conception of democracy, which needs to be rediscovered today. But going beyond that, we must also enlarge this vision in the light of recent developments. While Dr Ambedkar was ahead of his time in stressing the link between political and economic democracy, perhaps he failed to anticipate the full scope of political democracy itself. Indeed, he thought of political democracy mainly in terms of electoral and parliamentary processes. Today, however, we are constantly discovering new forms of democratic practice, in which people are often able to participate even if economic democracy is nowhere near to being realised.

The basis of economic democracy also needs some rethinking, with a little help from the libertarian socialist tradition. Dr Ambedkar pinned his hopes for economic democracy mainly on state action: collectivisation of agriculture, state ownership of key industries, central planning, and so on. This is understandable, considering that the developmental state seemed to have enormous potential at that time, not only in the Soviet Union, but also in much of the developing world. However, the limits (and indeed dangers) of state control of the means of production have now become clearer. At the same time, there is also greater clarity about the scope for expanding economic democracy through other means, such as worker management, producer cooperatives, non-profit associations, participatory planning, and community control of environmental resources. The state, of course, also has a role to play, for instance by providing universal basic services – one example of "revolutionary changes in the economic and social life of the people" that can be (and have been) brought about through democratic struggles. The battle for economic democracy is far from lost, but it requires a different approach from that envisaged by Dr Ambedkar.

Indian democracy is still relatively young – sixty-seven years is not a long time to make the transition from a society built around the privileges of a small minority to one governed "by the people for the people". Dr Ambedkar's thought is an invaluable guide on this unfinished journey. But it would be just as counter-productive to claim that he had the final word on democracy as to say that Marx had the final word on class. It would also be an insult to his appeal for critical thinking. The best answer we can give to this appeal is to enrich Dr Ambedkar's profound ideas and insights with those of other schools of thought.

## References


- Ambedkar, B.R. (1936), *Annihilation of Caste*; reprinted in Government of Maharashtra (1979-98), volume I.
- Ambedkar, B.R. (1948), "States and Minorities", memorandum submitted to the Constituent Assembly; reprinted in Government of Maharashtra (1979-98), volume I.
- Ambedkar, B.R. ( 1952 ), "*Conditions Precedent for the Successful Working of Democracy*", Speech delivered at the Poona District Law Library; reprinted in Bhagwan Das (2010 ).
- Ambedkar, B.R. (1957), *The Buddha and His Dhamma* (Bombay: People's Education Society).
- Das, Bhagwan (ed.) (2010) *Thus Spoke Ambedkar* (New Delhi: Navayana).
- Government of Maharashtra (1979-98), *Dr Babasaheb Ambedkar: Writings and Speeches*, 16 volumes (Mumbai: Department of Education).
- Rodriguez, Valerian (ed.) (2002), *The Essential Writings of B. R. Ambedkar* (New Delhi: Oxford University Press).

# 2

# Globalisation, the State and Dalits

*—Anand Teltumbde*

## Globalisation: Genesis of the New World Order

Although globalisation may be the most discussed word in the lexicon of the last quarter of the century, it still defies a precise definition. Various people refer to globalisation variously. Very often, one particular dimension of globalisation is taken as key. For instance, a politically-centred definition may underscore the decline of the Nation-state and the territorially-bounded societies; while economically-centred definitions may underscore capitalism and the expansion of the free-market system as the prime mover of globalising processes. For some, globalisation is best understood as a legitimating cover or ideology, a set of ideas that distorts reality so as to serve particular interests.[1] Thus Schirato and Webb (2003: 199) view 'globalisation' as a 'discursive regime' and suggest that it 'functions as a set of texts, ideas, goals, values, narratives, disposi-tions and prohibitions, a veritable template for ordering and evaluating activities, which is "filled in" or inflected with the interests of whoever can access it.'[2] For others, globalisation is a much more 'material' reality in the contemporary world.

The Social Sciences Encyclopaedia privileges economics in defining globalisation associating it with the economic and imperial expansionism of the great powers since the sixteenth century.[3] It takes globalisation as a more advanced stage of this process of development. Langhorne (2001) highlights the dimension of technological advance as impelling other processes[4]. The Dictionary of Social Sciences considers globalisation as 'A catch-all term for the expansion of diverse forms of economic, political, and cultural activity beyond national borders'[5]. In Bauman's (1999) Formulation, globalisation is about 'time-space compression'[6]. Roland Robertson, take it as 'the crystallisation of the entire world as a single place'[7]. Lechte (2003) accepts Marshall McLuhan's 1962 phrase 'the global village'[8], which refers to a number of things: communication networks and new technology; the speed of movement; the emergence and contemporary prominence of the multinational corporation; the idea that physical distances are no more relevant; an awareness of the finitude of global resources; and the threat of a standardisation of cultural life. Michael Mann (2001) views globalisation as the extension of social relations over the globe[9], as Held and McGrew's (2002) define it as growing world interconnectedness.[10] Even institutions have offered their own definitions. For instance, the United Nations Conference on Trade and Development (UNCTAD) defines it as "the process of increasing economic integration among nations through cross-border flows of goods and resources, together with the development of a complementary set of organisational structures, to manage the associated network of economic activities."

A definitions galore indeed! All these definitions plausibly describe contemporary globalisation, but very few have indicated its political content dictated by the crisis-ridden trajectory of capitalism.

This tends to define contemporary globalisation as a euphemism for the imperialist strategy of capitalism in a terminal crisis[11]. Capitalism, by its very nature, is a globalising system. Karl Marx, who provided us with a comprehensive analysis of the capitalist system, had provided this insight in his Communist Manifesto, way back in 1848:

"The bourgeoisie cannot exist without constantly revolutionising the instruments of production, and thereby the relations of production, and with them the whole relations of society. Constant revolutionising of production, uninterrupted disturbance of all social conditions, everlasting uncertainty and agitation distinguish the bourgeois epoch from earlier ones. The need of a constantly expanding market for its produce chases the bourgeoisie over the whole surface of the globe. All old-established national industries have been destroyed or are being destroyed. In place of the old wants, satisfied by the productions of the country, we find new wants. In place of the old local and national seclusion and self-sufficiency, we have intercourse in every direction, universal interdependence of nations. The bourgeoisie compels all nations, on pain of extinction, to adopt the bourgeois mode of production. to become bourgeois themselves. In one word, it creates a world after its own image.[12]

Therefore there is no point in describing it like a strange phenomenon. Globalisation is essentially capitalism and only needs to be seen in its evolutionary context. What is important is to comprehend its contemporary specificities and more importantly the process that has occasioned it. The reason this calls contemporary globalisation as a strategy of capitalism is that capitalism has skillfully used up the opportunity provided by advances in technology and the debacle of the Soviet system to give itself a new lease of life through a serious crisis, which could prove to be its death knell. It naturally subsumed a combi-nation of economic, technological, socio-cultural and political forces, focusing primarily on economics – the integration of national economies into an international economy through trade, foreign direct investment, capital flows, migration, and the spread of technology, and so on.

As we know, capitalism is inherently a crisis prone system. In its short history of some four centuries, it has faced several crises, one more serious than the previous one. In the well known history from the later ninteenth century, we see it suffering a long depression, a worldwide economic recession, beginning in 1873 and running through the spring of 1879, which particularly hit the United Kingdom, the citadel of capitalism, and the United States of America which had been experiencing strong economic growth fuelled by the Second Industrial Revolution in the decade following the American Civil War. Capitalism grew thereafter at the unprecedented pace, but gave rise to the World War-I and thereafter the Great Depression of 1930 only to be rescued by "Keynesian prescription", which may have been inimical to its nature otherwise. It survived almost the fatal blow, but only to give rise to another World War, which offered it huge opportunity to prosper through the reconstruction of the world devastated in the War.

Capitalism, having experienced its golden period from 1948 to mid 1960s, due to massive reconstruction of the world devastated in World War II and unleashing pent up aspirations of new colonies that were freed during the period, faced severe crisis of over-production, fall in profits, lack of Investment opportunities, and Consequently social unrest all over the world. The oil price hike that came in its wake in 1973 created unprecedented financial crisis in many developing countries, which they overcame by taking huge debts from the banks in developed countries that were already stashed with surplus funds. This process resulted in a severe debt crisis by the end of the decade. On the other hand, the oil exporting countries had deposited their wind-fall profits in western banks accentuating the crisis further due to lack of investment opportunities.

In order to save the global banking system from imminent collapse, the Bretton Wood institutions adopted the package which was designed and tested out by the 'Chicago boys' in post-Allende Chile under the CIA sponsored dictator Augusto Pinochet. Although the ideology and economics behind these package was in making for decades right since the ascendency of the socialist ideology, its introduction in the form of globalisation creed has been soaked in the blood on the streets of Santiago. It came as micro-economic stabilisation and structural adjustment programme and imposed upon the debt ridden countries that approached the IMF and the World Bank for rescue loans. The debt crisis erupted first in the Latin American countries and therefore, they were thus first 'globalised'. The collapse of the so called socialist regime, partly under inertia of its own ideological degeneration and partly as engineered by the resurgent capitalist camp, by the end of the decade removed even the symbolic resistance and rendered the world unipolar with its apex in the USA. The United States, with its unrivalled military might and ideological leadership, emerged as a global hegemon to make globalisation the default system of the new world order.

## The Religion of the Elites

In the new world order, globalisation has become the ruling creed, a veritable religion of the elites. In our country, these policies were formally adopted in July 1991, taking shelter under the fact that the country faced an acute crisis on Balance of Payment (BoP) and did not have enough foreign exchange to meet country's import needs even for a fortnight. These were attributed to the duo of Narasimha Rao, and Manmohan Singh, the then Prime Minister and Finance Minister respectively. While this is true, the adoption of some amount of deregulation and liberalisation had begun with the second tranche of IMF loan India took in 1981 after the second coming of Indira Gandhi. After Indira Gandhi's assassination soon thereafter, her son Rajiv Gandhi, who became the Prime Minister, had given a major push to these policies with a series of deregulation and liberalisation measures in terms of increasing the number of industrial areas where TNC's could invest; allowing 100 per cent foreign equity in export-technology oriented units; introducing tax concessions for TNC's, and so on. Arguably, at least in part, it was the financial profligacy these policies represented that rather pushed the country into the BoP crisis of July 1991.

These policies boosted the sagging morale of the elites, from the rich to the upper layers of the middle classes, who were experiencing discomfort for over a decade. Conversely, the ill effect of these policies had shown up immediately across the vulnerable sections of society, such as peasants, workers, women, children, and lower strata of middle class people. However, sometimes with the arguments like 'there is no alter-native' (TINA), or sometime by pointing at the glitter of 'foreign goods' being freely available in shops or the spate of foreign cars running on the newly constructed flyovers as a proxy for development, or asking counter questions like "what good did the forty years of 'Licence Raj' do to the poor?", the protagonists of globalisation have managed to keep people in the state of bewilderment. Meanwhile, with ideological maturation globalisation spread its wings to cover all aspects of life. The spread of globalisation (neoliberal) culture, predominantly through satellite television and other media, to the nook and corner of the country silently worked in benumbing the senses of people to the suffering around and converting them into consumers. While some conscious section of intellectuals and activists tried to mobilise resistance to these monstrous strategy, they could not thwart its dinosaurian sweep. Much of it was ignored as the old-fashioned leftist propaganda or opposed this with combination of counter-propaganda and brute force. Their feeble voices were effectively drowned in the cacophonic din of half-lies issued from Washington, duly amplified by the entire elite sponsored establishment in Delhi.

## Heuristic and a Strategy

While on the one side, globalisation has been pushing scores of poor people to the margin, on the other it has been fast transforming the country into something the elites always dreamt of. By now it is incontrovertibly established that globalisation has been having a devastating impact on the majority of people. This fact of devastation has even been acknowledged by the globalist establishment, which, scared by the possible adverse reaction, came out with a proposition of a 'human face' through none other than Wolfensohn, the then President, World Bank. The experience establishes the heuristic that the severity of the adverse impact of globalisation is inversely proportional to one's standing in the socio-economic scale. That is, if you are at the bottom of the pyramid, you would be hit the hardest and conversely, if you are at the top, you would face it in negative, i.e., prosperity. In India, Dalits and lower castes occupying the lowest rung of the socio-economic scale, the impact of globalisation on them has been, as expected, the severest. However, the propaganda machinery of the entire comprador network of imperialism all over the globe would not let people see such a heuristic in operation. Their strategy consisted in the first instance of countering the facts by whatever means; if it could not be done, then acknowledge parts of them and propose palliatives; trumpet success in other parts and thereby create a cobweb of social engineering around people to keep them in a confused state. One must say that the strategy has not been entirely unsuccessful; now that no such evaluative discussion appears to be taking place and globalisation is virtually taken as an inevitability, a natural order, to be lived with.

While there has been an overabundance of discussion on the impact of globalisation, both negative and positive, theoretical, as well as empirical, on secular parameters of development, such as poverty, employment, health, etc., there is a relative lack of it on the other non-secular factors, such as race, colour, caste, gender, etc., which in large measure determine the state of the former. Particularly, caste, which is unique to our subcontinent, and which has acknowledgedly large influence on the development state of our people, appears completely ignored in these discussions. If there have been some passing references to it by way of empirical evidence and piecemeal concerns for reservations being decimated through privatisation, there is absolutely none in systemic causal terms as to how globalisation influences castes. In terms of the rhetoric that globalisation is a 'great leveller', which has gained grounds among some Dalit intellectuals in India, often ready to tow the line of powers that be, it is argued, that much as it was done at the time of the advent of capitalism, that castes would be destroyed by the forces of globalisation. Despite contrary experience with this argument, the rhetoric still goes on.

## Deliberate Confusion

The confusion about globalisation is particularly confounded due to the peculiar life experiences of Dalits. They impel them to see any devolution the of power of the local elite (upper castes) in a positive light. Since globalisation is projected as devolving power from nation state controlled by local elite to the global arena, they tend to see it as advantageous to them. It is coolly assumed that globalisation brings about devolution of power of the native elite and that devolution automatically becomes advantageous to Dalits. It is easy to see that both are incorrect. Nevertheless, this notion promoted by some people has shrouded all other specific considerations, such as education, health, employment and even caste discrimination itself. It is however true that the reality of Dalits represent a socio-economic complexity that is unique. While they are among the poorest of the poor, their poverty is not purely an economic parameter; it is the complex result of the contemporary economic processes and the extra-economic exploitation they suffered, and continue to suffer, through history. Any study, therefore, needs to comprehensively address both these features of their being.

Indeed, this special state of Dalits and their consciousness provides ample opportunities for the comprador elements to confuse their gullible section about the real character of globalisation. The argument ranges from the stereotypical 'economic growth' assumed to flow from globalisation, and benefit Dalits through the 'trickle down' effect to the onslaught of modernity assumed to stem from its processes which would crush castes. Some of them have even cleverly invoked Babasaheb Ambedkar, the demigod of Dalits, by painting him in monetarist colours, because of his thesis titled *The Problem of Rupee,* so as to show him as one of the neo-liberals in support of their argument. Insofar as globalisation is associated with imperialism, some people have gone to the extent of arguing that Dalits should support globalisation as they supported the British during British colonialism. These arguments, untenable though, have certainly served their purpose in spreading confusion among the Dalits and befogging this discourse.

## Neoliberal Character of Globalisation

Globalisation, essentially, spells the rise of free market capitalism and hence is confused with liberalism. However, the creed of globalisation needs to be distinguished from classical liberalism. Classical liberals were committed to individualism, liberty and equal rights and did believe in a free economy with minimal government interference. But they had qualified each of their terms with human considerations. For instance, individual liberty of classical liberty was to transgress others' liberty. But the creed of globalisation does not regard such restrictions and extends familiar tenets of liberalism to extremity to almost mean the opposite. Its individualism grants full liberty to wreck havoc on the entire world. Its free competition (sans interference of the government in liberalism) almost becomes Spenserian 'social Darwinism', portending disastrous consequence not only to the human race, but to the planet earth itself. The creed of globalisation, therefore, is distinguished as neoliberalism, the epithet derogatively given to it by the Latin Americans to reject its liberal pretentions. Liberalism is liberal, flexible; neoliberalism is not, it is the social extremism in favour of the powerful.

Capitalism successfully survived competition with the lure of emergent socialism to the masses by flexibly diluting its ideological stances as reflected in Keynesianism. The welfare state within a mixed economic paradigm, that became a default model of the state during its golden period, is the product of this flexibility. Neoliberalism finds fault with this flexibility and insists upon its tenets with fundamentalist vigour. Individualism valorises the individual to the neglect of the social, which implies legitimacy to the existing exploiting order and condemnation of complaint or agitation against it. Social Darwinist competition justifies inequality and denies the right to non-competitive people to live. Free market fundamentalism considers the market to be the supreme institutional framework for facilitating right transactions among individuals in a competitive mode. The manifestation of this essential character of globalisation is reflected by two powerful and significant trends: the first, trade liberalisation, which has virtually removed all controls on business by national governments via an aggressive promotion of a view that the greatest good will come for the greatest numbers when business has the fullest freedom to act wherever and whenever it sees fit and the second, global cultural homogenisation, dominated by American and Western life styles of hedonistic consumerism that has been sweeping the world.

Globalisation has led to new competitive demands imposed on firms by technological innovations, an intensification of competition, swiftly changing market opportunities and demands due to greater volatility in the labour, capital, and product markets, plus profound transformations of production processes via outsourcing, downsising or subcontracting.[13] These developments have significantly increased the uncertainty of working lives.[14] Deregulation and flexibility of the labour market, coupled with cutbacks in welfare state provisions[15], have become a specific dilemma for young job-seekers and jobholders with little experience[16] and to those like Dalits with weak ties to the labour market. Due to these changes, the world of work has been transformed beyond recognition. This is reflected in the growing demand for flexible labour and labour relations, and an acceleration of the pace and flow of work, in general. The shift from national product, capital, and labour markets towards expanding global markets[17] and consequently, progressing retrenchment of the welfare state and increasing stifling of the voice of labour has been clearly discernible[18] during the globalisation era.

Although, various countries have responded to these global pressures differently due to country-specific institutions and historical path dependence[19], none could escape the repercussions in entirety on its vulnerable population. Likewise at the level of individuals, the impact of globalisation has been varied. While for those working in modern service jobs like Information Technology and Finance, globalisation may have been a boon as it has led to rise in their salaries, but for majority of people working in other sectors, it has been a curse as their wages have grown at a much slower pace than before and have, in some areas, even stagnated. That has been an unfortunate reality for the vast majority of workers in India, who are faced with an annual inflation rate of near double digit and have to contend with a decline in purchasing power each year as a result.[20] There is a greater redundancy risk for workers with low educational qualifications, lacking labour force experience, and employed in insecure job positions. Globalisation opens the way for new, soft options that flexibly facilitates layoffs, wage adjustments or temporary employment. The issue of unemployment is a serious theme, especially because it is an aggravating factor in the process of deepening inequality and social exclusion. The extremely serious problem is the so-called "structural unemployment", which is a consequence of both the loss of competitiveness of certain sectors of the economy which were formerly protected by almost unassailable tariff or non-tariff barriers and the enormous productivity gains per work unit, coupled with lower wages.

Globalisation has certainly exacerbated the issues of inequality and social exclusion. It is manifested both on the international plane and on the internal plane by both developed and developing countries. The worst thing is that it has lent legitimacy to these evils. In the dimension of interpersonal relations, inequality is regarded less as the product of "capitalist exploitation" or of distortions of the model of accumulation, than of the qualitative differences in labour and of innate, or acquired skills and abilities. In the dimension of the relations between states, inequality is perceived not so much as a historical, political, economic or cultural phenomenon, but rather as incapacity to adapt to the institutional and ideological framework which prevails in "nations who are winners". This waning of the economic, sociological, historical or ethical explanation for inequality leads to the growth of indifference and intolerance with regard to losers, who are classified as the only ones responsible for their own backwardness.

The grievous implication of this character of globalisation to the people like Dalits is clear.

## Indian State: Neoliberalism Personified

What has globalisation done to the Indian state? The Indian state formed after independence is a constitutional state, which is supposed to inherit its values and ideology and conduct itself as ordained by it. The Indian Constitution can be taken as the epitome of virtue within the liberal tradition. If we take an objective evaluation of the performance of the Indian state, we would come to an undeniable conclusion that it has miserably failed in meeting the constitutional expectations. However, benchmarking it to other liberal bourgeoisie states that were born in the erstwhile colonies, one may have to acknowledge that the Indian state has not done badly. Notwithstanding its socialist pretensions, the Indian state came into being quintessentially as the bourgeoisie landlord state in a delicate political context of traumatic partition, problematic of integration of nearly 600 princely states dotting its territory, armed peasant rebellions led by the communists, presence of politicised minorities and not the least, the politically awakened mass of Dalits, its organic proletariat. As such, it had to gain quick legitimacy with all classes and convince them that their interests would be best secured with it. It accomplished this through the Constitution that came to be the epitome of liberal ideals, with an imprint of a person of Dr Ambedkar's stature as its architect. Dr Ambedkar was not only adored by Dalits, but as the lifelong battler against the mighty Congress was respected by other minorities and others who were suspicious of the Congress. While the Constitution became a laudable document, the rest of the apparatus of the state–the structure, the bureaucracy, the processes, and the entire operative laws that relate with people—was adopted in toto from the colonial regime in order to lace itself with all the repressive power of the colonial state.

Under the cover of socialist rhetoric, the Indian state ensured to further the capitalist agenda. As a matter of fact what are identified as Nehruvian socialist markers, were actually proposed by the collective of capitalists in a document that anticipated transfer of power full three years before it actually happened. The document that outlined the investment plan for 15 years for independent India was prepared by the who's who of Indian industry (such as JRD Tata, GD Birla, Kasturbhai Lalbhai, Purshottamdas Thakurdas and Shri Ram) as well as top technocrats such as John Matthai, (Matthai, who drafted the document, later became India's Finance Minister) Ardeshir Dalal and AD Shroff and came to be known as Bombay Plan (1944-45). If you take a close look at this plan, you would realise that what followed for the next 15 years was the implementation of the blueprint given in the plan. Indians innocently believed that the model of mixed economy, with the public sector playing a key role, was the product of Nehru's socialist proclivities. Not only them, but also the world was befooled into believing when India adopted the system of Five Year Plan, which was identified then with the USSR, that India was inclined to go the Soviet way. They had better known that the Bombay Plan had itself advocated the central planning and a strong public sector. It stated, "that practically every aspect of economic life will have to be vigorously controlled by the government." Not only our first five year plan, which was launched immediately in 1947 adopted the Bombay Plan outlays in toto, the subsequent two plans, which were supposed to be guided by the celebrated Mahalnobis development model, also approximately confirmed to the Bombay Plan. It may be seen in retrospect that the next significant policy measure in the form of the Green Revolution, which ostensibly was to solve our food security problem, also served the capitalist interests by germinating markets (agro-input market, agro-output market, farm implement market, credit market, and of course, money economy) in the vast countryside and created huge investment opportunities.

Notwithstanding these sorry facts about the biography of the Indian state, the Indian state remained a capitalist state and largely behaved within the Keynesian framework that informed most non-socialist states then. Keynesianism, marked by full employment, had mandated the state to undertake huge investments, brought about a big state sector in the national economy. Eulogised as the modern temples in the Nehruvian rhetoric, the existence of the public sector lent credibility to the state being above society and particularly independent of the capitalist interests. As regards the feudal interests, the state had undertaken calibrated policy measures that would not dent their interests, but, at the same time, reinforce its credibility with the majority of people who thirsted for land. It had brought in Land Reforms that displaced the erstwhile upper caste landlords from villages to the urban areas which offered better prospects for their prosperity and replaced them with the people of middle castes, hugely altering the social and political configuration of rural India. The land Reforms created an illusion about redistribution through the slogans like 'land to the tillers' and reinforced the socialist rhetoric, but created a new class of rich farmers, from amongst the populous caste band of Shudras to have better control on the countryside. This class which was hugely enriched by the capitalist strategy of Green Revolution additionally wielded the baton of Brahmanism to keep Dalits, denuded of their traditional security of the *jajmani* system and who were reduced to rely on them as agricultural wage labourers, suppressed. They soon graduated to be the formidable political power block from panchayat to parliament and also as an economic power.

The state with its socialist rhetoric during Nehru's times gave systematic support for capitalist development in the country as willed by the nascent bourgeoisie. After Nehru, his daughter – Indira Gandhi- developed her own pro-poor rhetoric to decimate the political opposition and in the process ruffled feathers of a section of the bourgeoisie that were seen as supporters of the opposition, but promoted new genre of it represented by the likes of Dhirubhai Ambani. While some of them prospered with political patronage, the overall global crisis of capitalism after the mid 1970s could not be thwarted. After the second coming of Indira Gandhi, she took the then biggest loan IMF advanced to any country and with that, the policies had a subtle neoliberal tilt. When Indira Gandhi was assassinated and her son Rajiv Gandhi took the reins of power, they became visible as discussed before. It could not help in political management and the country plunged into turmoil, both politically and economically. Therefore, when after Rajiv Gandhi's assassination, Narsimha Rao became the Prime Minister; he adopted reforms as a no-alternative policy package and installed the neoliberal team to manage its implementation. All the key people in the Planning Commission, and Ministries like Finance, commerce and petroleum were with IMF/World Bank connection, many of whom still continue. With these new people in saddle driving the reforms, the state itself transformed itself into a neoliberal state.

Prabhat Patnaik noted two features of this neoliberal state: "One, the change in the nature of the state, from being an entity apparently standing above society and intervening in its economic functioning in the interests of society as a whole, even at the expense of the unbridled interests of finance capital to being an entity acting exclusively to promote the interests of finance capital. The second feature related to the fact that since finance capital in the contemporary era is not exclusively tied to any particular national domain (and its imperial adjunct), but has an international character, to protect and promote it on the global plane where it operates, a surrogate global state necessarily has to come into being; and this role is performed by the major capitalist states acting in unison under the leadership of the most powerful state, the U.S., and enjoying the support of the less powerful nation-states whose own large capitalists and financiers are in favour of such an arrangement."[21] What we call the unipolar world does not refer only to the end of cold war, but the nation states conceding the leadership role to the US to protect the interest of global capital. This arrangement itself reflects the existence of the surrogate global state that Patnaik refers to.

Many people erroneously take this change in the nature of the capitalist state as the retreat of the state. There is no retreat or minimalising of the state that has happened. On the contrary, the state has become much stronger in its core functions in its transformation into a neoliberal state. It has just discarded its role of spender or investor to produce goods and services on behalf of people and donned the role of executor of the neoliberal agenda on behalf of the global capital. In order to perform this new role it required far more strengthening of its core coercive function (All liberal political theorists from Locke to Hobbs grant the central role to coercion as a necessary part of a state's function) because the move to withdraw from the domains that benefitted people and to help private interests in taking them over for pursuit of profits would surely provoke resistance from the majority and the state needed power to repress it.

Even to perform this new role, the state had to have legitimacy, which could be secured through non-economic superstructural constructions. The new superstructural construction has been cleverly provided by the US in the form of 'War on Terror'. It created fear psychosis in people about security and made them reliant on the state which promised to fight the forces of insecurity on their behalf. In the name of security, the state could virtually do everything with impunity: curb fundamental rights, block democratic expression, assume totalitarian powers, etc. This security syndrome came handy for the states in developing countries for subjugating their large populations. They improvised it according to their needs and local conditions. Nowhere is it more pronounced than in India, where, apart from Islamophobia inherited from the global establishment, it has created a phantom of internal security threat to curb any kind of dissent. Anybody, who dared to ask radical question, could be termed Maoist and slapped with all kinds of charges under the draconian laws such that it terrorises scores of others against such acts. Adivasis and Dalits, who are the worst victims of the neoliberal policies and also potentially the most revolutionary mass, have been particularly targeted by it. Another superstructural ploy the state adopted to secure social legitimacy is to promote religious and communal consciousness and invoke the construct of a 'nation', which is essentially imperialist, racist and xenophobic conception and manufacture consent around it, through the use of the media controlled by the financial interests themselves.

The transformed state essentially internalised neoliberal ethos of social Darwinism that valorises the strong and condemns the weak. Although the Indian state had always promoted the interests of capitalists, it was aware that it could not be done by completely ignoring the interests of the working classes. The classical schema informed it that for the very survival of the capitalist system, proletariat needs to reproduce as the provider of labour and needs to have purchasing power in order to be the customer for its finished product. Howsoever, the capitalist might like to maximise surplus through exploitation of labour it could never ignore this constraint. Over the years, however, due mainly to the influx of advanced technology that not only displaced labour, but also the labourer, this schema is becoming applicable to an increasingly narrower section of the population, which has disposable surplus. The vast majority of impoverished people are pushed to the margins where the parallel subsistence economy, characterised by cheap and imitation goods, has come into existence, where producers and consumers lose distinction as in the agrarian subsistence economy. It is because of this changed configuration of the economy that neoliberalism is emboldened to ignore the poor. The state as a political entity, however, has to 'manage' them, which it does by providing 'targeted' support to them. It no more talks about the rights of people, but the dole such that its growth machine could go on unhindered.

## Dalits: Pushing into Dark Times

The impact of globalisation on Dalits will be evident even from the foregoing discussion on the nature of globalisation and the state. Nonetheless, we can review the same in specific and comprehensive terms. Although Dalits tend to be a complex subject, on a careful analysis, we can see that they are a part of poor people additionally handicapped by the social discrimination they suffer on account of the caste system. From their perspective, much of their woes, including poverty, is due to their caste. From purely a methodological viewpoint, we can isolate these two aspect of Dalit being, viz., they being a part of the poor, and being the socially oppressed people, and see how they are impacted by globalisation.

## Dalits as a part of the Poor

The biggest promise of globalisation is economic growth. This growth, as the protagonists claim, would trickle down to the lowest strata of the society making eventually all better off. Contrary to a commonplace notion prevalent among Dalits that economic condition of a person does not mean freedom from caste, it is futile to deny that economic condition does loosen a person's caste shackles. If Dalits were not economically dependent upon the caste Hindus, caste system would have found it difficult to survive. Caste system is rooted in the premise of a backward economy in which a large population, devoid of any means of living, is utterly dependent upon the higher caste people. If the entire country becomes economically developed so as to be capable of having reasonable distributive justice in terms of economic prosperity, the very base of the caste system would begin to crumble. The promise of economic prosperity of globalisation, therefore, becomes a welcome proposition in the scheme of annihilation of castes.

It is generally assumed that free trade and competition are conducive to economic growth.[22] Protagonists of globalisation pitch the state against the market and claim that the state is an inefficient institution that does little for society beyond providing stability and protection. The activities related to distributing resources and economic growth, they say, are better left to the "invisible hand" of the market. Globalist propaganda almost projects it as the undisputed premise. However, there is plethora of literature that disputes market prowess to produce growth without the unkind hand of the state. The entire free trade argument generally rest on the theory of comparative advantage, introduced by David Ricardo in 1821 in his *Principles of Political Economy and Taxation*. Now, even the undergraduate economics student also knows that Ricardo "proved" his theory of comparative advantage using a two country, static model of the world, using examples of Portugal as more efficient producer of both wine and cloth than England, but with greatest superiority in wine production. Ricardo demonstrated that, in his modified world, both Portugal and England would gain if Portugal concentrated on producing wine and England on cloth and traded their produce in a mode of free trade. There have been refinements to Ricardo's theory in mainstream economics in the form of the Hecksher-Ohlin theory[23], Stopler-Samuleson theory[24], etc., but still, Ricardo's conclusion is generally held valid.

Anybody can see that the theory of comparative advantage is based on a number of assumptions, such as there is perfect competition between firms, there is full employment of all factors of production, labour and capital are perfectly mobile within a country and do not move across national borders; a country's gains from trade are captured by those living in the country and spent locally; a country's external trade is always in balance, and market prices accurately reflect the real (or social) costs of the products produced.[25] Even a quick consideration of these assumptions reveals that they are extensive and unrealistic. Moreover, if they are not satisfied, there is no basis for accepting the theory's conclusion that free-market policies will promote international well being.[26] If the premise thus is shaky, the conclusions automatically ought to become suspect. The economic growth accruing through free trade is not necessarily held out either by theory or the practice.

This faltering of theory is corroborated by the empirical evidence. Martin Hart-Landsberg and Burkett (2006) show that even in the current phase of globalisation, this much claimed economic growth had not materialised and that the post-1980 neoliberal era has been marked by slower growth, greater trade imbalances, and deteriorating social conditions.[27] The following "Globalisation Facts and Figures" reported by the International Forum on Globalisation illustrates it further: "Excluding China, there are 100 million more poor people in developing countries than a decade ago.[28] "Since 1980, economic decline or stagnation has affected 100 countries, reducing the incomes of 1.6 billion people. For 70 of these countries, average incomes are less in the mid 1990s than in 1980, and in 43, less than in 1970."[29] For developing countries as a whole (excluding China), the average trade deficit in the 1990s was higher than in the 1970s by almost 3 per centage points of GDP, while the average growth rate was lower by 2 per cent per annum."[30] According to the 2003 *United Nations Human Development Report*, some 54 countries – mainly in sub-Saharan Africa – are poorer now than in 1990. In 21, countries, a larger proportion of people are going hungry. In 14, more children are dying before the age of five. In 12, primary school enrolments are shrinking. In 34, life expectancy has fallen. If present trends continue, this situation will only get worse.

This pattern was broadly similar in all developing regions. In Latin America, the average growth rate was lower by 3 per cent per annum in the 1990s than in the 1970s, while trade deficits, as a proportion of GDP, were much the same. In sub-Saharan Africa, growth fell, but deficits rose. The Asian countries managed to grow faster in the 1980s, while reducing their payments deficits, but in the 1990s, they have run greater deficits without achieving faster growth.[31] A study by Mark Weisbrot, Dean Baker, and David Rosnick on the consequences of neoliberal policies on third world development comes to similar conclusions. The authors note that, "contrary to popular belief, the past 25 years (1980–2005) have seen a sharply slower rate of economic growth and reduced progress on social indicators for the vast majority of low- and middle-income countries (compared with the prior two decades)."[32] India is normally cited as a bright example of economic growth, but, even here evidence during the first decade of globalisation was quite shaky, as could be seen from Table 1.

**Table 1: General Comparison of Pre and Post-Globalisation Periods**

| | ***Decade of 1980s*** | ***Decade of 1990s*** |
|---|---|---|
| GDP Growth Rate | 5.6 per cent | 5.9 per cent |
| Growth Rate of commodity production | 5.0 per cent | 4.3 per cent |
| Growth Rate of Agricultural production | 3.84 per cent | 1.24 per cent |
| Growth Rate of foodgrain production | 3.46 per cent | 1.22 per cent |
| Increase in employment in the organised sector over the decade | 16.8 per cent | 5.8 per cent |
| Growth Rate of industry | 7.7 per cent | 5.8 per cent |
| Rate of capital formation | 7.3 per cent | 4.2 per cent |
| Growth of electricity generation | 12.4 per cent | 3.5 per cent |
| Growth of imports per annum | 4.5 per cent | 8.0 per cent |
| Growth of exports per annum | 8.3 per cent | 8.4 per cent |
| Drop in value of the Rupee, *vis-à-vis* the US Dollar | Rs. 10 drop | Rs. 30 drop |

*Source:* Calculated from various figures in the Economic Survey of various years.

Before the growth premise could be firmly established, globalisation had rather pushed the world into deadly recessions since August 2008, wiping out millions of jobs, trillions of dollars of wealth and pushing majority of people to the brink of disaster. Mark Martinez, in his recent book *The Myth of the Free Market,* describes how the flawed myth of the "invisible hand" distorted our understanding of how modern capitalist markets developed and actually work. Martinez drew from history to illustrate that political processes and the state are not only instrumental in making capitalist markets work, but that there would be no capitalist markets or wealth creation without state intervention. He brings his story up to the present day to show how the seeds of an unprecedented government intervention in the financial markets were sown in past actions.[33] Indeed, today, there is no need to be labour for refuting the standard mantras of neoclassical free market economic theory that free trade automatically leads to economic growth. Although the hardcore neoliberals still shyly persist with their proposition of free trade, they cannot hide the obvious conclusion to the contrary. In the attempt of rescuing the institutions of globalisation, the States have been channelling trillions of dollars of public money and taking charge of these institutions. It is the State that is eventually saving the market.

The second argument of the protagonists of globalisation is that the growth trickles down to make all better off. Of course, if this is the state of growth, there is no question of anything trickling down to the poor. However, even if growth accrued, as it did in some countries like India (after 2000) and China, the trickle has not materialised. Instead, it has created a grotesque spectre of producing billionaires at the fastest rate, on the one hand, and farmers' suicides at an unprecedented rate, at the other. There is no theoretical basis, whatsoever for this metaphorical theory. This metaphor of trickle admits anyway that globalisation is not oriented to benefit the poor in the first place. It primarily benefits the better off and then only it reaches the poor through the trickling process. Further, this metaphor commonsensically assumes permeability of the medium (social structure) for the trickle to happen. At least in India it certainly does not exist with its impregnable caste layers. Leave aside India, nowhere in the world this 'trickle down' has happened. As a result, whatever growth that accrued during globalisation was increasingly pocketed by the rich leaving an ever wider gap between them and the poor. Inequality is the single biggest outcome of globalisation that stands acknowledged by even the globalist camp. Globalisation has engendered explosive patterns of social polarisation within and between nations. In 2001 itself, the 358 billionaires of the world had assets estimated at $760 billion equivalent to the wealth of the bottom 45per cent of the world population, that is about 2.7 billion individuals. The three richest people in the world owned assets that exceeded the combined gross domestic products of the world's poorest 48 Countries. This trend has persisted through later years until it met with recession from 2008 onwards. Obscene patterns of poverty and inequalities, amidst ostentatious wealth, are thus the very stuff of our global system.

The above discussion shows that primarily the much vaunted claim of economic growth through globalisation itself has not materialised. Even if it had materialised, as in some countries, there is no evidence, either in theory or practice, that it has trickled down to poor. It could be historically seen that economic growth does not automatically correlate with reduction in poverty. The only surest outcome of globalisation has been the galloping inequality at every level. The implication of these finding to the castes is clear, as corroborated by the experience that globalisation, rather than weakening the castes, may contribute to aggravation of their viciousness.

There is no point in talking about poverty, which has become a much abused statistic in the hands of the Indian government right since the advent of globalisation. Every government (and that is the evidence that the ruling classes in the country are united on it) has gone out of its way to prove how globalisation has helped bring down poverty. As the evidence of increase in poverty poured through the 53rd round of the National Sample Survey (NSS), marking the shocking reversal of the decades- long declining trend of poverty[34], the government had suddenly began claiming a ridiculous fall in poverty figures ostensibly to counter the rising anti-globalisation sentiment prompted by this evidence. It fraudulently claimed a drop in the poverty figures to less than half from 37.09 per cent in 1993/94 to 18 per cent in 2001-02. It took a while for the experts to know that the methodology of the survey was mysteriously changed. Since then, the game has gone on without any shame.

Recently, there has been a huge controversy over the issue of poverty line when the government declared Rs 32 and Rs 26 daily spend per person shall be the poverty line for urban and rural areas respectively. By its own reckoning using this basis, 40.74 crore people, i.e., one-third population of India, are below the poverty line. Although this definition is ridiculed widely by people, it innocuously showed how government has been playing with this vital parameter merely to claim how globalisation benefitted the people. The government may have succeeded in confounding the poverty issue among the experts, but the fact remains that the poverty has not come down (if at all it has come down) at the pace it had experienced during the earlier decades with much modest economic growth. Moreover, poverty is a vulgar parameter to assess a policy. Even if a person is better off today than yesterday in spending, it does not itself becomes a cause for celebration. The government should be concerned with what he/she is spending his earnings on. Everybody knows that the basic necessities of life have become expensive because of globalisation and hence, the per-capita spend will show a rise. It does not mean that the people are materially better off today than yesterday. What matters is whether they are getting more food to eat, more medicines for health care, better education, and so on. If you ask, such relevant questions, the answers will surely be in the negative. Speaking about Dalits, the gap even in the per capita spend between theirs and others still persists. Much of their earnings are eaten away by doctors, medicine, and education, leaving lesser food to eat.

Poverty could be assessed in other ways too. It is the cumulative result of deprivation on many counts. As for the rural population, the declining public investment in agriculture, trade liberalisation in many agricultural products, declining rural employment, sharp rise in prices of food items and the government's abdication of the responsibility to provide food security to people by performing 'funeral rites of the Public Distribution System', all under the dictates of globalisation, have been mainly responsible for their material deprivation. Because of the fiscal fundamentalism induced by globalisation, the public investment in agriculture faltered during the 1990s and resulted in wild fluctuations in agricultural growth, touching a deep trough in some years:

from 5.0 per cent in 1994-95 to a negative 0.9 per cent the following year then to a positive growth of 9.6 per cent in 1996-97 and again a negative 1.9 per cent in 1997-98. It rose in 1998-99 to 7.2 per cent, but fell to 0.8 per cent in 1999-2000. It was mainly attributed to the sharp decline in investment in agriculture: from the level of 2.2 per cent of GDP at the base year 1990-91 to as low as 1.4 per cent of the GDP in 1998-99. Foodgrain production fell, provoking IFRI to warn the country that it would face cereal deficits of 36 to 64 million tonnes a year by 2020.[35] A study by Utsa Patnaik had pointed out that the per capita availability of foodgrains for human consumption had fallen substantially during the globalisation-decade, most during the years, 1998-99 to 2000-2001, because of the aggressive income-deflating policies of the NDA government.[36]

The price rise for foodgrains, owing mainly to cuts in food and fertiliser subsidies, has particularly been harsh. In a single year between 1999 and 2000, the food prices had doubled.[37] As a result; the per capita consumption of foodgrains declined from 510 grams in 1991 to 458 grams in 2000. The ill effect of this decline was showing up in the National Family Health Survey (NFHS) in terms of alarming rate of malnourishment among children and incidence of anaemia among young mothers. For almost 90 per cent of Indians, the share of income that goes to buy food is more than 50 per cent. For the poorest 50 per cent of the population, expenditure on food is over 70 per cent of the income[38]. Thus, any food scarcity or a rise of food prices or any fall in wages has adverse conse-quences on food intake. Food scarcity affects women more and threats to food security will have a grave and immediate impact on women's health. It is under such circumstances the government, under the spell of globalisation, promoted production of cash crops for exports.

**Table 2: Sectoral Estimated Employment Elasticities with Respect to GDP - All India**

| *Period / Sectors* | *1977-78 To 1983-84* | *1983-84 To 1993-94* | *1993-94 To 1999-2000* | *1999-2000 To 2004-05* | *1993-94 To 2004-05* |
|---|---|---|---|---|---|
| Agriculture | 0.45 | 0.50 | - 0.10 | 1.52 | 0.36 |
| Mining + quarrying | 0.80 | 0.69 | –0.55 | 0.80 | 0.03 |
| Manufacturing | 0.67 | 0.33 | 0.30 | 0.34 | 0.32 |
| Electricity, gas, water (Utilities) | 0.73 | 0.52 | –0.13 | 0.32 | 0.02 |
| Construction | 1.00 | 1.00 | 1.11 | 0.85 | 0.97 |
| Trade | 0.78 | 0.63 | 0.54 | 0.61 | 0.57 |
| Transport and storage | 1.00 | 0.49 | 0.70 | 0.27 | 0.46 |
| Financial services | 1.00 | 0.92 | 0.80 | 0.94 | 0.86 |
| Community, social and personal services | 0.83 | 0.50 | 0.07 | 0.29 | 0.15 |
| **Total** | **0.53** | **0.41** | **0.15** | **0.48** | **0.29** |

*Source*: For 1977-78 over -1983 -84 and 1993/94 Over 1983 -84, Planning Commission, 2001.

For the balance periods: S.K. Sasikumar and Anup K. Karan, Global Downturn and Export Sector in India: Impact on Production, Export and Employment, V. V. Giri National Labour Institute, 2010.

Competitive pressure of globalisation has directly impacted employment through increasing capital intensity of investments, as revealed by the fall in the employment elasticities during the globalisation periods as shown by Table 2. During 1977-78 to 1983-84, all the sectoral elasticities were pretty much higher than those in later periods, except in the period 1999–2000 to 2004–05 For Agriculture, the elasticties fell just during the decade from mid-1980s 1983-84 to 1993/94), identified as informal globalisation and further in during the next decade 1993-94 to 1999-2000 of formal globalisation. Surprisingly during the next decade (1999-2000 to 2004-05), the elasticties show a drastic rise, mainly against Agriculture and during the next decade (1993-94 to 2004-05) they fall, but show a marked increase against construction. However, except for the decade 1999-2000 to 2004-05, there is a distinct tendency for the elasticties to fall. Notwithstanding these technicalities, many economists have concluded the employment scenario during the post-globalisation period as jobless growth. Even the results of the recent survey conducted from July 2009 to June 2010 by the NSS, has revealed that employment generation actually decreased sharply between 2004-05 and 2009-10, the period of exceptional economic growth, when compared to the earlier five-year period[39].

The fall in employment elasticities could be taken as a natural trend because of the increasing content of technology in the production processes. but what is clearly attributable to globalisation is the massive closure of the small scale industries, pervasive corporate downsising, outsourcing, and informalisation of jobs with the tacit consent of the government. The corporates feel unconstrained, as never before, in following any strategies like contractisation and casualisation of jobs while crying foul at the continuing constraints of labour laws. This trend is not confined to India; it is the scenario all over the entire world. The numbers of part-time workers, seasonal workers, home workers and subcontracted workers are growing in leaps and bounds all over the world.[40] This trend is confirmed by the helplessness of the working class as reflected in the wage squeeze experienced during the 1990s[41] and the tremendous fall in the ratio of the man-days lost due to strike and lockouts[42]. The rural employment growth fell to an alarming 0.67 per cent during 1993-94 to 1999-2000; urban employment growth fell equally sharply, to 1.34 per cent over the same period. These are far below the annual growth of population of the job seekers, thus causing huge unemployment year by year.

Thus, globalisation, not only in its ideological bias, but also in its empirical manifestation, can be seen against the poor. Its impact on Dalits, who are a part of the poor, rather the poorest, has to be the severest.

## Dalits as a Disadvantaged Social Group

The impact of globalisation on Dalits, as a socially excluded people, can be conceived in two domains: one, the constitutional space that signifies the current mode of their specific existence and two, the long term project of their emancipation.

The Constitutional space for the Dalits comprises mainly the provision of reservations in the state-aided educational institutions and in the employment of government and public sector companies. Notwithstanding the fact that these provisions can be faulted in their conceptualisation as well as implementation, there may not be much doubt that they have played a crucial role in the progress of a section of Dalits. Globalisation has variously constricted this space and as a result, without any actual change in the Constitution, has brought reservations to a virtual end.

During the globalisation period, the government appointed two committees: one, Punnayya Committee (1993) that looked into funding of central universities to recommend how education, especially higher education, should be financed and two, Swaminathan Committee (1994) which looked into possibilities of resource mobilisation in technical education, essentially through 'cost recovery' from students. The basic thrust of these committees was to term higher education as private good and hence to make a case for its marketisation. Many study groups and committees worked to reinforce this viewpoint that surfaced clearly in the recommendations in the Birla-Ambani report on the Policy Framework for Reforms in Education (April 2000). The very fact that the government solicited such a report from the representatives of global capital, and not from any expert in the education field or an academician, exposed the hidden strategies of globalisation. This report conceded that providing primary education was the obligation of the government, but advocated privatisation and total marketisation of the higher education including influx of foreign direct investment in it. It proposed the market for private credit under the alibi of providing financial assistance to the needy students. It is interesting to see how the recommendations of the various committees cohered with the World Bank opinion that the role of the government should be limited to providing only primary education.

While this was happening in respect of higher education, interestingly, there was considerable emphasis on spreading literacy. Guess why. The intention was to include people into the market net. The illiterates cannot read advertisements and hence remain out of the market net. The objective was clear: Literacy for the masses and the higher education to the classes who pay its 'commercial' cost. The increasing cost of education, on the one hand, and the drying up of the motivation for education because of no-job prospects created by globalisation on the other, is fast, proving the that reservation in education is meaningless. In addition, the generally pervading ethos of globalisation has marginalised the discourse of reservation. The recent court judgements removing reservation to the SCs and the STs in the minority-run educational institutions can be a example of this trend. Globalisation has created a neo-caste divide in education which is pushing them back into the dark times. It is going to effectively shut the doors of education to Dalits as they were in the reign of Manu!

The impact of this trend is seen in the alarming rate of school dropouts among the Dalits during recent years. This may be explained by the need for Dalit children to supplement their falling family incomes as also by the erosion of the faith that education could be the instrument to change the pathetic course of their lives. With primary education itself becoming an insurmountable barrier and higher education becoming a virtual taboo, Dalits are getting literally left out of the educational arena. The impetus that privatisation and commercialisation of education received during the globaliation period is literally pushing education out of public sphere and thereby neutralising the constitutional provisions for the Dalits. Left out of education, the only future that could be in wait for them is alienation, lumpenisation and criminalisation.

The spheres of education and jobs are mutually reinforcing. The winds of privatisation blown by globalisation have already shaken the foundations of reservations in the job sphere. The condition of Dalits in the PSU-companies that were privatised has been miserable; most of them having been driven out under the cover of VRS. But it is no more the same even in the PSUs. The globalisation ethos has emboldened PSU managements to unleash their anti-Dalit prejudices with an alibi of competition in the marketplace. The better ones of these PSUs have undergone restructuring investing managements with arbitrary powers to do what they liked with impunity. These developments have given managements a field day in operating their pent up prejudices against Dalit employees as evidenced by a sudden spurt in the cases of departmental actions against and dismissals of Dalit employees during this period, without resorting to outright sale of the PSUs, the government initially tried out the indirect method of privatisation by allowing these PSUs to form joint venture companies in the private sector by offering its private partner 50 per cent equity. As such, within a few years many profit making PSUs rushed in to form such joint venture companies (JVC) in the private sector. Theoretically, this provision could be extended to transform the business divisions of any PSU into private JVCs by reducing the parent company to a financial holding company with a Board of Directors and skeleton staff and effectively stave off the Dalit menace! Unfortunately for the companies this vile experiment of JVC has been a grand failure. It called the bluff of the management that the PSU framework shackled their 'competence' and the infusion of Dalits weakened their 'merit'. It also conclusively proved the protagonists of the private sector wrong.

## Project of Dalit Emancipation

Apart from the current concerns of Dalits as seen above, Dalits have an implicit long term project of their emancipation, which would mean their comprehensive empowerment to compete in the world as equals. For the sake of clarity, let us map this project by four empowerments, viz., personal empowerment, socio-economic empowerment, socio-political empowerment and socio-cultural empowerment. In terms of methodology, these empowerments could be represented by one or two proxy parameters, which then could be examined for the impact of globali-sation. The proxy parameters that best represented these empowerments were: health and education; land reforms and secure employment; democracy and modernity, respectively. Now, we can attempt to assess the impact of globalisation on the emancipation project of Dalits through its impact on each of these parameters.

## 1. Personal Empowerment- Health and Education

Health is the basic determinant of a person's capacity to realise his full potential in life and is particularly important for the lower social strata because they use the human body to the hilt. It also largely determines their educability and mental capacities to comprehend the world. The WHO-UNICEF Alma-Ata Declaration (AAD) in 1979 had affirmed health as a fundamental human right and Primary Health Care as the cornerstone of community self reliance, to be entirely supported by the government. Ignoring this, globalisation insisted on healthcare as a marketable service to be opened up for global capital. One of its key institutions, GATS brought various services hitherto in public domain into the international trade arena through government level commitment. Healthcare actually goes beyond the narrow definition of healthcare services or medical care, which only deals with the removal of disease and is, therefore, just its subset. Since health is influenced by a number of factors, such as adequate food, housing, basic sanitation, healthy lifestyles, protection against environmental hazards and communicable diseases, the frontiers of healthcare extend beyond the narrow limits of medical care. Healthcare is a basic public right, and it is the responsibility of the governments to provide it to all people in equal measure. These principles have been recognised by nearly all governments of the world and enshrined in many constitutions. Article 47 of the Constitution of India also makes it a fundamental duty of the state to raise the level of nutrition and the standard of living and to improve public health. Article 39 has also enjoins upon the state to ensure: "children are given opportunities and facilities to develop in a healthy manner and in conditions of freedom and dignity".

Healthcare cannot be measured in statistical terms like the number of doctors or hospitals beds available percapita. Although even on these counts, the Indian health care system was never satisfactory as in most other spheres, it may be said to its credit that during the post-1947 decades, it has made considerable progress in creating public health infrastructure in terms of primary health centres, community health centres, hospital beds, medical colleges, dental colleges, doctors, nurses, etc., but the advent of globalisation has reversed the trend giving renewed impetus to privatisation in the healthcare sector. The government policy driven by corporate designs is fast decimating whatever little existed in the name of public health care system. The corporate houses entered the healthcare area and created state-of-the-art hospitals with the most sophisticated technologies that cater to the wealthy few. At the same time, globalisation has impelled the government to cut already meager outlays on public health in the name of fiscal prudence. Public hospitals operating under tight cutbacks suffer shortages of equipment, deteriorating health care services, longer hours and less pay for health workers, and longer patient queues and waiting, forcing even the poor to go to private doctors. Healthcare has already become a big business dominated by insurance companies, pharmaceutical firms and enterprises. The market ethos have already raised the price levels all across which eats up much of the income of the poor, be the major cause of rising incidence of poverty according to some studies.

One researcher has noted the increasing privatisation of the health care system during the globalisation period as follows: "The decade to 1996 witnessed a steep decline in the market share of public health services. Private spending now accounts for over 80 per cent of health care spending, one of the highest ratios in the world. Some surveys estimate that more than 90 per cent of beds are in the private sector. The proportion of patients seeking ambulatory care in the public sector fell from 32 per cent to 26 per cent in rural areas and from 30 per cent to 17 per cent in urban areas. Similarly, by 1996, the private sector accounted for 54 per cent of rural hospitalisation and 70 per cent of hospitalisation in urban areas. There is strong evidence that such official statistics grossly underestimate the sise of the private sector which, through facility surveys in various states, has recently been estimated as high as 93 per cent of all hospitals and 64 per cent of all beds nationwide. This remarkable growth in private sector health services has occurred largely by accident as the private sector has stepped in to meet needs that the public sector could not address."[43]

The habitats of poor people, especially Dalits are in or near places where industrial or municipal wastes (mostly untreated) are discharged or dumped, or where industrial input materials are mined or otherwise drawn. The urban scenario is bad especially in metros where the exhaust emission of exploding vehicle populations of the rich is responsible for asthma and respiratory diseases, especially among children. All these are direct causes of ill-health and go beyond even the conventional public health care system. It necessarily brings in the entire gamut of public policy, which has been directly impacted by globalisation in favour of global capital. Under GATT, 'non tariff barriers', i.e., any measure that is not a tariff, but inhibits trade is forbidden by governments. Thus, it becomes illegal when governments ban dangerous technologies, contami-nated or toxic foods and products, and even culturally unsuitable TV programmes and films. Thus under the WTO, the rule of governments are weakened and the unfettered power of the transnational corporations are strengthened. WTO serves as the government of the world order for corpo-rate interests. Although it is an and inter-governmental body comprising member states, it is the TNCs that sit on the important advisory committees which decide policy and set the agenda. It can be seen that the WTO has far reaching implications for health and health policy. Notwithstanding these compulsions, the state governments in India proactively compete among themselves to attract foreign direct investments (FDI) which they, *inter alia,* by winking at the gross violation of the environment, pollution and effluent standards. Entire public policy is influenced by the globali-sation credo of GDP growth, howsoever injurious their consequences to the poor people may be.

In sum, one can see that on the parameter of health, the impact of globalisation has been totally deleterious to Dalits.

Education is another vital factor in an individual's development. In the Dalit movement, it was always highlighted as the single biggest instrumentality for their emancipation. Jotiba Phule, for instance, had attributed the miserable plight of the Shudras and Ati-Shudras (Dalits) to the denial of education to them by the Brahmins and had, therefore, opened schools for them. Every other leader who championed the cause of Dalits has stressed the importance of education. Babasaheb Ambedkar placed education foremost in his agenda, as his mantra – *educate, agitate and organise* - reflects. As a result of these reform movements and particularly because of the Ambedkar's role, many Dalits took to education as a key to their emancipation and made some progress during the post-independence decades.

Indeed, education is a comprehensive instrumentality in the emancipation project; its role in providing individual and social competencies is much bigger than as a means in the economic production. Fundamentally this paradigm is negated under globalisation, which has given impetus to 'human capital' discourse that measures the education system exclusively in economic terms particularly in responding to market needs. This discourse is fraught with several implicit dangers not only to Dalits, but also to the overall constitution of the civil society. As for Dalits, it totally demolishes the extra-market rationale for giving them preferential access to and certain concessions in education.

We have already discussed education briefly in relation to the reservations provided for Dalits in educational institutions. In the globalisation-schema education is no more a public good and under GATT, it is already reckoned as the service to be traded internationally. Even the Supreme Court could not remain uninfluenced by the neoliberal logic and legitimised providing education as occupation of private persons for profit motive in the Pai foundation case. Education is viewed by the capitalist sharks as a $ 50 billion opportunity and channeled their investment in a big way. There is a mushrooming growth of private universities in the country that nobody probably could count. Many of them flaunt collaboration with foreign universities. The government already has half a dozen bills ready to open up the education market for foreign players under various alibis, including raising standards of our higher education system. It is well known that top universities are not lured by such offerings as they experienced that they cannot replicate their success in an alien land. It is only the non descript universities who value them. The basic premise that the private universities improve education standards is fallacious even on the basis of our own experience over the last two decades. None of the private institution has really come up to the level of our famous public institutions like IITs, IIMs, AIMS, etc.

The implications to Dalits of these developments in higher education are twofold: One, they will be deprived of reservation in these private institutions and two, the expensive higher education will go beyond their reach. This is no more hypothetical and much of it is a part of our empirical experience. Just the market ethos has raised the fee structure even of the government educational institutions to be theoretically beyond the reach of more than 90 per cent Indian households. Already, less than 10 per cent Dalits reach higher education and nearly 70 per cent of them go to the humanities courses which are not valued by the market. In the coming days, even this representation of Dalits may not be possible, portending disasterous consequence to their emancipation project. Remember, Dr Ambedkar had ranked higher education very high in his scheme of Dalit emancipation and had opened up colleges to facilitate the same. He clearly saw that only higher education propelled one to positions of power and he wanted Dalits to get them.

More than higher education, there is a far bigger dangerous spectre before Dalits, which would deny them education altogether as in Manu's reigns that kept them in sub-human state for millenia. It is the so called Right to Education the government gifted to the people recently. I am sure it will puzzle you. But just consider two of its salient features: this Right takes away the right of the 0-6 years children, which was granted to them by our Constitution makers; this right legitimises the multi-layered education system right at the elementary stage, which means you would get the kind of education according to your economic standing. One needs to recall that the Constitution had uniquely mandated our rulers to complete universal, free and compulsory education to all the children up to the age of 14 within 10 years from its adoption, i.e., 1960. The rulers have committed a constitutional breach in totally ignoring this mandate for more than 30 years. It is only when the Supreme Court in a

Unnikrishnan case interpreted that the right to education, which was relegated to the Part IV of the Constitution, was actually a fundamental right being an integral part of the right to life, vide Art 21, the government woke up to its obligation and began strategising about it. True to its character, it brought an amendment to the Constitution neutralising the effect of the judgement by inserting Art 21A that restricted the age to 6-14. The Unnikrishnan judgment had further observed that the right to education existed and would not be contingent upon the economic capacity of the state up to 14 years of age. Article 21A said that it would come into force 'in such manner as the State may, by law, determine'. So it was made contingent on a law that the state may bring in. This Act is that law, and it took another eight years to come since the 86th amendment was passed. So it took seventeen years for the right to be enforced since the Unnikrishnan judgment, that too for the restricted age group of 6 to 14 years.

The exclusion of 0-6 years of children from the RTE itself amounts to a fraud on the people because it is this age which is crucial for the development of a child. It is said that by the age of five, 75 per cent personality gets formed. Proper nutrition, toys to play with, proper education in this age group is crucial for a child to grow with into a healthy human. Rather in the context of the harsh reality that India is a home to the maximum number of maximum malnourished children and to one-third stunted children in the world[44], who enter the world with irremediable disability, the state obligation should go back to the mothers' womb.[45] In order to ensure that no child is born with a handicap, the state, in the spirit of the Constitution, should take responsibility of providing proper nutrition and prenatal care to the pregnant women, who need it. The anganwadis just cannot meet these objectives.

The most treacherous content of the RTE is legitimising the multi-layered education system that grew during the globalisation-years. There is a huge continuum of schools with government run schools sans blackboard, roof, or teachers, at the one end and international schools that might shame the best of their breed in the advanced countries at the other. The spread of the notion that private is superior to public also could be attributed to globalisation. During the last two decades, there has been mushrooming growth of private English medium schools not only in urban areas, but also in villages, which have eclipsed the government vernacular schools to the extent that they are virtually closing down. In the hope of giving the children the best possible education, the poor people are fleeced by these schools both ways: they incur much higher costs and the children draw blank because of the alien language and there being no competent teacher to teach them. In short, the system violates the principle of the neighourhood common school system envisaged by the Constitution as seen by the Kothari Commission, the first Education Commission. The RTE, in effect, ordains the provision of education according to the class of people. Since class at the lower end corresponds to caste, it coincides with the Manu's code.

In order to thwart the criticism of innate inequity, RTE provides for 25 per cent reservation to the lower classes in any school. Reservation has really become a weapon with the government to use anywhere to neutralise the opposition. Nobody asked a pertinent question in this regard: How does this solve the basic problem of inequity? There are numerous other questions also about its implementability, given the fact that the government cost reimbursement formula does not match the expenses of the elite schools. The fact cannot be hidden that the entire rural area, where nearly 70 per cent of our population lives and more than 80 per cent Dalits live are virtually cut off from any meaningful education. Even in urban areas, the children from slums and working class localities will not have access to quality education. As a ritual, they would go to school (they must otherwise their parents will be arrested!), get promoted to higher classes (as there will not be any exam) and come out of the middle school so blank as to have no option than dropping out. There is no explanation required that majority of Dalit children will meet this fate.

Already this trend has created a permanent divide between urban and rural areas, the latter having been totally excluded from education of any consequence. The commercial ethos that entered the education field, through globalisation, has further created a divide between the haves and have-nots. The pay seats in the educational institutions have fortified the class basis of education. Dalits who have been barely able to afford schooling with the aid of freeship and scholarship are squeezed out from both ends. Firstly, education has become increasingly inaccessible and unaffordable to them. Even if they persist with it, they have to face several hurdles on the way to get education that would secure them gainful employment. The increasing opportunity cost of schooling is dissuading many Dalits from education resulting in an increasing numbers of dropouts. Even if they crossed all the hurdles as an exception, they would face a far bigger hurdle in the job market that tended to value one's family background more than one's scholastic performance. The economic globalisation has brought in a fundamental change in the composition of the job market. The manufacturing sector that valued the formal edu-cational inputs has been shrinking, whereas the service sector that required such attributes as one's looks, mannerisms, 'communication', connections, relationships etc. that could be summed up as one's class attributes, did not value educational qualification. This class divide cannot be easily crossed by Dalits. Globalisation has, thus, raised a neo-caste barrier for Dalits that may be far more difficult to cross than that of even Manu's.

## 2. Economic Empowerment- land Reforms and Employment

The economic dimension of the caste question is intimately connected with land reforms. Over 81 per cent of Dalits still live in rural areas of them, about 50 per cent are landless labourers and about 25 per cent are cultivators with marginal farms[46]. The dependency relationship of Dalits with the upper caste has been the significant factor in shoring up the economic basis of caste. As only the land reforms could feasibly break this relationship, they constituted a progressive agenda all through the post-independence years. Globalisation has not only eclipsed this agenda of land reforms, but also substituted it with corporatisation of farming for the global agricultural market. Globalisation goes beyond the skewed distribution of land among people and rather takes advantage of it to consolidate farms for capitalist agriculture. Globalisation has undone the ceiling on land holdings in state after state to allow corporate superfarms for luxury production for international markets[47].

The policy thrust of the World bank- IMF-WTO combine has always been clearly for the abolition of the land ceiling laws and for liberalising investment into agriculture. For example, Karnataka was one of the first states to amend its Land Reforms Act (1961) that aimed at removing the land ceiling for aquaculture in the Uttara Kannada and Dakshin Kannada districts and also for the horticulture, floriculture and agro-based industries. Despite the massive protests it met from Karnataka Farmers Union- the Karnataka Rajya Ryota Sangha (KRRS) who have been spearheading the movement against the entry of multinational corporations in agriculture, one finds the corporatisation process going ahead unabatedly. A massive displacement of farmers from their land has taken place, creating an explosive situation, socially, as well as politically.[48] Food-growing land is being diverted to non-food crops such as flowers or luxury commodities such as shrimp.[49] Corporatisation of agriculture, which is being pushed under trade liberalisation as a successor of the Green Revolution is leading to new poverty for small farmers as unequal and unfair contracts lock them into new forms of bondage.

The globalisation agenda is systematically driving against family farming as in vogue today. It is driving towards integration of Indian agriculture into global agri-market through contract farming and eventually towards corporatisation. Because of contraction of investment support by the government, rising prices of input and the fall of prices for many agri-products in the international markets created a veritable crisis in agriculture which manifested in an alarming phenomenon of farmers' suicides. It has reinforced the notion that small farm agriculture was infeasible and discredited the discourse of land reform. Globalisation also unleashed the unprecedented rush for land grab all over the country in garb of SEZ, infrastructure development, urbanisation and industrialisation. Already in the first decade itself more than one million hectares of agriculture land was lost to non-agricultural usage. It engendered resistance movements, but not powerful enough to completely thwart the process except in a few cases. The government is actively supporting the builders and corporates by declaring war on tribals to clear forest lands; driving Dalits and other poor out of their habitat by demolishing slums in urban areas and displacing entire communities in the name of SEZ.

Globalisation has thus, created opposite processes to that of land reforms. We have already discussed the jobless growth that occurred in the globalisation period. There has been a structural change in the sectoral composition of GDP during the globalisation years. As per 2011 estimation, the share of agriculture in GDP was 17. 2per cent, that of industry 26.4 per cent, and services is 56.4 per cent. In terms of workforce engagement we get almost an inverse picture. Agriculture still employs nearly 55 per cent workforce, the Industry 22 per cent and the Services, just 23 per cent. There was marked acceleration in services sector growth in the 1980s and 1990s, especially in the nineties. While the share of services in India's GDP increased by 21 per cent points in the 50 years between 1950 and 2000, nearly 40 per cent of that increase was concentrated in the 1990s. The boom in the services sector has been relatively "jobless". The rise in services share in GDP has not been accompanied by a proportionate increase in the sector's share of national employment. Services or the "tertiary sector" of the economy covers a wide gamut of activities like Trade, Hotels and Restaurants, Railways, Other Transport & Storage, Communication (Post, Telecom), Banking, Insurance, Dwellings, Real Estate, Business Services, Public Adminis-tration; Defence, Personal Services, Community Services and Other Services. While almost all service sectors participated in this boom, the growth was fastest in Information Technology and business process outsourcing which grew at over 33 per cent.

This change has serious implication for the Dalits and rather all people at the bottom of the social structure. Firstly, it indicates that while the share of income is falling for the majority of people a small minority is enjoying the fruits of growth in the economy. Secondly, the stagnation of the share of Industry indicates that there is contraction of employment in the country for the young people who are being added to the workforce in big numbers (demographic dividend). While the Services will take care of the highly educated youngsters from the elite background, all others will be pushed to the informal sectors or the other growing sector of crime, Agriculture being unattractive to the educated youngsters and is itself suffering a serious crisis. This is what globalisation would mean for the Dalit youth.

## 3. Political Empowerment-Democracy

The importance of democracy as a value in the emancipation project of Dalits cannot be over emphasised. Whatever hue it comes with, demo-cracy provides some space for the weak people to voice their concerns. It is the framework within which agitations germinate, movements are launched and struggles are waged. It may not be an exaggeration to say that the western liberal democratic ethos that pervaded the colonial rule, has greatly facilitated the birth and growth of the Dalit movement.

If the foregoing discussion on the ideological proclivities of globalisation or its genesis or its definition is accepted, there is no further discussion required on the impact of globalisation on democracy. The problem arises because of what is meant by democracy. For those who are enamoured with the outward exhibition of representational mechanics, the meaning of democracy is different from those belonging to the vast majority of people who have to wage a life and death struggle to make their representatives listen to their woes. The former are sanguine at India or the US being the great democracies while the latter lot may dismiss them and rather call them the worst kind of dictatorship. Such is the perceptual continuum over which the meaning of democracy differs according to the standing of people in the socio-economic scale. It must be emphasised here, although it should be obvious from the topic itself that the present discussion is from the viewpoint of Dalits about democracy. According to this viewpoint, democracy simply means having voice to common people; having freedom to protest, express dissent, to come out on the roads in anger and freedom to recall their representatives, if they do not perform.

Let us not be outright contemptuous of what the scholars say. Superficially, the theoretical (dominant liberal type) premise appears to be that democracy and globalisation go hand in hand. The scholars see the confirmation of it in opening of the countries of Central and Eastern Europe following the demise of Soviet-led authoritarianism and in the outward orientation of Latin America since the wave of democratisation began there in 1978.[50] They also contend that insofar as free international transactions benefit society as a whole, democracy that renders leaders more accountable to the citisenry should be conducive to the removal of restrictions on such transactions.[51] The democracy-globalisation nexus, it is further argued is reinforced by the exchange of goods and services which act as a conduit for the exchange of ideas, and a more diverse stock of ideas encourages political competition which is what democracy is.[52] Some observe that in financially open economies, the government and central bank are more sensitive to the markets. The transparency demanded by markets has impelled the autocratic regimes to go democratic. They obviously point at Indonesia where the expediencies of managing financial globalisation spurred the transition to a more open and competitive democratic system. Of course, they would not forget to say that between 1975 and 2002, there was a quadrupling in the number of democratic countries and that the share of countries open to international capital flows rose from 25 to 38 per cent. The powerful dynamics set in motion by globalisation is seen as driving democratisation of the world.

All this sounds impressive. But on careful analysis, one can easily see that these statements are either unduly exaggerated or simply wrong. When one speaks about opening of Central Europe, one has to also consider cases like Bolivia and Peru where democratisation has fuelled a popular backlash against opening to the rest of the world. Some studies not only reject the hypothesis that democratisation leads to openness, but in act conclude in favour of the opposite.[53] The empirical evidence shows that in countries where labour is the scarce factor of production, democratic reforms will encourage protectionism rather than opening to the rest of the world.[54] Others suggest that democratisation will not result in working class support for globalisation. These perspectives suggest that the relationship running from democracy to globalisation is at best ambiguous. The same can be said about the relationship running from openness to democratisation. While one speaks about Indonesia where financial opening led to precipitation of a shift to democratisation, one cannot overlook China where economic and financial opening have not undermined autocratic control. There are many economic studies that find no impact of trade openness on democracy or show even a negative relationship between them.[55] There is a scholarly support to the common-place observation taxation, regulation, and risk-sharing policies, thereby weakening support for democratic forms of governance.[56] It all should convince you that even the serious scholarly studies also refute the claim of the propagandists of globalisation that it leads to democratisation.

Leave apart scholars, it is not difficult to see the consequences of globalisation to democracy based on our own experience; they are evident in the manner in which it was imposed on the people. Globalisation has never been a democratic choice of the people anywhere. The imperatives of globalisation have been business driven, by business strategies and for business ends. Governments have helped them by policy actions that were often taken in secret, without national debate and discussion.[57] The manner in which globalisation was introduced in India in the garb of economic reforms, without any discussion in the parliament or with people, stands testimony to this fact. Globalisation rather has brought in new degree of falsehood into the polity: While our rulers still claim that the reforms they carried out were not imposed by anyone, but had come out of the indigenous wisdom, the fact remains that India displays one of few perfect examples in the world of compliance with the Washington Consensus that encapsulated globalisation. The intrinsic ant-democratic content of globalisation thus surfaces right from its birth.

Free market, the flagpost of globalisation grants more value to a moneyed person and thus is against the dictum of democracy of one person, one value. Democracy assumes community and existence of pluralist groups, but neoliberalism dismisses them and atomises population into discrete self-seeking individuals. This conception clearly favours business because it eliminates the concept of collective and thereby emasculates labour. Democracy was built on the nation state. Globalisation seeks to remove power from the nation-state and puts it in the global arena thus crippling the nation-state in meeting the democratic aspirations of its people. Today we experience that year-by-year, over the last couple of decades, the reality of the democracy is being weakened despite the loud talk on its glory.

The WTO, the IMF, and World Bank—the three most important international economic institutions that are the propellers of globalisation often described, as "institutions of global governance" are essentially unaccountable to any electorate. Indeed, one does not need a conspiracy theory to notice the progressive removal of economic-decision making from governments to unelected (and for most countries, foreign) officials. For much of the world, this is the face of globalisation that intrudes into civil society. The free market ethos of globalisation conceptually can neither conform to the democratic spirit of the Indian Constitution, nor can it coexist with the system of positive discrimination in favour of the Dalits.

The erosion of democracy under globalisation spells blockade of the very emancipation discourse of oppressed people like the Dalits. With powerful surveillance technologies at their disposal, they can nip any such attempts in the bud.

Globalisation being the spread and intensification of capitalist relations, one expected that it would promote modernity, weaken the caste-feudalism and thereby be beneficial to the Dalits in socio-cultural terms. This argument pretending to possess theoretical propriety inevitably turns out as naïve in the context of historical experience with capitalism which not only did not dent the castes, but also made skilful use of them in dividing the labour.

The phenomenon of emergence of religious fundamentalism in many countries and particularly in our country in the era of globalisation is not a chance happening. It is the imperative of globalisation that large multitude of masses is held in the conformist mode by whatever means. There is no potent and economical means as religion for the purpose. The rise of Hindutva forces, demolition of Babri Masjid, review of the constitution, denigration and harassment of minorities, saffronisation of education and generally communalisation of polity, are not to be taken as unconnected events. These are very much complementary to globalisation. The events if seen in totality show the deeper linkage and chronological order between the decline of state controlled economies, intensification of adverse effects of globalisation, rise of America as the lone super power of the world, decline of the authority of the United Nations, decline of Non-Aligned movement and rise of Fascist Fundamentalist politics in our own country.[58]

In the context of India, one can observe a weird phenomenon of emboldening of the casteist and communalist forces during the globalisation era. It may not be disputed that much of India's history is a history of defeat by outside forces. While many of them had made this country their home and ruled in small suzerainties, never the entire subcontinent, allowing the locals without much of social interference and a strong sense of defeat. British colonial rule was unlike it. It had defeated the natives with superior technology, organisation and discipline and established its unitary institutional authority on the entire subcontinent. Barring hardcore orthodox elements, the advent of Western liberalism during the colonial times had indeed rendered the Hindus defensive and somewhat apologetic about their traditions and customs. When the lower caste people through non-Brahman movement and later Dalit movement challenged their oppression, the conscious Hindus were further embarrassed. Came independence, the Constitution of India, the first-past-the-post type of election system valorised numbers and highlighted the importance of communitarian vote banks. As these processes suppressed the innate drive of caste customs and traditions, India limped on with its 'low income' status in the comity of nations with the so called 'Hindu' rate of growth, shaking the confidence of the Hindus in superiority of their past. The cumulative impact of all these develop-ments has been to render the middle caste Hindus, the opinion leaders, clearly defensive as regards the caste system.

While the above developments had their dialectical component in the rise of a section of the backward castes, who took over feudal reigns of power in villages asserting their caste superiority over Dalits, with their crudity, they could not articulate the argument for justifying caste system. It is only during the globalisation period, which brought unprecedented economic growth, international recognition as one of the fastest growing economy, a name in the areas of frontier technology like ICT and Biotech, fame to Indians as heads of MNCs and TNCs and generally established the Indian community as the most prosperous migrant community in the USA, the El Dorado of middle classes, that reversed the trend and boosted the middle class confidence in their culture, customs and traditions, which are nothing, but euphemism for the caste system. The new syndromes of 'India Shining' or 'India a becoming super-power' reflect this new found confidence in 'India'. The new generation of middle castes, whether in India or abroad, is devoid of sense of shame about India's past and rather appear vehemently justifying it, including the caste system. The ideology of globalisation with its social Darwinist ethos has certainly been instrumental in this reversal. Globalisation has thus reversed the century-long trend of building anti-caste ethos.

Not only in India, but also all over the world Neo-fascism and neo-Nazism is gaining ground. Glele-Ahanhanzo noted in a report to the U.N. General Assembly that the power of the extreme right-wing parties, which are thriving on "an economic and social climate characterised by fear and despair" was on the increase. Among the key factors fuelling the far right reaction, according to the U.N. report, are "the combined effects of globalisation, identity crises and social exclusion." Where local traditions lose influence; individuals tend to become atomised psychologically and thus more susceptible to the lures of ultranationalists who manipulate deep-seated anxieties.[59] The upsurge of fundamentalist, obscurantist and fascist tendencies the world over are thus occasioned by globalisation.

Those who pin their expectation on the cultural transformation through globalisation also commit an error. Cultural transformation does not take place from one discrete form to an entirely alien one. Cultural homogenisation indicated by the terms like McDonaldisation, Americanisation, Cocacolisation, etc., through globalisation also do not mean that the resultant culture is American culture. Cultures do change, but in a calibrated manner, resulting into hybrid cultures. There is an over-abundance of evidence in support of this thesis. While imbibing homogenisation influence from the 'core' every 'periphery', with its inertia preserves its core culture and creates hybrids. While there are inexhaustible examples of these processes the world over, in the Indian context, we could easily see the most striking cases of most 'globalised' people aggressively pursuing revivalism of the most decadent kind of Hindu customs and traditions and propagating most poisonous communalism of Hindutva. There are attempts at reviving unknown Hindu festivals and giving them mass forms. There is a spate of temple building/renovation activity everywhere and their promotion such that masses throng to them. In Mumbai, the systematic build up of an innocuous small temple of Siddhivinayaka until 1980s is a case in point. Today, the temple has become a complex in the busy central Mumbai, gobbling up the two streets and blatantly swallowing up an entire foot path and part of the main road, in the name of security. The temple is fast becoming one of the richest shrines in the country. The same is applicable to Shirdi, a place famed by a poor *sufi fakir,* tipped to become an international pilgrimage centre and scores of other places. The complicity of the State that is supposed to be secular is glaringly evident in all these processes. Over the last decade, there is a subtle attempt by the Shiv Sena to celebrate public Satyanarayan Poojas on the Republic Day clearly to undermine its importance. These were the means through which the Indian caste culture was preserved through the onslaught of alien influences in history. Therefore, it is a misfounded expectation to hope for globalisation weakening the castes.

Globalisation is thus full of contradictions; it generates tendencies of universalism and yet leads to re-assertions of profound particularisms because universalism itself is to a large extent an illusion. What we have in fact is the coexistence of a minority of rich nomads moving freely around the globe and an overwhelming majority condemned to confining spaces of poverty.[60] There is no scope even to speculate that globalisation would entail spread of modernity in society so as to bury castes. On the contrary, there is a good deal of evidence of caste discrimination getting accentuated during the globalisation period. The caste atrocities that best represent this menace have risen significantly rise during the globalisation period, as compared to the pre-globalisation period as shown in the Table 3.

**Table 3: Average number of atrocities per annum on the Dalits during the pre-Reform and the post-Reform years**

| *Year* | *Murders* | *Serious Injury* | *Rape under* | *Arson* | *Others* | *Crime POA* | *Total* |
|---|---|---|---|---|---|---|---|
| Pre-Reform years 1981-1986 | 523.17 | 1,416.8 | 666.3 | 1046.3 | 11,530.1 | 10,057.6 | 25,237.3 |
| Post-Reform years - 1995-1997 | 539.3 | 4197 | 929.3 | 449.3 | 12,356.3 | 10,458.7 | 28,929.9 |
| per cent Increase during Reform-years over the pre-Reform years | 3.1 | 196.1 | 39.5 | -57.1 | 7.2 | 4.0 | 14.6 |

*Source*: Computed from the figures from the reports of National Commission for SCs and STs.

The menace of Hindutva represents blatant anti-modernity and the worst kind of revivalism. It seeks to bring in the old obscurantist values that cannot exclude the code of Manu. Although the Hindutva project so far has not branded Dalits as their 'other' like Muslims and rather co-opted them as their cannon fodder against these religious minorities as in the recent Gujarat carnage, it certainly expects them to abide by the 'great' tenets of Hindu tradition. Insofar as there is a irreconcilable contradiction between the Hindu traditions and the Dalit aspirations, the Hindutva project shall mean negation of the emancipation of the Dalits. Not only that, it neutralises whatever progress Dalits made in challenging the system of caste exploitation, but also holds forth the horrific prospects of inhuman oppression that their ancestors faced. The 'journey in reverse gear' that we observe in every field is going to be detrimental to Dalits and the minority community.

## Conclusion

Globalisation, an agenda of capitalism in crisis, driven by imperialist institutions like IMF, World Bank, and WTO along the ideology of neo-liberalism has essentially a pro-rich bias. Wherever they were imple-mented, they have worsened the situation of masses of poor people in absolute as well as in relative, terms. Globalisation, contrary to the claims of its protagonists, has been a total failure even in generating growth or increasing productivity. It did not have anything to say about poor people, except for its 'trickle down' theory. Nowhere this trickle has materialised. On the contrary, it has created unprecedented amount of inequality in every possible sphere. It has been a social disaster, environmental disaster and a threat to stability of the world. The claim of its proponents that free trade with private enterprise is the route to economic growth is also confuted by longer historic experience. No country, past or present, has taken off into sustained economic growth and moved from economic backwardness to modernity without large-scale government protection and subsidisation of infant industries and other modes of insulation from domination by powerful outsiders.

In India too all the ill effects of the globalisation were experienced by the poor people in terms of inflation, de-industrialisation, casualisation of labour, unemployment, worsening food security, gnawing inequality, de-peasantisation, destruction of the environment and agriculture, suppression of democratic rights, pollution of culture and most importantly, its indigenous fall out in terms of fascist, fundamentalist, communalist and obscurantist programme of Hindutva. Since, the impact of all these is to be borne in direct proportion of the poverty and deprivation, the Dalits are naturally hit by globalisation the hardest. In addition to this impact, they have to carry the burden of their identity as socially oppressed people. The Constitution of India had certain mitigating measures, but globalisation has severally neutralised these and exposed the Dalits to brute market forces. It has similarly demolished their aspi-rations for emancipation.

Notwithstanding the contrary evidence even on the growth premise, (compared to an overall average of 2.04 per cent before reforms (1983-94), the annual growth rate was a mere 0.98 per cent in 1994-2000.) the government has launched the second generation of reforms which are nothing, but intensification of the globalisation-ordained policies. These reforms clearly appear to be the whole hog offering of our natural resources to global capitalists to loot. They are manifesting into the war on poor Tribals and Dalits with the 'biggest internal security threat' syndrome. People have experienced the backbreaking impact of the 'milder' version of the first generation of reforms from 1991; the second generation of them is surely going to be harsher, as the hazy markers like 'Operation Green Hunt' indicate.

The government is sanguine with the grace of its global masters. It is totally oblivious of the people's plight. It does not understand that it is the people who eventually constitute the market, whether free or otherwise. And market requires widespread purchasing power. It follows that the government should aim at empowering the masses and enhancing their capability. It should take effective measures for accelerated development of the disadvantaged sections like Dalits. The pre-requisite for even the 'free market' oriented reforms comes out to be the radical land reforms, massive investments in rural areas into agriculture-related infrastructural projects, universalisation of primary education through common school system, primary health care system and reinforcement of positive discrimination in favour of the Dalits in all sectors of the economy, etc. The devil of casteism could be tamed only by freeing the general masses of the people from the anxieties and uncertainties about basic survival. The general condition of deprivation has rendered them vulnerable to the frequent machinations of the vested interests that make them see the enemy within their own class. The relative equality thus can be the bedrock for launching the socio-cultural offensive in the form of mass-education programmes. But, surprisingly, globalisation is opposed to every bit of this logical programme for sustainability.

## Notes and References


1. Barrett, M. *The Politics of Truth: From Marx to Foucault,* Polity Press, Cambridge: 1991.
2. Schirato, T. and Webb, J. *Understanding Globalisation,* Sage, London, 2003. p. 200.
3. Kuper, A. and Kuper, J. (eds.) *The Social Sciences Encyclopaedia,* (2nd edn.,) Routledge,. London, 1996, p. 234.
4. Langhorne, R. *The Coming of Globalisation,* Palgrave Macmillan, Basingstoke, 2001, p. 2.
5. Calhoun, C. (ed.) *Dictionary of the Social Sciences,* Oxford University Press, Oxford, 2002, p. 192.
6. Bauman, Z. *Globalisation: The Human Consequences,* Polity Press, Cambridge, 1999.
7. Cited in Aaronson, S. A. *Taking to the Streets: The Lost History of Public Efforts to Shape Globalisation,* University of Michigan Press, Ann Arbor, 2002, p. 220.
8. Lechte, J. *Key Contemporary Concepts: From Abjection to Zeno's Paradox,* Sage, London, 2003.
9. Mann, M. 'Globalisation and September 11', *New Left Review*, 12 (2001) 51–72.
10. Held, D. and McGrew, A. *Globalisation/Anti-Globalisation,* Polity Press, Cambridge, 2002, p, 1.
11. I have used this definition consistently from 1995 onwards in my numerous articles on Globalisation. With regard to capitalist crisis Wallerstein perceptively observes, "At the turn of the twenty-first century, the capitalist world economy is in crisis;" therefore, the current "ideological celebration of so-called globalisation is in reality the swan song of our historical system." SeeWallerstein, Immanuel, *Utopistics, or, Historical choices of the twenty-first century,* New Press, New York, 1998, p. 32.
12. Marx, K. *Karl. Marx: Selected Writings*, (ed. By D. McLellan) Oxford University Press, Oxford, 1987, pp. 224-5.
13. Mill, M. and Blossfeld, H. P. Globalisation, Uncertainty and the Early Life Course: A Theoretical Framework, in Blossfeld, H. P., Klijzing, E., Mills, M. and Kurz, K. (Eds.). *Globalisation, Uncertainty, and Youth in Society*, Routledge, London/ New York, 2005; Heery, E. and Salmon, J. (Eds.) *The Insecure Workforce*. Routledge, London/ New York, 2000; Ladipo, D. and Wilkinson, F. 'More pressure, less protection', in Burchell, B., Ladipo, D. and Wilkinson, F. (Eds.) *Job Insecurity and Work Intensification*, Routledge, London/New York, 2002.
14. Blossfeld, H. P., Klijzing, E., Mills, M. and Kurz, K. (Eds.) *The losers in a globalising world: becoming an adult in uncertain times*. Routledge, London/ New York, 2005.

15. Esping-Andersen, G. and Regini, M. *Why Deregulate Labour Markets?* Oxford University Press, Oxford, 2000.
16. Golsch, K. *The Impact of Labour Market Insecurity on the Work and Family Life of Men and Women*, Europäische Hochschulschriften, Reihe 22: Soziologie, Frankfurt a.M.: Lang., 2005.
17. Blossfeld, H. P. 'Globalisation, social inequality and the role of country-specific institutions. Open research questions in a learning society', in P. Conceição, Heitor, H.V. and Lundvall, B.A. (Eds.) *Innovation, Competence Building and Social Cohesion in Europe: Towards a Learning Society*, Edward Elgar, Cheltenham/Lyme, 2002.
18. Esping-Andersen, G. *Welfare states in transition. National adaptations in global economies*, Sage Publications, London/ Thousands Oaks/ New Delhi, London/ Thousands Oaks/ New Delhi, 1996.
19. Blossfeld, 2002. *Ibid*; Esping-Andersen, *The Social Foundations of Post-industrial Economies*. Oxford University Press, Oxford, 1999.
20. Thomas Schmitt, *Meet the Losers of Globalisation*, Global Policy Forum, Interhemispheric Resource Center, March 8, 2006.
21. Patnaik, Prabhat. The State under Neo-liberalism, MRZine,http://mrzine.monthlyreview.org/2010/patnaik100810.html. Last Accessed: 03 August 2011]
22. Baumol, William J., *The Free-Market Innovation Machine: Analysing the Growth Miracle of Capitalism*, Princeton University Press, Princeton, New Jersey, 2002.
23. The theory based on a general equilibrium mathematical model of international trade, developed by Eli Heckscher and Bertil Ohlin at the Stockholm School of Economics that essentially says that countries will export products that use their abundant and cheap factor(s) of production and import products that use the countries' scarce factor(s).See Blaug, Mark. *The methodology of economics, or, How economists explain*. Cambridge University Press, Cambridge, 1992, p. 286.
24. It states that under some economic assumptions (constant returns, perfect competition, equality of the number of factors to the number of products), a rise in the relative price of a good will lead to a rise in the return to that factor which is used most intensively in the production of the good, and conversely, to a fall in the return to the other factor.
25. Martin Hart-Landsberg, Neoliberalism: Myths and Reality, *Monthly Review*, Volume 57, Number 11. April 2006.
26. *Ibid.*
27. Martin Hart-Landsberg and Paul Burkett, *China and Socialism: Market Reforms and Class Struggle*, Aakar Books, New Delhi, 2006.
28. The World Bank, Annual Review of Development Effectiveness, 1999 cited in *IFG Bulletin*, 2001, Volume 1, Issue 3.
29. United Nations Human Development Report, 1999 cited in *IFG Bulletin*, 2001, Volume 1, Issue 3, Available at http://www.thirdworldtraveler.com/Globalisation/Globalisation_FactsFigures.html. [Last Accessed: April 12, 2009]
30. UNCTAD, *Trade and Development Report 1999*, (New York: United Nations, 1999), vi. Cited by Martin Hart-Landsberg (2006), *Op. Cit.*

31. UNCTAD, *Trade and Development Report 1999* (New York: United Nations, 1999), vi. Cited by Martin Hart-Landsberg (2006), *Op. Cit.*
32. Mark Weisbrot, Dean Baker, & David Rosnick, *The Scorecard on Development: 25 Years of Diminished Progress*, Center for Economic and Policy Research, Washington, D.C., 2005, 1.
33. Martinez, Mark A., *The Myth of the Free Market: The Role of the State in a Capitalist Economy,* Kumarian Press, *2009.*
34. Proffesor S. P. Gupta had estimated the poverty figures for the rural area having gone up to 45.3 per cent in 1998 from 35 per cent in 1990 while that for the urban areas remaining the same at around 35 per cent.Many surveys and studies independently corroborated the significant rise in poverty figures after the launch of globalisation. A survey carried out by the NCAER along with the International Development Research Centre of Canada also drew similar conclusions. Yet another study by the International Food Policy Research Institute (IFPRI) notes that while overall economic growth has been impressive since the start of the reforms in the early 1990s, this has not had a positive impact on rural poverty. See Teltumbde, Anand, Impact of New Economic Reforms on Dalits in India, in *New Economic Policy and Dalits*, (ed.) Jogdand, P.G., Rawat Publishers, New Delhi, 2000
35. IFPR 2020. Gloomy Outlook for Malnourished Children, *New report projects slowing progress against world hunger*, Washington, D.C., 28 August 2001. http://srd.yahoo.com/goo/per cent22International+ Food+Policy+Research+ Instituteper cent22per cent 2b2020per cent2bindia/4/T=1011371526/ F=d9d141a12ede609f27c794ec5c2a603d/* http://www.futureharvest.org/health/ impact_release.shtml. [Last Accessed: April 12, 2009]
36. Patnaik, *Utsa, Falling Per Capita Availability of Foodgrains for Human Consumption in the Reform Period in India*, Akhbar, No. 2, October 2001 also available on http://www.ercwilcom.net/~indowindow/akhbar/2001-02/ global.htm.
37. Shiva, Vandana. *Poverty & Globalisation*, available on http://news. bbc.co.uk/ hi/English/static/events/reith_2000/lecture5.stm.[Last Accessed on 09 November 2011]
38. *Jan Swasthya Sabha* 2000: 43-44.
39. Press Note: Key Indicators of Employment and Unemployment in India, 2009-10, National Sample Survey Office, Ministry of Statistics and Programme Implementation, Government of India, New Delhi.
40. Klerck, G. Casual Labour (draft paper) cited in Jauch, Herbert, Globalisation and employment: New opportunities or Continued Marginalisation, Labour Resource and Research Institute, Presentation at a Panel Discussion of the Namibia Economic society, Windhoek, 7 March 2000.
41. Wages as a per centage of net sales of the private corporate sector declined from 6.0 per cent in 1991-92 to 5.2 per cent in 1997-98. CMIE, Corporate Sector, May 1999.
42. This ratio, which was 0.74 in 1998, fell to 0.65 in 1999 and further to 0.25 in the first nine months of 2000· See Research Unit for Political Economy, *Aspects of India's economy*, Nos. 30 & 31, p. 132.

43. Marikkani M., Scenario Of Rural Health Care System In India: *Indian Streams Research Journal* (June; 2012)
44. According to NFHS III, 78.9 per cent children in the age group of 6 to 35 months were anaemic. India has 61 million stunted children, one-third of the total in the world.
45. NFHS III revealed 57 per cent of pregnant women between the age group of 15 to 49 years were anaemic.
46. The problem of landlessness is more serious among the SC as compared to the ST and the Muslims, as 70per cent of the SC rural households are landless and near landless (owning less than 1 acre). Government record on land redistribution has been quite disappointing. So far, only 2per cent of the total cultivable land has been distributed under the ceiling to landless and the share goes up marginally to 10per cent if we include government land. Only 18 lakh acres of land have been distributed so far to 18.5 lakh SC beneficiaries with 0.977 acre per beneficiary. Therefore, it is a cause for concern that a large section of SC households remain without viable land even today. For example, there are large tracts of customary lands whose rights were given to SCs, but which were encroached upon by the high caste landlords. These lands include Mahar Vatan land in Maharashtra, Panchami land in Tamilnadu, and Depressed Caste land in A.P. The government through the new organisation should release these lands from the encroachers and hand these to their legitimate owners.
47. Shiva, Vandana, *Ibid.*
48. Shiva, Vandana, Radha Holla and Kusum Menon, *Globalisation and Agriculture quoted in TWN, Globalisation of Agriculture and Rising Food Insecurity,* http://www.twnside.org.sg/title/food-cn.htm. [Last Accessed: 9 November 2011]
49. Shiva, Vandana, *Ibid.*
50. Munoz, Oscar. "Toward Trade Opening," in Joan Nelson (ed.), *Intricate Links:Democratizatio and Market Reforms in Latin America and Eastern Europe,"* Transaction publishers, New Brunswick, 1994, pp. 61-104.
51. Milner, Helen and Keiko Kubota. "Why the Move to Free Trade? Democracy and Trade Policy in the Developing Countries," *International Organisation,* (2005), 59:157-93; Garrett, Geoffrey. "The Causes of Globalisation," *Comparative Political Studies* 33, (2000) pp.341-391.
52. Dailami, Mansoor. *"Financial Openness, Democracy, and Redistributive Policy,"* Policy Research paper No. 2372, Washington, D.C.: The World Bank. (2000), p. 4.
53. For example see Yu, Miaojie. "Trade Globalisation and Political Liberalisation: A Gravity Approach," unpublished manuscript, University of California, Davis, (2005).
54. O'Rourke, Kevin and Alan Taylor. "Democracy and Protectionism in the Nineteenth Century," unpublished manuscript, Trinity College, Dubin and University of California, Davis (September 2005).
55. Bussmann, Margit. "Examining Causality among Conflict, Democracy, Openness, and Economic Growth," unpublished manuscript (2001), Univer-sity of Alabama, Li, Quan and Rafael Reuveny (2001), "Economic Globali-sation and Democracy: An Empirical Analysis," unpublished manuscript, Penn State

and Indiana University and Rigobon, Roberto and Dani Rodrik (2004), "Rule of Law, Democracy, Openness and Income: Estimating the Interrelationships," NBER Working Paper No. 10750 (September).

56. Dailami, Mansoor. *"Financial Openness, Democracy, and Redistributive Policy,"* Policy Research paper No. 2372, Washington, D.C.: The World Bank, 2000.
57. Herman, Edward, S. *The Threat of Globalisation, New Politics*, Vol. 7, No. 2 (new series), whole No. 26, Winter 1999.
58. Puniyani, Ram. *Globalisation and Politics of Identity, Akhbar*, No. 3, November 2001 available on http://www.ercwilcom.net/~indowindow/akhbar/2001-03/feature.htm. [Last Accessed: 9 November 2011]
59. Lee, Martin A. *Fascism and globalisation: The World / Europe; The Fascist Response to Globalisation, Los Angeles Times,* November 28, 1999, Sunday, Home Edition.
60. Robert Fatton Jr., *Globalisation, Poverty, and Terror,* SEPTEMBER 25, 20001. http://faculty.virginia.edu/mesp/Fatton-Globalisation-Terror.pdf. [Last Accessed: April 12, 2009]

# 3

# The Politics of Human Rights in India

—*Ajay Gudavarty*

## Introduction

At the heart of thinking, practicing and implementing human rights is the dilemma between making these sufficiently general, abstract and universal so as to entitle individuals and collectives across gender, race, colour, class, language, age, sexual preferences, and religious distinctions, and the imperative of making them context specific, concrete and particular so as to effectively implement these to protect specific individuals and groups experiencing particular modes of marginalisation and denial of socio-economic mobility. Human rights, therefore, essentially refers to those rights that are accrued to us for just being human, and thus, 'the subject of human rights are not members of this or that society, but of the community of humankind' (Vincent 1986: 9).[1] 'It is this vision that is enshrined in the Universal Declaration of Human Rights (UDHR) as a 'common standard of achievement for all people's and all nations'.[2] Various conventions, declarations and other documents further developed rights based on this vision. The most prominent among these being the International Covenant on Civil and Political Rights (ICCPR) and the International Covenant on Economic, Social and Cultural Rights (ICESCR) that were adopted by the UN in 1966, and came into force, after being ratified by the UN member states, in 1976. There were conventions that focused on the rights violations of specific social groups such as the various misrecognised racial, ethnic, and indigenous groups, women and those that were relegated to a minority status, such as the immigrants. For instance, the International Convention on the Elimination of All Forms of Racial Discrimination (ICERD) was adopted by the UN in 1965, and the Convention on the Elimination of All Forms of Discrimination Against Women (CEDAW), in 1979.[3] The international discourse on human rights underwent a transformation with the addition of the 'third generation rights' that yet again focused attention on the common concerns of the humanity by foregrounding issues of interdependence. This was reflected in the various declarations and protocols on environmental issues, along with the Declaration on the Right to Development that was adopted in 1986 by the UN.

Much of the International human rights law has close connection, both conceptual and in terms of its actual implementation, 'with the principles of domestic constitutional law embodied in the fundamental laws of various countries'. Domestic laws have been both the source and effects of international human rights laws. It is significant to note, with reference to India, that the Indian Constitution was framed at a time (1947-49) when the General Assembly of the United Nations had given its approval to the UDHR. However, the Constitution making process was also preceded by a struggle for civil liberties as an integral part of the anti-colonial struggle. The first probable organised initiative was taken by Jawaharlal Nehru to form a civil liberties organisation on November 7, 1936, by founding the Indian Civil Liberties Union (ICLU) with Rabindranath Tagore as its president. Rights were articulated not only as guarantees against arbitrary state action that was so much part of the British colonial rule, but also as necessary means to achieve a more just and egalitarian socio-economic order. It was this two-pronged strategy that was the basis of the anti-colonial struggle and the various instruments it set up, including the Motilal Nehru Committee of 1928, and the Karachi session of the Congress in 1931, which adopted the resolution on funda-mental rights. The strategy was a derivative of the conceptual distinction between the natural rights and the positivist tradition of articulating rights. In the natural rights tradition, rights are envisaged as inalienable, having their own origins in nature, while in the positivist tradition 'rights not only originate in the action of the state, but are also entirely dependent on it for their existence' (Singh 2005: 32). The state is the source and arbiter of rights and therefore, can legitimately even take them away in certain rare and well-specified situations. It is this conceptual distinction that the Constitution of India has enshrined in the various principles and provisions of human rights in Part III (Fundamental Rights) and Part IV (Directive Principles of State Policy). Fundamental rights protect broadly six types or categories of rights that include right to equality, right to personal liberty, right against exploitation, right to freedom of conscience and expression, rights dealing with cultural and educational rights (with special reference to minorities), and finally the right to judicial or constitutional remedies. Based on the Constitutional vision, the Supreme Court in India, besides review of legislative and administrative measures, gave the writ jurisdiction a creative shape, entailing judicial activism for protection and expansion of human rights, through the innovation of *public interest litigation* (PIL) or *social interest litigation* (SIL) since the 1980. In the cases of *Gupta V. Union of India* (1982) and *Nakara V. Union of India* (1983), the Supreme Court did away with the 'orthodox bar of *locus standi*' and it extended the possibility of approaching the Court even by a letter (named by Upendra Baxi as *epistolary jurisdiction*), which can be 'treated by the Court as a writ petition' (Singh 1999: 75). The Courts also expanded the scope of enumerated rights by reading in new rights into the fundamental rights. Among others, they included, the right to literacy and primary and secondary education; right to health, right to food, drinking water and integrity of the environment, right to minimum wages, right to compensation for torture, cruel treatment; right to speedy trial (including the right to free legal aid) (*Ibid: 79*). These efforts to both protect and expand the content of rights by the courts was possible, apart from the pressure from the civil rights and other political groups and movements such as that of women and Dalits, due to the fact that India is a signatory to the major International human rights instruments including the UDHR, ICCPR, IESCR, IERD, and CEDAW, to name a few. The Supreme Court has invoked the Articles of International Conventions to pronounce judgments. For instance, relying on Article 24 of the ICCPR, the Supreme Court expanded the ambit of Article 21 that refers to the 'right to life and personal liberty'. In *Sheela Barse V. Secretary, Children Aid Society,* the court made stringent provisions for protecting the rights of children detained in observation homes. Similarly, in *Jolly George Verghese V Bank of Cochin,* the Supreme Court relied on Article 11 of the ICCPR, which provides that no one shall be imprisoned merely for inability to fulfill contractual obligation, in interpreting section 51 of the Civil Procedure Code of India (Joshi, 1999:97).

However, notwithstanding these invocations, what these rights actually refer to depends on the more specific historical, social and cultural context, both across and within particular societies. The interface between global and domestic human rights, while enabling the implementation of human rights, continue to raise politically and philosophically significant questions (for the jurisprudence of rights) regarding the Eurocentric character of the global human rights. For instance, Immanuel Kant argues, 'Freedom (independence from being constrained by another's choice), insofar as it can coexist with the freedom of every other in accordance with a universal law, is the only original right belonging to every man by virtue of his humanity' (Kant 1995: 238). Such a foregrounding of the idea of freedom could be problematic, in the sense of being Western and Eurocentric, from the point of view of those societies that wish to protect their communities and pose certain limits on free speech, or for certain sections within a society, such as women, who might argue that a notion of freedom without obligations presupposes atomistic individuals hyper-separated from the complex network of social relations.[4] Thus, *"the question that begs attention is how do we retain the emancipatory, rather than the hegemonic, potential of the universal nature of human rights, and transmute them into particular, rather than localised, mechanisms accessible to different social groups in varied political contexts."*

It is this 'dilemmatic situation' that translates, more specifically, into a series of debates on human rights. This paper will focus on three such significant issues that are particularly relevant to the emerging discourse and politics of human rights in India.

(a) The debate on the centrality of the legal ( concrete) dimension of the human rights, as against the moral ( abstract) dimension that translates into preeminence for civil-political rights since these are the only rights that are justiciable. Is rule of law guaranteeing basic civil-political rights, even at times of crisis, an effective check on state power or can it be overcome by the 'normalisation of the exception'? These issues will be explored in the context of the growing `war` against militancy, terrorism and armed struggles in India.

(b) (b) The debate on universal human rights versus cultural relativism is espoused by many states in the non-European part of the world. While cultural relativism poses challenges to the liberal-universal discourse of human rights, what has it meant to the various marginalised social groups in these societies? We shall focus on an issue of cultural relativism with reference to the recent debate on caste and race carried out by the Dalit groups in the Durban conference in 2001.

(c) Finally, the debate on the 'third generation' human rights, as articulated in the 'Right to Development' foregrounds the, original idea of *indivisibility* that is constitutive of human rights. Does the language of development as a right offer a model of development different from market-oriented neo-liberal reforms? How does such a discourse interact with grassroots political movements that operate at national and local levels? It will be pointed out that the discourse, politics and practices of human rights emerge from a complex and continuous exchange between political movements, and institutions, both at the national and international levels, by drawing continuities between the discourse around 'Right to Development' and taking the instance of the anti-liquor movement led by women in Andhra Pradesh.

## Civil-Political Rights, Rule of Law and the 'War on Terrorism'

Cranston, in his celebrated essay 'Are There Any Human Rights' argued that human rights need to have a restricted reference to only the 'first generation rights' such as freedom of speech that are based on the principle of non-interference and therefore are cogent and encompass the 'feasibility of guaranteeing complete and comprehensive fulfillment', which, in turn, makes it possible to legislate and make these rights justiciable. Without legality being the defining feature of human rights they end up, as Bentham once put it, as 'bawling upon paper'. Human rights become effective only as legal rights emanating either from national legislation or international conventions and declarations 'rather then on the basic humanity (or humanness) of the persons involved' (Sen 2006: 2). According to Cranston, "The traditional political and civil rights are not difficult to *institutionalise* for the most part, they require govern-ments, and other people generally to leave a man alone...The problem posed by claims to economic and social rights, however, are of another order altogether" (Cranston 1983: 13). This centrality of legality seems to be linked to a certain understanding of not just human rights, but of law itself. The idea that law by its very nature 'holds for everyone' and it is a 'sort of thing that demands equality in its application' (Bilgrami 2007: 318). Further, it is abstract enough to inform us, or enable us to make sense of uncertain situations and institutionalise certain standardised practices, even in conditions of emergency or social crisis of various kinds. It is with this understanding that the International Convention on Civil Political Rights (ICCPR) in Article 6 explicitly states : 'Every human being has the inherent right to life. This right shall be protected by law. No one shall be arbitrarily deprived of his life'.[5] Similarly, it states in Art 9 that 'No one shall be subject to arbitrary arrest or detention. No one shall be deprived of his liberty except on such grounds and in accordance with such procedure established by law'.

In contemporary liberal democracies, it is the principle of rule of law that assures the individuals the 'government's respect for the sovereign authority of the people', and therefore the guarantee against the violation of 'basic' civil and political rights. It is this promise in rule of law that the Marxist historian Thompson attempted to foreground and extrapolate, contrary to either reducing it to a mere 'juridical illusion' or ideological hypocrisy of liberal democracies. Thompson, therefore argued that rule of law meant 'the imposing of effective inhibitions upon power and the defence of the citisen from power's all-intrusive claims' (Thompson 1975: 266). With the growing global 'war on terrorism'[6], analysing rule of law, in order to comprehend the efficacy of human rights (civil-political rights) as legal rights, would perhaps point towards two dominant forms that it has taken in contemporary times, quite in contrast to its promise of 'inhibiting' the 'all-intrusive powers'. First, the rule of law is 'receiving so much attention now because of its centrality to both democracy and the market economy in the era marked by a wave of transitions to both' (Carothers 1998: 97). Strengthening the rule of law refers to institutionalisation of the 'basic elements of a modern market economy such as property rights and contracts' (*Ibid*), making it possible therefore to 'export' rule of law (and democracy), and confirming its inextricable link with market that Hayek had proposed in his campaign for the libertarian-right. Second, (in many complex ways linked to the first) is the very erosion of law as norms outside of exception, and instead becoming a mark of 'normali-sation of the exception'. As Agamben has pointed out, the 'state of exception' 'is not a special kind of law' meant to deal with conditions like war, but normalised to the extent of becoming 'a paradigm of government', and 'constituting the very basis of modern state power'.

The plight of human rights-civil political rights- in India is marked expressly by this shift to the 'normalisation of exception'. The growing war on terror has translated into a situation, where on issues of 'national security' and public order, there can be no constraints that law can impose. In fact, in its renewed avatar, the raison d'etre of law has to be to protect security and order. Various Acts have been promulgated to put this new role of law into action. Among them, the Terrorist and Disruptive Activities (Prevention) (TADA) Act, the Prevention of Terrorist Activities (POTA) Act, and Armed Forces (Special Powers) (AFSPA) Act, have gained prominence in terms of their role in the violation of the civil and political rights of citisens of India, as well as the activists struggling on behalf of the citisens as part of a vibrant human rights movement in India (Gudavarthy 2008). These violations are not aberrations, but implicit in the way these legislations have been both envisaged and put to use. For instance, AFSPA Section 4(a) states: that any commissioned officer- 'if he is of opinion that it is necessary so to do for the maintenance of public order, after giving such due warning as he may consider necessary fire upon or otherwise use force, even to causing death, against any person who is acting in contravention of any law or order for the time being in force in the disturbed area prohibiting the assembly of five or more persons or the carrying of weapons or of things capable of being used as weapons or of firearms, ammunition or explosive substances'. This can be contrasted with, as Noorani has argued, with the provisions of the CrPC, wherein Section 130(3) explicitly states that officer of the armed forces should use 'as little force and do as little injury to person and property' (Noorani 2009:9). In spite of the contrast with the CrPC and the outrageous powers to kill, the Supreme Court has upheld the constitutional validity of AFSPA in the *Naga People's Movement of Human Rights vs Union of India* (1998) (2 SCC 109).[7] The process of 'normalisation of exception' is being further entrenched in not only upholding 'special powers', but in fact making them part of the CrPC itself through the recently constituted *(Malimath) Committee on Reforms of Criminal Justice System*, which has proposed extensive changes to the criminal procedure code carrying in many of the 'special powers' into regular criminal justice system. It suggests some very fundamental changes in its proposals-

(a) To dilute the provision of 'guilty beyond reasonable doubt' and replace the Evidence Act with the provision that it is sufficient that 'the court is convinced that it is true' (Para 5.13).

(b) Withdrawal of the right to silence to the accused by 'amending the code to provide for appropriate inferences from the silence of the accused' (Para 3.40).

(c) Removal of the distinction between 'cognisable' offences and 'non-cognisable' offences.

(d) 'The confession before a Superintendent of Police or a higher ranking official should be admissible in evidence subject to the condition that the accused is informed of his right to consult a legal practitioner'( 7.35.2).

(e) Review of the sunset (time bound expiration) provision in Acts such as the POTA.

## Universality, Cultural Relativism and the 'Caste is Race' Debate

Human rights are also unique in as much as they allow for imagining human rights to be universal as much as being culturally relativistic to each individual society with their different social traditions. It is therefore possible to argue that the notion of human rights to be found in the UDHR of the United Nations can be traced to the historical experience of Western Civilisation. When the UDHR was adopted most 'third world' countries were still under the yoke of colonial rule. However, does this historical fact make human rights essentially Western, in the sense, that they originate exclusively from Western culture or tradition and therefore, there is nothing universal about human rights?

Donnelly, in one of the early intervention to the debate on 'cultural relativism versus universal human rights', argued that there are broadly four ways to approach the interface between them. Through 'radical cultural relativism' culture becomes the sole source of human rights[8], while a 'radical universalist' approach argues that culture is irrelevant and there are values and rights that are eternal and relevant across space and time. Contrary to the above approaches are two other approaches, namely 'strong cultural relativism' and 'weak cultural relativism'. While the former argues rights are culturally determined, but universality of rights serves as a check on 'potential excesses of relativism', the later foregrounds culture as an important source, but allows 'relatively rare and strictly limited local variations and exceptions' ( Donnelly, 1984). According to Donnelly, the weak cultural relativism is possibly the best way to reconcile relativism and universalism. Such an approach, while emphasising the need for universalist categories allows for variations in 'form'. For instance, right to work needs to be recognised a universal right in all societies, encompassing issues such as right to seek employment, right to be compensated for unemployment, among others. However, further specification regarding the length and amount of unemployment benefits could vary (*Ibid*).[2]

In the more contemporary of debates, scholars have attempted to foreground principles around which a universal framework of human rights can be sustained. Nussbaum has argued, based on her Aristotelian approach of 'general characteristics of human beings', that it is possible to identify characteristics that are fundamentally human and 'not as a member of a particular group or local community' (Gould 2004: 55). She says, "my proposal is fairly universal and 'essentialist'. That is, it asks us to focus on what is common to all, rather than on differences (although, as we shall see, it does not neglect these), and too see capabilities and functions as were central, more at the core of human life than others" (Nussbaum 1995: 63). She believes that needs such as food, drink, shelter, sex, mobility, relatedness, humour, among others are common across societies. Sen, has further argued, in basic agreement with Nussbaum's approach, that there is an impending need to develop common standards in accessing development, such as nutrition, and education, as they form the 'capabilities' to function in various ways and are essential to the universal 'freedom to achieve'. Cultural relativism, therefore, cannot be meaningful in contexts where it undermines the 'capabilities' necessary to function. Thus, for instance, Okin argues, that the 'respect for cultural practices must be subordinate to the requirements of women's equality' (Okin 1999: 12).

Universality in such a framework emerges 'as a potential framework or horizon for interaction', which grows with inter-societal conversations. In contrast to abstract universality, we could, following Gould, refer to it as 'concrete universality' that is 'constructed by individuals in concrete and differentiated social relations in networks' of relationships and networks of engagement, themselves interconnecting' ( Gould 2004: 62). It could be possibly developed around the universal values of care, sympathy and solidarity, which was referred to as 'non-Eurocentric universality' by Parekh, premised on a unique dialectic between the particular and the universal where 'particularity or difference is valued, but not particularism, which absolutises it. The universal is valued, but not universalism, at least not of the kind that sets itself in opposition to and despises the particular' (Parekh 2008: 3).

This discussion is of particular significance in understanding the politics and discourse of human rights in India. As the State increasingly becomes non-responsive and governs through a paradigm of 'state of exception', marginalised social groups access rights moving beyond the nation and talking of a language that is post-Westphalian in nature, playing out the unique dialectic between the universal and the particular. At the World Conference against Racism, Racial Discrimination, Xenophobia and Related Intolerance (WCAR), held at Durban in August 2001, Dalit organisations, led by the National Campaign on Dalit Human Rights (NCDHR), spearheaded a campaign to include caste discrimination as part of racial discrimination and discuss the modes of eliminating it by putting international pressure on the Government of India, as its obligation for having ratified the International Convention on Elimination of All Forms of Racial Discriminations (ICERD) in 1969. The United Nations (universal) framework to understand discrimination based on birth was exclusively west-centric in its recognition of only race and colour, and in ignoring experiences that were specific to Asia and Africa. Article 2 of the Convention proclaims : 'No state, institution, group or individual shall make any discrimination whatsoever in matters of human rights and fundamental freedoms in the treatment of persons, on the ground of race, colour or ethnic origin.' Though racial discrimination was defined in terms of exclusion based on descent, the Convention did not mention or include 'discrimination arising from non race-colour-ethnic identities' (Thorat 2004: xvi). It was only in 1996 that the Committee on the Elimination of all forms of Racial Discrimination (ICERD) made an explicit reference to caste-based discrimination and the practice of untouchability: "The committee states that the term 'descent' mentioned in Article 1 of the Convention does not solely refer to race. The Committee affirms that the situation of the Scheduled Castes and Scheduled Tribes falls within the scope of the Convention". The Dalit groups in India, taking a clue from this demanded a more elaborate discussion on caste-based practices under Paragraph 109 of the agenda of the Durban conference, which referred to 'discrimination on the basis of work and descent'.

However, the Government of India objected to this demand of the Dalit groups. Caste was described as strictly an 'internal' matter, not to be debated in international fora. The official position of the government clearly stated, 'Communities which fall under the definition of Scheduled Castes and Scheduled Tribes are unique to Indian society and to its historical process and do not come under the purview of Article 1 of the Convention. Caste-based discrimination should not, therefore, have been brought within the discussion in this committee, which is charged solely with the responsibility of looking into racial discrimination' (Thorat 2004: xxiii). In claiming caste as 'unique to Indian society' Government of India was making a cultural relativist argument that cannot be easily made sense by the international organisations that function with a universalist discourse of human rights. Intriguingly, while the Dalit groups themselves had to puncture the western-centric bias to get caste included within the scope of ICERD, the Government of India was also critiquing the universalist nature, but precisely not to debate caste within the purview of ICERD. The debate took interesting twists in India, many of the scholars, sensitive to protecting the 'self-determination' of India, argued that taking caste to international fora also meant that 'we are looking for foreign help to fight everything, including the caste system' (Gupta 2004: 53).

Similarly, those alert to the 'imperialism of categories' objected to the forceful reading of caste as race, while the weakening of the caste system is possible only 'if caste is presented as a caste and not forcibly fitted into the category of race, and at the same time, an attempt is made to promulgate an international charter against caste discrimination' (Seth 2004: xxvii). This alone would actually make the initial attempts of the Dalit groups to recognise the specificity of caste based discrimination, rather than conflate caste with race. Further, this kind of a conflation may even lead to a change in the way caste is understood and provide an opportunity for the State to withdraw some of its social welfare policies, such as affirmative action.

Dalit groups and activists, working on their behalf, were attempting to foreground a 'concrete universality' that is sensitive to the specificities of caste-based discrimination, but comprehend universalisation as increasing interconnections and looking for commonalities in discrimination practiced in various social contexts. They therefore argued that 'whether it is Australian attacks on Indians or atrocities committed on Dalits by Indians or discrimination and oppression of the people of the north-east ( which is racial in nature- my addition), they are basically issues that concern humanity and cannot be prevented from being internationalised' ( Teltumbde, 2009: 18). While there is commonality as discrimination against humanity, which is important to recover, there is distinction in the way they are privileged or neglected in concrete social and historical contexts. Therefore, while caste based discrimination is neglected, racial discrimination of Indians living elsewhere gets focused since they belong to specific (privileged) caste backgrounds. In essence, what Dalit groups were attempting was a double-edged approach of distinguishing caste from race, yet using race, which is globally a more recognised form of discrimination, by reading caste unto race to make use of the political spaces opened by the latter.

## Third Generation Rights, Right to Development and Domestic Violence

Third generation rights were not merely new, or rights that were not covered under the first two generation of civil-political and social-economic and cultural rights, but signified radically new principles beyond the scope of the language of rights in the first two generations. Apart from the end of cold war, there were various social and political developments that led to a new language of rights, among which prominent was the rise of movements for environmental justice, for peace and for nuclear disarmament. Environmental struggles brought into relief the principle of 'intergenerational equity' further problematising the idea of equality. The World Commission on Environment and Development stated that 'needs of future generations will not be compromised while the present generation's needs are met' (Brundtlard Report 1987: 170). Movements for peace articulated new ideas about 'collective interests' that have to be fought by humanity as such and there are no natural (social) consti-tuencies that would struggle for peace. Such issues could be fought not solely around interests, but common concern about the well-being and the very future survival of humanity. It is the spirit and the vision of some of these novel principles that got encapsulated in third generation rights, such as the Right to Development.

The Right to Development (RD), adopted in 1986 by the UN General Assembly and reaffirmed in the Vienna Declaration of 1993 World Conference on Human Rights, marked a new beginning. It envisaged a new model of development around principles of fair and equitable distribution, political participation, social well-being, cultural recognition and dignity beyond the parameters of development as expansion of GNP, industrialisation, export-growth and capital flows, and marking a break from the top-down process of 'developmentalism'.[10] It is indispensable to recognise the strong interdependence of various kinds of civil-political and socio-economic rights and the futility in attempting to either achieve one against the other or selectively privilege a set of rights. Amartya Sen refers to them as 'substantive freedoms', which includes the idea of 'human dignity' that refers, along with access to resources, health, education, equity of opportunities, also to the participation in the life of the community and the freedom to speak without fear. They should all finally contribute towards 'giving individuals greater control over his/her environment and thereby increase their freedom'. Sen considers both a 'sense of self' and the capacity 'to appear in public without shame' as relevant to the 'capability to function', and hence as falling within the scope of an account of justice and development (Sen 1998). This shift towards integrating rights in redefining justice underscores the changes not only in the discourse on development, but also the liberal theory through the Rawlsian theory of 'distributive justice' and his 'difference principle', and the discourse on human rights itself founded in the international declaration on the 'Right to Development'.

In order to effectively convert this vision into tangible policies, the Declaration on Right to Development made, among others, four funda-mental formulations. First, RD reiterated the principle of indivisibility of rights.[11] Article 6(2) stated that the prime object of the Declaration is to 'eliminate obstacles to development resulting from failure to observe civil and political rights, as well as economic, social and cultural rights'. In other words, RD works as a hinge connecting various rights into a 'vector' that 'measures' human well-being. 'The value of the vector improves if at least one right improves and no right deteriorates. If any right is violated, the vector deteriorates and the Right to Development is violated' (Sen Gupta 2006: viii). Second, the emphasis on the right to participate replaced the human being as an object of development and made him/her an active subject. Article 1 states that 'right to Development is an inalienable right, by virtue of which every human person and all peoples are entitled to participate in, and enjoy economic, social, cultural, and political development, in which all human rights and fundamental freedoms can be fully realised'. Without the right to participate, human, societies are reduced to 'target groups' to be administered state-initiated policies and bureaucratic intervention. For instance, peasants are reduced to 'pure' economic categories such as 'small farmers', undermining, as Escobar argues, a 'whole way of life' ( Escobar 1997).[12] The societies are made 'manageable' and the imperatives of 'governmentality' undermines the agency of social groups reducing them to the status of mere 'populations' (Scott 1998).

Third, RD recasts development as neither a means nor an end, instead it lays premium on development as a process. In other words, 'the outcomes of the process are human rights, but the process itself would also be claimed as a human right' (Sen Gupta, 2006: 12). As we understand democracy not only as an end, but also as a means to an end, development is also 'not a finite event, but a process over time' (*Ibid: 17*). This mode of approaching development make it open to 'social ethics and public reasoning', as well as make it as much a collective right to be available to specific social groups as much as individuals within those groups (Sen, 2006: 2).

Finally, RD lays emphasis in its realisation on the mutual interdependence within the 'international community of states'. RD argues for the primary responsibility on the individual national states and cooperation from the international community. It expects 'policies at the national level with equitable economic relations and a favourable environment at the international level' (Sen Gupta, 2006:18). The responsibility of international community is articulated as an 'imperfect obligation', addressed to all those states which are in a position to help. An instance of such a role by the international community could be found in the recently forged alternative regional organisations such as MERCOSUR and ALBA in Latin America. With the initiative under these regional organisations, there has been, for instance, extensive medical services made available by Cuba to Venezuela, keeping in mind not merely profit, but social benefits to the people of both the countries (Gudavarthy, 2009).

Increasingly, there has been the realisation that any effective and meaningful implementation of human rights has to integrate various aspects including the civil-political rights for political participation with social and economic rights for fair distribution, means with ends as an on-going process, and domestic policies with international cooperation. This move towards integrating various rights is visible in some of the prominent judgments by the Supreme Court in the recent past. For instance, in the *Francis Coralis Mullin vs Union Territory of Delhi,* the Supreme Court argued that, 'The Right to live is not restricted to mere animal existence, but it also includes the right to live with human dignity, and all that goes along with it, namely, the bare necessities of life such as adequate nutrition, clothing and shelter and facilities for reading, writing and expressing ourselves.' (SSC. 608, 1981 1). Right to Education was read into the fundamental rights through Right to Life. Art. 21A was inserted that recognised the Right to Education as a fundamental right and imposed a duty on the state to provide free and compulsory to all children from the age of six to fourteen years. It is these judgments that led to the 86th Amendment to the Constitution in 2002, granting legislative recognition to the Right to Education, finally fructifying in the Right to Education Act, 2010. While state institutions such as the judiciary have, to some extent, demonstrated an integrationist framework, political movements of various hues have worked for long with such a framework.

Women's struggles at the grassroots, for instance, have been for long indicating that domination and systematic marginalisation of women has been possible due to complex interaction between the political, economic, social and cultural dimensions. Therefore, in dealing with specific forms of violations of rights, such as dowry-related deaths, domestic violence, sexual harassment among others, and their manifold interactions have to be taken into account in developing strategies that can effectively undermine the entrenched modes of domination. It was such an integrationist strategy that was being proposed in a struggle that drew incisive links between a political economy driven by collection of revenues from the sale of liquor, and the masculine culture of controlling the 'private' sphere through physical violence against women. The anti-arrack movement, as it was referred to, began in August 1992, in a remote village of Dubagunta of Nellore district in Andhra Pradesh. Women of the village stopped vending of arrack in their village after three men lost their way and drowned in a tank. Women stopped arrack carts and jeeps from entering the village, and demanded complete prohibition of the sale of liquor in the state. The movement went beyond the traditional and conventional divisions between the public and private, in order to comprehend the hidden linkages between family, domestic violence, the state and the liquor lobby. They understood that behind their abusive husbands was the whole support structure led by the arrack contractors, police, goondas, legislators, ministers, officials and bureaucrats (Reddy and Patnaik, 1993:1064). Women consistently articulated the language of including various social (domestic stress, dignity, mental anguish, education and health), economic (constant debt, hunger, falling standard and quality of living) and political (unholy nexus between the politicians-representatives, police, and the liquor lobby-contractors) issues in the developmental agenda. They further argued that, without necessary economic empowerment, social change, political participation, and struggle against cultural practices, mere legal (rights) intervention can be formal and counter-productive. Thus, when the Government of Andhra Pradesh refused to prohibit liquor and restricted women's right to forge political movements, and instead suggested availing legal options by making use of the Domestic Violence Act (2005), women's groups argued that it has the effect of making law insular to the needs of women.

Firstly, the victims become more 'vulnerable' by the compulsion of opening up before an unsympathetic judiciary and police stations. Secondly, the provisions of the law are incapable of addressing the larger issues of women. "A close look at the appeals that women have made in relation to the domestic violence law 498A in the last two decades shows that they are seeking relief which extend beyond those that can be offered by courts and police stations. Women are seeking responsible husbands, a role in decision-making, self-respect and a dignified family life, which, in itself, often contributes to the violence they experience" (Suneetha, 2005: 102). Finally, such legal interventions add to the logic of the technocratic State in pulling social problems outside the domain of politics and projecting solutions in fine technical interventions. "Such an 'enclosure' in the legal realm individualises the woman into a caste and leads to a depoliticisation of the discussion of women's battles in the family. Is it this closure, which is producing the silence that we are noticing?" (*Ibid: 4103*). Thus, women's movements at the local level are reiterating the points made at the international level in the Declaration on Right to Development that development needs to be posited around principles of indivisibility, right to political participation by the agents, and perceive it as an ongoing process, forging complex links, rather than a single event.

## References and Further Readings


Agamben Giorgio, *State of Exception*, University of Chicago Press, Chicago, 2005.

Amnesty International India, *The (Malimath) Committee on Reforms of Criminal Justice System: Premises, Politics and Implications for Human Rights*, AII, Delhi, 2003.

Baxi, Upendra, *Human Rights in a Post-Human World*, Oxford University Press, Oxford, 2007.

Bilgrami, Akhil, '*Secularism and the Very Concept of Law*' in Rajeshwari Sundar Rajan (ed) Secularism, Permanent Black, Delhi, 2008.

Bielefeldt, Heiner, '*Western versus Islamic Human Rights Conception*' in A.Pollis and P.Schwab (ed) Human Rights: New Perspectives, New Realities, Lynne Reinner Publishers, London, 2000.

Carothers, Thomas, '*The Rule of Law Revival*', Foeriegn Affairs, March/April 1998, 77(2).

Cranston, Maurice, '*Are there any Human Rights?*' Daedalus, fall, 1983.

Donnelly, Jack, '*Cultural relativism versus Universal Human Rights*' Human Rights Quaterly, 6, 1984.

Donnelly, Jack, '*In Search of the Unicorn: The Jurisprudence and Politics of the Right to Development*' California Internal Law Journal, 1985.

Escobar, Arturo, '*Planning*' .Sachs (Ed) Development: Dictionary, Orient Longman, Hyderabad, 1997.

Fischlin, Daniel and Nandorfy, Martha, *The Concise Guide to Global Human rights*, Oxford University Press, Delhi, 2007.

Gould, Carol, *Globalisation, Democracy and Human Rights*, Cambridge University Press, Cambridge, 2004.

Gudavarthy, Ajay, '*Human Rights Movements in India: State, Civil Society, and Beyond*' Contributions to Indian Sociology, April, 2008.

Gudavarthy, Ajay, '*Gandhi, Dalits and Feminists: Recovering the Convergence*' Economic and Political Weekly, May 30, 2008.

Gudavarthy, Ajay, '*Globalisation and Regionalisation: Mapping the New Continental Drift*' Economic and Political Weekly, June 19, 2009.

Gupta, Dipankar, '*Caste is not Race:,,,,, but, Let's Go to the UN Forum Anyway*' in Sukhdeo Thorat and Umakant (Ed) Caste, Race and Discrimination, Rawat Publishers, Delhi, 2004.

Haragopal, G, '*Terrorism and Human Rights: Indian Experience with Repressive Laws*' Economic and Political Weekly, July 11, 2009.

Joshi, Sanjay, '*The right to Equality, Life and Liberty under the Constitution of India*' in Abdulrahim et.al (Ed) Perspectives on Human Rights, Manak, Delhi, 1999.

Noorani, AG, '*Armed Forces (Special Powers) Act: Urgency of review*' Economic and Political weekly, August 22, 2009.

Nussbaum, Martha, and J.Glover (Ed) *Women, Culture and Development*, Oxford University Press, New York, 1995.

Parekh, Bikhu, *A New Politics of Identity*, Palgrave Macmillan, New York, 2008.

Reddy, Narsimha, and Arun Patnaik, '*Anti-Arrack Agitation of Women In Andhra Pradesh*', Economic and Political Weekly, May 22, 1993.

Scott, 1998 James, *Seeing Like a State*, Yale University Press, London.

Sen, Amartya, *Development as Freedom*, Oxford University Press, Delhi 1998.

Sen, Amartya, '*Human Rights and Development*' in B. A .Andreassen and S.P.Marks (Ed) Development as a Human Right, Harvard University Press, Harvard, 2006.

Sen Gupta, Arjun, '*Right to Development as a Human Right*', ', Economic and Political Weekly, July 2001.

Sen Gupta, Arjun, '*The Human Right to Development*' in B. A. Andreassen (ed).

Suneetha, '*Adjudicating (Un) Domestic Battles*', Economic and Political Weekly, No 38 September 17, 2005.

Seth, D.L, '*Caste in the Mirror of Race*' in Sukhdeo Thorat (ed)

Singh, Ajay, '*Role of Judiciary in the Protection and Promotion of Human Rights*' in Abdulrahim et.al. (ed) Perspectives on Human Rights, Manak, Delhi, 1999.

Singh, Ujjwal Kumar. 2005. *Democratising state and society: role of civil liberties and democratic rights movements in India. Contemporary India*, January-June.

Susan, Muller Okin, *Is Multiculturalism Bad for Women?* Princeton University Press, Princeton, 1999.

Teltumbde, Anand, '*Race or Caste, Discrimination is a Universal Concern*' Economic and Political Weekly, August 22, 2009.

Thompson, EP, *Whigs and Hunters*, Allen Lane, London, 1975.

Vincent, RJ, *Human Rights and International Relations*, Cambridge University Press, Cambridge, 1986.

Kant, Immanuel, *The Metaphysics of Morals*, Cambridge University Press, Cambridge, 1995.

# 4

# Language Rights: Implementing Worldwide Language Rights and to Promote Social Justice

*—Tania Hossain*

## Abstract

One of the most influential movements on language in recent years has been the growing attention to language rights, particularly as they affect linguistic minorities (both indigenous and migrant groups). Research on language rights has focused on formal language-rights statements (e.g., by the Council of Europe), on legal and constitutional guarantees of language rights (e.g., in South Africa), and on the use of language rights as a rationale for efforts by linguistic minorities to preserve, reinvigorate, and expand the functional range of minority languages. Among the most influential scholars working within a language-rights framework are Skutnabb-Kangas (2000; Phillipson, 2000) and May (2001).

Skutnabb-Kangas, May, and others have argued that language rights offer a reasonable framework for the protection of minority languages. In contrast, Brutt-Griffler (2004) argues that a focus on language rights is neither theoretically justified nor useful as a means for protecting the interests of linguistic minorities. This paper would focus on the debate between Brutt-Griffler (who is highly critical of language rights) and Skutnabb-Kangas with the reference of linguistics minority rights in Bangladesh.

## Introduction

One of the most important issues in language-rights research is the question of whether language-rights efforts can affect changes in language policies and in the systems of inequality that currently characterise many language situations. Many students in the world enter the school where there is a difference between the language used in the school and the language they speak at home. When dealing with the issue of education and language, it is important to differentiate between the right to get an education which is necessary for social, economic and political partici-pation and mobility and the right to an education through the mother tongue(s). These two rights are essential for language minorities to participate in a broader society as well as retain connection with their home or community language (Wiley, 2002).

This paper will address the following questions:

What are the major aims of the language-rights movement?

What are the major accomplishments of the language-rights movement to date?

What are the main problems or limitations with the language-rights movement?

Tove Skutanbb-Kangas has worked for the education of linguistic minorities worldwide throughout her career. In her article, "Marvelous human rights rhetoric and grim realities: Language rights in education," she raised a question: "Can a human rights (HRs) approach to language planning and policy promote educational equity for diverse student populations?"(Skutnabb - Kangas, 2002, p.179). She argues that most of the indigenous and minority education in the world meets the UN defini-tion of linguistic genocide and the dominant language is often turned into a killer language. To her, the most important linguistic human right (LHR) which is needed to maintain the world's linguistic diversity is the unconditional mother tongue medium (MTM) education. The pedagogical reasons for the lack of literacy in the world, as well as the economic and other factors, are responsible for the denial of this right. In the linguistic and cultural diversity, it is presumed that children learn their language from their parents, as well as their community. It happens in the societies where children do not commonly attend school. But when most of the children start attending school, if the minority and indigenous children are educated through the dominant language (often the official language), it is unlikely that when they will be adults they will continue to speak to their own children with their own language. So the home language is not transmitted, and children are forced to become part of another linguistic group. In Skutnabb-Kangas' opinion, the schools, the media and the world's economic, military and political systems are the main agents for this linguistic genocide. Fishman has mentioned many times that languages cannot be saved by schools, but they sometimes act as an agent for killing language in one or two generations. Krauss (1995) argues, 90per cent of today's spoken languages may no longer be spoken or learnt by the children by the year 2100 (Skutnabb -Kangas, 2002).

According to Skutnabb-Kangas, it is necessary for the children to learn the home language, as well as the dominant language. Most of the minority children need to learn the dominant language along with their own language. Additional languages enrich people's live and give people more choice, more freedom, but these additional languages should be learned additively, not subtractively. They should not replace mother tongues. Skutnabb-Kangas believes that everyone who resides in a country where a mother tongue is not an official language has the right to become bilingual in the mother tongue and the official language. English can be one of the possibilities as it has an official status in 70 countries of the world (Skutnabb-Kangas, 2004). Subtractive formal education which teaches children a dominant language may cause the linguistic genocide and the dominant language like English, Chinese, Hindi, etc., turns into a killer language. Educational linguistic human rights which guarantees the additive language learning is needed to prevent linguistic genocide and also for linguistic diversity to be maintained on the earth (Skutnabb-Kangas, 2002).

Proponents of the monolingual instruction such as English-only often express economic reasons to show that MTM education is impossible. They often describe MTM instruction is a naïve and romantic dream which misleads linguists and educationists. They argue that Asian and African poor countries cannot afford to teach many languages. Thus, it is better to teach students one language only, preferably English. According to Skutnabb-Kangas, the economic rationale for not organising MTM is actually a fraud. Irrational policies are adopted which fail to support multilingualism or ensure school achievement for indigenous people, national immigrants and refugee minorities. Politically dominated groups adopt these irrational language policies, particularly in many Asian and African countries. These educational policies may cause linguistic and cultural genocide. The United Nations 1948 special definition of genocide is as follows: "Article III (1) prohibiting the use of the language of the group in daily intercourse or in schools, or the printing and circulation of publications in the language group". Prohibition can be direct or indirect. It would be regarded as a question of linguistic genocide if in the schools there are no minority teachers, if the minority language is not used as a medium of education and if indirectly, in the daily intercourse in schools, the use of the minority languages is prohibited. The dominant language medium of education for the minority child may cause mental harm and in future students will start using the dominant language with their own children when they will be adults. In this process, within two or three generations, linguistically (as well as in other ways) individuals are forcibly transferred to a dominant group (Skutnabb-Kangas).

Suresh Canagarajah (2004) points out that certain languages can enjoy higher linguistic capital than other languages. But this concept does not express that the child whose mother language is suppressed by education will suffer psychological damage. Much research shows that knowledge of an additional language is needed for primary socialisation. For example, in Sri Lanka, Hindu reformists started an educational system which is different from education system offered by the British, i.e., it includes both English and Vernacular education. The new educational system includes Tamil and local culture content in a constructive way. It ensures additive bilingualism (Canagarajah, 2004).

Language has positive rights and positive right means the rights which would create obligations for the state. The state have a firm duty to ensure the rights. Negative rights prevent linguistic discrimination. Positive right is required for education through the medium of minority languages. MTM education is one of the most important demands presented by many indigenous and minority people all over the world. But in the HR approach, educational equity for the diverse students does not seem to be very promising. Discrimination in education based on language, class and gender still exists in the world. MTM education is also linguistic human rights (LHR) but very few people in the world enjoy this right. Skutnabb-Kangas complains that, though the UN talks about human rights and democracy, many governments spend more money on the military rather than on education and health (Skutnabb-Kangas, 2002).

Tomasevki (1996) mentioned, "the purpose of international HRs law is to overrule the law of supply and demand and remove price-tags from people and from necessities for their survival"(p. 104, quoted in Skutnabb –Kangas). These necessities are not only for the basic food and housing, but also for the dignified life such as civil, political and cultural rights, as well as LHRs. At present, however, many states refuse the HR of access to free and compulsory education by putting price tags on education. In the last two decades, several countries have introduced school fees for the basic primary education, but the UN Special Rapporteur on the rights to education, criticises this fact. This necessary right is not being implemented or being respected by the governments today. MTM education is not today a HR in practice (Skutnabb-Kangas, 2002).

Many governments claim that HRs can be defined according to their own cultural norms and other governments claim that human rights must be respected by other countries. Unfortunately, international and regional conventions and charters give very poor support to the LHRs education. Language is given little attention. Sometimes language is present in the preambles of HRs instruments, but completely disappears when it comes to the educational document. In some cases, language may be clearly mentioned in the articles dealing with education, especially the right to MTM education, but this article may be emphasised less than other articles (*ibid*).

Skutnabb-Kangas talks about the worldwide linguistic human rights for minorities. At the same time, she describes the failure of states in implementing education using non-dominant languages. In spite of her frustration, she recommends adopting and implementing worldwide language rights. She believes that adopting such language policy will promote greater social justice (Tollefson, 2004).

Bangladesh offers an example of how such language rights as human rights that transcend social, religious, ethnic boundaries have been truncated, necessitating, as it were, a constrained national dialogue on the merits of national-education policies that seemingly exclude minority languages and position the country on the brink of economic disarray and social chaos, and negating the very essence of procedural and distributive justice. The ensuing muted debates in that country are not rife with procedural and distributive justice, in that equity in access to schooling does not loom large in those debates. There is also hardly an acknowledgement that less dominant (or minority) languages need to be more seriously considered in the education policy of a nation with 48 ethnic minority groups, each with its own language. Even with such a large number of traditional languages, historically, debates still focus, *mutatis mutandis*, on Bengali and English, making minority children, particularly those from rural areas, almost personally responsible for learning at least three languages. It is, therefore, important that more extensive work be undertaken to inform the process for instituting national-language policies that will expand educational opportunities to multi-cultural societies; foster inter-ethnic relationships; create synchronous dialogues among multicultural groups; prepare them to respect LHRs and synchronise them with, social equity; and encourage them to participate more actively in an increasingly global marketplace.

The national language and the most widely used home language in Bangladesh is Bengali, spoken by approximately 130 million people out of a total population of approximately 160 million in the country. (An additional 150 million in the neighbouring countries also speak Bengali.) Bengali is an Indo-Iranian language of the Indo-European family. Sylhetti is the second important language which is spoken by 5 million people and it is also an Indo-Iranian language. 14 million people use Chittagonian as their mother tongue and it is widely considered a dialect of Bengali, but it is not mutually intelligible, and most of its speakers do not use standard Bengali. Bengali plays a central role in most institutions in Bangladesh, but in reality, other languages also are central to life in rural areas, with consequences for education and literacy. According to the census of 1991, sixty language varieties are spoken in Bangladesh (Humayun, 2003). Of these, thirteen languages are spoken by ethnic minorities in the hill regions of the country (Hossain & Tollefson, 2006).

Culturally, ethnically, religiously and linguistically Bangladesh is a diverse country. More than 48 ethnic groups are living in Bangladesh. They constitute approximately 2 per cent of the population of the country. These groups are known within documents and literature in Bangladesh as, 'Adivasi', or indigenous' or 'ethnic minority' or 'tribal' people. These minority people basically live in Chittagong Hill Tracts and the total population is about 1.3 million people. 90 per cent people among them live in rural areas. Most of them are not literate in any languages-their mother tongue or in Bangla, the state language. 30 per cent of them are literate in Bangla. Literacy rate is very low in Chittagong Hill Tracts. 60 per cent enrolled student drop out from the early primary school which is twice than the national dropout rate. One of the major reasons is children need to educate themselves in Bangla which is totally unfamiliar to them as their mother tongue is other than Bangla. Except language barriers, there are also some other barriers like irrelevant curriculum which does not go along with the local culture. There is also the language barrier between teachers and students. Bangladeshi educational system is mainly managed by one central system which does not give special importance to the minority language rights. Although Government of Bangladesh has tried to increase the enrollment and quality of education, especially girls' education, but unfortunately it has not been implemented effectively (Tripura, 2008).

There are many minority languages in Bangladesh, which include varieties from different language families. Several are Sino-Tibetan (Tibeto-Burmese) languages, including Arakanese, Garo, and a number of varieties of

**Table List of languages of Bangladesh (Table retrieved Sep, 10 from ethonologue, webpage, 2013, (<http://www.ethnologue.com/show_country.asp?name=Bangladesh>)**

| Language name | Population | Region | Alternate Name |
|---|---|---|---|
| Bengali | 207,000,000 including 211,000,000-second language. | Almost all over Bangladesh. | Bangla-Bhasa, Bangala |
| English | 3% of the total population | All over Bangladesh. | |
| Chak | 909(1981) | Tropical forest area. | |
| Chakma<br>Garo | 260,577(1991)<br>102,000 (1993) | Tropical forest area<br>In the hill tracts | Takam<br>Garrow, Mande |
| Khasi | 85,088(1961) | | Kahasi, Khasiyas, khuchia, Kyi, Oossyah, |
| Kok/ Barok | 78,000(1993) | | Tripuri, Tripura, Tipura, Mrung, Usipi |
| Meitei | 92,800 | | Meithei, Meithe, Mitei, Mithe, Meiteiron, Manipur, Kathe, kathi, Ponna |
| Murung | 20,000 | Southerneastern, Chittagong Hill tracts | Mro, Murung, Mrung, Maru, Niopreng |
| Pankhu | 2,278 | Tropical forest | Pankho, Panko, Pangkhu |
| Sadri, Oraon | 84,000 to 200,000 | Through out the RajshahiDivision, InChittagong Division, Moulovibazr, Khulna, Khustia, Magura, district,Jhenaidah district. | Borail Sadri, Nurpur Sadri, Uchai Sadri, Mokkan Tila Sadri. |
| Santali | 157,000(1993Johnstone) | In Chitatgong Hill tracts | Hor, Satar, Santali, Sandal, Sangtal, Santal, Har, Sonthal. |
| Sylhetti | 5,000,000 | District of Sylhet | Sylhet, Sylhetti Bangala |
| Tangchangya | 17,695(1981 census) | Tropical forest area | Tanchangya |
| Tippera | 105,000(1993 Johnstone) | Chittagong Hills | Tippera- Bangali, Tipperah, Tipra, Tipura, Triperah, Tippurah, Tripura |
| Usui | 4,010(1981 census) | Chittagong Hills | Ushio, Unsuiy, Unshoi |

Chin. Austro-Asiatic (Mon-Khmer) languages include Khasi and Mundari (Munda). Though proficiency levels vary widely, many speakers of the minority languages speak some Bengali as a second language, many speakers are not literate in any language (Hossain & Tollefson, 2006).

People who use these dialects do not know Bengali language well. Bengali is the second language of these people. Though Humayun, in his seminal paper, *Bangladesh er Bivinna Jatishotta o Tader Bhasa* (The Language of different ethnic groups and their language), stated that one standard language is necessary for minority groups of Bangladesh, it is also necessary to collect the writing systems of those languages. He also argued that it is necessary to decide on a proper language policy for them and as there is no similarity between their writing systems with Bengali, it is better to use Bengali as their medium of Instruction for the time being (source: Humayun, 2003, p. 12). Humayun urged that since the ethnic minorities of Bangladesh do not have an alphabetical script, it will be one of the duties of the institute to develop alphabets of that minority groups such as Chakma and Marma. There are roughly 48 minority groups in Bangladesh and they do not know Bengali. It is reasonable that they should be taught in their own languages and then Bengali can be introduced and English, afterwards. Though many proposals like this have already been proposed, practically the Government has pursued no policy for the minority peoples of Bangladesh.

Bangladesh Constitution recognises no minorities in the country and also does not give any special provision for their protection and promotion. Minority groups are generally deprived from their rights all over the world and Bangladesh is no exception. Problems of Bangladesh are human right issue. Education is a basic human right and a large number of minority child are deprived of this right. Also, this educational policy may create linguistic genocide in Bangladesh.

On the other hand, Brutt-Griffler holds a different view. The inadequacy of theory in language planning and policy (LPP) is her primary concern (Tollefson, 2004). She argues that a focus on language rights is not theoretically justified, and that it cannot protect the interest of the linguistic minorities. She said that linguistic human rights had little impact on peoples live at the same time, it offers inadequacy for language policy and planning (LPP) theory. She also mentioned that language rights can never be effective for social change and that a focus on language rights perpetuates inadequate LPP theory. She mentioned that states often adopt language policy which may not favour ethnolinguistic minorities even though these states support language rights. For example, the rationale for official-English laws and prohibition of bilingual education in the United States is that it will improve education quality, economic opportu-nity and equal rights for linguistic minorities (*ibid*).

In her article, "Class, ethnicity, and language rights"(2004), Brutt-Griffler gave two examples of Lesotho and Sri Lanka- colonial contexts, where a form of industrial education used the local mother tongue and restrictions blocked teaching of English for the working class people (Brutt-Griffler, 2002). Phillipson (1992), in *Linguistic Imperialism* argues that English-speaking countries tried to impose English on the world in the colonial period and he also argued that this notion still exists in the world. But it seems to be different in colonial Basutoland (Lesotho) and Ceylon. British colony authorities tried their best to keep English out of reach of the vast majority of the population in each colony (see Brutt-Grifler, 2002). The British took this policy to maintain the necessary linguistic conditions for the colonial exploitation of the working class. In 1920, the British discovered an alarming trend in Basutoland. The mountain habitat had gone into precipitous decline. The entire mountain ecosystem irreparably changed. The British found that the Basuto had started to use the mountain for extensive agricultural development. Because Basuto people were starving in the valleys, they had moved to the mountains. This adaptation by the Basuto people was unexpected by the British, who had exploited them as manual labourers working for the enrichment of colonising European nations (*ibid*). Brutt-Griffler argues that the migrations to the mountain of the Basuto people is the same sort of adaptive system that led other Africans and Asian peoples subjected to colonial rule to gain access to English. Skutnabb-Kangas (2000), in her book, *Linguistic Genocide in Education-Or Worldwide Diversity and Human Rights,* argued that linguistic diversity, like biodiversity, is necessary for the existence of our planet and it is more than a matter of human interest. In some measure, the future of the planet depends on the preservation of the world's linguistic diversity and the bearers of linguistic and cultural diversity of the world are the indigenous and minority people. In such a notion, linguistic adaptive response of the Basuto people their socio-economic oppression within the world economy have relevancy for the natural environment, as well as their natural migration. Like the migration of the Basuto people, people's decision around the world to learn English language is one kind of adaptive responses which is taken by the people's own initiative to the socioeconomic forces; their adap-tation is reasonable and at times, effective within the conditions they face. According to Brutt-Griffler, these underlying contexts are not addressed by the language rights. Thus, to spread and maintain one's own language does not depend only on the ideological imperatives. It is also determined by complex socio-economic factors.

In many postcolonial countries, the English language seems to be an inseparable part of sociocultural and economic realities (Canagarajah, 1999, 2000; Kachru & Nelson, 1996). What is the impact of language on identity? One of the problematic assumptions of language rights is that it tries to reduce the language rights to national and national minorities ethnic group affiliations (May, 2000). It is assumed that language policy should serve interests equally and uniformly for all the members of the group. May (2000) points out, "advocates of linguistic human rights tend to assume the identity of linguistic minority groups as given, the collective aims of linguistic minority groups as uniform, and the notion of collective rights as unproblematic" (pp. 371-372, quoted in Brutt-Griffler, 2002). Kontra et al (1999) mentioned that the aim of the language policy should be ensure the equity for all language groups (*ibid*). May (2000) remarks:

The question of the link between language and identity needs to be critically examined, not just assumed, while the contingent nature of linguistic identity-as one of many (sometimes) competing identities available to minority language speakers-needs to be acknowledge and accommodated (p. 372, quoted in Brutt-Griffler, 2002).

May points out that many in a society may not accept that identity is inherited or rooted in the mythological past. Rather, identity is constantly being socially or individually constructed. Self-interest of individuals in a group may differ. If the unit of analysis of the language policy is ethnicity, nationality or minority status, it would seem that all people in the group have the interest to maintain their mother tongue. On the other hand, if the unit of analysis is class, the interest of some may be to maintain the dominant language. Thus, ethnic-national analysis and class analysis exist in an uneasy alliance. According to May and Brutt-Griffler, the language right movement concentrates on the deprivation of the rights of the linguistic minorities and depends on ethnic-national analysis. On the other hand, the class perspective concentrates on the way language policy differentially affects disempowered members of the linguistic minorities. Kontra *et. al.*, (1999) and Pennycook (1998) point out that language rights should be and are concerned with both. Thus, language policy should focus not only on language groups, minorities and ethnic affiliation, but also on its impact on the disempowered socio-economic groups within language groups (Brutt-Griffler, 2002).

Both Skutnabb-Kangas and Brutt-Griffler are not concerned with the formal declarations of language rights, but with concrete language policies and practices which focus on the individual's choices about language acquisition, use, maintenance and loss. Brutt-Griffler strongly suggests that within the current global contexts English should be central to any equitable language policy. She views English education as economic capital for social mobility. However, Tollefson (2000) mentioned that when English is widely seen as a key to the success of a nation and the economic well being of individuals, the spread of English could create social, economic and political inequalities. Bruthiaux (2002) argued that many of the worlds' poor see English language education as a tool of poverty reduction deserving major layout of the public resources. In the end, it may prove to be misguided and wasteful. Grin (2001) argues that the more people learn English, the less the skill of knowing English will count. Thus, it is important to distinguish between the role of English in individually-oriented escape from poverty and class-oriented arguments about large scale poverty reduction (Pennycook, 2004).

## Bangladesh can be one of the examples of this situation

English was introduced into South Asia by the British. Almost all post – colonial countries in South Asia like Bangladesh, India, Pakistan and Nepal faced a long period of economic, linguistic and political domination. In Bangladesh, English plays an important role in everyday activities, along with Bangla. Like many other Islamic countries, English plays an important role in the educational systems of Bangladesh. It is used as a second-language, although it is spoken only by 3per cent of the population. Bangladesh suffers from continual poverty and more than half of the population is living under the poverty line. English plays two important roles in Bangladesh. The medium of education-Bengali or English-distinguishes the well-educated and economically advantaged urban dwellers from the undereducated and economically distressed rural population.

English is linked with the individual opportunity. Bangladesh takes English as the medium of instruction in education not because this country has a huge contribution in the global economy, but because English is necessary to survive in Bangladesh. Bangladeshi students have a positive attitude toward English, which is regarded as a language of opportunity and is no longer regarded as a burden of colonialism. In South Asia, English is generally not viewed as a colonial burden, but as an international or neutral language. English offers significant economic opportunity and privileges for its speakers. Thus, public pressure for English language teaching at an early age is widespread (Hossain, 2015).

Primarily, Skutnabb-Kangas was concerned with the activist goal of social justice and Brutt-Griffler's main concern is to develop an adequate theory of the spread of English. Tollefson (2004) mentioned that her claim about inadequate language policy theory is important as William (1992) points out, "LPP remains on the margins of social sciences"(Tollefson, 2004, p. 153). Fishman (1992) point out that it is necessary for the LPP researcher to develop a more sophisticated social theory which is drawn from the advanced work of sociolingistics. The lack of interest in LPP among the sociolinguists indicates that LPP theory has little to offer to their field (Tollefson, 2004).

Both Skutnabb-Kangas and Brutt-Grifller's are frustrated with the failure and with the inadequacy of the LPP theory. Inspite of this, Skutnabb-Kangas supports adopting and implementing worldwide language rights and to promote social justice, adaptation of such language policy is necessary. In contrast, Brutt-Griffler argues that focus on the language rights offers an insufficient direction of LPP theory and it cannot be an effective path for meaningful social change.

## References

Bruthiaux, P. (2002). Hold your courses: Language education, language choice, and economic development. TESOL Quarterly, 36, 275-296.

Brutt-Grifler, J. (2002). *Class, ethnicity, and language rights. Journal of Language, identity, and Education 1* (3), 207-234.

Canagarajah, A.S. (1999). *Resisting linguistic imperialism in English teaching.* Oxford, England: Oxford University Press.

Canagarajah, A.S. (2000). Negotiating ideologies through English: Strategies from the periphery. In T. Ricento (Ed.), *Ideology, politics and language policies: Focus on English* (pp.121-132). Philadelphia: Benjamins.

Canagarajah, A.S. (2004). Language Rights and postmodern conditions. *Journal of Language, identity, and Education 3* (2), 141-145.

Donahue, T.S. (2002). Language planning and the perils of ideological solipsism. In J. W. Tollefson(Ed.), *Language policies in education: Critical issues* (pp. 137-164). Mahwah, NJ: Lawrence Erlbaum Associates, Inc.

Fishman, J.A. (1992). Forward: What can sociology contribute to the socio-linguistic enterprise? In G. Williams, *Sociolinguistics: A sociological criti-que* (pp.vii-ix). London: Routledge.

Hossain, T. (2015). Education Systems in Bangladesh: Major Issues and Concerns,Vol.7,(p-29-39), *Global Japanese Studies Review, Meiji University*

Hossain, T., & Tollefson, J. W. (2006). Language policy in education in Bangladesh. In J. W. Tollefson & A. B. M. Tsui (Eds.). *Language policy, culture and identity in Asian contexts* (pp. 241-257). Mahwah, NJ: Lawrence Erlbaum Associates Inc.

Janks, H. (2000). Domination, access, diversity and design: A synthesis for critical literacy education. *Educational Review*, 52, 175-186.

Kontra, M., Philipson, R., Skutnabb-Kangas, T., & Varady, T. (1999). Conceptualising and implementing linguistic human rights. In M, Kontra, R, Philipson, T, Skutnabb-Kangas, T, & Varady, (Eds.), *Language: A right and a resource. Approaching linguistic human rights* (pp.1-21). New York: Central European University Press.

Krauss, M. (1995, February 19). Paper presented at a conference of the American Association for the Advancement of Science, reported in Philadelphia Inquirer, p. A15.

Lin, A. (1999). Doing-English-lesson in the reproduction or transformation of social words? *TESOL Quarterly*, 33,393-412.

List of different languages of Bangladesh

http://www.ethnologue.com/show_country.asp?name=Bangladesh

May, S. (2000). Uncommon languages: The challenges and possibilities of minority language rights. *Journal of Multilingual and Multicultural Development*, 21, 366-385.

Pennycook, A. (1998). The right to language: Towards a situated ethics of language possibilities. *Language Sciences*, 20, 73-87.

Pennycook, A. (2004). Beyond mother tongue and access of English. *Journal of Language, Identity, and Education 3*, (2), 145-149.

Phillipson, R. (1992). *Linguistic Imperialism.* Oxford, England: Oxford University Press.

Phillipson, R. (1999). Heroes, rebels, communities and states in language rights activism and litigation. In M. Kontra, R. Philipson, T. Skutnabb-Kangas, & T. Varady(Eds.), *Language: A right and a resource. Approaching linguistic human rights* (pp. 28-51). Newyork: Central European University Press.

Skutnabb-Kangas, T. (2000). *Linguistic genocide in education-Or worldwide diversity and human rights?* Mahwah, NJ: Lawrence Erlbaum Associates, Inc.

Skutnabb-Kangas, T. (2002). Marvelous human rights rhetoric and grim realities: Language rights in education. *Journal of Language, Identity, and Education 1*, (3), 179-205.

Tripura, M.B. (2008). UN Forum on Minority Issues. RetrievedNovember 11, 2005, from http://search.yahoo.co.jp/searchper cent3b_ylt=A2RACGT9UC 9VtUkAhgGk_Op7?p=linguistics+rights+for+Bangladeshi+people+ &search .x=1&fr=top_ga1_sa&tid=top_ga1_sa&ei=UTF-8&aq=&oq=&afs

Tollefson, J. W. (2000). Policy and ideology in the spread of English. In J. k. Hall & W. Egginton (Eds.), *The sociopolitics of English language teaching* (pp.7-21). Clevedon, UK: Multilingual Matters.

Tollefson, J. W. (2004). Theory and action in language policy and planning. *Journal of Language, Identity, and Education 3*, (2), 151-155.

Tomasevki, k. (1996). International prospects for the future of the welfare state. *In Reconceptualising the welfare state* (pp.100-117). Copenhagen: Danish Center For Human Rights.

Wiley, T.G. (2002). Accessing language rights in education: A brief history of the U.S. contexts. In J. Tollefson (Ed.), *Language policies in education: Critical Issues* (pp. 39-64). Mahwah, NJ: Lawrence Erlbaum Associates, Inc.

Williams, G. (1992). *Sociolinguistics: A sociological critique*. London: Rout-ledge.

Acknowledgement: Some parts of the kutnabb-Kangas and Brutt-Grifller's argument were published in *Educational Studies*, International Christian University, Vol. 53, Tokyo.I am pleased that editor allow me to use those information for this book chapter too.

# 5

# 'We are not what we were': The Nicobarese Socio-cultural Milieu Post the Tsunami, 2004

*—Ajay Saini*

### Abstract

*The post tsunami socio-cultural change among the Nicobarese inhabiting the southern Nicobar islands has remained unresearched and undocumented. This paper will inquire into the post-tsunami socio-cultural milieu of the Nicobarese and narrate the changes brought in the socio-cultural domains of the community,. post the governmental humanitarian interventions undertaken in the islands. This paper will give an account of the change by juxtaposing the pre and the post-tsunami spatial location, subsistence, housing, economy, social structure and political organisation of the community. The paper is based on an ethnographic research being conducted by the writer in the Nicobar Islands since 2011.*

## 1. The Nicobarese

The Nicobar Islands are located in the south-east part of the Bay of Bengal between 6° to 10° N latitude and between 92° to 94° E longitude. There are twenty two islands, of which only twelve are inhabited by human population. The islands are divided as northern (Car Nicobar), central (Chowra, Teressa, Bompuka, Katchal, Kamorta, Nancowry and Trinket) and southern Nicobar (Pulo Milo, Little Nicobar, Kondul, Great Nicobar, and so on). The Nicobars stretch over 36 miles, with an aggregate land area of 635 sq miles (Justin, 1990; Saini, 2012, 2013). The islands have been divided into six divisions on the basis of cultural and linguistic features of the Nicobarese (Sinha Roy and Datta Chaudhuri, 2007:45). An inscription dated 1059 A.D. indicates that some of the Nicobar islands were a part of the Chola King of Tanjore's empire. As per the accounts of the Cholas, the islands were used as base shelter stations for war purposes and for keeping control over the territories of Malaysia (Justin, 1990: 10-11).

The Nicobarese and the Shompen are the indigenous communities which inhabit the Nicobar Islands. Ethnically, both the communities belong to same genetic stock. However, some anthropologists argue that the Shompen are Malays and the Nicobarese belong to the Mangoloid race (Kaul and Dilwali, 1989:21). Anthropologists posit that the Nicobar Islands have been visited by travelers since time immemorial. The first documented visits were recorded by the Chinese pilgrims around the seventh century. During the mid eighteenth century, the islands were colonised by the Danes and the Austrians; and the British in the second half of the eighteenth century. During this period, there was an occasional bartering of goods between the British and the Nicobarese. *Copra* (smoke dried coconut) production was introduced to the community at the turn of the twentith century and half a century later, the barter system was replaced by monetary exchange. The Japanese also had a stint in the islands before the Andaman and Nicobar Archipelago became a part of independent India in 1947 (Singh, 2006:52).

Post the independence of India, the Nicobar Archipelago became the territory of India and was recognised as a tribal reserve by the Andaman and Nicobar Islands (Protection of Aboriginal Tribes) Regulation Act, 1956 (Saini, Forthcoming b). Naidu (1998) and Mann (2005) argue that in order to populate the islands, the government rehabilitated ex-servicemen from the mainland India to the Great Nicobar. With the resettlement of 337 families in 1971, some areas of the Great Nicobar were declared unreserved. Later, some people from mainland India voluntarily migrated to the islands. All these migrant people are known as settlers and live at Campbell Bay and the areas extending 35 km from it (Saini, 2014).

## 2. The Tsunami and the Nicobarese of the Southern Nicobar

The Indian Ocean tsunami of 26 December, 2004 virtually destabilised the entire Nicobarese society by destroying human lives, houses, live-stock, fertile lands and vegetation. The geography of the islands has been altered due to the submergence of land areas. All these changes posed solemn threats to the Nicobarese and their continuity in the islands (Sinha Roy and Datta Chaudhuri, 2007:62). The demolition of age old traditions, indigenous knowledge, indigenous natural resources and the deaths of traditional experts left a void in tribal communities. The deaths of the elderly, who possessed technological knowledge about canoe making, medicine and magico-religious practices, adversely impacted the indigenous societies (Das, Barik, and Biswas, 2007:17-9). The catastrophe not only destroyed the culturally significant objects and killed people in the islands, but also depleted the livelihood options of the survivors, as their kitchen gardens, coconut plantations, poultry and drifts of pigs were washed away (Sahani and Prasad, 2007:75-8).

The Nicobarese community that belongs to the southern group had 20 villages in the Little Nicobar and 14 villages in the Great Nicobar Islands, before it was hit by the tsunami. The catastrophe subjected the Nicobarese to several hardships and disabilities including the destruction of property, lives, livelihoods and ecology. As per the Census 2001, their total population was 1,181 (Census 2001) which reduced to 990 (Census 2011). However, the settler population in the islands, which was 6,635 in 2001, increased up to 7153 in 2011 (Directorate of Economics and Statistics, Andaman and Nicobar Administration, 2010/2011; Saini 2014). The tsunami caused large scale interventions in the area that involved relief drives and the initiation of various welfare and develop-ment activities. Apart from shelter, the Nicobarese were provided with free rations, monetary compensations and amenities like water, health and electricity (Saini, 2013, forthcoming). More than nine years have elapsed since the tsunami and many welfare activities undertaken by the adminstration like free ration supply, have been discontinued. The Nicobarese, who were once self-sustaining in the pre-tsunami phase, are now displaying signs of utter dependence in the post-tsunami phase. Many of them have been gripped by consumerism and have lost interest in their indigenous sources of livelihoods (Saini, 2013b, 2014, forthcoming).

## 2. Research Inquiry and Methodology

The post tsunami socio-cultural changes among the Nicobarese inhabiting the southern Nicobar Islands have remained unresearched and undocumented. This paper will inquire into the post-tsunami socio-cultural milieu of the Nicobarese and narrate the changes brought in the socio-cultural domains of the community post the humanitarian interventions undertaken by the island administration. Grounded in qualitative paradigm, the research used an ethnographic approach. Three categories of respondents for the study were identified as- the Nicobarese, Administrative Staff (GOs, INGOs, NGOs) and the non-Nicobarese populations (settlers). Theoretical sampling technique was used for data collection and the samples were chosen purposely. Methods such as participant observation, in-depth interview and focus group interview were triangulated. Content analysis (official documents, announcements, schemes or programmes) and discourse analysis were also used.

## 3. The Politics of Disasters: A Literature Review

This section will give an account of politics of disasters by reviewing numerous research studies conducted post three major disasters. (Mehta, 2005) argues that the aftermath of the Kuchchh earthquake (2001, Gujarat, India) reveals a second disaster after a disaster that occurs because of flawed relief/ rehabilitation measures and poor distribution of aid, especially by state and official agencies. Simpson and Corbridge (2006) also elaborate on the politics of reconstruction by the right wing in the aftermath of the Kuchchh earthquake. Letukas and Barnshaw (2008) argue that post the Indian Ocean tsunami, a systematic social change was orchestrated through humanitarian aids through influencing the political and economic structures across long periods of time. Rigg, Law, Tan-Mullins, and Grundy-Warr (2005) also find that post-tsunami recon-struction never meant the recreation of pre-tsunami state of affairs in Thailand.

Silva (2009) reflects that the post Indian Ocean tsunami reconstruction in Sri Lanka was motivated by a neo-liberal ideology, which the research of Kelman, Spence, Palmer, Petal, and Saito (2008) also supports. Hilhorst and Jansen (2010) also argue that the government of Sri Lanka and the rebels of Liberation Tigers of Tamil Eelam (LTTE) used the language of humanitarian space to reinforce their claims on territories and the people. The common concern with the 'Indian Ocean tsunami' involved poor regard for a complex ecological system and the consequences of human action'. A flood of aid workers and attendant problems swept across Southeast Asia; Kennedy, *et. al.* (2008, cited in Williams 2008:1127) called it "the second tsunami" and Clark (2007, cited in Williams 2008:1127) termed it "other tsunami". The research conducted post the Katrina hurricane (2005) shows that class and racial differences determined the magnitude of the aftermath experienced by the victims (White, Philpot, Wylie, and McGowen, 2007:523-34). The succeeding 'recovery disaster' that gripped the city in the aftermath of Katrina were of human, rather than natural origin (Tierney 2008:183, as cited in Williams 2008:1127).

The research studies conducted, post three major catastrophes- Kuchchh earthquake, Indian Ocean tsunami and Katrina hurricane, have concluded that the post-disaster socio-cultural changes were not the spontaneous corollaries of disasters. These changes were guided by numerous factors, agents and agencies. Disasters have been taken as an opportunity to orchestrate the socio-cultural, economic and political order which suits the interests of hegemonic forces or maintains status quo. The review of research concludes that the post-disaster changes, which seem an apolitical aftermath, have layered meanings and purposes which reflect numerous political and ideological interests.

## 3.1 The Post-tsunami Aid in the Nicobar Archipelago: An Aftermath

The research conducted on the aftermath of the humanitarian interventions in the Nicobar archipelago concluded that the frame work toward recovery and rehabilitation had little accounting for the socio-ecological characteristics and resilience of the native islanders. It delayed the process of recovery and the self-reliance of the community was threatened by the dominant system of governance. The intervention of government and various other agencies created new social and economic linkages, while various indigenous social networks came under pressure (Chandi, 2006). The immediate humanitarian aid focused on rescue and relief for the victims. Some of the Nicobarese villages were entirely evacuated and the inhabitants were resettled in relief camps or temporary shelters. The Nicobarese came to the relief camps with a notion that they would soon go back to their places and start afresh, but they were stuck in relief camps for too long (Gupta and Sharma, 2006:71).

Chandi (2006) argues that the post-tsunami management in the islands was top-down and bereft of sufficient consultation with the affected communities. The Nicobarese were given little chance to decide for themselves, as the initiative of the Nicobarese was obscured by adminis-trative authority that drew up plans in accordance with its convenience. The subsistence of the Nicobarese after the tsunami was not easy, Chaudhry and Thukral, (2006: 1-24) associated their sufferings with the ineffective management of the situation post the disaster. The local administration had an overwhelming focus on immediate relief, the long-term impacts of which on the victim communities were not considered. Many agencies entered the affected zones, provided immediate relief and then made an immediate exit. Such interventions left the communities to tackle the problems themselves, most of which were created by the post-tsunami interventions.

The way humanitarian aid was provided had solemn implications on the Nicobarese which ruptured the Nicobarese society in various forms. Singh (2009:53) and Ramanujam, Singh, and Vatn (2012) found that monetary aids and relief resources were distributed on the basis of norms and formal rules that overlooked the Nicobarese local context and caused social upheaval in the traditional communities by diminishing the stature of their joint family system. The humanitarian interventions also shifted the relationships of power in the community as the educated Nicobarese were preferred to participate in disaster management over the uneducated, nevertheless experienced elderly. The Nicobarese were provided monetary compensations post the tsunami, but the very compensation which was supposed to help the Nicobarese impacted them adversely.

The study of Singh (2009) in Car Nicobar concludes that a continuous flow of aid and adoption of affluent and high consumption behaviour among the Nicobarese have changed their lifestyle. The Nico-barese dependency on the market has increased manifold, but capital accumulation is not so visibly seen among them (Singh, 2006:54-6). Ramanujam, *et. al.*, (2012) further argue that though the tsunami was a severe blow to the Nicobarese, but the community had enough resilience to rebuild itself with initial humanitarian assistance from outside. The post tsunami intervention of the administration caused distress to the Nicobarese community as a whole by causing unprecedented change in their internal institutions and power relations.

## 4. The Post-tsunami Socio-cultural Change

This section of the paper will narrates the post tsunami change that the Nicobarese of the southern group have experienced in the socio-cultural milieu, especially-spatial location, subsistence, housing and economy (livelihood, crops and agricultural practices, technology/housing and other construction activities, food habits/pets and livestock, death, illness medicine and funeral practices, recreation, body adornment and decorative art), social structure (sise of the community and settlement patterns, household composition/ marriage and divorce practices, ceremonies, social stratification and law and order) and political organisation.

## 4.1 Spatial Location

The Nicobarese inhabited various places both in the Great and the Little Nicobar islands in the pre-tsunami period. There were fourteen Nicobarese villages and 2 or 3 small single house hamlets in the Great Nicobar Island, which were sparsely populated and destroyed during the tsunami. At present, there are three Nicobarese villages: New Chingenh Basti, Afra Bay and Rajiv Nagar. There were twenty villages in the Little Nicobar Island, which have now been reduced to five (Makachua, Pulo Panja, Pulo Patia, Puloulo, Pulobha.) post the tsunami. These original habitats of the Nicobarese were devastated during the tsunami and the communities were evacuated and relocated; the Nicobarese of Chingenh were relocated at New Chingenh and the rest to intermediate shelters in Rajiv Nagar. The Nicobarese spent six years in these temporary shelters before they were provided permanent shelters at specific places (Maka-chua, Pulo Panja, Pulo Patia, Puloulo, Pulobha, New Chingenh and Rajiv Nagar) in the Great and Little Nicobar islands. Some of the former places of residence are currently rendered uninhabitable because of the topographic changes that took place. Though the Nicobarese do not inhabit these islands, they still have their plantations there.

The Nicobarese relocated to Rajiv Nagar are living at the most accessible and well connected places. New Chingenh is another place which is accessible through road, though it does not have a metal road. Only a *kacha* (unmattled) unleveled road leads to New Chingenh, a 30 minute walk from the metal road. The accessibility to permanent shelters at Makachua, Pulo Panja, Pulo Patia, Puloulo, Pulobha is grossly inade-quate. Although a speedboat sails to these islands thrice a week, it is irregular and transportation among these five villages is very difficult with no emergency helicopter facility for the Little Nicobar islands. Accessibility to communities living in Rajiv Nagar has increased, whereas accessibility for those living in other parts is comparatively difficult.

## 4.2 Subsistence, Housing and Economy

### 4.2.1 Livelihood

Forests and the sea were an integral part of the Nicobarese life and this was evidenced in their culture. The traditional economy of the community has sustained, flourished and developed on the resources available in the ecological setting of these islands. The traditional economy could be broadly categorised as horticulture, herding, coconut plantation, hunting and fishing. The Nicobarese society was self-sustaining prior to the tsunami, but has now emerged as a dependent society in the post-tsunami phase. Coconut plantations and *copra* (smoke dried coconut) production was a major livelihood activity. Coconuts were grown for personal and commercial consumption, whereas jackfruit, banana, Malaya potato, pendanus and pineapples were generally grown for household consumption. The money procured by selling *copra* was used to buy essential commodities. The community's needs were rudimentary and most of these were fulfilled by the available natural resources provided by the ecosystem. The Nicobarese lost their plantations during the tsunami and their livelihood was jeopardised. The new plantations have not yet borne fruit and the production of *copra* has not been resumed.

In the pre-tsunami phase, the Nicobarese were both sellers and buyers in the market and exchange between the Nicobarese and the non-Nicobarese was bidirectional. In the post-tsunami phase, however, the exchange in the market has become unidirectional as the Nicobarese are solely buyers. Fishing and hunting were the other chief activities for subsistence; this has now become sporadic. Since the communities (the Nicobarese of Rajiv Nagar and New Chingenh) have been rehabilitated far from sea, they now purchase fish from the open markets. The hunting of wild boar has declined as well, particularly among the Nicobarese of Rajiv Nagar and New Chingenh. The main reason for the absence of game hunting is the relocation of the Nicobarese in areas where wild boars are not available. Thus, traditional fishing and game hunting techniques have been declining in the post-tsunami phase.

The accessibility to indigenous resources has also undergone major changes. Only four hectares of land is given to each family rehabilitated at Rajiv Nagar for their plantations, and most of the Nicobarese living at New Chingenh have become landless, post the tsunami. There is, however, no delimitation of land for the Nicobarese located at the villages of Maka Chua, Pulo panja, Pulo Patia, Puloulo and Pulobha.

The communities have been quite dependant on governmental humanitarian aid for their survival and although lakhs of rupees were given as compensation, most of the money is now depleted. As per the Prime Minister's Press Meet Note (4th, January 2006), an ex-gratia of Rs 2 lakh was given to the next of kin of all who died, went missing/orphaned during the tsunami. Unmarried girls (above 18 years of age) and widows were disbursed ex-gratia at the rate of Rs 1 lakh. Rs 22,231 (per hectare) and Rs 90,465 (per hectare) were given for loss of paddy/vegetables and plantation crops (coconut and areca nut), respectively. Post the tsunami, some of the community members work on their plantations, but majority of them are not engaged in any livelihood activities and have become sedentary (Saini, forthcoming). A percentage of the population is engaged in daily wage labour under the Mahatma Gandhi National Rural Employment Guarantee Act (MGNREGA), which was not a phenomenon in the pre-tsunami period. MGNREGA has failed to attract the Nicobarese, since wage labour had never been the part of their indigenous culture. In the absence of promotion of indigenous livelihoods, the unemploy-ment rate has increased among the Nicobarese in the post-tsunami period, along with a tremendous increase in their needs.

### 4.2.2 Crops and Agricultural Practices

Agricultural practices among the Nicobarese were not advanced, but were sustainable and eco-friendly. They were non-mechanical and labour intensive, wherein the entire family would work in the plantations with no stringent division of labour. Every member of the family contributed according to her/his capacity. There has been no substantial change in agricultural practices in the post-tsunami phase and the Nicobarese are still utilising the same traditional knowledge and practices.

### 4.2.3 Technology/ Housing and other Construction Activities

Pre-tsunami, the Nicobarese enjoyed a simple and traditional lifestyle. Through cultural contact with the non-Nicobarese populations at intermediate shelters, they have now adopted modern and sophisticated technology. There has been a tremendous surge in the purchase of modern gadgets that include washing machines, mobiles, televisions, mixers, DVD players, refrigerators, and so on. However, there are no substantial technological modifications in livelihood-generating activities such as coconut plantations, fishing or pig rearing.

Housing among the Nicobarese has undergone a complete change. Pre-tsunami, the communities used to live in huts, which were built on stilts about 2–2.5 meters off the ground. The traditional Nicobarese huts had one big hall where all the activities were conducted. Now, the shelters, though built on stilts, have multiple rooms. Traditional houses were constructed with local material, whereas these shelters are constructed with wood, iron, tin, concrete and other non-indigenous materials imported from other states. The traditional Nicobarese huts were independent units, whereas the new shelters are two separate units adjoined together. They are also built on stilts, but unlike the traditional huts, these shelters shake and rattle when exposed to wind and rain.

### 4.2.4 Food Habits/Pets and Livestock

The traditional food comprised potato, coconut, guava, papaya, fish, pork, chicken and pendanus. Now, the Nicobarese have acquired a taste for fast food and relish *pani puri*, chow mein, noodles, egg rolls, chapati, rice, *dal* and various vegetables. These changes in food habits are associated with the unavailability of traditional food and the availability of easy-to-cook food in the market.

Pigs and poultry were reared prior to the tsunami; each family used to have twenty five to thirty pigs. The numbers have reduced considerably now. The reasons are the unavailability of pigs, lack of coconuts to feed the pigs, lack of space and change in environmental surroundings and a general disinterest among the people.

### 4.2.5 Death, Illness, Medicine and Funeral Practices

The communities have a practical approach towards death. Birth and death are both accepted as natural phenomena and this belief has not changed, even after the tsunami. Traditional funeral practices among the Nicobarese have also undergone many changes. The Nicobarese practice of abandoning the house (where death has occurred) for some time after a death is not observed so stringently now due to altered housing patterns. Given that they now live in permanent shelters, it is virtually impossible for the bereaved family to leave their house for long. The social support system among the Nicobarese has also altered significantly, and a bereaved family cannot expect to receive the kind of empathy and support it received prior to the tsunami. The lifestyle of the people has recorded changes and consequently, there has been a rise in lifestyle diseases as well. Given their proximity to nature, the Nicobarese used to eat non-processed food, but now they have acquired a taste for junk food, spice and flavours usually consumed by other communities. As a result, they frequently fall sick and suffer from mild headaches, stomach aches, obesity, indigestion, gastric problems and fatigue.

### 4.2.6 Recreation, Body Adornment and Decorative Art

Indigenous recreation and decorative art had been an integral part of the Nicobarese culture, but both these practices have waned in the post-tsunami phase. Ceremonies were a major source of recreation (detailed discussion on this subject is provided in the section on the post-tsunami structure). Now television has overshadowed all indigenous sources of recreation. Outdoor games like volleyball, cricket, kabaddi, kho-kho and football were quite popular and although they still play some of these games, the lack of space to play has dramatically reduced the frequency of these activities. Singing and dancing were other indigenous means of recreation; these too have witnessed changes since the communities now sing Hollywood and Tollywood songs instead of folk songs. While celebrating various ceremonies, the Nicobarese play many Hindi, Tamil and English songs. Although they could barely understand the lyrics, they have developed a liking for the fast beats and their rhythm. The traditional art of house decoration has been replaced by modern art. Houses are decorated with posters of film celebrities and sport stars. The women now wear modern apparel and use cosmetics and most of the youth have tattoos. All modern cosmetic products like face wash, gel, body lotion etc., are used by both males and females.

## 4.3 Social Structure

### 4.3.1 Size of the Community and Settlement Patterns

The casualties during the tsunami decreased the sise of the Nicobarese community considerably. Pre- tsunami, the population of the Nicobarese in the southern group was 1,181 and maximum deaths were recorded among the elderly. The settlements located on far flung islands in the pre-tsunami period have been consolidated at particular places which led to an increase in physical proximity between the settlements. The Nicobarese of Rajiv Nagar and New Chingenh feel suffocated in their new compact homes and the permanent shelters in the tribal reserve area are located far from the sea, usually at higher altitudes. There have been cases of landslides and trees have fallen on the settlements, causing much damage. There were three cases in Makachua, wherein one shelter and a staff quarter of primary school were reduced to rubble. Many activities associated with space like pig rearing, fishing, hunting and plantations have been adversely affected by the new settlement patterns.

### 4.3.2 Household Composition/ Marriage/Divorce Practices

Household composition was complex in the pre-tsunami period as the Nicobarese followed the *tuhet* (extended family) system and lived in extended families. The *tuhet* has been weakened significantly due to the death of its members during the tsunami and the introduction of nuclear families. The Nicobarese, who used to live together in the pre-tsunami period, now live in nuclear families, as the space in a shelter is sufficient for a single family only.

Divorce practices among the Nicobarese have remained more or less the same and there have been no substantial changes in the marriage practices either. Post marital residence among the Nicobarese was both patrilocal and matrilocal as per the convenience of both parties and this has not undergone any change.

### 4.3.3 Ceremonies

The Nicobarese used to celebrate many ceremonies and rituals in the pre-tsunami period including *hodi* making- *hodi* is the canoe made by digging wood from a log of tree. *Hodi* making was a ceremony when the Nicobarese would make beautiful canoes, Stick fighting- a traditional festival when the Nicobarese would playfully fight with big sticks, Pig festival- a festival celebrated in the memory of ancestors. The Nicobarese from various villages would gather at a particular place and bring pigs with them for a communal feast, Christmas, Easter, All souls' day- celebrated in the memory of the Nicobarese who have died (usually ancestors), New Year, Canoe race- celebrated by organising a canoe race where the people compete among themselves, Independence day and Republic day.

Traditional ceremonies like stick fight, canoe race and pig festival have not been celebrated since the tsunami. However, the communities will resume the pig festival once they restart pig rearing and related livelihood activities. December 26 is now observed as Mourning day. It is a day which the Nicobarese observe in remembrance of the people they lost during the tsunami on 26th December, 2004. Candles are lit and a communal feast is held. The ceremony is held at the house of the village captain and all village members attend it. Sometimes it is held at two to three places in a village. People attend mass and pray for the people who lost their lives during the tsunami.

There has been a considerable change in the manner and the spirit of celebration among the communities. In the post-tsunami period, the devotion and fervor with which each festival was celebrated has now diminished. The Nicobarese expressed that pigs had always been a part and parcel of all their festivals, and lack of pigs and other traditional food products like *toddy*, pandanus and coconut have curtailed the spirit of festive celebrations. Since indigenous ceremonial items are not available in the post-tsunami period, they have been replaced by items such as biscuits, candies, cake, alcohol, rusk and so on. Moreover, due to the exposure to other cultures and festivals, the Nicobarese have become apathetic towards their own indigenous festivals and ceremonies.

### 4.3.4 Social Stratification

The tribal social organisation of the Nicobarese community is not complex and stratification is generally based on age. The elderly are highly revered and an adult earns respect with age. Economic status or material possessions were not considered as dominant factors for stratification, as everyone had more or less equal possessions along with unlimited land. The social status of a family depended on a combination of the number of plantations, number of pigs and contributions made during local festivals and feasts. Post-tsunami, an individual's status is determined by economic considerations wherein an individual possessing more material goods and money is considered rich.

### 4.3.5 Law and Order

The Nicobarese were governed by a set of informal laws and oral codes of conduct acquired through the process of socialisation. Social norms were generally enforced by village captains, elderly members of the community or priests of the church. Post-tsunami, the administration and the non-Nicobarese communities have emerged as the enforcers of social control. The administration, through a series of formal and informal mechanisms has influenced social norms by virtue of the authority it commands; for instance, by prescribing certain conditions in the allotment order of permanent shelters. As per new conditions stipulated, the Nicobarese cannot make any modifications in the structure of the 'shelters'. The Nicobarese are not satisfied with the structures of shelters. They say that the shelters make too much noise during rain and wind and the community feels cramped in the shelters.

The lifestyle of the Nicobarese is considered unhygienic and the non-Nicobarese say that the former do not keep their surroundings neat and clean. The Nicobarese are instructed by the administration to maintain their surroundings and keep it neat and clean. The non-Nicobarese populations too play a pivotal role by displaying gestures of acceptance and rejection of certain behavioural at patterns of the Nicobarese. Many food habits among the Nicobarese like raw fish and pork changed owing to the stigmatisation by the non-Nicobarese. The Nicobarese concept of nudity and their self-identity was also compromised to a considerable extent. Previously, disputes were resolved by the elderly and captains of villages. These disputes have escalated, post the tsunami, as the society is under pressure due to rapid acculturation, changes in spatial location and alcoholism.

## 4.4 Political Organisation

The Tribal Council, the Great and the Little Nicobar Islands, is the political organisation of the Nicobarese of the southern group. The office bearers in the Tribal Council comprise the Chairman, the Secretary and the Village Captains, who are democratically elected. The majority of the office bearers of the present Tribal Council were elected in 2003 and no elections were conducted after that. The chairman of the Tribal Council said that the structure of council would be changed, hence fresh elections are not conducted yet. There are currently eight villages in Great and Little Nicobar Islands and each village elects two captains, the First and the Second Captain. At present, there are sixteen captains in the Tribal council and the Chairman is the head of the council who works in collaboration with the administration.

In the pre-tsunami phase, the elderly were chosen as captains, by virtue of their knowledge and experience. The captains are now selected on the recommendation of the Assistant Commissioner, the Great and Little Nicobar Islands. Due to the shift in the leadership pattern, the authority and control of the captains has declined across villages. Captains of Makachua, Pulobhabi, New Chingenh and the chairman and the secretary of Tribal council narrated their own experiences of decline in their control over villages in addition to the difficulties they encountered. The death of the elderly during the tsunami has significantly altered the power dynamics. The administration plays a pivotal role in choosing young captains who are literate and can communicate in the Hindi language. These young captains are not resistant to change as they are less aware about their own customs and rituals.

## Conclusion

The juxtaposition of the pre and the post-tsunami socio-cultural milieu of the Nicobarese shows that the spatial location of the Nicobarese has been thoroughly altered, along with a decrease in the sise of the community, with a significant reduction in the old age group. There have been changes in settlement patterns, in addition to the disintegration of joint families and the emergence of nuclear families. Indigenous sources of livelihood, destroyed during the tsunami, have not been replenished and most of the Nicobarese are surviving on monetary compensations. Wage labour, which is of recent origin, is a harbinger of further change in the Nicobarese socio-cultural milieu. Although the Nicobarese have hastily embraced modern technology in their lifestyle, technology in crop and agricultural practices has not been adopted. Livestock was reduced considerably and no efforts have been made for its revival. The influx of money into the Nicobarese society, through compensations, triggered consumerism, leading to the obliteration of various indigenous practices. For instance, traditional decorative art has been replaced by modern art and traditional body adornment practices have become redundant.

Indigenous food habits have been influenced by the food habits of the non-Nicobarese populations and lifestyle diseases have recorded an increase among the Nicobarese. Television has significantly influenced the community in their social and cultural spheres, particularly with regard to recreational activities. Although death, conception and marriage practices among the Nicobarese have not undergone any change, traditional funeral practices are affected. Festivals and communal ceremonies have lost their original spirit of celebration, and many traditions are on the verge of extinction. The post-tsunami phase has also replaced the traditional authority of the elderly with bureaucracy. The change ushered into the economic structure of the Nicobarese has adversely impacted the social stratification causing the erosion of various traditions and social norms.

## Acknowledgement

The writer expresses deep gratitude to Professor S. Parasuraman (Director, TISS) and Professor Surinder Jaswal (Dean, writer Research and Development, TISS) for their mentoring and guidance. The author thanks the Andaman and Nicobar administration for permitting him to conduct field work in the tribal reserve of the Nicobar archipelago. The support received from the people of the southern Nicobar, especially John Robert and the Chairmen of the Tribal Council, the Great and Little Nicobar Islands, Barnabas and Late Paul Joora, is humbly acknowledged. Discussions with Tim, Tam, Nene and Ipanema, while drafting this paper, made writing a joyous experience.

## References

1. "Basic Statistics 1/2011." *Directorate of Economics and Statistics, Andaman and Nicobar Administration*, Viewed on 15 January 2014 (www.and.nic.in/stats/BasicStatistics/index.htm).

2. Chandi, M. (2006): "*Rehabilitation and change in the aftermath of a tsunami: a return to Little Nicobar Island.*" Paper presented at the First India Disaster Management Congress, Organised by the National Institute of Disaster Management, New Delhi, India. November 29th.
3. Chaudhry, S., Thukral, E.G. (2006): *Battered Islands: Report of a Fact Finding Mission to Tsunami-Affected Areas of the Andaman and Nicobar Islands.* (New Delhi: South Asia Regional Programme, Housing and Land Rights Network, Habitat International Coalition).
4. Das, B. K., Barik, S. S., & Biswas, S. (2007). "*Impact Assessment of Tsunami: A Demographic Study in Southern Group of Nicobar Islands*". in Anthropological Survey of India (ed) *Tsunami in South Asia: Studies on impact of Tsunami on Communities of Andaman and Nicobar Islands* (Kolkata: Allied Publishers). 8-21 pp.
5. Gupta, M., & Sharma, A. (2006 ). *Compounded loss: the post tsunami recovery experience of Indian island communities. Disasters Prevention and Management* , Vol. 15 (1): pp 67-78.
6. *Hilhorst, D., & Jansen, B. J. (2010). Humanitarian space as arena : a perspective on the everyday politics of aid. Development and Change* , Vol. 41(6): pp 1117-1139.
7. Justin, A. (1990). *The Nicobarese* . Calcutta: Seagull.
8. Kaul, R., & Dilwali, A. (1989). *Andaman and Nicobar: Islands in the Sun* . Surrey: Spantech.
9. *Kelman, I., Spence, R., Palmer, J., Petal, M., & Saito, K. (2008). Tourists and Disasters: Lessons from the 26 December 2004 Tsunamis. Journal of Coastal Conservation* , Vol. 12(3): pp 105-113.
10. *Letukas, L., & Barnshaw, J. (2008). A World-System Approach to Post-Catastrophe International Relief. Social Forces* , 87(2): pp 1063-1087.
11. Mann, R. S. (2005). *Andaman and Nicobar Tribes Restudied: Encounters and Concerns.* New Delhi: Mittal Publications.
12. Mehta, L. (2005). *The Tsunami and Globalised Uncertainity . Economic and Political Weekly* , Vol. 40 (3): 194-195.
13. Naidu, T. S. (1998). *The Endangered Aborigines and Environment of Andaman and Nicobar Islands: A Futuristic Study on Health Nutrition Demography Culture Environment* . Pondicherry: Pondicherry University.
14. "Population Enumeration Data (Final Population)." *Census of India 2011*, Viewed on 4 April 2014 (http://www.censusindia.gov.in/pca/final_pca.aspx).
15. "Prime Minister's Press Meet Note", 04 January 2006, Viewed on 16 May 2014 (http://www.and.nic.in/Announcements/post-tsunami.pdf).
16. Ramanujam, R.V., Singh, S.J., & Vatn, A. (2012): "*From the Ashes into the Fire? Institutional Change in the Post-Tsunami Nicobar Islands, India*". *Society and Natural Resources*, 25: pp 1152-66.
17. *Rigg, J., Law, L., Tan-Mullins, M., & Grundy-Warr, C. (2005). The Indian Ocean tsunami: socio-economic impacts in Thailand . The Geographical Journal* , Vol. 171(4): 374-379.

18. Sahani, R., & Prasad, D. V. (2007). "Impact Assessment of Tsunami on Car Nicobarese. In Anthropological Survey of India (ed) *Tsunami in South Asia: Studies on impacts of Tsunami on Communities of Andaman and Nicobar Islands* (Kolkata: Allied Publishers) pp64-89.
19. Saini, A. (2012): "*Thus Spake the Nicobarese*", *The Indian Journal of Social Work*, 73 (2): pp 287-94.
20. Saini, A. (2013a): "*Post-tsunami Socio-cultural Changes among the Nico-barese: An Ethnography of the Nicobarese of the Southern Nicobar Islands*" TISS Working Paper Series No.1, *Tata Institute of Social Sciences*, January.
21. Saini, A. (2013b): "*A Nicobarese Tribal Leader Who Lived Two Lives*", *Economic and Political Weekly*,48(51) 21 December. Viewed on 14 May 2014 (http:// www.epw.in/web-exclusives/nicobarese-tribal-leader-who-lived-two-lives.html).
22. Saini, A. (2014a): "*A Nicobarese Tribal Leader Who Lived Two Lives*", *Economic and Political Weekly*,49(5), 24-26.
23. Saini, A. (2014b): "*The Southern Nicobar Islands as Imaginative Geogra-phies*", Unpublished Manuscript.
24. Saini, A. (Forthcoming a): "*The Post-tsunami Phase: A Dawn of Consumerism among the Nicobarese*", *Economic and Political Weekly.*
25. Saini, A. (Forthcoming b): "*The Post-tsunami Humanitarian Aid: A Trojan Horse in the Southern Nicobar Islands*", *Economic and Political Weekly.*
26. Silva, K. T. (2009). '*Tsunami third wave' and the politics of disaster management in Sri Lanka. Norsk Geografisk Tidsskrift- Norwegian Journal of Geography* , 63(1): pp 61-72.
27. Simpson, E., & Corbridge, S. (2006). *The Geography of Things That May Become Memories: The 2001 Earthquake in Kachchh-Gujarat and the Politics of Rehabilitation in the Prememorial Era. Annals of the Association of American Geographers* , Vol. 96(3): pp 566-585.
28. Singh, S.J. (2006): *The Nicobar Islands: Cultural choices in the aftermath of the Tsunami* (Vienna: Oliver Lehmann).
29. Singh, S.J. (2009): "*Complex Disasters: The Nicobar Islands in the Grip of Humanitarian Aid*", *Geographische Rundschau* (International Edition) 5(3): pp 48-56.
30. *Sinha Roy, K M and S S Datta Chaudhuri (2007): "A Disaster Unparallel: A Case Study of Katchal and Nancowry Islands*" in Anthropological Survey of India (ed) *Tsunami in South Asia: Studies on impacts of Tsunami on Communities of Andaman and Nicobar Islands* (Kolkata: Allied Publishers) 43-46.
31. White, I. K., Philpot, T. S., Wylie, K., & McGoween, E. (2007).

# 6

# Gender and Educational Policy: A study of dropout girls from rural Andhra Pradesh and Telangana state

*—Nagaraju Gundimeda*

## Introduction

Education is the cornerstone of national development. It enables men and women to respond to the opportunities, prepare them to face traditional challenges and modern opportunities. Education has been viewed as a potential agent of transformation of the marginalised and oppressed socio-religious categories. Education has a profound effect on girls' ability to claim other rights and status in the society, such as economic independence and political representation. So it can be said that education is the effective means to counter gender discrimination and enhance status of women in the society. UNICEF Report (2004) on the status of the World's Children highlighted the importance of girls' education for the progressive society. It says, 'Girls education is the most effective means of combating many of the most profound challenges to human development'.

The importance of girls' education for economic and social development is well known. Development economists have emphasised the importance of girls' educational attainment in reaching overall development goals. Investment in girls' education may well be the highest return investment available in developing world (World Bank 2008). At this juncture it is very much important to examine the manifestations of Millennium Development Goals and its relevance for education of girls. Millennium Development Goals highlights the significance of basic needs of people and concerns for sustainable social and environmental orders of the societies across the globe. Goal 1 to Goal 8 demonstrates the role of girls/women as agents of development and active partners of social change. Gender inequality in education is one of the crucial challenges for developing countries. The famous Dakar declaration of education for all[1] highlights the significance of achieving goals pertaining to children education are as follows:

- The expansion of early childhood care and education,
- The achievement of universal primary education,
- The development of learning opportunities for youth and adults, the spread of literacy,
- The achievement of gender parity and gender equality in education and improvements in education quality.

The Global Monitoring Report of EFA claims that this declaration marks an ambitious international movement to expand learning opportunities for every child, youth and adult in the world by 2015. Although the international bodies initiating a wide range of programmes to address the regional disparities, still the educational gaps between boys and girls remain significant due to constitutional laps and socio-cultural burden in addition to economic marginalization. Although South Asia[2] as a region comprises only 10 per cent of the Asian continent, but its population accounts for about 40 per cent of Asian Peoples.

According to UNESCO study[3] South Asia is a home to one-quarter of the world's primary school-age population. The study found that this region accounts for the highest absolute number of out-of-school children: 42 million out of 162 million school-age children in this region (or 26 per cent) were out of school in the year 2001-2002. The boys and girls of these region accounts for almost 1/3rd's (36 per cent) of the world have deprived school children. In other words, on an average one out of three school-age children in the region did not attend school. The report claims that more than 8 million of almost 20 million school-age children (or 40 per cent) are out of school in Pakistan which stand first in South Asia, where as Nepal has the second-highest (34 per cent) number of out-of-school children in the region. India being the second most populous country in the world is also the home for large number of out of school children. This country has the highest absolute number of out-of-school children. According to the MICS 2000 survey[4], almost 27 million school-age children in India do not attend school, or one out of four. India alone accounts for 23 per cent of the global total. In Bangladesh, one out of five or 3.7 million primary school-age children are out of school. Educational performance in Srilanka and Maldives show near-universal primary school participation.

## Conceptual framework

Although the broader theoretical debates on sociology of education have mapped the structural concerns and constrains associated with educational problems of girls in primary stages and women at higher stages of education, only with the intervention of feminist scholarship on education from a gender perspective unfolded new ways of looking and articulating the theoretical concerns and methodological challenges embodied in the male stream sociological discourses. However, the mainstream feminist epistemology of sociology of education also critiqued for not recognising the multiple sociological categories such as class, race, religion, region, sexuality and ethnicity in the context of west and caste/tribe in India in addition to the above mentioned categories which have concerns of contradictory as well as composite in nature.

Off late, sociologists have recognized the application of inter-sectional theory for mapping the multiple voices and their concerns which are unique to their particular social identity. In this paper, intersectional theory has been used as theoretical framework for mapping the educational deadlocks of rural girl children belonging to multiple social groups such as religion, caste, tribe, and region and class background. The sociological and anthropological writings by scholars such as Karuna Chanana (2001), Amit Choudhury (2006), Indira R (2013) Nagaraju Gundemeda (2014), *Sarangapani Padma (2003), Sadhana* Saxena (2012) Sengupta and. Guha (2002), Sharma, Neerja and Nandita Chaudhury (2003) Sinha Shanta (2008), Ratna Sudarshan (2000) Padma Velaskar (2012), Vimala Ramachandran (2004) Wazir, Rekha (2000) Gaby Weiner (1997) to name a few have discussed in detail the issues and challenges associated with educational deprivation and discrimination of girls in South Asian countries in general and India in particular. However, there are very few studies focused on the educational policies such as DPEP, SSA, KGBV. Krishna Kumar and Sarada Balagoplan have dealt with questions of girls schooling in residential educational system.

## History of girls Education in India

Although in the Vedic period women had access to education, they had gradually lost this right due to different cultural factors like the social evils of caste system and the subordination to men in the family as well as in the society. However, during the British rule both the state and civil society made an effort to spread literacy and propagate the primary education among girls and women. By this time, "Educating a girl means educating a family" had come to be the slogan of Indian leaders and social reformers. At that period, the women's movements in India also took education of women as their agenda and their struggle for the education of women cannot be ignored. Their desire was to change the existing state of things which was the cause of women's sufferings at that time. Father of India, Mahatma Gandhi also stressed the need for educating women as a part of nationalist movement. His call to women to join the political movements brought women out of their homes in large numbers from all parts of India from all backgrounds. During the same time various socio-religious movements led by eminent social reformers like Jyotiba Phule, Raja Ram Mohan Roy, Iswar Chandra Vidyasagar emphasized the centrality of women's education for emancipation in different spheres of life. However, women's education got a fillip after the country got independence in 1947. The vision of national leaders and the aspirations of the common masses have reflected in making the Indian constitution which proclaims compulsory free education for all the children up to the age of 14 years.

## Status of Girls Education in Post- Independent India

After the attainment of independence in 1947, women's education received fresh impetus from the government of India. A number of commissions and committees were appointed to look into the various aspects of women's education and also to make recommendations for its improvement and expansion. The goals and objectives of women's education took a new mode in independent India's educational goals. Education of women was no longer seen exclusively as an instrument for inculcating values appropriate to women's roles in society. It was seen as a means of providing equality of opportunity to women as the title of the report of the Committee on Status of Women (1974) was 'Toward Equality'. This conceptualisation has been further refined to underscore the role of education for women's equality in the New Educational Policy, 1986 which emphasised on women's education as it will lead to their empowerment.

## School Drop-out in India

The history of education reveals the alarming trends in the form of higher dropout rates. Dropout is a major educational problem faced by both boys and girls in India. Although they may be enrolled in the beginning of the year, they don't always remain in schools. The potential factors which pulled the children out of schools are social, cultural, economic, political and educational. Different studies have also found that dropout rates are very high among girls. It is estimated that 45 per cent of girls and 41 per cent of boys' dropout of school between grades I and V (The World Bank, 1997). Studies have also found that the rate of dropout also depend on the background indicators such as gender (male/female), caste, locality (rural/urban), type of family, religion, parental education, parental occupation, household income, birth order of the child, number of siblings and students work participation (domestic/outside).

The World Bank (2002) and UNESCO (2002) study reports on the educational status in the developing countries revealed that 115 million children between the age group of 6 to 11 are out of school every year and another 150 million of those currently enrolled will drop out before completing the primary level, out of this 2/3rd of these children's are girls. Girl's education has been acknowledged as one of the most important developmental challenges of the world societies. Education for all Global Monitoring Report (2003-04) viewed that gender equality in education is essential for sustainable development.

Gender equality in education would imply that girls and boys are offered the same chances to go to school and that they enjoy teaching methods and curricula free of stereotype and academic orientation and counseling unaffected by gender bias. But in actual practice this equality is yet to be achieved, one of the best indicators of gender disparity in education is evident even at the entry level of education. World Education Forum in Dakar, Senegal in the year 2000 also emphasized on the gender parity in education as one of the six goals of the Education For All (EFA) programme. India is positioned almost at the bottom of the heap in measures of the Gender Parity Index which traces the growth of female enrolment in schools. And to add to this dubious distinction is India figures nowhere in the list of countries that have shown the greatest improvement in girls' enrolment (Rawat 2004).

According to census of India 2001, the female literacy has come up to 54 per cent in 2001 from 39 per cent in 1991, along with this the enrollment rate of girls in primary and upper primary schools also improved from 35.3 per cent in 1980-81 to 67.5 per cent in 2000-01[5]. The initiates of state and the efforts of civil society, definitely strengthen the educational system at the gross root level. While the education system has no doubt phenomenally increased its outreach and coverage at the primary level and enrollment rates have also gone up apparently, but the massive drop out of enrolled girls have also continued to drain the system which needs attention of all sort to make the system with more success. Recognizing the importance of girl's education the government initiated number of programmes to encourage the educational participation of girls and launched innovative schemes aimed to maintain higher retention rates in the schools. In the broadest sense education is not simply an agent of socialization rather it is a means of knowledge acquisition and the learning skills, thus broadly education is a human right.

**Table No. 1: State-wise Number of Out of School Children by Gender (annexure)**

**Number of Out of School Children by Gender (6-14 years Age) In India- (As on 31.03.2008)**

Class I-V

| | *States/UTs* | *Boys* | | *Girls* | | *Total* |
|---|---|---|---|---|---|---|
| 1. | Andhra Pradesh | 130112 | 45.7 | 154861 | 54.3 | 284973 |
| 2. | Arunachal Pradesh | 10733 | 48.6 | 11337 | 51.4 | 22070 |
| 3. | Assam | 178281 | 52.6 | 160819 | 47.4 | 339100 |
| 4. | Bihar | 493127 | 48.8 | 517603 | 51.2 | 1010730 |
| 5. | Chhattisgarh | 84891 | 50 | 84862 | 50 | 169753 |
| 6. | Goa | 873 | 44.3 | 1096 | 55.7 | 1969 |
| 7. | Gujarat | 79834 | 52.2 | 73245 | 47.8 | 153079 |
| 8. | Haryana | 76499 | 47.6 | 84337 | 52.4 | 160836 |
| 9. | Himachal Pradesh | 1984 | 48.7 | 2091 | 51.3 | 4075 |

*(Contd...)*

| | | | | | | |
|---|---|---|---|---|---|---|
| 10. | Jammu & Kashmir | 31309 | 46 | 36741 | 54 | 68050 |
| 11. | Jharkhand | 71060 | 49.6 | 72083 | 50.4 | 143143 |
| 12. | Karnataka | 36561 | 50.1 | 36406 | 49.9 | 72967 |
| 13. | Kerala | 11946 | 61.9 | 7352 | 38.1 | 19298 |
| 14. | Madhya Pradesh | 92521 | 51 | 88903 | 49 | 181424 |
| 15. | Maharashtra | 37070 | 52.9 | 33017 | 47.1 | 70087 |
| 16. | Manipur | 25108 | 47.3 | 27972 | 52.7 | 53080 |
| 17. | Meghalaya | 14267 | 52.8 | 12761 | 47.2 | 27028 |
| 18. | Mizoram | 6113 | 51.3 | 5807 | 48.7 | 11920 |
| 19. | Nagaland | 17121 | 48.4 | 18264 | 51.6 | 35385 |
| 20. | Orissa | 177152 | 50.5 | 173551 | 49.5 | 350703 |
| 21. | Punjab | 53565 | 53.3 | 46892 | 46.7 | 100457 |
| 22. | Rajasthan | 71221 | 45.8 | 84117 | 54.2 | 155338 |
| 23. | Sikkim | 1017 | 55.3 | 822 | 44.7 | 1839 |
| 24. | Tamil Nadu | 43397 | 50.2 | 43017 | 49.8 | 86414 |
| 25. | Tripura | 2049 | 50 | 2052 | 50 | 4101 |
| 26. | Uttar Pradesh | 247728 | 52.3 | 226321 | 47.7 | 474049 |
| 27. | Uttarakhand | 7558 | 47.5 | 8338 | 52.5 | 15896 |
| 28. | West Bengal | 235787 | 51.7 | 220428 | 48.3 | 456215 |
| 29. | Andaman & Nicobar Islands | NA | NA | NA | NA | NA |
| 30. | Chandigarh | 2832 | 49.1 | 2933 | 50.9 | 5765 |
| 31. | Dadra & Nagar Haveli | 122 | 28.8 | 301 | 71.2 | 423 |
| 32. | Daman & Diu | 85 | 54.5 | 71 | 45.5 | 156 |
| 33. | Delhi | 12810 | 54.4 | 10718 | 45.6 | 23528 |
| 34. | Lakshadweep | 80 | 51.3 | 76 | 48.7 | 156 |
| 35. | Puducherry | 636 | 60.6 | 414 | 39.4 | 1050 |
| | India | 2255449 | 50.1 | 2249608 | 49.9 | 4505057 |

Data from above table (T1) imply wide variations in terms of access to schools. Access to education is primarily determined by the availability of school and social categories such as class, gender, caste, region, religious backgrounds of the children. Educational policy reports, research finding noted that gender inequalities determine degrees of access ranging from primary education to higher education. Realising the importance of girls' education for their own empowerment and also for the overall development of the society, Government of India has been formulating different plans and programmes to secure women's education. The national commitment to provide free and compulsory education to all children in the age group of 6-14 years is now a fundamental right to every child in India after the passing of 86th Amendment of Constitution in December, 2002. Sarva Shikshya Abhiyan or "Education for All" which was launched in 2003 recognises that ensuring girls' education requires changes not only in the education system but also in societal norms and attitudes. Under this umbrella programme free text books to every child is given and free uniforms to every girl is provided. National Programme of

Education for Girls at Elementary Level (NPEGEL) was launched in 2003 by the Government of India for providing additional components for progress of girls' education in educationally backward Blocks and in the blocks in which SC/ST population is found to be more. In order to realise the universalisation of primary and secondary education for girls the government of India introduced a new scheme named after *Kasturba Gandhi* wife of Mahatma Gandhi.

## Kasturba Gandhi BalikaVidyalaya - Brief Historical Note

This scheme drew its inspiration from Kasturba, who contributed in promoting education among the people of Champaran, especially when Mahatma Gandhi was busy in addressing the causes of the indigo farmers of West Champaran[6]. She took the initiative of running the Ashram, Hospital and School for the children. She specially made efforts to educate girls. KGBV is a scheme started in July 2004 by Government of India for setting up residential schools with boarding facilities for girls belonging to SC, ST, OBC, minorities and BPL categories in all over India. The scheme provides a minimum reservation of 75 per cent of the seats for girls belonging to SC, ST, OBC or minority communities and priority for the remaining 25 per cent, is accorded to girls from families below poverty line.

Around 3000 KGBVs were sanctioned by Government of India till the year 2014. Of these, 427 KGBVs have been sanctioned in Muslim concentration blocks, 612 in ST blocks, 688 in SC blocks. As on 31st January, 2009, 2423 KGBVs are reported to be functional (i.e. 94 per cent) in the States and 1, 90,404 girls enrolled in them (50,630 SC girls (27 per cent); 58,682 ST girls (31 per cent); 50,161 OBC girls (26 per cent); 18,206 BPL girls (9 per cent); 12,725 Minority girls (7 per cent). Out of the total 2578 sanctioned KGBVs, 547 KGBVs have been constructed + 1262 are in progress and 769 have not been started. The Kasturba Gandhi Balika Vidyalaya scheme is merged with Sarva Shiksha Abhiyan in the XI Plan with effect from 1st April, 2007. The scheme is aimed to improve the educational conditions of girls in Educationally Backward Blocks (EBBs). The aim of scheme is to set up schools in areas which fulfill the following criteria:

- Concentration of tribal population, with low female literacy and/or a large number of girls out of school;
- Concentration of SC, OBC and minority populations, with low female literacy and/or a large number of girls out of school;
- Areas with low female literacy; or areas with a large number of small, scattered habitations that do not qualify for a school.

## Aim of the scheme

Gender disparities still persist in rural areas and among disadvantaged communities. Looking at enrolment trends, there remain significant gaps in the enrolment of girls at the elementary level as compared to boys, especially at the upper primary levels. The objective of KGBV is to ensure access and quality education to the girls of disadvantaged groups of society by setting up residential schools with boarding facilities at elementary level. This innovative policy attracted the attention of children, parents, policy makers and political leadership. This scheme became a benchmark for launching of the prestigious Navodaya Vidyalayas across the country which are known as the centers of excellence. However, most of the schemes initiated by government are oriented towards education of boys, whereas the educational of girls didn't get adequate importance in policy making and implementation for education of girls from primary to post graduate education. At this critical juncture the central government initiative to introduce residential school for girls who are dropped out from schools due to various reasons is laudable. Renowned educationalist and scholar of eminence professor Krishna Kumar's reflections on KGBV highlights the significance and critical role of this scheme in shaping the future of rural society and family of these deprived girls.

> KGBVs are meant to serve rural girls belonging to families whose economy is Below the Poverty Line and others who come from Dalit and minority communities. Now they provide a full-time residential facility and regular education from classes VI to VIII. Girls who never enrolled in a primary school or who dropped out before completing Class V are eligible for enrolment in a KGBV. By any standards, it is a bold and imaginative scheme and over the recent years, it has gained both popularity and status in State after State. There are some 2,500 functioning KGBVs in rural India today. Visit any of them, and the one demand you will hear from residents and their parents is that they want the school to go up to Class XII or at least Class X. They also want more money to expand infras-tructure. 'Though run on the minimalist principles of SSA, the KGBVs have been a spectacular success', especially in States where the Mahila Samakhya (MS) is managing them. (Hindu-31-08-2010).

Kumar comments signify the role of KGBV as an agent of social transformation of Indian society in general and rural girl's in particular. With foregoing account the following data provide an outline about the nature of enrollment across the castes in KGBV across the districts in Andhra Pradesh. Though Andhra Pradesh has been considered as one of the key and leading states in advancement of technical and higher education in order to institutionalise the ongoing achievement state should strengthen the primary education at gross root level by including the educationally deprived categories such as girls, SC, ST, minorities and other poorer (educationally) sections of rural areas. The undivided Andhra Pradesh broadly consists of three distinct regions namely Andhra, Telangana and Rayalaseema. The literacy levels in Telangana is 49 per cent, as against 55 per cent in costal Andhra, and 51 per cent in Rayalaseema. Government of Andhra Pradesh is one of the leading states in evolving innovative educational scheme like Andhra Pradesh Residential schools[7] (APRS) for talented rural children in general and marginal groups such as, Scheduled Castes, Scheduled Tribes and Backward Castes in particular. Over a period of time chain of residential schools for general, SC, ST and BC students has been started across the state to cater the educational needs of the rural children.

A cursory look at the above table (T-3) and the pattern of enrollment in KGBVs indicates that most of girls are hailing from socially marginalised communities and followed by religious minorities particularly Muslims of India. Data has been generated by using the government information related to number of KGBV and nature of enrollment. Majority of the girls are hails from backward castes followed by ST, SC, BPL and minorities. The trend implies that the government has been successful in taking the scheme to the social groups who come under Below Poverty Line across the castes, religious and economic conditions.

## Methodology and Methods of Data Collection

Exploratory research design has been used to map out the functioning and evaluate the performance of KGBVs in the state of Andhra Pradesh. The aim of the study is to understand the issues which prevents or hinder the educational advancement of girls and critically analyses the possibilities and limitations associated with government policies or schemes such as KGBV. The central government sanctioned around 2500 schools across the states, currently the government of Andhra Pradesh running 395 KGBV across the districts especially in the mandals (administrative blocks) which are marked as EBBs (Educationally Backward Blocks) by the government on the basis of women literacy levels.

## Methods of Data Collection

The study used both qualitative and quantitative research strategies to comprehend the reasons for dropout rate among rural girl children. Structured questionnaire, semi-structured interview guide, were to elicit the quantitative data whereas participant observation method and focused groups interviews enabled to access information related to school infrastructure, patterns of enrolment across the caste, class, religion and region.

Rationalise behind the application of qualitative techniques like semi-structured interviews, participant observation is to access the inside stories of girl students, teachers who are the main actors of schools. Girl students were asked to reflect upon their views on the functioning of schools, their individual stories behind joining the schools, family conditions and parental support for their education, problems they encounter in their everyday were encouraged to reveal for comprehensive understanding of the stakeholders reactions and levels of acceptance. The sample of the study is 427 girl children enrolled in

## Table No. 2: Category-wise Enrollment of Children in KGBV across the Districts in united Andhra Pradesh[10]

| District | SC | Per cent | ST | Per cent | OBC | Per cent | BPL | Per cent | Min. | Per cent | Total | Per cent |
|---|---|---|---|---|---|---|---|---|---|---|---|---|
| 1. Adilabad | 569 | 28.8 | 888 | 45 | 488 | 24.7 | 28 | 1.4 | 2 | 0.1 | 1975 | 6.2 |
| 2. Khammam | 373 | 19 | 1137 | 57.9 | 389 | 19.8 | 65 | 3.3 | 0 | 0 | 1964 | 6.1 |
| 3. MNagar | 903 | 29.5 | 773 | 25.3 | 1013 | 33.1 | 200 | 6.5 | 171 | 5.6 | 3060 | 9.6 |
| 4. Medak | 427 | 22.1 | 630 | 32.6 | 599 | 31 | 79 | 4.1 | 200 | 10.3 | 1935 | 6 |
| 5. Nalgonda | 618 | 27.9 | 812 | 36.6 | 574 | 25.9 | 35 | 1.6 | 178 | 8 | 2217 | 6.9 |
| 6. Nizamabad | 481 | 28 | 418 | 24.3 | 659 | 38.4 | 107 | 6.2 | 50 | 2.9 | 1715 | 5.4 |
| 7. Rangareddy | 288 | 21.4 | 551 | 40.9 | 359 | 26.7 | 33 | 2.4 | 116 | 8.6 | 1347 | 4.2 |
| 8. Warangal | 373 | 23.8 | 823 | 52.6 | 345 | 22 | 25 | 1.6 | 0 | 0 | 1566 | 4.9 |
| 9. Anantapur | 509 | 22.7 | 649 | 28.9 | 677 | 30.2 | 221 | 1 | 188 | 8.4 | 2244 | 7 |
| 10. Chittor | 288 | 21.7 | 179 | 13.5 | 586 | 44.2 | 197 | 14.9 | 76 | 5.7 | 1326 | 4.1 |
| 11. Kadapa | 392 | 17.9 | 159 | 7.3 | 936 | 42.8 | 646 | 29.5 | 56 | 2.6 | 2189 | 6.8 |
| 12. Guntur | 324 | 20.9 | 554 | 35.8 | 322 | 20.8 | 293 | 18.9 | 55 | 3.6 | 1548 | 4.8 |
| 13. Kurnool | 697 | 29.6 | 202 | 8.6 | 809 | 34.4 | 192 | 8.2 | 451 | 19.2 | 2351 | 7.3 |
| 14. Nellor | 165 | 40.7 | 56 | 13.8 | 121 | 29.9 | 56 | 13.8 | 7 | 1.7 | 405 | 1.3 |
| 15. Prakasam | 426 | 21.8 | 316 | 16.2 | 531 | 27.2 | 591 | 30.3 | 86 | 4.4 | 1950 | 6.1 |
| 16. Srikakulam | 86 | 6.4 | 300 | 22.5 | 913 | 68.3 | 35 | 2.6 | 2 | 0.1 | 1336 | 4.2 |
| 17. Visakhapatnam | 75 | 4.7 | 923 | 57.7 | 493 | 30.8 | 109 | 6.8 | 0 | 0 | 1600 | 5 |
| 18. Vizianagaram | 226 | 17.7 | 400 | 31.3 | 632 | 49.4 | 21 | 1.6 | 0 | 0 | 1279 | 4 |
| **Total** | **7220** | **22.6** | **9770** | **30.5** | **10446** | **32.6** | **2933** | **9.2** | **1638** | **5.1** | **32007** | **100** |

*Source*: percentages were generated from basic data –accessed from -www.ssa.nic.in

40 selected KGBV schools across the five districts. An attempt has been to map out the reasons from drop out at primary and secondary stages of education. The following table and analysis provides the factors pushes girl children out of school from early stages of their education.

**Table No 4 Reasons for Dropout from the School**

| ***Reasons for Dropout from the School*** | ***Frequency*** | ***Percent*** |
|---|---|---|
| Financial Problems | 63 | 25.7 per cent |
| Family problems | 55 | 22.4 per cent |
| Own Health Problems | 37 | 15.1 per cent |
| School is located very far | 16 | 6.5 per cent |
| Mother Health problems | 15 | 6.1 per cent |
| Sibling Health Problem | 15 | 6.1 per cent |
| Didn't like schooling/ Teaching is not good | 11 | 4.5 per cent |
| Father health problems | 8 | 3.3 per cent |
| Parent death | 8 | 3.3 per cent |
| Child Labour | 7 | 2.9 per cent |
| Parents are illiterates | 6 | 2.4 per cent |
| Due to Migration | 4 | 1.6 per cent |
| **Total** | **245** | **100.0 per cent** |

## I. Financial Problems

The study found that the primary reasons for higher levels of dropout rate is financial problems (26 per cent), family problems (22 per cent) and one's own health problems (15 per cent). Parental health and wellbeing, health conditions of self and siblings are some of the key factors to determine the educational opportunities of girl children. Degree of school distance from one's own residence and teaching methods and teacher attitude towards the girl children discourage these marginal communities to continue in school and complete their education. Death of parents, illiteracy and migration tend to affect the life chances of girls children from completing their schooling.

The following narrative highlights the lived experience and their expectation from the education system. The narratives are direct trans-lations without disturbing the basic essence.

> ***L. Kasilakshmi, 9th class-*** *I was a worker before joining in this school. Principal Sir came to our home and requested my parents to join me here I was drop out for 2 years after completing my 5th class. I want to become a teacher in my life. My family depends on agricultural labour.*

*We are 4 children including 3 girls and one boy. My elder sister got married and other sister used to work in the field. Only my brother is going to school. We are very poor family. Everyone in the family has to go to work. My parents are illiterates, we only started education. My elder sister has studied 5th class; second sister has studied 7th class, now they dropped out. I studied 5th class and started working in home and fields.* ***My father did not send me to 6th class and he could not spend money also.*** *I was without schooling for one year. I like education, discipline and neatness in this school. Here teaching, food, medical facilities, and rooms are good. We have classes and study hours.*

***K. Manasa, 7th class--*** *I am from a very poor background. I like education very much. My father is mason and my mother works as an agricultural labourer in fields. I have one younger brother, he is studying 4th class. I am in 7th class. My father studied only 1st class and my mother is an illiterate. I studied L.K.G to 4th in Avenue Grammar School. I studied my 5th class in Primary School. I have studied 6th class in Lingasa-mudram and joined here for 7th class. I like the facilities and system here. I like the discipline and subject teaching here.* ***I have joined here because the government provides everything without any fee. I am dropped out in 5th class due to my brother's death.*** *Again with uncle's support I am back to education. I want to become doctor in my life. I want to keep the word given to my teachers. I wanted to be an independent.*

The foregoing case studies reveal the role of economic factors in shaping the success of educational journey of rural girls from under privileged background. This conforms the position of the Marxist feminist and their emphasis on the economy as the base and how the material conditions determine the other social cultural and education spheres.

## II. Family problems

Family plays an important role in construction and reinforcement of gendered ideologies in traditional societies in general and Indian society in particular. The success and failure of girls' education in India to a large extent determined by the prevailing conditions and support of family. Around 1/4th of the girl children said that they were forced to stop school because of the manifest and latent problems. The following case studies highlight some of the major problems confronted by the children at the early age.

***P. Sudharani, 9th class-*** *My parents are illiterates. We are from a very poor background. We are 5 members and live in a very small room. Our school has up to 7th class. We are provided meals in the school. My sister and I are studying in my family. My father studied 5th class. He works in agriculture; my mother is an illiterate and helps my father in agriculture. I like education and discipline in the school. I was given cloths, bed sheets, text books, and notebooks free. I was engaged in* *domestic works. I was a drop after my 5th class. My family circumstances did not permit me to study further. Now I am in K.G.B.V. School. I want to study well to pass 10th and 12th. My future will be decided by brother. I will go for engineering after intermediate.*

***K. Aswani, 9th class**-I was engaged in Buffalo rearing. My family is a poor family. My father works in agriculture. We are 4 children to my parents. Out of them **3 are girls 1 boy**. My father studied 3rd class and my mother and my sister are illiterates. My brother and I are studying. I have studied my primary education in my village and after that I was sent to work. **I was not allowed to go to next village for study. This school is good because it provides free education**. My principal sir convinced my parents to join me here. I studied 5th class in my village and stopped further education. I want to become a police in my future.*

***Bharati, 9th class**- My life was a very troublesome. **My mother was not well. I dropped school to cook food for family. I was so depressed for not being to school**. I want to become police in my life. I am expecting support from my family. My family is depended on agriculture. We are four children to our parents and they are struggling to provide education for us. My brother is studying Intermediate in Guntur and my sister is in 7th class. My father has studied 10th class and my mother is illiterate. I have studied in M.P.U.P School in my village. I like the education over there.*

***G. Rajakumari, 9th class**- I was engaged in buffalo rearing. We are 4 girls to my parents. All my family members go to daily labour. I was also engaged in domestic work. I did my primary schooling in my village M.P.U.P. School I want to become a doctor in my life; I am from a very poor background. My brother is studying in Narsaraopet. My parents spent money on my sister's marriage. My brother is also dropped out college because of financial problems. My father, brother and I are studied in my family. I did my primary schooling in our village and dropped out for one year after my 5th class. I was not sent to school in neighbouring village because I have to walk. We have no money for private school. My uncle got to know about this school.*

The foregoing analysis clearly shows how the economic and family problems push girls from primary and secondary stages of schooling across the villages of Andhra Pradesh and Telanagana states.

## I. Own Health Problem

Malnutrition is the major health problem confronted by a sizable proportion of children in South Asian countries; India is not an exception to this process. The poor economic conditions and coupled with demographic family size affect severely the health status of girl children at the very young years. Therefore, ill health is one of the root causes of higher levels of dropout rate from schools. The following case studies show the rural reality of Indian society.

> ***P. Jaavani, 7th class-*** *I want to get fame as a good teacher. I expect respect in the society. I do not know what will happen in the future. My family consists of mother, brother and myself. My mother goes to fields and my brother is studying in 1st class in government school. I have studied (1 to 4 classes) in government school at my village. I have continued my study up to 6th. I am a dropout in 7th class because of my* ***ill health****. Later I have joined here with support of my aunty. Facilities are good in this school. We have teachers for all subjects.*

## IV. Lack of availability of school and bad teachers & teaching

Most of the UN and World Bank studies on developing countries pointed out the issue of schools without schooling. The ASER and PROBE studies on government schools across the states in India also highlighted the poor quality of education system. Interestingly several girl children said the indifferent attitudes of teachers and lack of proper infrastructure in government/ private schools in Rural India are some of the major reasons for the higher levels of dropout rate. Here are the cases related the teachers and teaching in Andhra and Telanagana.

> ***K. Sivakumari, 9th class-*** *I have studied up to 5th class in my village and stopped education. Principal Sir in my village convinced my parents to send me here. We are two children to our parents. We also work in agriculture to manage our family. My parents are illiterates. Now we are coming to school. High school is located within* ***radius of 5 km from our village****. My father also cannot join us in private school. So we dropped school. I am very much benefited here. I learnt discipline here, food is good, medical facilities are there, good teaching, and neatness are there. We can study under any tree happily.*
>
> ***M. Siva Parvathi, 9th Class-*** *I had dropped out after 5th class and engaged in domestic work and agricultural work. My family could not bear the expenditure to send me to our next village for education. I am very lucky to join this school. Everything is free in this school. Teachers are really good and maintain discipline. I was not aware of the value of education, now I am studying well.*
>
> ***Kumari, 9th class-*** *I was completely involved in domestic work and go to school whenever I get some time. Other time I used to play with my friends. I like science subject very much, that is why I want to be science teacher in the future. My father goes to field in the morning and comeback in the evening. I used to prepare food for my family members. We used to have combined lunch. No one in our family got educated. My brother dropped out in 9th class. My primary education was in Uyyalawada.*

*Teaching was not good in that school. Teachers never care the children. Children were always playing. I was not allowed to go to the next village for my further education. We have to go by walk. So, I became a dropout. My brother is studying Intermediate.*

***M. Radha, 9th class-*** *My family depends on agricultural labour. I am from a poor family. My mother's health is not good. We are three girls to my parents. We all engaged in domestic work. My parents are illiterates and we three children are studying. I am a drop out for one year after completing my primary education in our village. I was supposed to send Mundlamuru village for my high school. I have to go on walking. We have no money for private schools. So I dropped. My principal sir encouraged all of us joins here. My life was a very troublesome life. I was engaged in domestic works. My life is good in K.G.B.V. I want to become science teacher in future.*

Content analysis of an in-depth interview with girl children from KGBVs revealed that there are multiple factors responsible for children dropout from schools at an early age. Non-availability of primary schools also forces poor parents to opt for private schools and search for alternative educational spaces.

**Table No 5- Class in which Children Dropped out from School**

| *Class* | *Frequency* | *Per cent* |
|---|---|---|
| 1 | 1 | 0.4 |
| 2 | 7 | 2.7 |
| 3 | 17 | 6.5 |
| 4 | 28 | 10.6 |
| 5 | 87 | 33.1 |
| 6 | 70 | 26.6 |
| 7 | 35 | 13.3 |
| 8 | 18 | 6.8 |
| **Total** | **263** | **100.0** |

The above table (T-21) presents the patterns of dropout rate with reference to class at which the children are dropped out from schools. It has been noticed that most of the girls are dropped out of school during 5th and 6th standard compared to other classes of study. There are multiple factors which are responsible for dropping from school. More than economic factors, access to school, and changes in the biological cycle of girls are also responsible for drop out. The foregoing children narratives reveals that majority of the cases drop out cases starts from class 5th standard and go up with higher classes of study. Lack of school in one's own village forces girls to dropout from further studies.

**Table No 6: Nature of Building**

| *Building* | *Frequency* | *Percent* |
|---|---|---|
| Pucca | 29 | 72.5 |
| Kacha | 11 | 27.5 |
| | 40 | 100 |

One of the major concern shared by children and teachers is that most of the KGBV' are functioning under rented buildings. Major problem with these buildings is that they are not meant for catering the educational needs of schools. These buildings also lacks school ambiance. Thus, the environment is not conducive for educational empowerment. Almost 1/3rd of the buildings are Kacha building where the issues of children safety are under question. Location of school building and associated basic facilities such as water, number of bathrooms, toilets not only influence educational quality but also determines the health conditions of girls children. The following paragraphs present children perceptions and their experiences with hostel life.

V. ***Amulya, 9th class*** *-I have joined here for 9th class. I was supported by Sujatha Madam to join this school. I was given bed sheets, plate, uniform and books. We have teachers for every subject. We also have study hours. As the school is located near the tank, water is blocked during rainy season. So we are often affected by snakes. I like the food here. We request the officers to complete the construction of building work as soon as possible. I want to become a drawing teacher in the future. My father works as security guard in Bangalore. My mother is looking after the milk business.*

***K. Madhavi, 9th class****-My family is with parents and sisters. My father is a shepherd and my mother goes to fields. My elder sister is in 7th class and younger sister is in 2nd class. I have studied 6th to 8th in Z.P.P.H. School in Rompidodla. Later I have joined here. My teachers teach well in this school. We are often scared of snakes as our school in outskirts of the school. I request for a new building as soon as possible. We are also affected mosquitoes. Please try to understand our problems. I want to become teacher in life. I want to bring good name to my family.*

***D. Bhagyalaxmi, 9th class****- I am shifted here while I was studying 9th class. My parents joined me here because children of our village were also joining here. We have teachers for every subject. Our food is also good. My school located at the outskirts of the village, and frequent visit of snakes is creating fear in us. That is why many students did not join here. I request you change this place very soon. I want to become teacher in my life. I want to reach a very good stage in my life.*

Thus, the location of school building is very important issue from the girl's perspective. Children reflections highlights that some of the children are living with fear.

## Number of rooms in school building

Critical size of rooms in a school is always desirable to create an excellent educational ambiance. We have also collected data regarding the number of rooms in schools. It has been observed that 17 per cent of the schools have more than 6 rooms, followed by 7 and 8 room schools are 13.8 per cent. On an average around 50 per cent of the schools have basic number of rooms whereas remaining 50 per cent do not have critical size, which would definitely influence the educational atmosphere. On an average more than 100-150 students are accommodated in the same hostel where number of rooms also very less or not adequate.

> ***K. Sukanya-*** *I want to score good marks in 10th class. I want to become teacher in the future. I am enjoying the stay and comforts in this school and hostel. We are also given cosmetics per month. We are given soaps, bed sheets, school dress and pencils. We need a permanent building as soon as possible. We also do not have proper water facility. Sometimes we are going to nearby boys' hostel to bring the water.*
>
> ***R. Lalithabai, 6th class, MettaboodaThanda-*** *Rooms are not adequate here, no playground, and drenched during rainy season. No proper water facility. Teachers are good here. I want to study well and I am updated with all works. We need a new building immediately. I want to become a teacher.*
>
> ***M. Saraswatibai, 7th class-*** *My parents are labourers. We are 5 members in the family. One brother is in 3rd class and other is in 4th class. I have completed 1-5th class in our village school. Rooms are congested and rain water is coming into room. We do not have space to keep our boxes. Snakes are entering our rooms and classes. I want to become doctor in future.*

**Table No 6— Compound Wall**

| *Compound wall* | *Frequency* | *Percentage* |
|---|---|---|
| Yes | 28 | 70 |
| No | 12 | 30 |
| **Total** | **40** | **100** |

Almost 1/3rd of the schools do not have compound walls (30 per cent), whereas 70 per cent of schools do have compound wall. This is so important from the gender perspective.

***K. Govindamma**, 6th class- I have studied up to 5th class in Government School. I got 3rd rank in the school. My seniors in K.B.G.V. from village asked my mother to join me here. I was given Plate, water glass and 3 bed sheets. I could able to understand the teaching here. I like the food here. I was also given Rs 50 p.m. and Notes. My school is located outside the village and near the tank. Our compound wall is very small, snakes are coming in. We are scared of it every time. We need a new school building. I want to become a science teacher in future.*

Children reflections highlight the significance of compound wall in every school. Since girl's security is under threat, children feel a sense of lack of security in respective schools.

## Availability of Water in the School.

Although water is an important and inseparable component of human life, empirical observations highlight the lack of water facility in some of the schools. Some of the schools fail to provide not only drinking water but also daily use water. As a result girls' students finding extremely difficult to fulfill their every day basic needs such as bathing, toilet, etc.

**Table No 7— Availability of Water in the School**

| *Water* | *Frequency* | *Per cent* |
|---|---|---|
| Yes | 35 | 87.5 |
| No | 5 | 12.5 |
| **Total** | **40** | **100** |

Almost 75 per cent of children in KGBV are using or depending on ground water for daily use, followed by tank water which accounts for 21 per cent and only 4 per cent of children have access to purified drinking water. An attempt has been made to reflect the experience of children with water in KGBV.

***Gangabai D, 7th class-**My parents are labourers. We are 7 members in the family-I have studied 1-5th class in Yarragondapalem by staying in SC hostel. I like everything there. We do not have enough bathrooms-We do not have good drinking water. Water is coming into rooms during rains and we could not sleep. Scorpios and snakes are coming to rooms- I want to study well and get good job to support my parents. I want to become a teacher.*

***P. Nireekshana-** I am aiming to get good marks in 10th class. I want to become a doctor. I am in K.G.B.V because of my parents and uncle. They have joined me here because of the good education provided here. School is fine here. But we have a water problem here. I have a request for a* *permanent accommodation. I am satisfied with the education here. We are given books, texts, dress. Teachers are cooperative. We have study hours in 5 to 6.30 morning and evening. We are very much encouraged by our teachers.*

***S. Prasanthi, 8th class-*** *I want to score good marks in 10th class. I would like to continue my studies. I have joined KGBV for 6th class and I will continue till 10th class. I have joined KGBV with grandfather's initiative. I am enjoying the stay and comforts in this school. We are also given cosmetics per month. We need a permanent building as soon as possible. We also do not have proper water facility. Sometimes we are going to boys' hostel to bring the water.*

The study team also observed that girls in some of the KGBVs in Ananthapur district find it extremely difficult to take bath a day and they tend to wait for a day to two days to access drinking and usable water.

## Availability of Toilets in the School

Toilet facility is one of the essential component of the schools particularly so in the case of the girl children. Two issues need to be discussed here; one is availability of toilet and secondly usability of the toilet.

**Table No 8 Availability of Toilets in the School**

| *Toilets* | *Frequency* | *Per cent* |
|---|---|---|
| Yes/ usable | 31 | 81.6 |
| No/ unusable | 7 | 18.4 |
| **Total** | **40** | **100** |

The study found that almost 80 per cent of schools provided toilet facilities compared to 10 per cent failed to provide the same. More serious issue is that 10 per cent of the toilets are not usable at all. Some of the children shared their experiences with hostel facilities in general and toilet facilities in particular. Below are some snapshots highlights the ground realities in the field.

***AnanthaLaxmi, B. 8th class-*** *I want to do nursing in the future. My father works in Photo studio and mother is a tailor. I have joined here for 8th class. My father's friend referred this school. I did not like any other facility other than education. We have 3 bathrooms and 2 latrines. We are adjusting with them. We were given only 15 notebooks. It is difficult to buy the note books after that. We are scared of snakes, insects, and Scorpios especially during the rainy season.*

***M. Jyothibai, 7th class-*** *We are 7 members in my family. My father works in agriculture. My sister is in 8th class in KGBV. I have studied in private* *school till 5th class. Madam from here came to our school and told us about free provisions of KGBV. After joining here I understood problems in rainy season. We have very small ground. Food is not enough. Bathrooms are very less. Here, education is poor (quality) compared to private school in our village. They do not repeat the explanation and I am afraid to ask them.*

***Gunti Galamma, 9th class***-*We are 4 members in my family. My family wants me to study well and have studied 1-6th class staying in SC hostel and joined here for 7th class. My aunty helped me in joining this school. My madam takes care of us nicely. We do not have enough bathrooms. I am here because everything is free. We have water problem. We bring water from outside. I prefer to go home to avoid troubles here.*

The major implication of this findings and reflections demonstrations that girl children are forced to go out for toilet which might lead to social tensions and other human problems.

## Conclusion

Though India is one of the developing countries, the education scenario indicates the backward position on the various issues of education. One of the major problems faced by the Indian education system is higher dropout rates at the lowest levels of education i.e. primary education.

Universalisation of primary education has become a reality in independent India. Children across the rural-urban, caste, gender, religious and ethnic background enroll at primary stage of their education. However, most of the developing countries in general and South Asian countries in particular face multiple challenges in enrollment and retention of girls from rural India in secondary education. Though government of India and state governments have been designing and implementing multiple education policies to achieve universalisation of secondary education, most of those policies are aimed towards boys whereas the state is either indifferent or blind to the specific needs policies for girls at secondary education. At this critical juncture of the KGBV scheme designed to meet the secondary educational needs of the rural girls from the Adivasi, dalit, backward castes, minatory and children of below poverty line received a critical appraisal for scope and scale of coverage of the program. Agenda of this programme is to brick back those girls dropped out from primary and early stages of higher grades to secondary schools. The design of the scheme is inclusive economically and educationally.

However, an in-depth analysis of the functioning of KGBV schools across the Andhra and Telangana states reveals a wide gap between the policy proclamation and implementation. The paper found that there were multiple factors which determine the continuity and degree of girls' dropout. The primary factors of dropout were family economic and socio-cultural conditions. More than 40 per cent girl children dropout due to economic vulnerability and the family size pushes the parents to stop the girl's education at an early stage. Girl children are the first victims of the major crisis in family. Death of a father, mother, brother or sister and child caring and buffalo rearing, parent's migration to other villages affects the educational chances of rural girls. The reflection of the rural girl children on the nature of instruction and infrastructure reveals the dilemmas and discontent against the methods of teaching and means of learning. Most the school buildings are functioning in private rented buildings with very modest infrastructure. There is a mismatch between the number of children studying in a schools and number of classrooms and hostel rooms including bathrooms are very few in number. Water, unusable toilets and lack of proper usable and drinking water are the major problems faced by children in everyday schools life. The paper strongly recommends the proper infrastructure facility and tools of learning for the holistic development of children from multiple socio-cultural backgrounds. Although the constitutional framers recognised the critical role of education for economic modernisation and social transformation, lack of political will and structural inequities in policy framing tend to reflect on the functioning and performance of the government schemes in general and educational programmes in particular.

## References

Balagopalan, Sarada (2010): "Rationalising Seclusion: *A Preliminary Analysis of a Residential Schooling Scheme for Poor Girls in India"*, *Feminist Theory,* 11(3): 295-308.

Chanana Karuna (2001) Interrogating Women's Education: Bounded Visions, Expanding Horizons.Jaipur: Rawat Publications.

Choudhury, Amit. 2006. 'Revisiting Dropouts: Old Issues, Fresh Perspectives', *Economic and Political Weekly,* 41 (51): 5257-5263.

Indira R (2013) Themes in Sociology of Education. Newdelhi: Sage publication.

Krishna Kumar. Empowerment by verbal chicanery (Hindu-31-08-2010) http://www.thehindu.com/opinion/lead/empowerment-by-verbal-chicanery/article605995.ece

Kumar K and Litika Gupta 2008. What Is Missing in Girls' Empowerment? Vol. XLIII No 26-27.

Nagaraju Gundemeda (2014) Vulnerability and Education: A Study of the Patterns of Discrimination in Government Schools in Andhra Pradesh. Social Action 64:1.

Ramachandran Vimala (2004) Hierarchies of Access: Gender and Equity in Primary Education (ed); Sage Publications, New Delhi.

Sarangapani Padma (2003) Constructing School Knowledge: An Ethnography of Learning in an Indian Village. Newdelhi: Sage publication.

Saxena S.2012. Is Equality an Outdated Concern in Education? Economic & Political Weekly VOL XLVII NO 49.

Sengupta,P and G.Guha.2002. 'Enrolment, Drop out and Grade Completion of Girl Children in West Bengal,' *Economic and Political Weekly,* 37(17): 1621-1637.

Sharma, Neerja and Nandita Chaudhury. 2003. *'From Home to School*: Circumstances in the Lives of children from poor families', *Seminar.*

Sinha Shanta (2008) Children's Right to Education and Democratisation of Schools. http://www.ncpcr.gov.in/view_file.php?fid=79

Sudarshan, Ratna M.2000. *'Educational Status of Girls and Women:* The Emerging Scenario' in Rekha Wazir (ed.): *The Gender Gap in Basic Education: NGOs as Change Agents* (38-79). New Delhi: Sage Publication.

Velaskar Padma (2012), Education for Liberation: Ambedkar's Thought and Dalit Women's Perspectives Contemporary Education Dialogue July 2012 9: 245-271,

Wazir, Rekha. 2000. *The Gender Gap in Basic Education: NGOs as Change Agent,* New Delhi: Sage Publication.

Weiner, G.1997. 'Feminisms and Education' in Halsey et al (eds.). *Education, Culture, Economy, Society,* pp. 144-153. New York: Oxford University Press.

## Notes

1. In April 2000 in Dakar, 164 governments together with partner institutions adopted a Framework for Action focusing on the strategies to achieve Education for All. UNESCO Publishing-Oxford-2008.
2. Afghanistan,Bangladesh, Bhutan, India, Nepal, the Maldives, Pakistan, and Sri Lanka.
3. Children Out of School- Measuring Exclusion from Primary Education-http://www.uis.unesco.org/template/pdf/educgeneral/OOSC_EN_WEB_ FINAL.pdf (29-8-2010).
4. Multiple Indicator Survey – 2000-(MICS-2000)-INDIA-Summary Report-Department of Women & Child Development & United Nations Children's Fund-*November-http://www.childinfo.org/files/india.pdf*
5. Selected educational statistics, Government of India (GoI) 2000-01s, and Report of Dept. of Women and Children; 2002).
6. In Champaran, a district in state of Bihar, tens of thousands of landless serfs, indentured labourers and poor farmers were forced to grow indigo and other cash crops instead of the food crops in 1914. Mahatma Gandhi visitied villages of Champaran and fought against the British raj politics.
7. APRS-1971- sarvel of Nalgonda district of A.P.

# 7

# Right to Language in the context of Globalisation and Democracy

*—Dr Avinash Pandey*

The scholars of linguistics very often reflect on 'language' and the future of languages. This engagement has been more prominent during the modern times. The reasons for this increasing engagement are not hard to find. Modernity, characteristically, foregrounds the historicity of languages and concerns about the future of our languages. The realisation of the historicity of language, especially in the modern age, has brought to the fore concerns about the future of our languages. Modernity constitutes an awareness regarding the responsibility and consequences of our actions. If languages do not have a divine origin but are a result of the efforts of mankind, the future of our languages depends on our actions. We are directly responsible for our languages but any discussion regarding the future of our languages presents before us some peculiar difficulties. These difficulties are mainly due to the omnipresence of language in our social world. We do not know of any social group, which does not have language(s). This omnipresence of language makes it difficult to come up with a particular conceptualisation of language, which can be applied across the board. Further, even within a social group, we have existence of social cleavages of caste, class, gender, region, religion, etc. Linguistic divisions do not always coincide with these social divisions. Therefore language forms an arena of struggle. The awareness regarding the historicity of language ultimately leads us to the appreciation of the fact that 'language' is a word in our language and that it acquires its meaning like any other word of our language: alternative conceptualisations compete with each other to count as what constitutes a language.

The two articulations are relevant in this debate that arises within the framework of the nationalist agenda and globalisation. These two interpretations have dominated in this discourse regarding language and are, today competing for social space and imagination. One has to only look at the varying interpretations of the Right to Education Act, 2009, to get an idea about this struggle. This article will seek to understand the forces underlying these articulations and their implications for the future of our languages, as well as the social fabric of our country.

In a nationalistic framework, the emphasis is on the creation of the citisen of the nation-state. Eurocentric theories correlate the emergence of the nation-state with industrialisation, modernisation and democracy. A single ethnic group, shared culture (religion, language, etc.), clear territorial boundaries, citisenship and equal rights supposedly form crucial ingredients of the process of emergence of nation-states. However, the emergence of nation-states, especially in the continents of Asia and Africa, present a different picture from that of Europe. Nation-states in Asia and Africa emerged through the experience of colonialism. It was a typical 'change-from-above' sort of scenario. There was no churning of society, no re-allocation of material and cultural resources but rather a capitalist sort of structure (modern?) was super-imposed on the already existing social formations to benefit the colonisers. The new structure, thus, was introduced through the traditional fault lines, along which society was already divided. Thus, for example, in India, the new class structure was introduced through the already existing caste structures. This explains the great degree of overlap between class and caste in India.

Needless to say, what one gets is a nation-state but no citizenship. Citizenship was achieved through a protracted struggle with the colonisers. A consequence of this situation is that people organised themselves against the foreign rule not as citisens of a nation, to which they had no access but on the basis of the traditional cleavages of society, based on religion, caste, gender, etc. This strengthened the already existing fault lines, albeit in a 'modern' set-up. The project of making of the citisen, in countries like India, began after these countries gained independence. The colonisers are often given credit for the process of formation of nation-states in the colonial countries but it would do us a world of good to remember that when 'transfer of power' took place in the Indian Subcontinent, it was not clear whether two nations were gaining independence, or about 565 principalities. The issue was undecided till then. It was the *anti-colonial struggle* that gave shape to our nation.

As far as languages were concerned, the project of nation-building also involved the development and standardisation of our languages. Language, in the nationalist framework, is conceptualised as a system. The standard picture of the linguistic world is a Herderian conception of the world as composed of individual language-and-culture units.Such a conception deals with speech community as equivalent with language. The boundaries between speech communities are thought of as boundaries of communication (mutual intelligibility). Such an orientation towards language is based on a monolingual perspective of the user of the language. It assumes that the system of language is imminent and can be understood in its own terms. Any reference to extra-linguistic categories is deemed unnecessary. Mutual intelligibility is seen as a function of some objective degree of linguistic difference. Thus, communication is equated with a common language.

The project of making the citizen involves, developing an environ-ment where the citisen could exercise his/her rights and fulfill the responsibilities in a manner which would empower the citisen socially, politically and economically. The linguistic reorganisation of states can be seen as a move in this direction. The language policy of India has been deeply influenced by that of USSR. The reasons are not difficult to imagine. The USSR was arguably the first and at the time of our indepen-dence, the only country to actively engage with the issue of multilingualism and make it central in its language policy and planning.

The dual movement of nation-building, as well as development of the citisen,is clearly reflected in the linguistic scenario of India. The Census of India reports around 10,000 labels for mother tongues in India. These labels are then rationalised into around 3500 labels, out of which 1700 odd languages are treated as unclassified. The remaining1600 odd labels are classified into 200 odd languages. It is on this basis that we can say around 200+ languages are spoken in India. The Census of India reports only those languages which have more than 10,000 speakers. The recent People's Linguistic Survey of India, which does not follow any such restriction, puts the figure at 750+ languages. These languages have been recognised by the Indian State in various capacities: India doesn't have a national language. Hindi and English serve as official languages of India. The VIII schedule of languages, which reads "Languages", in 2013 recognises around 22 languages, whose development and enrichment the Government of India actively promotes. And then there is the rest of the lot. So we have a pyramid like arrangement, with Hindi and English forming the apex of the pyramid, the schedule languages, the mid-part and the rest of the languages, as the base of the pyramid.

As one would expect, given the socio-economic framework adopted by the Indian State, there was a great degree of elitism in the selection and development of languages. Thus, for example, out of the 40+ languages spoken in Maharashtra, it was Marathi which was selected as part of the VIII Schedule. Further, the particular variety of Marathi chosen to be developed and standardised reflected the dominance of particular social groups, rather than the entire population. Groups such as linguistic minorities, migrants, marginalised communities have been vulnerable vis-à-vis the dominant community in a given region and often, in the name of social integration, the needs and rights of these groups have been sidelined.

It is from this crucible of struggles, identities, adaptations, etc, that the relationships between nation development, citisen, identity and language have emerged. The struggle, for many, right from the beginning, was two-fold: one was against the colonisers and the other against the elite within the same society. Thus, while the elites and the lower classes/castes in India collaborated against the colonial rule, it often happened that the new institutions and practices, especially in the field of education and the army, introduced by the colonisers, often had the effect of providing space for the lower classes/castes to break free from the oppressive practices of their community. Savitribai Phule's poems on 'Mother English' can be seen in this context.

Given this sort of dynamics, the issue of making of citizens, as well as identity, can no longer be seen in terms of homogeneous communities, as often is the tendency but rather as a process of negotiation between different interests among and within communities. Identity is not always something which people seek to preserve and maintain but it can be something which one might want to discard, at least some aspects of it. One may not always find something valuable in the traditional notions of identity, especially if one belongs to the oppressed classes which have suffered hundreds of years of backwardness at the hands of elites of their own community. The process of demarginalisation may involve throwing away one's ethnicities, traditions and cultures. The issue of citisenship is inherently linked with this oppression and backwardness. Citisenship without social justice is just not possible.

The deepening of the democratic processes and the partial empowerment of the middle and lower strata of society led to the demand for a greater and more meaningful access to the institutions and processes of democracy. A logical consequence, in the field of languages, would have been to extend access to the developed languages to these strata as well as include the language varieties used by these strata in the scheme of things and develop them for use in government and other formal occasions. This move would have, in tune with the letter and spirit of the Constitution, strengthened the promise of nation building and citisenship, within the framework of social justice. But what happened instead was a shift in the function of nation-states. The processes of globalisation gathered momentum in the last quarter of the twenteeth century. This was accompanied by the defeat of socialism in the Soviet Union, which gave the forces of globalisation a free hand. These events meant that the conceptualisation and development of languages in the nationalist framework took a backseat in the light of an alternative conceptualisation in the framework of globalisation.

Globalisation, most commonly, refers to a wide range of human activities, incorporating distinct socio-political, economic and cultural trends which are related to the spread of "free" market policies in the world economy to an extent never experienced before. Accompanying this economic liberalisation is the perceived domination of western forms of political, economic and cultural life. One also talks about the development and spread of new information and communication technologies throughout the world. One of the most dominant images of globalisation is that of the uninhibited flow of capital, labour, resources across national and natural boundaries. The huge asymmetry in the directionality of flow and transfer, and the socio-economic distress that it is creating are real issues, but there is no denying the fact that the scale at which different forms of human labour and natural resources are being *transferred* is unprecedented. This flow is characterised by:

1. *Deterritorialisation.* According to which, a growing variety of social activities takes place, irrespective of the geographical location of the participants.
2. Growth of social *interconnectedness* across existing geo-graphical and political boundaries.
3. The *speed* or *velocity* of the flow. There seems to be a compression of space and time made possible by social and political developments, accompanied by technological advances.

Globalisation should be understood as a *multi-pronged* process, since deterritorialisation, social interconnectedness, and acceleration manifest themselves in many different (economic, political, and cultural) arenas of social activity. The concept of globalisation preserves the existence of nation-states as units and presupposes a stratification and compartmentalisation of the world for its *space of experience*. The modern state is likely to look more like a source of continuing globalisation, or more accurately, a vehicle of globalisation, than its victim.

Globalisation is also a *transformation* of the available structures and it is this property which sets it apart from the previous stages of capitalism. If the term globalisation is used as shorthand to a cluster of arrangements and priorities, which promotes a transnational global mobility and a massively increased intensity of commercial and cultural exchange, then these arrangements and priorities have changed in order to perpetuate the ability of flow to transgress the stratification and compartmentalisation, which globalisation presupposes for its functioning. One witnesses a shift from building a sovereign nation and citisens to creation of conditions for 'free markets' and management of 'labour markets, without changing their basic identity, or fundamentally disrupting their capacity to act. The vagaries of the stock market and speculative capital keep the governments on their toes, for now they need to ensure that there is no panic which would lead to the flight of capital. The flow of capital seems to be the determining factor as far as government actions are concerned and not the needs of its own people, who may have elected the government. In other words, globalisation both presupposes the existence of nation-states and transgresses its sovereignty. If the basis of nation states is no longer the creation of sovereign, then the citisen can only be defined in cultural terms, rather than in terms of rights and duties. This explains why economic liberalism has often been inaugurated during periods of sustained right wing/conservative periods of political office (as in many countries of Europe) or with the entire society taking rightward 'tilts' (as in India). This connection can easily be understood if we grasp the anti-democratic nature of globalisation.

We have observed that globalisation is a multi-pronged process and that it has effects in the domain of culture. It is important to note that cultures of globalisation, as opposed to global cultures, are distinct expressions of particular cultures, now projected as universal, but every culture needs a space to be experienced and spaces are local in nature. Therefore, the cultures of globalisation are indigenised, with local cultures providing the necessary 'tadka' and also an illusion of authenticity. Such 'glocal' processes can be clearly seen in cultures of food, clothing, music, films, lifestyles, etc. As far as languages are concerned, we have forms like Hinglish and Pinglish which serve as labels to the language-use of Hindi/Punjabi and English speakers. Globalisation, thus, produces hybridity and multiplicity through its homogenising tendencies.

This is not to claim that previous cultures were 'pure' and that pure is in some way better. In fact, pure cultures do not exist. It is in the nature of humans to interact and diffuse, But, historically, this process of diffusion has been 'bottom-up' in nature and a gradual one, i.e., initiated by people over a period of time. The hybridity produced by globalisation is basically 'top-down' in nature, i.e., brought in by market forces with ferocity hitherto unknown to mankind. So what we have is a network of cultural flows which is undoubtedly hegemonic and imperialistic as it seeks to impove-rish and even destroy the cultures which have evolved over centuries.

The effect this clash of 'hybridities' has on languages depends upon the communicative potential of languages. The communicative potential of languages is not an intrinsic property of languages but is determined by the socio-economic conditions of their existence. These conditions enhance or constrain the linguistic capital of languages i.e., the linguistic resources available in the language. Languages offering opportunity for direct communication with the larger number of people are believed to have a higher communicative potential. This communicative potential of a language, rather than depending upon the number of native speakers of the language, depends upon whether the language has been acquired as a foreign one by a large number of bilingual individuals. Such languages provide an indirect connection with a third language, through interpretation or translation. Thus, though German and Punjabi have similar number of native speakers (around 90 million), the communicative potential of German is higher as German is acquired by a larger number of second language learners and thus offers a wider communication access.

Let us see the effect of the clash of hybridities on languages with high, medium and low communicative potential.We have identified globalisation with flow: the flows across territories and social spaces are that of resources – natural and cultural – in a commodified form. This is more so *vis-a-vis* language especially with respect to 'knowledge economies'. If the flows are to be uninhibited, there is a need for effective communication systems. This involves access to 'international' languages – mainly English - which is then commodified and sold by various agencies such as British Library through activities like TESOL and TOEFL. But these international languages are not rooted in the spaces where they are consumed and are something imposed from above. Therefore, these international languages have to engage with the 'local' languages for social space, through which 'authentic experience' needed for creation of meanings to the consumer can be obtained. The effect this engagement has on English is multi-fold. For one, English is indegenised, creating multiple standards of speaking English. Of course, 'proper English' is marked and sold but one cannot really control the production and English as per the 'standard norms', as English is itself despatialised. One can easily imagine a situation where English is indegenised in so many local spaces that it would make no sense to call it 'one' language. This sub-version of English language, as a system, would pose a real danger to the unity of the language-system, making English an 'endangered' language is a very special sense.

From an institutional perspective, the rapidly expanding reach of English would provide English with a level of communicative potential not seen before. This is because language is a resource which gains in utility as it gathers more users. As a result of the expansion of English due to globalisation, we are witnessing a huge expansion in the number of texts available in English. Larger the number of text available, greater will be the tendency to learn the language, rather than depend upon the availability of translations. A speaker of English has to spend little effort to access much of the cultural resources across the globe. This leads to a rise in second language learners of English. With the increase in second language learners, the communicative potential of the language increases. The process spirals up exponentially. The success of English will no longer depend upon the nationality of global powers. Even if countries like USA decline as global powers, the domination of English will continue as long as we look upon language as a commodity. This is another sense in which English is despatialised: its power no longer depends upon the economic status of its 'native speakers'.

Languages like Marathi find themselves in an intermediate position. Marathi has been developed and standardised. It is the language of the state and, therefore, receives state patronage. This makes Marathi an attractive option for the non-Marathi speakers living in the state, especially those who speak languages with low communicative potential. This includes dialects of Marathi, languages spoken by tribals, etc. This process has increased the reach of Marathi, and thereby its communicative potential, at the expense of other languages spoken in Maharashtra. This increase in potential of Marathi makes it a viable object of engagement as far as the international languages are concerned. Given the power and reach of English, this engagement affects Marathi in several ways:

We observe a language shift as far as the domains in which Marathi is used. To observe the tussle between English and Marathi over domains, one has only to visit a mall in Mumbai and Pune. Inside the mall, English is replacing Marathi as the language of the market. A similar effect can be observed in the field of knowledge: knowledge production is increasingly being made in English. The effect of this can be observed in the enrolment levels of Marathi schools, which have till now been known to have imparted good quality education to its students. A recent obser-vation in a school in Mumbai indicates that the enrolment rates per standard have fallen from 150 to 50 over the past 15 years. Where have the students gone? The answer is pretty obvious. The domain of Marathi use is shrinking rapidly. Marathi is increasingly being relegated to the domain of culture': a marker of authenticity (which is then commodified and sold), a language for subjective attachment towards local roots, while English is 'objective' and the language of knowledge. The division of labour is clear: English offers economic progress and Marathi spiritual progress. What is this means in a world which is projected as moving towards 'knowledge economies' is not hard to predict.

A corollary of this division is that the users of Marathi depend upon English for information and knowledge. A visit to any newspaper office will give us a fair idea of this process. For national and international news, papers are increasingly depending upon English sources. This makes Marathi newspapers a major centre for translation. This is, of course, true not only for newspapers but other forms of media too. Publications in Marathi are carrying content obtained from English to a much larger extent than before. The danger in this sort of engagement is brought out clearly in an anecdote involving the noted write U.R. Ananthmurthy. Once on a visit to Seoul, Ananthmurthy visited a three storeyed Korean bookshop. He asked for a book which had Korean 'content' but failed to get one. The bookshop had books like 'Dummies....', 'Chicken Soup for the Soul...',etc, all in the Korean language but not in content. So the bookshop sold Korean language books in a formal sense but not in any substantive one. Given the rising dominance of English in the field of knowledge production, languages like Marathi too are facing the same danger. An hour with a Marathi RJ on F.M. radio should be enough to convince us of that. Of course, form cannot be totally divorced from content. Content influences form, it creates its own structures of expres-sion. We can, therefore, expect English like expressions in Marathi. The process, of course, is underway: consider the use of pronouns, adjectives, inflections on nouns, etc, in Marathi - they are becoming more like those of English.

What this indicates is that the communicative potential of English increases by impoverishing languages like Marathi. Therefore, the spread of English is imperialistic in nature. But given the huge gap between the linguistic capital of English and Marathi, one would not see a struggle between the two languages. Marathi would rather seek to find its place in the imperial network of world languages, rather than struggle with the more powerful languages. Language struggle exists only between languages which compete for use in the same power related function. English, in this sense, is far beyond its reach. The demand for Marathi as one subject in English medium schools, instead of a demand for good quality Marathi schools, clearly defines the scope of the struggle. The struggle is more intense with languages like Hindi, with which Marathi has to compete for its place. It is in this sense that Hindi is seen to pose a challenge to Marathi, rather than English.

Let us now consider the situation of the less powerful languages: those languages with low communicative potential. These form more than 90 per cent of the world's languages and are spoken by less than 4per cent of the world's population. Many of these languages function almost entirely without script, media, or records. Most of these languages have been brought to the brink of extinction. The situation is quite alarming. UNESCO's Safeguarding Endangered Languages website estimates that "over 50 per cent of some 6,700 languages spoken today are in danger of disappearing," and that "one language disappears on an average every two weeks."According to more pessimistic, but still realistic, estimates, there might be only 300 to 600 oral languages left in 2100 A.D. as unthreatened languages, transmitted by the parent generation to children.These would probably include most of the languages that have more than one million speakers today. Almost all languages about to disappear would be indigenous, and most of today's indigenous languages would disappear, with the exception of very few, which are strong numerically (for example Quechua, Aymara, Bodo, Mapuche) and/ or have official status (like Maori, and some Saami languages). Tribals, who constitute about 8 per cent of our population, account for about 75 per cent of our languages. Most of these languages face extinction in the near future. They just cannot survive the onslaught of the market forces without the help of state intervention. The amount of damage this loss would create can only be imagined. It is here that the effects of globalisation of language conflicts become evident. As we have seen, globalisation seeks to change the function of the state. The state can no longer be primarily concerned with the welfare and needs of its people, but rather with maintaining favourable conditions for the market. So any space for development and maintenance of languages outside the ambit of the market is necessarily diminishing. This is where globalisation is different from the previous versions of capitalism. The advent of capitalism and nation-states led to the development of certain widely spoken languages under the state's patronage. The peripheral languages were woefully ignored and left to fend for themselves. Development and maintenance of these peripheral languages seemed to be the step forward, but what actually happened was that the states relinquished their function to the market forces. So what we get is a vicious circle, a black hole created by globalisation which seeks to suck in the majority of human languages into extinction.

Thus, the forces of globalisation create a hierarchical order of languages where the international languages, mainly English, rapidly grow in their communicative potential and, in the process, impoverish languages like Marathi and bring 90per cent of our languages on the verge of extinction. Thus, the accumulation of the linguistic capital of English is taking place by the deflation and dispossession of the linguistic capital of other languages.

Whether the local/national languages will continue to subsidise the richer languages or find a social space to develop on its grounds, will depend upon the outcome of the struggle between the nationalistic agenda, based within the framework of social justice, and that of the market. One can observe this struggle in the varying interpretations of RTE. Some wish to interpret the provisions of RTE through the rationality of the market –education vouchers, English medium schools, etc., – while others see RTE being interpreted as a right to mother tongue education. Which interpretation gains an upper hand will decide to a large extent the future of our languages: the latter will lay the foundation for enrichment and development of our languages, while the former will make RTE an engine for linguistic genocide in this country. The choice is, of course, ours.

## References:

Bartelson , J. ( 2000 ) Three concepts of globalisation. *International Sociology* 15 (2): 180 – 96 .

Bauman , Z. ( 1998 ) *Globalisation: The Human Consequences*. Cambridge : Polity

Blommaert , J. ( 2003 ) A sociolinguistics of globalisation. Commentary . *Journal of Sociolinguistics* 7 : 607 – 23 .

Castells, M. (1991) *The Informational City: Information Technology, Economic Restructuring, and the Urban-Regional Process*. Oxford: Blackwell.

Friedman, T. (2000) The Lexus and the Olive Tree: Understanding Globalisation (New York: Anchor Books).

Hannerz , U. ( 1996 ) *Transnational Connections*. London : Routledge .

Krauss , M. ( 1992 ) The world ' s languages in crisis. *Language* 68 (1): 4 – 10.

Lash , S. , and Urry , J. ( 1994 ) *Economies of Signs and Space* . London : Sage.

Mufwene , S. (2008) *Language Evolution: Contact, Competition and Change*. London: Continuum.

Mühlhäusler , P. (2003) *Language of Environment – Environment of Language. A Course in Ecolinguistics*. London: :Battlebridge .

Panitch, L. (1994) 'Globalisation and the State', *Socialist Register*, pp. 60–93. London: The Merlin Press.

Phillipson , R. ( 2008b ) Lingua franca or lingua frankensteinia? English in European integration and globalisation. *World Englishes*27 ( 2 ): 250 – 84.

Sassen (1996) *Losing control? Sovereignty in An Age of Globalisation* (New York: Columbia University Press, 1996) Series : University seminars — Leonard Hastings Schoff memorial lectures.

Scholte, J.-A. (1996) 'The Geography of Collective Identities in a Globalising World', *Review of International Political Economy* 3(4): 565–607.

Scholte, J.-A. (1997) 'Global Capitalism and the State', *International Affairs* 73(3): 427–52.

Skutnabb - Kangas , T. ( 2000 ) *Linguistic Genocide in Education – Or Worldwide Diversity and Human Righs?* Mahwah, NJand London, UK : Lawrence Erlbaum Associates . [South Asian updatededition: Delhi, Orient BlackSwan, 2008.]

Thompson, G. (1999) 'Introduction: Situating Globalisation', *International Social Science Journal* 51(2): 139–52.

Wierzbicka , A. ( 2006 ) *English: Meaning and Culture*. Oxford: Oxford University Press.

# 8

# Dalit fiction and the Urban Problematic: Reading Manu Joseph's 'Serious Men'

—*Abhishek Das*

In his seminal work, *Homo Hierchicus*, Louis Dumont attempted to define the mechanism of caste in the Indian society by positing that the principle of hierarchy in the caste system was the conflict between the 'pure' and the 'impure'. He claimed that, under such circumstances, the concepts of 'superiority' and 'superior purity' became synonymous in their implication and ideologically, the distinction of purity became the foundation of *status* in the society. Dumont's exposition highlighted the inherent exploitative hierarchy that has plagued the Indian society for long and through the ages, and has threatened to destroy the *fabric of the nation* with unhindered arrogance. The asymmetrical access to authority and influence was posited as a normative social requirement and with the onset of the colonial rule, it attained the institutional backing of the alleged 'secular' administrative set up.

However, fortunately for the persecuted section, there have always been voices of dissent in several eras who virulently criticised the inhuman and dehumanising practice of caste in the Indian social landscape. Several voices were brutally stifled, strangulated and eventually silenced, but a few escaped and through their perseverance tried to chart a path of rebellion and redemption. Dr B.R. Ambedkar's status as such a visionary who fought to defy the dictums of traditional caste satraps and dared to envision a radical future for his systematically denigrated brethren, needs no new fillip. His tireless efforts to ensure that the victims of history got their human dues and his corresponding quest to comprehend the fundamentals of the caste problematic made him the towering figure and a luminary who illuminated the lives of millions. His prescriptive discourse premised upon the narrative of self-dignity of the untouchables and his monumental contribution towards metamorphosing the untouchables into Dalits would stand any rigorous historical yardstick. Dr Ambedkar realised, much before his contemporaries, that the oppressive potential of the caste machinery was embedded in the characteristically 'isolated' and 'self-contained' peasant communities in the pre-dominantly rural hinterland of India. Hence, in several of his corrective discourses, he urged the Dalits to migrate to the urban space and fervently argued that the urbane ethos and the solace of anonymity offered by the cosmopolitanism of the cities would act as a curative to reverse the ills of the diabolical caste system.

This paper will attempt to interrogate the potential of the urban space as a neutralising entity, and would try to unravel the insidious manner in which the caste system operates, thereby continuing the narrative of victimisation. The Ambedkarite discourse of progress premised upon a 'right-based' understanding of the caste problematic and which depended substantially on the success of the secular state as a guarantee for mitigating caste from the national consciousness would also be analysed. It would endeavour to argue that in an acutely casteist nation that organises all its spaces-rural and urban, isolated and cosmopolitan in a manner that replicates the 'asymmetrical relations', the access to social, cultural and national resources are manipulated in a covert and overt manner, bypassing the constitutional safeguards assured by the state executive. This paper would look at, Manu Joseph's 'Serious Men', a possible entrant to the Dalit cannon. Through a minute textual analysis, the paper would try to support its proposition that the urban and rural sphere, irrespective of their respective idiosyncratic functioning, are united in their redundant association with casteist values. However, the intention is not to indulge in a superficial act of comparison but to point at the tragic irony that binds the two spaces, notwithstanding the giant strides the nation claims to have taken in the realm of material progress. Instead, this is precisely the Achilles' heel that the paper wants to highlight: Caste operates at the ideational, level, as well as in the material, and any attempt to rectify the system without taking both the aspects into consideration would only belie the possibility of resuscitation. This paper will also explore the traditional modes of protest which need to be reanalysed and new subversive carnivalesque spirit, infused in the already existing narrative of rights.

The narrative of material progress that the urban centric model induces as part of its promise to mitigate the effects of caste hides the primary fact that part of that growth can be attributed to the *cheap* labour of the Dalit migrants from the villages who are only allowed to earn the right to live a life in the ghettoes in return.The illumination of the glittering city life perennially escapes them and they are forced to wallow in the reality of unfulfilled dreams. It is within this condition of apathy that we first encounter Ayan Mani,the Dalit protagonist of Joseph's novel. Mani lives the death of his ambitions every day in a *chawl* where the 'congestion of *hopeless* shuffling human bodies' regularly quarrelled with fate in 'small dark rooms' and the '*endless* corridor of gloom'. It is the tragic irony of *modern* India that an author,writing about a Dalit protagonist, is more often than not forced to envision a *living hell* as the space his character inhabits.The permanent residence in the City's dark underbelly becomes a *de-facto* setting for the struggling Dalit humanity.Thus even when the city of dreams, Mumbai, reveals herself in all her magnificence, the readers encounter Ayyan Mani as an *outside observer* struggling to gain an entry and a subsequent foothold in the urban social scape. It is only telling that we first meet Mani sitting in the crowded sea-beach in Mumbai, observing the multitude from a distance. To a conscious reader, the implication would be unmistakable. Mani himself is *invisible* in the whole process, a situation the Dalits have always faced in a society that has worked over time to deny them visibility. Even within the *great corridors of power* in the institute where Mani works for his living, his presence is *ghost-like,* merely like a fleeting 'shadow' leaving no permanent mark of his existence. One is almost reminded of the practice whereby the Dalits were forced to tie a broom to the waste to wipe off their *footmarks* from the earth they walked upon. The figurative *erasure* once practiced enters the urban,educated world as a metaphor for *inconsequence.* The razzmatazz of Mumbai leaves out the Dalit who is accorded the *fate* of a man where the "...frailties of the male folk showed all the time in the tired faces of the newly dead, or in the vacant eyes of drunkards, or the resigned calm of jobless boys who just sat for hours watching the world go by". So much for the affirmative actions proposed by the Indian polity!

In this world of low expectations and resigned fatalism and even lower material achievements, the threat of potential emasculation looms over permanently as a deathly pall. Joseph's acerbic description of Mani's young son, Adi's childish re-enactment of the act of copulation on the terrace of the *chawl* and the *curious* acceptance of it by the onlookers is a depiction of a wretched reality where even the most private act of marital consummation becomes a public affair owing to the lack of living (and breathing) space. This merging of the public and the private realms is not a matter of choice for the Dalits, but a tragic reaffirmation of their *dehumanised* reality. Even in the sprawling urban space, they suffer from a form of forced spatial segregation owing to their lowly professional prospects, a direct corollary of their caste position. It is the illogical insistence on the continuity of caste based professional scheme that a sweeper's son is still expected to take up a broom and sentence himself to a life committed to hardships. Even an exception like Ayan Mani who achieves a *legendary* status in his *chawl* by becoming a government peon cannot afford a world outside the slime and grime of the BBD slum, an erstwhile prison building under the British.

Sukhdeo Thorat's investigative work, '*Dalits in India: Search for a common Destiny*' seems to unravel a similar roadmap on probing the *problematic* in the context of the *neoliberal* Indian state, the product of the liberalisation, Globalisation and privatisation policies of the 1990s introduced with much fan-fare. Recent surveys by leading newspapers have shown how the Indians have merely embraced the economic and cultural dimension of globalisation and, at the same time, fervently *guarded* their private space from being *contaminated.* It is against this background of deliberate refusal to look beyond the veneer that Manu Joseph's protagonist functions. He is the alleged *beneficiary* of the opportunities provided by an egalitarian welfare state, but yet his extraordinary talent, reflected in his IQ score of 148, merely invokes a sneer in the highest intellectual echelon.The contempt that the upper caste intellectuals shower him with at hearing about his accomplishments is followed by a snide remark on his 'reserved' status, amply reflecting the epidemic refusal of Dalit talent even in the alleys of a cosmopolitan space!

In fact, one could like to argue that in the post 1990 world of economic liberalisation and Globalisation, a new hostility has been systematically ingrained in the social matrix against the Dalits who sought material accomplishments. The curbing of economic *profligacy* on the part of the state since *that* era had, on the obverse side, the overwhelming emergence of the private sector as the mightier employer. Subsequently, as Tapan Basu points out, "For the urban middle classes (*predominantly upper castes, one may add*) in India, the single largest constituency for university level education globalisation betokened new aspirations, as well as new anxieties". The reduction in Government spending and the fast vanishing prospects of a secure Government job for the upper caste irked them immensely. This resulted in a heightened sense of enmity towards the Dalits who were then construed as the 'illegitimate' beneficiaries of State's largesse and violent protests were organised to *rectify* the imbalance. However, the historical truth that was conveniently forgotten in this melee and which comes out in a telling fashion in Meillasox's observation in Tapan Basu's argument is "That the constraints imposed by caste already ensured the siphoning of surplus wealth by a few sections of the Indian society at the expense of very many sections. Hence, in the context of such a society, analysis of material power cannot be divorced from an analysis of the ideational power, each of which inextricably expresses itself through the caste system".

But the intention of this paper is not to endorse the disproportionately large emphasis on *reservation* as a tool of Dalit empowerment. Instead, one may point out that the political and economic impetus that the state can provide in the name of *positive discrimination* is only a partial solution. The Dalit predicament cannot be understood within the rubric of class mobility. Instead, the psychological implications of being a Dalit should be emphasised upon. In the new economic scenario where monetary considerations and the ethos of economic utilitarianism becomes the watchwords, the pain of social rejection of Dalits, their inability to participate in community rituals, the claim for belonging in the intellectual space must not be overlooked. It is callously assumed that moving up the class ladder will automatically ensure gradual erasure of the Dalit identity. A country like India is characterised by an ardent and hypocritical orthodoxy where the public space alone is exclusively reserved for business and the market and deliberate amnesia regarding, caste is accepted and in the more private temple of personal dealings, casteist understanding of reality is rampant. But we need to ask if the personal and the public spheres are as separate as they are portrayed to be. Isn't the public dictated by the personal, and *vice versa*? And if that is so, doesn't the public sphere merely bear the illusion of castelessness? Godelier points at this when he observes, "in a society such as that of India, in which there is not yet a decisive differentiation between the ideational and material levels of existence, the institutions of family and business, for instance, often intertwine and impinge upon either level, caste too belongs to both strata."

The misplaced notions about a kind of 'intellectual purity' instil in the benefactors of casteism, an arrogance which allow them to claim the nation with its urban and rural spaces as their realm of dominance. Even an supposedly democratic instrument like the media, which dominates much of the urban social psyche, is inflicted by a similar sense of apathy and suspicion towards the Dalits, albeit under the guise of benevolent wonder. Thus, Adi's *supernormal* achievements as a wonder kid gets subsumed by the consideration that such an *achiever* came from a yet ignored corner of the city scape inhabited by the lower castes. This is an attitude that finds frequent mention in several reports in the same media, about talented Dalit students who commit suicide within the sanctified precincts of prestigious institutes of higher education, being unable to cope with nagging casteist taunts. This is the urban cosmopolitanism that promises to accord a sense of comforting anonymity. In reality it thus remains a persistent space of exploitation with modified punitive measures for *transgressors* who defy caste. We have to stop here for a moment and ask ourselves and the polity if India has *really* put the past of Omprakash Valmiki behind where the lower caste children were made to sit in segregated class-rooms and who survived on the morsels left over by the upper castes? Unlike the children of yore the lower caste students reach the thresholds of universities though, but to what avail? The taunts and the persecution still persist!

It would not be out of place to mention, at this juncture, a recent media report about casteist arrangements within a police barrack situated in a prominent north Indian capital city.This is the evident form of extreme institutionalised violence within the urban realm which co-exists with other surreptitious forms of casteist discrimination, both religious and secular in nature.

Thus, even in the twenty first century, several prominent north and south Indian religious shrines in the cities and outskirts openly assert their right to refuse entry to Dalits and the government determinedly looks on the other side unsure of its potential to fight the casteist populace. This is a severe reminder of the continuing existence of deplorable practices forced on the Dalits in the 19th and 20th century, India by the upper castes to ensure that the *polluting* contact with the Dalit was mitigated. India might not have the practice of tying spittoons around the necks of the *untouchables* to save the upper caste from contamination from contact anymore, but stopping a devotee of the almighty from entering the premises of a temple, even decades after the Temple entry movement, does provide a ludicrous picture like the one seen by Fa- Hien on his visit to India, in the medieval era. The spectacle of a human being with a broom tied to his back, an empty plate in his hand and a broken drum to warn people of his presence is a tragic instance of physical denigration of a human being, forcing him to look and act like a strange animal, and not a biped with human consciousness.

However, the emergence of organisations withThe *Bahujan samaj* vision and the ideological impetus provided by the Dalit Panther movement and other subsequent Dalit Rights group has instilled a certain degree of radical political consciousness that is reflected more in the activities and ideological moorings of Dalit individuals inhabiting the urban terrain and less so in the rural areas. This might have to do with the slightly increased degree of literacy in the towns and cities, as compared to the villages. It may also be because of the general degree of political awareness that a city can enforce, owing to its proximity to the seat of political power.This can often be construed as an empowering prospect for an otherwise marginalised Dalit individual.

Thus, we see how Ayyan Mani can manipulate the Brahmanised institution of higher science through his clever use of technology, media and his ability to create a network *of* oppressed individuals. It is also significant that Mani can ensure the support of the local Dalit politicians to triumph over the casteist scientists. But Mani's machinations and his subsequent triumph can't be perceived as instances of absolute success. Under the veneer of Bakhtinian *carnivalesque*, it should not escape the notice of the informed readers that Mani is still left with a minor job of a peon and a life of ever imminent poverty and a sub human prison cell like room at the very end. He might have played a decisive role in the battle of Brahmins in the institute, but it is still Arvind Acharya who reclaims his life at the end after his *Mani-aided* triumph over Jana Namboodiri. Though Mani is given the *right* to look after the acharya, it is by no means a fitting job for an exceptionally talented individual like Ayyan Mani. Even the political help he garners from the local leader is of little symbolical significance, as the leader's own credentials are suspect and Mani might well be the scape-goat in the future if the leader need-based disposition and preferences for ally changes consequent to demands of politics. Even the promise of mass based Dalit organisation in the urban setting seems like a far cry, as the youth who turn up for the riot might have been the same listless and purposeless boys from BBD *chawl* resigned to an eternal fate of joblessness, and ironically, it is the inability of the city to accommodate the material demands of its oppressed inhabitants that turn them into weapons in the hands of scheming leaders of dubious credibility. There are ample examples from contemporary Indian political scenario, whereby uneducated as well as educated, jobless sections of the Dalit youth has been used by opportunist mass leaders to further their own selfish aspirations.

Does the urban space provide any guarantee against such a possibility? In fact, recent experiences point towards the opposite. Unlike that in the west, industrialisation-induced rapid urbanisation in India has failed to overhaul the retrograde mind-set of the city dwellers. It is primarily because the migrants to the city were accorded jobs on the basis of the caste that they failed to wipe off during their city-ward journey. Therefore, rarely have these been instances where the village washerman's son has taken up the job as a school teacher or a cobbler or tanner's son was allowed a position in the city's temples. The best that may be claimed is that the city space for the Dalits is only infused with a problematic potential. The problematic potential or the problematic and potential thus needs more probing before we lose ourselves in the euphoria of development. Our failure to do so would be a sad reflection of our partial attitude to a vast multitude of our historically deprived countrymen and I am sure this is an image we cannot afford to live with any longer.

# 9

# Dalit Movement in Gujarat: Response of the Society and State- An Overview

*—Rajesh Lakum and Jagannatham Begari*

This paper is an attempt to examine the notion of caste violence and atrocities on Dalits and the response of the state and society in Gujarat. The Dalits face humiliation and discrimination based on their social status which raises the question of human rights violence. It is found that it is because of multiple forms of discrimination that had taken place against Dalits. This further gave the scope further to interrogate dalit assertions from the perspective from below. This paper also an attempt to critically examine the notion of caste violence and atrocities on Dalits in India. Notwithstanding these, the paper examines the concept of identity, movement, political mobilisation, institutional inequalities, caste discrimination, deprivation and violence which persists in India. It further evaluates the notion of purity, pollution, humiliation and deprivation. It further envisages the social, economic, political and cultural aspects which are responsible for the violence on dalits. The study is based on both the secondary sources and empirical study and used the purposive sample and exploratory method. To study the notion of humiliation, exclusion and marginality, this paper focuses on caste violence and Dalit movement in Gujarat. It is found that not many studies which explored the dalit movement in Gujarat, therefore, this paper is an attempt to fill the research gap.

## Conceptualisation of Caste

India has the world most popular democracy continues to have a vibrant media, an active civil society, a respected judiciary, however, witness human rights violations. According to 2011, custodian killings, police abuses including torture on dalits and failure to implement policies to protect vulnerable communities in India. It is interesting to note that India has yet to abolish laws or change policies that allow de jure and de facto impunity for human rights violations and the State has failed to prosecute even known perpetrators of serious abuses (HRW, World Report, 2012, pp. 328-33).

Violence could take place on individuals and groups such as domestic abuse, homicide, threats, robbery and so on. however, in the legal institutions, veryoften, carry out organised violence based on the notion of racist and sexist principles. The institutional violence in the world persists systematically which is more powerful. Institutional violence take place on the weaker sections who are usually weak. The rich powerful elites are rarely subjected to institutional violence because of their dominant position. The atrocities and violence carried out by powerful institutions but they don't defend atrocities by the claim of self-defense (Chomsky)[1]. Therefore, it argues that by using democratic space and with the help of political weapon, the violence could be reduced (Schwarzmantel, 2011, p. vii. The violence is not limited to areas of militarised violence. However, it expanded gender violence, class and caste violence; social violence; political instability; state-sanctioned intimidation; structural violence; unorganised crime and genocidal violence (Kenneth Bush, Colleen Duggen , 2013, p. 7). In the view of violence, it is pertinent to evaluate the caste violence conceptualised by Ambedkar.

B. R. Ambedkar argued that Caste has anti-social and "Caste has killed public spirit. Caste has destroyed the sense of public charity. Caste has made public opinion impossible. A Hindu's public is his caste and his responsibility is only to his caste and his loyalty is restricted only to his caste. Virtue has become caste-ridden and morality has become caste bound. There is no sympathy to the deserving and there is no appreciation of the meritorious and there is no charity to the needy. Suffering as such calls for no response. Though there is charity, however, it begins with the caste and ends with the caste. There is sympathy but not for man of other caste" (Ambedkar, 1979, p. 56). Caste violence erupted involving various caste groups to fight for their share in the resources of production and power in society. While caste conflicts might have existed for centuries, it has become heavily accentuated and has assumed endemic properties in contemporary times. The growing politicisation of the socially backward, economically aspiring, politically ascendant and traditionally weaker castes of Indian society, especially the scheduled castes, had led the members of these castes to assert and secure their lawful right and to resist any oppression by the dominant upper castes. Caste violence is a violence of the oppressed against the oppressor and demand for equality and justice (Verma, 2011, pp. 52-53). In any society dominant and subordinated classes, as well as their ideologies and narratives of the past and present do not exist in isolation but exist in conflict. Oppressors cannot be with the oppression as being against the oppressed is essence of oppression. Thus is ideology that serves the interests of one group subverts the interests of the other (Mani, 2005, p. 13).

The terms exclusion and marginality refers to the humiliation faced by the marginalised sections since the ages. The Dalit assertion is active basically through asymmetries of intersecting sets of attitudes- arrogance and obeisance, self-respect and servility, and reverence and repulsion. It continues to survive in different forms depending upon the specific nature of the social context. This involves the dynamics of social life with contradictory responses offered by the modern elite. Thus, on the one hand, the dynamics of social life shakes this social elite from the humiliating social protocols that regulate feudal society, on the other, these so called modern social elites tend to reproduce structures, both institution (state) and moral (friendship), that underlie and renew the phenomenon of humiliation. The reorganisation of modern society based on the division between the private and a public sphere which was accompanied by the possibility of misrecognition, degradation and humiliation. Transgression of the boundaries between the private and the public was considered as the context for humiliation. Secondly, the capacity to control the corporeal body in the public domain defines individual dignity and decency of the bourgeoisie society (Guru, 2009, pp. 1-2). In the light of this juncture, it is necessary to evaluate and interrogate concepts: such as dalits, exclusion and marginality.

## Interrogating the Dalits, Exclusion and Marginality

It seems that Indian society is highly stratified. The socio-economic situation of dalits and tribals is in the worst situation. Stephen Fuchs has argued that the caste system and untouchability developed after the arrival of the Aryans. The caste system, in India, is unique and not found elsewhere in the world (Michael, 1999, pp. 15-16). Significantly, the caste system segregated the Dalits from the rest of the society to such an extent that they were denied even the basic human rights. Denial of the right to drink water from any public well and to walk on the road were some of the notable examples of social persecution of the Dalits at the hands of the upper-caste Hindus (Mungekar, State, Market and the Dalits: Analytics of the New Econpmic Policy , 1999, p. 289). In the right to this, it is pertinent to explain and Conceptualise the term 'dalit'.

The term 'Dalit' is a Sanskrit term which means broken, crushed and oppressed. It also refers to burst, split, broken, downtrodden, scattered, crushed and destroyed. The word was first used by the British and then by Dr B.R. Ambedkar in his Marathi speech, *The Untouchable*, published in 1948. Later, the Dalit Panthers revived the term in their 1973 manifesto, extending its definition to include Scheduled Tribes, Neo-Buddhists, the working class, landless, poor people and women all those who are being exploited in terms of social, economic, political and cultural spheres in the name of religion (Jaganntham, 2009, pp. 257–280). The term implies a condition of being underprivileged and deprived of basic rights and refers to people who are suppressed on account of their lowly birth. It is understood that Dalits have been called by various names like untouchables, Harijans, depressed classes, outcastes and pariahs. In more ancient times, terms such as *Mlechha, Chandala, Panchama, Nishada, Avarna, Antyaja,* and *Atisudra* were the other names used for Dalits (Makawana, 2011). The Hindu religion is divided on the basis of the *Varna* system, as prescribed in the *Manusmiriti.* Evidence of caste hierarchy can be seen in the *Vedas.* The British Empire further recognised them as a depressed class in the 1931 census (Michael, 1999, p. 14). The term Scheduled castes appeared for the first time in April 1935, when the British government issued the Government of India (Scheduled Castes) Order, 1936, specifying certain castes, races and tribes as Scheduled Castes. Prior to that these groups were known as 'Depressed Classes'. Mahatma Gandhi coined them as Harijans, but B.R. Ambedkar did not accept the word '*Harijan*' and identified them as depressed classes (Michael, 1999, pp. 12-13). In the light of this, it is pertinent conceptualise the terms: marginalisation and social mobility.

## Marginalisation and Social Mobility

Marginality means location of a person, group, or a community practically "outside" the mainstream, through ideally the orientation may be towards it (Ram, 1995, pp. 200-201). Marginality may further be viewed in terms of relations between the centre and the periphery where a marginal man, or group, or community, located at the periphery, is practically deprived of all resources and opportunities, including the prestige esteem, though he/she or it may be part of a total system consisting both of the centre and the periphery. Therefore, marginalisation of such group of the people has been termed as marginality (Ram, 1995, pp. 202-203). Marginality has, however, been analysed qualitatively in the case of certain communities in India on the basis of their place in the economically productive roles, ethnic composition and cultural specification (Ram, 1995, p. 205). Considering marginality even in the sense of being "outside" the mainstream or located at the periphery either social or physical, it may be argued that the Scheduled Castes and more so the less mobile ones are marginal (Ram, 1995, p. 209).

S.K. Thorat argues that the exclusion and the denial of opportunity in economic spheres, denial in labour market in hiring for jobs, in capital market and through denial of access to capital, in agriculture land market and through denial in sale and purchase or leasing of land, in input market and consumer market denial in sale and purchase of commodities (Thorat, *ibid.*, p. 5). He further argues that in the present situation, the persons from Scheduled Castes suffer from discrimination and even exclusion from access to agricultural land. Evidence from the studies indicates that a high proportion of atrocities and violence against them are mainly related to issues of land. Therefore, the problem of landlessness of Scheduled Castes still continues in a serious proportion (Thorat, *ibid.*, p. 11). It is recognised that prevalence of market discrimination of certain social groups creates adverse consequences for economic growth, income distribution and can lead to inter-group conflict. Market discrimination can lead to income inequalities and high degree of deprivation for discrimination groups and induce inter-group conflict (Thorat, *ibid.*, p. 14). In the light of the conceptualisation of humiliation, exclusion and marginality, it is essential to probe by taking Gujarat state which is considered as a developed state and named the state as vibrant of Gujarat. However, it is found that there is a severe social discrimination and caste violence still take place in the Gujarat state. In this regard, it is necessary to evaluate the history of dalit movement and caste violence in Gujarat.

## The History of Dalits in Gujarat

The state of Gujarat is located in westernpart of India and shares a border and coastline line with Pakistan. The state of Gujarat is divided into three regions: Saurastra, North Gujarat and South Gujarat. The settlements probably started from the time of Indus valley civilisation. There were also *Harappan* centres[2], *Chandra gupta Maurya* assimilated Gujarat as an integral part of his empire which is an evident from several inscriptions. *Kumar Gupta*[3]-I, son and successor of *Chandra gupta*-II, ruled over Gujarat. Rocky inscriptions in the *Girnar* Hills show that the *Maurya* Emperor *Ashoka* extended his domain to Gujarat[4]. After the fall of the *Maurya* Empire, the *Sakas* and *Scythians* controlled the region[5]. Under *Rudradaman*, the area formed part of the *Gupta* Empire which was succeeded by the *Maitrika* dynasty. The Solanki[6] dynasty came to power when the state flourished in all fields. This was followed by the *Muslim* rule; *Ahmed*-I, the first independent *Muslim* ruler of Gujarat who founded Ahmedabad[7]. The *Mughal* Emperor *Akbar* conquered *Malwa* and Gujarat in the region remained under *Mughal* rule[8].

Gujarat was divided into several small princely states and the architecture of Gujarat is famous for its fine detail. Besides, the region has a long tradition of handicrafts, such as *Bandhini* (tie-dyed cloth), *Jari* (gold and silver embroidery), *Patola* (a beautifully patterned silk for which the thread is tied-dyed before being woven), perfumes and wood carvings. Gujarat was the chief centre of wood carving in India from at least the fifteenth century. Under *Mughal* rule, the region has developed foreign trade and commerce and initiated domestic manufacturing units and Gujarat the *Rajputs (Darbars)* who replaced the old *Zamindars,* survived feudal and locals. The state again got united in the twelfth century under *Muslim* rule as *Gurjar Rashtra* and signs of later *Mughal* rule. Wood carving in Gujarat in the *Mughal* Period[9] shows a beautiful synthesis of the indigenous and *Mughal* styles. Jain wooden pavilions of the late 16th and 17th centuries are richly sculptured with scenes from Jain mythology and contemporary life and with imaginative floral animal and geometrical motifs; figural sculpture has a great vivacity and rhythm.

After 1700 A.D., the *Dutch, English, French* and *Portuguese* established their bases along with the coastal region. The East India Company had set up its first headquarters[10] in India. As British maritime supremacy developed, the other European powers[11] went back. The state came under the control of the British East India Company in 1818.The land owning *Patels* benefited more from the land settlements under the British rule, and became landowners. The wealthiest of these are the Patidars. The region was divided into '*Sarkars' Paraganas* and *Mahals* for administrative convenience. This system had continued even in the British period. The land owning classes shifted from *Muslim Zamindaris* to *Hindu Rajput* chiefs. Under the British regime, the central and southern parts of Gujarat came directly under the British administration as part of the Bombay presidency, while other areas remained as princely states. After the First war of Indian independence in 1857, the British government ruled Gujarat directly and divided it into a number of princely states. Many wooden facades of the 19th century have been preserved, however, the ornamentation lacks the grace and movement of the earlier works (Edalji, 1986).

Followed by Indian independence in 1947, all parts of Gujarat, except *Saurastra* and Kutch, became part of Bombay state. The Bombay state was bifurcated into Maharashtra and Gujarat on 1st May 1960. More than half of Gujarat's population lives in the rural areas and is engaged in agriculture. The state has been divided into two distinct economic and geographic regions, namely, the main land Gujarat comprising *Mehsana, Sabarkantha*, and *Banaskanth*a on the northern border, *Ahmedabad, Gandhinagar, Kheda* and *Vadodar*a in Central Gujarat, *Panchmahal* in Eastern highland, Bharuch, *Surat, Valsad, Dang* Districts and *Navsari, Tapi* (*Vyara*) newly declared districts and divided from Surat in south Gujarat which includes coastal as well as hill regions.The peninsular Gujarat comprise *Kathiawad* (Saurastra) and *Kutch.* However, the development in the state is uneven.

> The Scheduled Caste population is stated to be 7.09 per cent and Scheduled Tribes comprise 14.76 per cent. The sex ratio has declined from 942 female per 1000 in year of 1981 to 920 female per 1000 male as per 2001 census. Gujarat consists of twenty four districts; the total villages of the state are 18,225. Out of these, 42.58 are urban and the rest rural. According to 2011 census, the population of Gujarat is 60,383,628, out of which 34,670,817 from the rural and 25,712, 81 from the urban. The total male population is 31,482,282; out of which 17,802,975 from the urban and 13,679,307 from the rural. The total female population of Gujarat is 28,901,346; out of which 16,867,842 from rural and 12,033,504 from urban.
>
> *If one interprets the population in of percentage, terms, total population is 60.38 million, out which 34.67 million from rural and 25.71 from the urban. The total literacy is 79.31; 73.00 for rural and 87.58 for urban.*

*The male total literacy rate is 87.23 out of which 83 from the rural and 97.44 from urban. The total female literacy rate is 70.73 out of which 62.41 from rural and 82.08 from urban.*[12]*According to 2011 census, total SC population in Gujarat is 6.75 per cent, in Kutch 12.37, Banaskantha 10.43, Patan 9.18, Ahmedabad 10.53, Surendranagar 10.22 and Junagadh 9.69 per cent SC population in Gujarat (Representative, 2013, p. 3). While the literacy rate in the State has increased, the gap between general and Scheduled Caste literacy rate has widened. The literacy rate among SCs 61.07 per cent, while the literacy among SCs male has been at par with general population, (61.29) the literacy among SC girls and women continues to lag behind. The State Government has to take effective measures to promote literacy amongst SCs girls and women* (Dr. P.L. Punia, Dr Shyam Agarwal, Mangat Ram Bali, Mange Ram, Arunkumar Singh, January-March 2012, p. 1).

**Table: 1. Population and Decadal Growth of SC, ST and Total Rural Population-All India**

| *Census* | *Population (Number in Lakhs)* | | | *Decadal Growth Rate (Per cent)* | | |
|---|---|---|---|---|---|---|
| | *Total* | *SC* | *ST* | *Total* | *SC* | *ST* |
| 1981 | 5238.66 | 912.05 | 504.48 | - | - | - |
| 1991 | 6286.91 | 1123.43 | 627.51 | 20.01 | 23.18 | 24.39 |
| 2001 | 7410.00 | 1330.11 | 773.39 | 17.86 | 18.40 | 23.25 |
| 2009-10 | 7417.38 | 1622.49 | 806.49 | - | - | - |

*Source:* Planning Commission, Tenth Five Year Plan 2002-07, Volume-2 and NSSO, Unit level data on Employment and Unemployment.

The total population of Gujarat according to 2001 Census is 50,671,017. Out of which 3,592,715 is from Scheduled Castes constitutes 7.1 percentage of the total population. In 2001 Census, of the total of 3,592,715 Scheduled Caste population 3,585,380 are Hindus constituting 99.8 per cent of the total SC population. Besides, 7,144 SCs are Buddhists and 191 Sikhs accounting for negligible percentage[13]. The state has registered 17.4 per cent growth of SC population in 1991-2001. There are thirty notified Scheduled Castes. If one can see the caste wise population among Scheduled Castes, the Mahyavansi caste has the highest population (43.2 per cent) out of the total SC population of the state, Bhambi (29 per cent), Bhangi (11.3 per cent), Meghval (4.9 per cent), Senva (3 per cent), Garoda (1.9 per cent), and Nadia (1.3). Among the districts in Gujarat, Kachchh (11.7 per cent), Surendranagar (11 per cent), Banaskantha (10.8 per cent), and Ahmadabad (10.7 per cent) have higher percentage of SCs population to their total population.

If one intends to assess in terms of percentage, the distribution of the total SCs population, Ahmedabad has returned the highest (17.3 per cent), followed by Banaskantha(7.6 per cent), Rajkot (6.8 per cent), Junagadh

(6.6 per cent), Vadodara (5.7 per cent), and Kachchh (5.2 per cent) district. Gujarat is one of the few states having high urban concentration of SCs population. In 2001 Census, 39.3 per cent of the total SC population has been registered in urban areas. Individual Scheduled Caste wise, highest 53.6 per cent urban population has been recorded among Nadia caste followed by Bhangi caste with 53.1 percentages. On the contrary, Senva (82.8 per cent) are predominantly found in rural areas. The sex ratio of total Scheduled castes the average population in the state is 925, which is below national average (936). Quite lower sex ratio has been recorded among Senva (916) and Mahyavansi (919). The child sex ratio (0-6 age group) for SCs in the state is alarmingly low (885). One of the seven major SCs, Garoda has recorded the lowest child sex ratio (864). However, Nadia (946), Meghval (925), and Bhangi (900) have recorded comparatively higher child sex ratio than the state average.

In Gujarat[14], 70.5 per cent of the SC population is literate. It is higher than the aggregated national figure for SCs (54.7 per cent). The gender gap in literacy rate among SCs is conspicuous with male and female literacy of 82.6 and 57.6 per cent respectively. Among the seven major SCs, Garoda with 82.4 per cent literacy rate, are not only on top but above the state average followed by Mahyavansi with 73.9 per cent literacy rewarded on the other hand Meghval is at the bottom of the list having only 58.1 per cent of their population as literates. The gender gap in literacy is very conspicuous among Meghvals. The male and female literacy rate at 73.5 per cent and 41.8 per cent respectively show that Meghval female are lagging behind their male counterparts by 31.7 percentage points. Three fourth of SCs (74.8 per cent) in the age group 5-14 years have been recorded as attending school.

The individual SCs, Garodas has recorded the highest school attending population (5-14 years) of 80.9 per cent, followed by Mahyavansi (78.3 per cent), Bhambi (76.2 per cent) and Senva (73.3 per cent). On the other hand, this proportion among lower castes is Meghval (66.4 per cent), Bhangis (66.5 per cent), and Nadia (69.5 per cent). In terms of the level of education, 4.2 per cent of the SC literates in Gujarat have recorded above the graduation. Individual caste wise, Garodas with 5.6 per cent and Mahyavansi with 5.5 per cent are on the top. In this respect, Bhangis are at the bottom with just 1 per cent of their total literates having graduation education. The percentage of SC workers to total population is 39.6 per cent, which is slightly lower than the aggregated figure of SCs at the national level (40.4 per cent), out of the total workers 79.7 per cent 20.3 per cent from marginal workers. The female total population is only 27 per cent, which is lower than their male counterparts (51.3 per cent). The year 1990 period from 2012, total incident of 459 murders and 548 rapes of Dalits in Gujarat state.[15]

**Table: 2 Incidents of Murder and Rape of Dalits in Gujarat**

| No. | Year of Period | Murder | Rape |
|---|---|---|---|
| 1. | 1990-1994 | 102 | 90 |
| 2. | 1995-1999 | 119 | 112 |
| 3. | 2000-2004 | 108 | 95 |
| 4. | 2005-2009 | 80 | 127 |
| 5. | 2010-2012 | 50 | 124 |
| | **Total** | **459** | **548** |

*Source:* State Crime Records Bureau, Gandhinagar (year -2001 to 2012) RTI Act-2005 and Balatkaragrasta Dalit women: aadhyana (Do. Hasmukha Parmar), this information was provided by KiritRathod - Navsarjan Trust, Gujarat.

It is interesting to note that the average Scheduled Caste population at the national level is 13 per cent; Scheduled Tribes population is 5.5 per cent. In contrast, the population of Scheduled Castes in Gujarat is 5.5 per cent and Scheduled Tribes population is 14.5 per cent. The level of the consciousness of Dalits in Gujarat is relatively less compare with southern states and other states of India. It is argued that atrocities on Dalits in Gujarat have increased but the assertions of Dalits are relatively less compared with other states. It is further found that the greater percentage of Scheduled castes in Gujarat stays in rural areas and a less percentage of population stats in urban areas, but the problem of untouchability and discrimination are found in both: the rural and the urban. It is further seen that in rural areas it is visible but in urban areas, one could find social discrimination is invisible. Notwithstanding, the literacy rate of scheduled castes is high, caste discrimination is also much in Gujarat, thus, it is argued the educated youth and employees knowingly or unknowingly became the part of *iniquitous* social system which is considered to be prime violator of the rights of Dalits. In this regard, it is pertinent to contextualise economic status of dalits in Gujarat.

## Economic status of Dalits in Gujarat

They are not homogeneous in their economic condition. 51 per cent of the SC population literates as against 61 per cent the state total population, but less than 1.5 per cent, have acquired higher education. In urban Gujarat, nearly one-fifth of SCs have settled as teachers, doctors, journalists, lawyers, etc. The rest of them are in the organised and unorganised sectors. Six per cent of Dalit households in rural areas can be called as relatively well-off farmers hiring labour and producing marketable surplus. Fifty per cent of the SCs workers are agricultural labourers and they earn Rs 200 per day. They are not paid the stipulated minimum wages. Three out of four SC households have less than 2000 rupees income per month and 82 per cent live in *Kuchha* dwellings. In the light of this, it is vital to study the caste system and untouchability in Gujarat.

## Caste system and Untouchability in Gujarat

The Hindu social order is based on three interrelated elements, namely, predetermination of social, religious and economic rights based on birth; the unequal and hierarchical division of and provision of strong social, religious and economic ostracism supported by religious ideology to maintain order. It is argues that as like other parts of the country, social evils like the caste system, hierarchy and discrimination very much persists in the state. They are trying to be assertive about their rights and need to live with dignity. The Hindus in Gujarat are divided into several castes- *Brahmins* (priests), *Vanias* (traders), *Rajputs* (warriors and rulers), *Kanbi*, and *Kathis*, *Kolis* (peasants) *Sonis* (goldsmiths), *Suthars* (carpenters), *Valands* (barbers), *Chamars* (leather workers), *Vankar* (weavers), and *Bhangis* (scavengers). The communities like *Brahmins*, *Vanias* and *Rajputs* are known as upper castes, while *Chamars*, *Vankar* and *Bhangis* are known as lower castes. Other castes like *Valand*, *Suthar* and *Kumbhar* etc. are included in the list of other backward castes (OBCs). It is found that there is a division among *Brahmins*, *Vanias*, *Kanbis* and *Patidars* (*Patels*) are considered as peasants. Within the *Patel* community, the *Kadva* and *Leva* sub-communities exist.

*Brahmins*, *Vania*, and *Rajput* communities control the economy and polity of Gujarat state. Total thirty one castes are included in the list of Schedule Castes in the state of Gujarat (Shah, 2010).

> (1) Bakad, (2) Brant (3) Bhambi, Bhambhi, Asadur, Asoli, Chamadiya, Chamar, Chambhar. Chamger, Haralapya, Harali, Khalpa, Machiger, Mochiger, Madar, Madig, Mochi, Naliya, Telugumochi, Kamtimochi, Ranigar, Rohidar, Rohit, and Samger, (4) Bavadhed, Dhed Sadhu (5) Bhangi, Mahetar, Olga, Rukhi (6) Chalwadi, Chatrya (7) Chena Dasar, Holayadasar (8) Dangshiya (9) Dhor, Kakya, Kankaya (10) Garmatang (11) Goroda, Garo (12) Hallir (13) Halsar, Haslar, Hullaslar, Halswar (14) Holar, Valhar (15) Holaya, Holer (16) Laugadre (17) Mahar, Naral, Dhegumegu (18) Mahyavanshi, Dhed, Vankar, Maruvankae, Atyanj (19) Mang, Matang, Minimading (20) Maang, Garudi (21) Meghaval, Meghawal (22) Mukri (23) Nadiya, Hadi (24) Pasee (25) Shenva, Chenva, Sedma, Rawat (26) Romaliya (27) Thori (28) Tiger, Tribanda (29) Turee (30) Turubarot (31) Barot

The domination of upper castes on the lower castes have been continuing for centuries but after the independence, it further gained the momentum as the economic development is confined merely to urban areas and upper castes. The caste system further accelerated in rural areas of Gujarat. Due to uneven development, it had an adverse impact on Dalits. Hence, it further continued the caste system, hierarchy and social inequalities in Gujarat. Inter-caste marriages in the villages are discouraged. Many couples who entered into inter-caste marriages were subjected to violence and often have had to leave the village. It is even difficult for them to get houses on rent, particularly, in upper caste localities as it is found that the upper castes practice the principle of purity and pollution. Dalits were asked to serve the upper castes and they were never allowed to enter and celebrate the religious ceremonies in villages. The *Panchayat* members elected by the voters from Dalits were served tea in separate designated cups and in some villages; Dalits were not even allowed to have tea along with upper caste men. If they were allowed, they have to wash their cups and keep them separately. Even in the government schools, Dalit children were served food separately and there was no clubbing of upper caste students with Dalit students[16] (Kennedy, 2010, pp. 1-59).

There have been agitations against this type discrimination. They are strong enough to fight the upper castes as the term Dalit give them confident, self-respect and dignity. Martin Macwan argues that the term 'Dalit' is rather a moral position of people who believe in equality of all human beings and freedom from oppression (Fernando Franco, Jyotsna Macwan, Suguna Ramanathan, 2004, p. 314). The study in Gujarat in the year of 1971 and 1996 found that rural villages in Gujarat practice untouchability, 75 per cent Scheduled Castes are not allowed entry beyond the threshold and they have to worship from a distance. The Scheduled Castes members of village society do not get entry beyond the outer room of the upper castes. A number of villages observe untouchability in public spaces. As many as 30 per cent of the village *Panchayats* still observe open or subtle discrimination with their elected members belonging to Scheduled Castes. The practice of untouchability has strikingly declined in occupational activities, for example, in buying and selling commodities. In 1971, 85 per cent of the villages, the Scheduled Caste members were barred from entering shops. This figure came down to 30 per cent in 1996 (Thorat, 2007, pp. 107-110). Every year in Gujarat state around 1100 of such cases are arising. The Scheduled Caste Commission Report is that 3.5 per cent cases are only getting resolved.[17]

A survey on untouchability in Gujarat, conducted by I. P. Desai, found this to be widespread in the rural areas in public places like buses, school seating arrangements and seating at *Panchayat* meetings (Fernando Franco, Jyotsna Macwan, Suguna Ramanathan, 2004, pp. 6-8). I.P. Desai observed that "There may be less untouchability cases between the Savarnas and the untouchable workers engaged in the similar work, but the personal relations among them are based on their social status (Shah, 2000, p. 467). In this connection, it is necessary to assess the Dalit movement which took place in the pre-independent Gujarat. Several social reformers and activists emerged whose concern for deprived communities, created consciousness among these sections, mobilised and organised and prepared them to fight against the social inequalities and injustice during the pre-independence era. This paper is an attempt to examine these movements to critically and contextualise the present Dalit movement.

## Assertions of Dalits against Caste Discrimination

There were several personalities who fought against the social evils in Gujarat state. The social reformers like *Narashiah Mehta, Shidhraj Solanki, Vir Megh Maya, Sayajirao Gayakwad* and *M K Gandhi* endlessly resisted the inequalities, discrimination, untouchability and struggled for the overall development of the under privileged communities and further created awareness among them and propagated values like equality respect and dignity. Dalits in Gujarat were for long forced to live an almost inhuman existence. An earthen goblet hung below the mouth and brooms tied behind were the signs of their accursed lives. In the early nineteenth century, a British officer, James Forbes, remarked on the plight of the Dalits in the *Dadhoi* region of *Vadodara* district thus: "The untouchables were prohibited from entering through the '*Hira Bhagol*' gate" (Forbes 1813). When there was a drought at *Patan*, the *Shidhraj Solanki* king of *Patan* had decided to sacrifice *Vir Megh Maya*, a Dalit to the local Goddess. There was a belief that the people of *Patan* would be saved from the drought if they sacrificed a life. *Vir Megh Maya* agreed to sacrifice himself but he had put the condition to *Shidhraj Solanki* that thereafter, the Dalits should be respected and argued for equal treatment for Dalits on par with other upper strata in *Baroda*. Because of his commitment towards Dalits, the Dalits constructed the temple of *Vir Megh Mayavat* in *Patan* and considered him as a source of inspiration.

*Achyut Yagnik* explains that *Mahyavanshi* means descendants of *Mahya*, a legendary Dalit martyr of eleventh century. The great *Chalukya* king, *Siddharaj*, built a huge step well in Patan, the capital of his kingdom. It required that a man of exceptional qualities to be sacrificed for the water to burst forth as this dugout. After a great search they found one such man, a Dalit *Vir Mahya* hailed from the *Vankar* community. He was ready to give his life, but in exchange for his sacrifice, he laid down several conditions for the betterment of his community such as the removal of the broom that Dalits had to tie behind their back and the spittoon around their neck. He further demanded that a part of the harvest be given to them (Fernando Franco, Jyotsna Macwan, Suguna Ramanathan, 2004, p. 9).

In the eighteenth century, the problem of untouchability existed in the form of caste system. The *Hindu* community of Ahmedabad boycotted English schools with the support of the Ahmedabad Merchants Association in protest against the admission of Dalit children. Against these social practices, the priests from Britain, who settled in Gujarat, took the initiative to admit untouchable students in the schools. But they faced opposition from the upper castes who believed in traditions and customs in the year 1845 at Ahmedabad.

The press too was influenced by untouchability. A report carried in *Gujarat Mintra*, a daily published from Surat on 12 February 1871, read thus: Though the merchant class has repeatedly complained to the government, they still have to sit in railway compartments beside low class people like *Bhangis* (Gurjar, 2004, p. 345).

During the nineteenth century, the *Ahmedabad Samachar* reported that untouchables were not allowed to enter the Court Hall and walk on the carpet in the court rooms in Ahmedabad[18]. Against this discrimination, untouchables started the movement against such social evils and demanded complete social change in Gujarat (Makawana, 2011, p. 16). The Dalits did not even have the freedom to choose their mode of wearing dresses, since the upper castes could not tolerate Dalits wearing good dresses. If the Dalits in *Hathijan*, a village near Ahmedabad, wore their dhotis with one end tucked in, the *Patels* would fall upon them saying. 'Bloody Dheds want to become Patels'. It they tucked both ends of the dhoti to escape the wrath of Patels, the *Thakordas* would attack them, 'Bloody *Dheds* went to become *Tharkardas*'. The Dalits had to wear their dhotis high above their knees. Dalits continued to put up with the ridicule and hatred of the *Savarnas* (Gurjar, 2004, p. 345).

## Dalit Movement in Gujarat in Pre and Post-Independence India

It is a fact that during the freedom struggle, there were anti-caste movements against the social evils. Even during the freedom struggle, there were leaders who raised the issues of the rights of untouchables in the country. There movements ignited the passion in the Dalits to fight for their rights. The state of Gujarat is not exception from these anti-caste movements.

## Mayavat Rajput Movement 1890 to 1939

In 1872, the population of depressed castes in *Surat* was 31,643 or 5.81 per cent. Initially, Surat and Bharuch districts were included in the erstwhile *Bombay* presidency. The south region of Gujarat was the Centre of industries, commerce and education. All these industries were owned by the upper caste *Hindus*. Hence, depressed castes had to depend upon the mercy of upper caste *Hindus* for their survival. The *Mayavat Rajput* movement was led by *MakanjiKuber Makawana* who fought for respect and dignity for the Dalits. The members of the *Vankar* caste were deprived of economic, social and political rights. They came out of the traditional socio-religious disabilities and stigma of untouchability after the introduction of western education and it led them to change their professions based on social status and joined the professional or skilled jobs, rather than traditional jobs like cooks, butlers and teachers. Further, they have joined councils, politics and national movement and contributed to nation building. Apart from these occupations, most of them became priests, government employees, businessmen and textile workers (Parmar, 1987).

All these positive deeds created awareness among *Vankars* in Surat and encouraged them to know their history and rewrite their history. *PrithvirajRao* hailed from the *Mayavansi* community and he has was the original king of *Bengal's Mayavatpuri* state and come under the ancient genealogy of *Kshatriya* but when they migrated to *Surat*, they were considered as an untouchable community. Against this, they started the movement and demanded the revival of their old status which they enjoyed when they were in Bengal. A historian, *Kanaiyalal Munshi*, delivered a lecture and supported their demand[19]. As a part of the movement, youth from *Vankar* caste started *Young men Mayavanshy Association*. The members of the Association started a long march from *Surat* to *Mumbai* on bicycles[20] and they not merely got the support from the natives of the country, but also from abroad. During the long march, they demanded respect and recognition of their social status in mainstream society. They further demanded change in their old name '*Dhed*' to *Mayavanshy*. The Government had changed their name on 25th October 1939 and used the term *Mayavanshy* in all official correspondence. This movement not merely created the consciousness among the *Dhed* community, but also inspired the people of Gujarat, particularly, Dalits to assert their rights and achieve their long pending demands from the government (Makawana, 2011, pp. 16-17). To critically analyse the atrocities on Dalits and caste discrimi-nation, it is essential to understand the Dalit labour movement in pre independence Gujarat.

## The Dalit Labour Movement in 1895

Most of the workers who were working in the Textile Mill industry at Ahmedabad were Dalits and the working conditions in the industry were worst. There was no ventilation, no minimum facilities that were provided for workers and they had to work for fourteen to eighteen hours every day. Women were not exempted from these barbaric working conditions. According to the industry rules, they were supposed to get the salary once in a week, but they used to get their salaries once in fifteen days. Due to the negligent attitude of the management of the industry, both the workers and their families suffered and in many cases, the children stopped going to the schools. Against this negative attitude of management, 9000 Mill workers from the Dalit community started an agitation in Ahmedabad[21] against the anti-worker attitude but the management closed the Textile Mill industries and removed the Dalits from work. The workers became helpless due to closing of the industry workers were denied of their right to work. Hence, against the closure of the industry and workers from Dalit community once against started the agitation. During the agitation, *Jethabhai* and *Haribhai* were in the forefront of the movement. They were beaten up badly by the police and they died after a couple of days.

Though, this movement did not succeed in its effort, it created enormous awareness among the Dalits (Makawana, 2011, p. 18). Other movement like

*Valmiki* movement in 1911 equally contributed to create consciousness among Dalits and asserting their rights. The sweepers who were working in Ahmedabad Municipal Corporation belonged to the *Valmiki* community and were not given the wages continuously for two months. Against this move, the sweepers from Dalit community started the agitation[22] at Ahmedabad under the leadership of *Dhana Balu*, *Kashiya Deva* and *Maphatiya Nana*. The police arrested them and kept them in the jail. The Municipal authorities brought the sweepers from other places like *Kheda*, *Nadiyad*, *Bharuch* and *Poona*. But they failed in continuing the workers brought from the other places. There went back to their native places. The city of Ahmedabad became dirty and shabby and this bad condition gave rise to health problems in Ahmedabad. At last, the Health Officer had to appeal to the sweepers to join the work. Finally, all workers from Dalit community rejoined duty (Makawana, 2011, pp. 18-19). These two cases reflect the assertion of Dalit women and sweepers against the casteist mindset of the administration and their negative approach toward the Dalits. This case also showed the way for Dalits to fight for their rights and resist exploitation in any form.

## Ambedkarite Agitations in Gujarat

The Dalits of Gujarat were greatly influenced by Dr. B R Ambedkar and his ideology after 1920. Though the *Bahiskut Hitkarihi Sabha* was established on 20th July 1924, it was only after the arrival of Dr. B R Ambedkar in Ahmedabad[23] on an invitation from *Dariyapur Navayuvak Mandal,* that it started its activities rigorously. Regular contacts led to reading of Ambedkarite literature and a new Ambedkarite generation begun to take shape. As a result, the state Scheduled Castes Federation (*Gujarat* Region) was founded in Ahmedabad[24]. All India Scheduled Castes Federation founded by Dr. B R Ambedkar in Nagpur[25] was also influenced by its counterpart in Gujarat. The *Saradhav-Kalol* bus agitation[26] was a result of Ambedkarite activities. The leadership of the Hotel entry agitations and Scheduled Castes Federation in Ahmedabad provided enormous strength to Dalit activists. Though the *Swaminarayan* Temple Entry agitation in 1948 was headed by Gandhian workers, Ambedkarites were active in the movement. The temple entry in *Kheda* village in 1946 was also carried out under the banner of the Scheduled Castes Federation. However, The *Satyagraha* for 'Wasteland for the landless' that took place in Ahmedabad in 1960 on account of the Republican Party's new ideology for social justice, may be considered a pivotal one (Gurjar, 2004, p. 362). As like in other states in India, people of Gujarat were influenced by Dr. B.R. Ambedkar and converted into Buddhism and followed in his footsteps and fought against social-economic inequalities. Against this backdrop, let us now focus on the relevance of *Buddhism* and Ambedkar's legacy.

## Buddhist Conversions in Gujarat

The legacy of Ambedkar and the ideology of *Buddhism* have a major impact on dalits in Gujarat. The dalits have followed the footsteps of Ambedkar. They strongly believe in Ambedkar's statement that 'Though I was born a *Hindu*, I shall certainly not die as a *Hindu'*. This announcement of Dr B. R. Ambedkar at *Yevla* village *Nasik*[27] district was to divert lakhs of Dalits from Hinduism forever. Lord Buddha who preached the superiority of man through equality had embraced untouchability such as *Sunit Supak* and *Nai Upali*. It was in his refuge of compassion and grace that the courtesan *Amrapali* was to find dignity in her last moments. Ambedkar looked upon Buddhism as a li'berat-ing force. Among the lakhs of Dalits who embraced Buddhism the day after Dr. B R Ambedkar converted to Buddhism and with blessings of the Buddhist monk *Mahasthivar Chanramani* in *Nagpur*[28], many were from Gujarat.

Since 1945, many Dalits opt for Buddhist rites and ceremonies on occasions of marriage, death, pregnancy and so on. In Saurastra, the bride and groom were made to seek blessings of Lord Buddha and Dr Ambedkar. On wedding cards, Lord Buddha was given the pride of place. Many parents named their children according to the Buddhist tradition. A large number of *Gujaratis* were among those who converted to Buddhism[29] at the *Dadar* crematorian on the occasion of the *Parinirvana* day of Dr B R Ambedkar, with the blessings of *Anand Kaushalyavan*, a Buddhist Monk. The elderly Ambedkarite, *GovindjiR.Parmar* (*Guruji*) from Gujarat, *Sadhu Shri Muldas* from Gujarat adopted Buddhism[30] at the conversion function in Nagpur. With Buddhism gaining ground, many Buddhist monks started visiting Gujarat to preach and convert people. The Japanese Buddhist monk *TenjoWaten* Abe arrived in Ahmedabad in 1957. Buddhism started flourishing after the world famous Buddhist monk Anand *Kaushlyayan* visited Ahmedabad in 1958. Later, the chairperson of *Ceylon Mahabodhi* society, the monk *Buddhrakshit*, addressed a public gathering[31] at a function of the *Mahabodhi* Ambedkar Mission. The Buddhist monk Shri *Sanghrakshit* from England, monk *VivekNanda* from Thailand and monk *Kshantipulo* visited Ahmedabad in December 1960. Frequent visits of and regular contact with Buddhist monks were responsible for the increasing number of Buddhist converts. Five educated youth from Ahmedabad were bestowed the Buddhist *PanchaseetTriharan* in December 1960 at the hands of monk *Sangharakshit*. *ShriDharmabandhu* '*Pagalbaba'*, a well-knows Buddhist from Gujarat, toured from village to village of *Saurastra* in 1958 and invoked the Dalit community's interest in Buddhism through soul-stirring songs, *Bhajans* and *Kawalis.Buddha Jayanti- Buddha Purnima* celebrations were held for the first time in Ahmedabad on 21 June 1951 under the auspices of the Scheduled Caste Federation. A religious procession was organised in Ahmedabad by the Ahmedabad *Boudhjan Samiti* and the 2500 birth anniversary of Lord Buddha. *Buddha Jayanti* programmes continued to be held in village after village in Gujarat.

The *Mahabodhi* Ambedkar Mission was founded[32] to enhance the spread of Buddhism. This was the first Buddhist institution of its kind in Gujarat. Subsequently, several institutions[33] were founded in Gujarat. The idol of Lord *Buddha*[34] was installed in *Ramai Mandir*[35] due to the efforts of the Buddhist devotee *Ramjibhai Meeowala*. This was the first idol-installation in Gujarat. Weekly *Buddha Vandana* programmes begun in Gujarat at the office of *Jyoti* a weekly. A *Maharahstrian* Dalit *Buddhist Vihar* at *Bakrawadi* in Baroda was founded on 30 June 1963. The foundation stone of *Bapunagar Prachsheel Buddhist Vihar* was laid by *Bhaiyasahed*[36] in 1974. About 1000 *Maharahstrian* Dalits embraced Buddhism in the Presence of *Dhdasahed* Gayakwad at *Ramni Chali* in Ahmedabad on 18 November 1956. Subsequently, innumerable Dalits converted to Buddhism under the leadership of *Krishana Sardare*. A programme was held on *Vijaya Dashmi* at *Vir Bhagat shih* Hall[37], in which monk *Shantrakshak* performed the conversion rites, the programme was the result of the efforts of Dr P G Jyotirkar. Although the exact number of Buddhists in Gujarat is not known, the number is estimated at about 50,000-60,000. This may be termed as a direct antipathy to Hinduism. Apart from this, lakhs of Dalits have distanced themselves from Hinduism. Instead of accusing Christian and Buddhist conversions as a conspiracy or challenge, Hinduism needs to do some soul searching. A decadent culture and religion are injurious not only to people, but also to the notion (Gurjar, 2004, p. 365 to 367). There were two cases that reflect the assertions of Dalit workers and sweepers against the caste mindset of the administration and their negative approach towards Dalits. These two cases show that the way the Dalits started asserting their rights and resisted against injustice being done to them.

## Naroda Bus Entry Movement (1931) & Hotel Entry Movement in 1938

The labourers from the depressed classes were living at *Naroda* in east Ahmedabad. They was more than working there. Every day, they had to travel from their village to town to go to the industry but they were not allowed to enter the government and the private buses. Then *Shri Krishna Sharma* and *Shri Premdas Sadhu* from the Dalit community started the agitation in January 1931 with the support of the labourers against the denial of bus entry, After this long struggle, the owners of the private and the Government buses agreed to start the buses and allowed the workers from Dalit communities to travel from in the buses (Makawana, 2011, p. 23).

Apart from the bus entry movement, there were other movements like hotel entry movement which were directed against the denial of hotel entry in Ahmedabad. The owners of the hotels believed in the principle of purity and impurity and hence, they did not allow Dalits to enter hotels and enjoy themselves like upper caste members. Hotels like *Radio* hotel (*Delhi Chakla*), *Chandravilash* and *Laxmi vilash* hotel (*Gandhi* road), and *Sankarvijay* hotel

(*Karanj)* and *Surati Khaman house* (*Raipur*) are famous in Ahmedabad. It was the general trend of upper castes that if the untouchables entered hotels, the response would be physical assault on them and many times Dalits were thrown out of the hotels. The *Kher* ministry had passed the Hotel Entry Law in 1938 in Bombay. On the basis of this, the collector of Ahmedabad, Mr. Drew, made a public declaration to inform the hotel owners that they would not be able to prohibit any Dalits from entering their hotel and if they did, the license would be confiscated (Gurjar, 2004, p. 348). Against this denial, the Dalits started agitation against the hotel managers who did not allow the untouchables to their hotels. Due to the agitations, the police arrested and filed the cases against one hundred fifty hotel managers in Ahmedabad who practiced untouchability. The leaders emerged from the deprived communities like *Mohanbhai Dugarbhai Parmar* and *Keshavji Ranshodji Vaghela.* Thus, it emerges that the movement really gave the confidence to the weaker sections in and around *Nadiyad, Kalol* and *Viramgam* and united them not merely on the issue of the hotel bus entry, but in asserting their rights in Gujarat in general (Makawana, 2011, pp. 21-23).

## Bus Entry Movement at Saradhav (Kalol) in 1946

There are Textile *Mills* such as *Navjivan mill, Bharat Vijay Mill* and *Chhotalal Mill* in *Kalol* in Gandhinagar district and most of the workers are from Dalit community who used to come from their villages but it understood that they were not allowed to enter the bus by the dominant castes. Against this denial, Dalits organised themselves and started the *Saradhav* bus entry movement[38] under the leadership of *Govind Shamji Parmar* who was the member of Scheduled Caste Federation along with other Dalit leaders[39]. The workers dared to go to the village as a group and enter the bus. In the village called *Kotha,* when the Dalit leaders[40] tried to enter bus, they were beaten up badly by the dominant caste men, severely injured and later on they died due to the major injuries. The properties of Dalits were destroyed and were attacked by the upper caste men. The leaders[41] emerged from these movements. Under their leadership, the movement continued for a couple of months against the upper castes[42] as they were primarily responsible for the discrimination. It was for the simple reason that the Dalits were not allowed to enter the buses to continue their superior status, their domination on Dalits in terms of social, economic, political and culture. The upper castes also thought that if Dalits would get consciousness, it would threaten the existence and continuance of their supremacy on Dalits (Makawana, 2011, pp. 23-25). Because of the agitations and direct action by the Dalits and their relentless struggles, the government of Mumbai enacted the Social Disability Act in 1947 and implemented it strictly. The government had put its efforts to create the consciousness among the people about the Act. This Act become an important step in annihilating the caste system.

## The Swaminarayan Temple Entry Movement 1947

One of the important Dalit movements in Gujarat was the *Swaminarayan* temple entry movement at *Kalupur* in Ahmedabad[43]. It has been considered as the spiritual place for Hindus. In this temple, Dalits were not allowed to enter the temple. After the *Harijan* Temple Entry Law came into existence,[44] the Mumbai Assembly tried its best to spread the news about the law among the Dalits and that they could enter temples like *Swaminarayan* temple. Because of the efforts of the Government, Dalits tried to enter *Swaminarayan* temple but they were not allowed to enter the temple. Dalit leaders[45] started the '*Harijan Mandir Pravesh Sanchalan Samiti'* (Committee for *Harijan* Temple entry). About five hundred Dalits gathered and tried to enter the *Swaminarayan* temple[46] but the priests of the temple closed the temple and locked the doors. Against this negative response of the temple priests and Management of the temple, several Dalits and their leaders gathered in front of the temple[47] and got the support from Ahmedabad Mill workers as most of the workers hailed from the Dalit community. More than twenty five thousand Dalits met near the *Swaminarayan* temple against the negative response of priests. The irritated workers of Ahmedabad Mill industry damaged the property of the temple[48].

Nevertheless, the management of *Swaminarayan* temple did not allow Dalits to enter the temple. The workers from Ahmedabad Mill Industry got the support and solidarity from *Kalol*, *Petlad* and *Kadi* mill workers. Apart from these, they got support from several quarters like the print media[49]. Home Minister of India blamed[50] *Swaminarayan's* approach towards Dalits for not allowing them to enter the temple. This movement became a success under the leadership of *Muljibhai Vaishya*[51]. Though the Dalits started the movement with entering temple, this culminated in a legal battle. The legal battle had continued for eighteen years. In this battle, Dalits won the case and got the right to enter the *Swaminarayan* temple (Makawana, 2011, pp. 29-31).

## First Anti-Reservation Agitations in 1981

To assess the assertions of Dalits, it is necessary to comprehend the anti-reservation movement in Gujarat in 1981. As a part of this movement, anti-reservation movement directly confronted the Dalits. Whatever the frustration of the upper castes had on Dalits got reflected in this movement. They attacked Dalits, manhandled them and burned their houses. Apart from the physical assault, they attacked the self-respect and dignity of Dalits as they were in the forefront of the movement and demanded reservations for OBCs. This is an example of how the upper castes who opposed reservations and did not tolerate the overall development of Dalits. Hence, it is imperative to critically look at the anti-reservation movement.

During this period, the elite classes of Gujarat started losing power and felt insecure as their control on the political, economic and educational fields gradually came down. But it is understand that the state government stopped the implementation of OBC reservations declared by the Union government. Fearing the mounting tensions in the state, the Prime Minister gave a hint of the possibility of undertaking a fresh review in the matter of OBC reservation. The union government also asked all the states to maintain status quo regarding OBC reservations till the consensus could be arrived at (S.Rana, 2008, pp. 121-129).

The agitation was initially launched by the professional Medicos for abolition of reservations in the Post-Graduate medical colleges[52] implemented by the Government of India. The agitations were started against the reservations seats for SC candidates in Pathology Department. It may be mentioned that some students of this college had filed a case in the Gujarat High Court[53] against the carry forward, roster and interchangability system of reservation seats. They lost the case in the High Court and therefore resorted to direct action. The Medical college students[54] went on the strike[55] demanding abolition of reservation system for SC and ST Candidates for post 1987-graduates (Shah, 1987, p. 167). They gradually spread to the residential localities of major cities in the state. The closing of schools and colleges became a trend in the Gujarat during the movement. Against the anti-reservation movement, about 75,000 Dalit Textile Mill workers observed a lightning strike[56] in support of reservations. Counter to Textile Mill Workers Agitation, the workers from upper castes in India observed a three days strike[57] (S. Rana, 2008, pp. 121-134). Indira Gandhi[58] intervened in the situation and sent the emissary, *Jaisukhlal Hathi* to Gujarat in March for deliberations with students and later on, invited students and the chief minister of Gujarat to New Delhi for further negotiations. After several round of talks both the parties reached a 12 point agreement accord[59] which agreed[60] to increase additional non- reserved seats to general category against the number of reserved seats claimed by SC, ST and other backward caste students. Three months later, the anti-reservation agitation came to halt (Shah, *Middle Class Politics: Case of Anti- Reservation Agitation in Gujarat*, 1987, p. 167).

It is understood that the post-independence decade opened up new vistas of growth and development of lower caste along with upper castes. The provisions of reservation provided opportunities for SC/STs in the government services, new jobs were opened up in nationalised banks and the insurance sector. All these played a crucial role in the conflicting and turbulent situation right from the beginning of the eighties. This created an atmosphere that scheduled castes are progressing and keeping most of the other castes behind them. Hence, it posited that all these developments put together led to develop a negative bias in the minds of upper castes on Dalits in Gujarat (S.Rana, 2008, pp. 121-129).

Most of the districts in the state were affected by the anti-reservation agitations. The *Kheda*, *Ahmedabad* and *Mehsana* districts became the epicenters of the anti-reservation movement where many atrocities on Dalits took place. These three districts were having very high rate of education and urbanisation. The number of Scheduled Castes also more, therefore, educational and economic progress of scheduled caste was enviously noticeable. One more feature of their widespread atrocities on scheduled Caste was that these three districts are having commonly highest population of Patel community among the upper castes. This community was in the forefront of the anti-reservation movement in the state. During the movement[61], Gujarat witnessed caste hatred and communal violence. First incident[62] concerned *Shakarabhai Premabhai Sonar*, a Scheduled Caste man employed as a watchman in the local Gram Panchayat He was locked up in the *Gram Panchayat.*[63]*Kerosene* was poured on him and he was burnt to death by a mob of local residents. In the second incident,[64] a Scheduled Caste lady teacher, *Ushaben Bhalchandra*, who ran away from the back door was caught by the mob and virtually stripped naked. In the third incident,[65] the village main light switch was put off at night and a mob in thousands attacked the locality of Dalits and three pucca houses were broken into, a few others were forced to migrate to the villages. The shops of the *Muslims* and a *Sindhi* were also put to fire. The Dalits ran away from the village for a quite some time due to atrocities on them. In another incident,[66] the anti-reservation stir turned into anti-government agitation in Gozaria village in *Mehsana* District. There was a clash between the police and the upper caste mob. As a result, two persons were killed in the police firing. The whole anger of upper castes got reflected in stopping milk supply and vegetables (S.Rana, 2008, pp. 123-125).

## Second Anti-Reservation Agitations in 1985

After the 1981 the Anti-reservation movement gained momentum in 1985 and organised agitations against the reservations for OBCs. The main reason for the 1985 anti-reservation agitation by the medical and engineering colleges was the hike in OBC reservation quota from 10 percentage to 28 per cent in the state. The students from upper castes intensified the agitation under the banner of State Parent's Federation. Students boycotted the examinations in the state. The agitations witnessed violent incidents this time. The worst affected sector was education as all the education institutions were continuously closed. The leaders of the elite class were able to organise and mobilise the support of upper class students, government employees and other sections of the society against the OBC reservations. All these and agitations spread strong feeling of hatred in the minds of upper castes. The anti-reservation agitations once again destabilised end the normal civic life in the state with repeated call offs, rallies, disrupted educational institutions and imposition of restrictions. There were clashes between pro- reservation and anti- reservation groups and also incidents of individual attacks involving stabbing, beating, damaging of property. Economic activities came almost to a halt. In such situations of chaos and anarchy, as usually happens, anti-social elements took over the command on the situation which further worsened the civic life and law and order in the society (S.Rana, 2008, pp. 129-134).

The student from *Ahmedabad* launched *All Gujarat Educational Reform Agitation Committee (AGERAC)*. It gave a call for Gujarat bandh[67] which received partial response from the people. Junior doctors of the civil hospital supported the agitation and abstained from duty. The bandh triggered off violence in different parts of the state. During the day, the events of violence were of a minor nature, such as throwing stones on public buses, clashes between police and students etc. Business organisations of Ahmedabad[68] observed bandh for five days[69] in protest against the government failure to protect the life and property of the citizens. Because of the pressure from the students and youth from upper castes, the government agreed not only to the abolition of the 18 per cent hike in reservation quota, but also to review the reservations (Shah, *Middle Class politics: Case of Anti- Reservation Agitation in Gujarat*, 1987, pp. 167, 169 and 170). It is felt that though the reservations were meant for three categories SCs, STs and OBCs, the main targets of attacks were the Scheduled Castes. Even the media, supposed to be neutral and report the facts to the people, failed in reporting the facts in an objective manner[70] (S.Rana, 2008, pp. 129-134).

## Fight for Self-Respect of Sambarda Movement in 1989

Sambarda village is in *Sabarkantha* district of Gujarat, *Palanpur* block Feudalism in this village has been continuing for centuries. The population of the village is about 550, out of which 55 per cent are Dalits and 45 per cent belong to the *Gandhavi* community (OBCs) (Chandu Maheriya, Harshad Desai, 1995, pp. 1-124). The *Gadhavi* were the supreme masters in Sambarda. Instances of eve-teasing of Dalit women and beating up Dalit youth was the general trend in the village (Gurjar, 2004, p. 375). The tortures of *Gadhavi* in the village on Dalits were prevalent and several incidents took place. *Rajanikant* from Dalit community was attacked by *Ranjitsinh Hamirdan Gadhavi* and injured severely but with a lot of difficulty, he was saved from the assault of *Gadhavi* group and was taken to Civil Hospital of *Palanpur*. The people of the village gave a complaint to the District Collector.

Due to the torture of his family members, it is understood that 332 Dalits from 32 families have migrated[71]. Four months after their migration, the Government allotted the land at *Palanpur*. The Dalits organised a meeting[72] and decided to migrate to that place. The entire Dalits of Sambarda village set off for the office of collector, *Palanpur*[73] under the leadership of Professor *Panachand Parmar* and demanded lodging and boarding for the migrant Dalits (Chandu Maheriya, Harshad Desai, 1995, pp. 1-124). Among the refugees were eighty year olds, pregnant women and five to seven month olds infants. The crusade for justice lased for 131 days. The refugees lived in tattered tents in sun and rain, sometimes nights in knee-deep water. But they refused to budge. The Dalits who had left all they possessed in *Sambarda* said, 'The geography needs to be changed if history has to be changed'. Tribal Chief Minister and three Dalits cabinet ministers had lost their moral strength and did not visit the Dalit *Satyagrahis*. Women gave birth in tents. Dalits from every village in *Banaskantha* flocked to the spot. The *Sambarda Swaman Jyot* incident roused the Dalits (Gurjar, 2004, p. 375).

There Dalits have mentioned that they do not want to go back to their native place and demanded permanent accommodation at *Virpur* near *Palanpur* and they were supported by an opposition party. Thereafter, they organised a silent rally[74] in which more than one lakh Dalits joined and it exhibited the strength of the Dalits under the leadership of *Fakirbhai Vaghela*. On 30th July, the Oppression Resistant Committee organised a silent rally to support the Dalits against domination of the *Jan Morcha*. The women from the various villages of *Banaskantha* observed the fast[75] rally and demanded that the oppressors of the Dalits should be punished, no departmental inquiry should be conducted against Dalits who are in government service, sanction their leave, withdrawal of police cases filed against the sympathisers of Dalits and no transfer of Dalits in the government service, etc., the re-habilitation for Dalits who faced violence from to the upper castes who indulged in harassing Dalit youth. The committee which constituted by the government recommended 98 plots, the new housing society[76] for government servants from Dalits called Gram Gruh Nirman Board. The Home Minister of Gujarat promised security for them in the village. Under the leadership of Chetandasji, 10,000 people from Dalits demanded rehabilitation. It was on *Vijya Dashmi* on 3rd November 1989 that the victorious Satyagrahis went to the new colony in Virpur and named it as *Swaman Nagar*. In this case, the Dalits of Gujarat exhibited unity and succeeded in the fight against the feudalism of elite classes. This movement was considered as a historical milestone in the campaign to attain respect and dignity for the Dalits (ChanduMaheriya, Harshad Desai, 1995, pp. 1-124). Dalit movement in Gujarat was influenced by the neighbouring state of Maharashtra and Ambedkarite ideology. It the forum of Dalit organisations: (1) The Republican Party (2) Dalit *Panthers*. Though their approach may be different, they certainly helped the Dalit movement in Gujarat. Though the Republican Party was a political party, its contribution in the march for social justice is historic and other hand. The Dalit *Panthers* gave militant strength and a boost to Dalit youth and activists.

## The Republican Party in Gujarat

All The branches of the Schedule Castes Federation in Gujarat were converted to branches of the Republican Party. The Bharatiya Republican Party was actually founded[77] in Nagpur to fulfill Dr B.R. Ambedkar's unfinished social agenda. The party was founded in Gujarat on 1st June 1958 in Ahmedabad. *GovindjiParmar* was its Vice-Chairman and; *Karsandas U.*

*Parmar*, its general secretary. Under the banner of Republic Party, Gujarat branch, several agitations and movements took place. The Satyagraha at Ahmedabad *Sachivalaya* on 18th August 1960 to demand land for the landless, the Saradhav bus agitation, the Enter Hotel agitation, the *Swaminarayan* temple entry were the prominent agitations of Gujarat which were led by RPL, a part from other Dalit organisations and activists. The entire credit for the spread of Buddhism in Gujarat goes to the Republican Party or the Scheduled Caste Federation. The Republic Party challenged *Majdoor Mahajan* (Labour Union) which was led by dominant castes that had ruled single handedly over the mill workers. It was due to the moral support of the Scheduled Castes Federation that the mill workers went on a nine day strike during the Swaminarayan temple entry agitation and had dared to go against *Majdoor Mahajan* (Labour Union). It also participated in the Lok Sabha, the legislature, the municipal corporation and local government- the district Panchayat and the block *Panchayat* elections in Gujarat. By participating in the elections, the party has mobilised and created consciousness among dalits and encouraged them to take part in electoral politics to raise their voice in policy making bodies in Gujarat.

## The Dalit Panthers movement

The unity and fury of the Dalits in Bombay took the shape of the Dalit *Panthers* in reaction to *Worli* massacre case in Bombay. Its ripples were felt in Gujarat. The seeds of the Dalit panthers were sown in Gujarat where Dalit leaders invited the Dalit Panthers leaders *Raja Dhale* to Ahmedabad on 14 April 1974 and organised a large procession to mark the birth anniversary of Dr Ambedkar. Dalit activists of Ahmedabad and Dalit leaders[78] organised several public meetings for the spreading the ideals of the Dalit Panthers. *Rameshchandra Parmar* and *Naran Vora* of the Republican Party were attracted to the Dalit panthers and all those leaders strengthened the foundation of the Dalit panthers in Gujarat. These leaders worked to establish the reputation of the Dalit panthers in Gujarat as a powerful and militant organisation. Its aim was to reach the remotest village, even at the risk of death and help the victims to get justice (Gurjar, 2004, pp. 375-376).

## The Atrocities against Dalits of *Kadi* in Gujarat

In the incident[79] in *Kadi* village, upper caste mobs attacked and looted property of the Dalits and injured several Dalits[80]. There are two versions of what actually preceded the events which culminated in the destruction of the properties of Dalits. The version of Dalits is that when a young Dalit boy and girl went to the shop, the owner from upper castes harassed her. She protested against this. Infuriated by the arguments, the *Patel* shop-owner called the shopkeepers hailing from his community. They beat up the Dalits who came in to support of the Dalit girl. Two Dalits came in support of the girl. Meanwhile, *NitinPatel*[81] also appeared there, the agitated mother of the girl protested against him. The supporters of *NitinPatel* manhandled her and other Dalits in the presence of police officers. The mob of upper castes systematically armed with weapons went and looted shops and workshops of Dalits for four to five hours continuously. The Dalit groups launched a agitation demanding removal of *Nitin Patel* from the Cabinet, file a case under the SC/ST Atrocities Act against those who were involved and withdrawal of false cases filed against Dalits, arrest the culprits, compensation for damages, suspension of police officers who had acted in alliance with the *Patels* and setting up of inquiry commission headed by a retired high court judge (Kiran Desai, RasikParmar, 1995, p. 1558). In other words, this paper has explained the dalit movement in Gujarat starting from the eighteenth century till 1990s and argued that all these movements are the basis for dalit assertions in Gujarat and made them dalits to aware of their rights and encouraged them question the dominance of upper strata or the state in any form.

In sum, Indian society is highly stratified and inequalities among different socio-economic groups are still very much in existence. Social identify of the people in India determines their status in society. Dalits are still being excluded from the public domain, whereas people of upper castes continue to enjoy all the privileges because of their social status. It is seen that Dalits, women and Tribals are generally in a disadvantaged position compared with those of other communities. They face discrimination, exclusion, exploitation and alienation. The caste system has further kept the Dalits away from the rest of the society to such an extent that they are generally denied even the basic human rights that one must enjoy in order to lead a life of dignity. Still in some villages evil practices like denial of the right to drink water from any public well by Dalits and denial to walk on the road are some of the notable examples of social persecution of the Dalits at the hands of the upper-castes. The study has brought out that Dalits are more effectively asserting their rights. It also maintains that the deprived communities in the country have been continuously denied their rights, deprived of education, employment opportunities and not allowed entry to public spaces like temples, hotels; schools, etc. In the past, they were pushed outside the political arena and excluded from the public domain. They have gained their present position in India through their continuous struggles since the mid-nineteenth century by setting their own agenda in the public sphere.

According to National Human Rights Commission, Gujarat has performed poorly in the area of implementation of rights given to Dalits and tribals, as enshrined in the Constitution of India. Caste system still persists and still one could see the two glass system, denial of temple entry is still observed for Dalits in rural Gujarat. The study has brought out that workers from the deprived communities in textile or in any industries are being discriminated against by the contractors and managers from the higher castes in Gujarat It also emerged from the study that now Dalits are being mobilised and campaigning for their rights with the help of NGOs, Dalit leadership, Dalit youth and Dalit social workers. However, in the case of the Sambarda movement, the political parties used this for gaining political mileage. It also emerged that both electronic and print media are biased towards upper castes and never consider the problems of Dalits seriously and highlighted their problems.

In post-independence India, a number of social legislations have been enacted to improve the lot of Dalits. These include: making the practise of untouchability a cognisable offence and attempts to substantially improve their socio-economic status. The provisions of voting rights, reservation in education and jobs and in the political fields, are the steps which have been in existence since the adoption of the Constitution. Efforts are still going on to remove different discriminatory practices against them. Scholars argue that notwithstanding provisions in the Indian Constitution, protective provisions, laws modernity, modern education, science and technology, powerful state machinery, atrocities on Dalits in one form or the other are still continuing.

## References

1. A.M. Shah (2010) *the Structure of Indian Society: Then and Now*, Routledge, New Delhi.
2. B. R. Ambedkar 1979 (2014) *Annihilation of Caste*, Dr Babasaheb Ambedkar: Writing and Speeches Vol. 1, Education Department, Govt. of Maharashtra and Dr Ambedkar Foundation, Ministry of Social Justice & Empowerment, Govt. of India, New Delhi, p. 56.
3. Braj Ranjan Mani (2005) *Debrahmanising History: Dominance and resistance in Indian society,* Manohar Publications, New Delhi, p.13.
4. Census of India in 2011, Government of India.
5. Chandu Maheriya, Harshad Desai (1995) *Samabardathi Swamanagar* (Samabarda to Swamanagar), (Gujarati), Centre for Social Studies, Surat.
6. Dosabhai Edalji (1986) *History of Gujarat from the Earlier Period to the Present time*, Asian Educational Services.
7. Fernando Franco, Jyotsna Macwan, Suguna Rammanathan (2004) *Journey to Freedom: Dalit Narratives,* Samya Publications, Kolkata.
8. Ghanshayam Shah (1987) *Middle Class Politics: Case of Anti- Reservation Agitation in Gujarat,* Economic and Political Weekly, 22, AN, pp. 167, 169, 170.
9. Ghanshayam Shah (2000) *Hope and Despair: A study of Untouchability and Atrocities in Gujarat,* Indian School of Political Economy.
10. Ghanshayam Shah (2001) *Dalit Politics: Has it Impasse?* In edited by Sudha Pai and Niraja Gopal Jayal *"Democratic Governace in India: Challenges of poverty, Development and Identity"*, Sage Publications, New Delhi, p. 223-24.
11. Gopal Guru (2009) *Introduction: Theorising Humiliation*, In edited by Own books *"Humiliation: Claims and Context"*, Oxford University Press, New Delhi, pp. 1-2.

12. HRW (2012) *World Report*, Human Right Watch, USA, pp. 328-33.
13. Indian Express News, Newspaper, Ahmedabad, Gujarat, 24 February 2013.
14. Jagannathem Begari (2009) *The Human Rights Implications of Dalits Self-Assertion in India*, Cambridge Scholars Publication, New Delhi, pp. 257-280.
15. Jag Mohan Singh Verma (2011) *Social Justice in India: A case for equality through privilege*, edited by MH Makwana and Richard Pais, *"Backward Classes and Social Justice"*, Rawat publications, New Delhi, pp. 52-3.
16. James Forbes (1813) *Oriental Memoirs*, 4 Vol. ii, Landon, pp. 310-81, 514.
17. John Schwarzmantel (2011) *Democracy and Political Violence,* Edinburgh University Press Ltd, Edinburgh, p. vii.
18. Kenneth Bush and Colleen Duggen (2013) *Evaluation in Conflict Zone: Methodological and Ethical Challenges,* Journal of Peace Building and Development, Special issue: Evaluation in Violently Divided Societies: Politics, Ethics and Methods, Volume: 8 number 2, Rutledge Taylor and fancies group, Canada, USA, p. 7.
19. Kiran Desai, RasikParmar (1995) *Kadi: Signs of Dalit Assertion*, Economic and Political Weekly, 30, p. 1558.
20. Makawana, M. (2011). *Dalit's in Western India*, Shanti Prakashan, New Delhi.
21. M.H. Makawana (2011) *Gujarat Na Dalit Andolano*, (Dalit Movement in Gujarat) (Gujarati), Surat.
22. Mungekar, B. L. (1999) *State, Market and the Dalits: Analytics of the New Economic Policy*, In edited by S.M. Michael, *"Dalits in Modern India: Vision and Values"*, Vistaar Publications, New Delhi, 289.
23. Nandu Ram (1995) *Beyond Ambedkar: Essays on Dalit in India*, Revised Edition 2009, Her-Anand Publications, New Delhi.
24. Nitin Gurjar (2004) *Dalit Movement in Gujarat*, Appendix 2, Edited By Fernando Franco, Jyotsna Macwan, Suguna Rammanathan, "*Journey to Freedom: Dalit Narratives"*, Samya Publications, Kolkata.
25. Noam Chomsky interviewed by Sparrow McLeod, entitled *"Institutional Violence"*, undated citations from the transcript of an interview from "*Democracy is coming to the USA"* a film by Walter Miale, Website: http://www.greenworld-center.org.
26. P.L. Punia, Shyam Agarwal, Mangat Ram Bali, Mangu Ram, Arun Kumar Singh (2012) *Anusuchit Jati Vani*, Ministry of Social Justice and Empowerment, National Commission for Scheduled Castes, Government of India, New Delhi.
27. R.F. Kennedy (2010) *"Understanding Untouchability: A Comprehensive Study of Practices and Conditions in 1589 Villages"*, Navsarjan RFK center Publications.
28. S.M. Michel (1999) *Dalits in Modern India: Vision and Values*, Vistaar Publications, New Delhi, p. 28-9.
29. S. Rana (2008) *Reservations in India: Myths and Realities,* Concept Publishing Company, New Delhi, pp. 129-34.
30. State Crime Records Bureau, Gandhinagar (year -2001 to 2012) RTI Act-2005 and *Balatkaragrasta Dalit women: aadhyana (Do. HasmukhaParmar),* this information was provided by KiritRathod - Navsarjan Trust, Gujarat.

31. SukhdeoThorat (n.d). *On Economic and Inclusive Policy*, New Delhi.
32. SukhadeoThorat (2007) *Human Rights of Ex-Untouchable in India: Violations and Enforcement,* Vol. 10 & 11, No. 1& 2, Jan. 2006- Dec. 2007, Indian Journal of Human Rights, p. 107-110.
33. Sudarshan Iyenger and Sujata Patel (1986) *Golana: Symptoms and Crisis,* Economic and Political Weekly, Vol. 21, No. 7 (Feb. 15, 1986), p. 287.
34. Y. A. Parmar (1987) *The Mahyavanshi: The Success Story of a Scheduled Castes,* Mittal Publications, New Delhi.

## Notes

1. Noam Chomsky interviewed by Sparrow McLeod, entitled "Institutional Violence", undated citations from the transcript of an interview from "Democracy is coming to the USA" a film by Walter Miale; sourcehttp://www.greenworld-center.org.
2. Lothal, Rampur, Ameri, Lakhabanal and Rozdi.
3. 415 A.D.
4. 250 B.C.
5. 130 to 390 A.D.
6. During the period 900 A.D.
7. 1411 A.D.
8. Nearly 200 years.
9. 1556- 1707.
10. 1612 in Surat.
11. Daman and Diu.
12. Census of India in 2011, Government of India.
13. Census of India 2001.
14. *Ibid.*
15. The study of Navsarjan RFK center in the year of 2010 reveals.
16. Indian Express news, Newspaper, Ahmedabad, Gujarat, 24 February 2013.
17. 4th June 1873.
18. 30th November 1931.
19. From 16th February to 23th February 1933.
20. 30th June 1895.
21. 17th September 1911.
22. 28 June 1931.
23. 1942.
24. 1947.
25. 13 October 1935.
26. 14 October 1956.
27. 6 December 1956.
28. 14 October 1956.

29. 18 January 1959.
30. 21 October 1958.
31. Ahmedabad Bouddhijan Samiti, Bharatiya Bouth Mahasabha, Mahabodhi society in India, Mahabodhi Prathana Samaj, Buddist society of Gujarat, Trailokya Bouddh Mahagan, Gujarat Dhamma Society and Buddhist Academy.
32. Jaipur in Rajasthan.
33. Kakol on 17 April 1956.
34. Yashawant Ambedkar.
35. Gomtipur, Ahmedabad in 1974.
36. 13th December 1946.
37. Ramjibhai Mevuvala, Ganapatbhai Makawana, Karsanbhai Levuva, Trikambhai Bhagat, Ratilal Rathod and Ghelabhai Seijvala.
38. Viraji Manaji Bhagat and Ghelabhai .
39. Nagjibhai Arya in Baroda, Parikshitlal Majumdar in Harijan Sevak Sangh and V.T. Parmar.
40. Patel, Darbar and Thakore.
41. In year of 1947.
42. 11th September 1947.
43. Keshavji Vaghela.
44. 14th January1948.
45. 15th January 1948.
46. 18th January 1948.
47. Times of India, Gujarat Darpan and Gujarat Mitra.
48. 21st January 1948.
49. Dalit MP (Member of Parliament).
50. 17th May 1985.
51. B J Medical College, campuses at Ahmedabad.
52. November 1979.
53. Ahmedabad, Vadodara and Jamnagar.
54. 12 January.
55. 20 and 21 February 1981.
56. 23, 24 and 25 February 1981.
57. Prime Minister.
58. 13th April 1981.
59. Besides that early January had accepted of government employees and police association too pressed for abolition of the roster, interchangeability, carry forward and further demanded total scrapping of reservations.
60. April and May of 1981.
61. Jabalpur village is situated about 12 km. away from Ahmedabad district with a population of about 3000 to 4000 of whom 500 to 600 belong to the Scheduled Castes.

62. 26th December 1980.
63. Detroj Village is some 50 km. away now an Ahmedabad district. The village consists of upper caste is Kshatriyas and Patesl, OBC category Thakors and also SC category in Vankar and Rohits, etc.
64. Pij village in Kheda district of central Gujarat is having a population of 10,000 upper caste Patels and about 500 for lower caste population.
65. 16th March1981.
66. 18 March.
67. Cloth merchants, foodgrain dealers, dealers in book and stationeries, edible oil, spices, electrical appliances, radio and television, laundry owners, footwear dealers, bullion merchants, etc.
68. 5th to 10th June.
69. Attack on Gomtipur at post office on 29th January 1981, attack on Jain temple on 2nd February 1981, attack on marriage party at Khambhatwala hall, Gita Mandir.
70. 26th June 1989.
71. 15th June 1989.
72. 26th June 1989.
73. 10th July 1989.
74. From 1st August to 31st August.
75. 5th September 1989.
76. 3rd October 1957.
77. Naginbhai Parmar, Dalpat Shrimali, Valjibhai Patel, BakulVakil and P. D. Vaghela.
78. Kadi is a small town place of Mehsana district of north Gujarat region.
79. 12th May, 1995.
80. Local MLA and Health Minister of Gujarat.

# 10

# Globalised Rights and Localised Violations: The Case of Palamur Labour in Telangana

—*Dr Venkatesh Nayak*


## Abstract

One of the assumed ideologically de-contested universal discourses on globalisation has been regarding human rights. But such universalisation has its own politics of rights prioritisation. Civil and political, or the first generation liberal rights, have been projected in a de-contested mode. The cost of such projection could be undermining the second generation socio-economic and cultural rights. Such truncated promotion and prioritisation of rights could prove incapable for establishing a regime of genuine global human rights. Such projection helps in offering legitimacy to the 'state withdrawal' syndrome in a welfare economy. In such a situation, people from a backward socio-economic region like Telangana, having the experience of colonial and post-colonial uneven development trajectories might become the victims of such myopic human rights vision. Such is the case of Palamur labour, which is forced to lead a nomadic life due to the existing distressed socio-economic and geographical conditions. This article will attempt to spot the gap between universal claims of human rights (de jure rights) and localised violations of Palamur labour rights (de facto rights) at the structural, as well as at the agency, levels.


"Human dignity is the quintessence of Human Rights."[1] The distress labour migration from Mahabubnagar district is called Palamur labour[2]. Migrant labourers, as a category of rights bearers, do have certain recognised rights to be promoted and protected. In the absence of human rights observance, 'human beings' would cease to be called 'human.' Natural rights theory is the accepted basis for the human rights discourse. Natural rights emanate from the natural law. Both natural rights and natural law provide a reasonable basis for the human rights language. In this context, there are two arguments. Firstly, human rights emanate from the rights, and rights emanate from the human rights. The first argument seems to be the more accepted position. The universal nature of human rights discourse is seriously contested from the cultural relativist angles and by postmodern thinkers.

Migration is a natural and universal phenomenon. The basic motivation behind all types of migration is the migrant's assumption of 'better' livelihood opportunities available elsewhere. The migration theories deal fairly with two streams of migration causes and motivations. At the individual level, the rational-individual chooses migration as a way out for betterment of the life. This position has been held by the neo-classical theory of migration (see Lewis, 1954). Even Todaro's (2005)[3] model resembles a refined position in this connection. The new economics of migration gives the family a prominent place in the determination of reasons for migration (see Joaquin, 2000)[4]. On the other hand, the structuralist argument, put forth by Marxism, stresses on the structural causes of migration. It emphasises on the capitalist mode of production's law of the uneven-development and assumes that social, historical, cultural factors work behind migration agency (see Iyer, *et. al;* 2005)[5]. It stresses on the distressful conditions of the migrating societies as the causes for the migration.

## Conceptualising Human Rights

All rights are moral standards and these norms are to be recognised, observed and promoted by the individuals and the institutions. Different approaches to rights indicate this point. "One approach sees rights as normative attributes 'belonging to self-conscious human beings'. Another approach regards these as entitlements to choose have, enjoy or have done. One more approach explains rights as the valid claims".[6] Some see human rights as the subset of rights, but human rights are the most basic, pertaining to what is essentially human, while other categories of rights are more specific, limited and derivative. Labour rights, in general, and migrant labour rights, in specific, are part of it. Rights are not only directed towards protecting the individual from the state organised power, but more so, to create the societal conditions by the state in which individuals may develop to their fullest potential. "Human rights have become a universal ideology."[7] Rights involving protection of certain human and social attributes will be having deeper implication for the right bearers and those who exercise rights. "Rights are rational/logical derivation of human and social attributes and also the alternative would ground on axiological or deontological foundations, but some would refer to ideological considerations."[8] Rights and human rights of all shades are requiring equal consideration and protection. Protection may be through formal institutions or public opinion for which moral imperatives are needed. Rights recognise individuals in their protective capacity and work as signals towards the passive individuals. These also prescribe the behaviour of 'right' towards rights in the form of duties. The abundance of human rights is self-destructive, but not logically impossible, and would deprive the community of its rational goal. Rights are equal claims and all individuals of the society require recognition of each member as the rights bearer and enjoyer. Basic rights theory has to attain three propositions before it is elevated to the level of rights. On the philosophical dimension, it will have to meet the minimum rational and logically, standard, by couching the ideological and cultural boundaries. Legally, it has to be translated into an enforceable code of action. And last one is to encoding the rights into different categories.

The philosophical basis of human rights is grounded in universal values and absolute priorities In Lockean Rights Theory, the basic argument was that all individuals are endowed by nature with the right to life, liberty and property. To protect these rights, they entered to in a contract. The duty of the rulers is to protect these rights. In these propositions, two things come into observation. "First, the individual, as an autonomous being capable of exercising choice, and second, the legitimacy of government depends upon the will of the people, as well as the governments' willingness and ability to protect those individual natural rights."[9] Thomas Paine, in his *Rights of Man,* saw rights origin in divine, by the equal rational human beings. They are imprescriptibly-rights which were 'those which appertain to man in rights of his existence'. In support of the French revolution and declaration of rights of Man, Paine asserted, 'each generation had the right to make rational decisions,for itself'. His rights include Lockean natural rights to life, liberty, property all intellectual rights and pursuit of individual happiness, without harming others' natural rights.The philosophical implication for this is the sequencing from natural rights or natural law to positive law. "The natural rights doctrine serves as a paradigm for a theory of rights."[10] Firstly, it argues that human beings are born with the rights. Secondly, they are pre-social in the sense they are not the product of any artificial edifice or contract. Thirdly, they are absolute non-negotiable, non-compromisable or non-negotiable. Fourthly, they are universal also. Irrespective of their contextual backgrounds, all human beings possess these. Utilitarian thinkers, like Jeremy Bentham, attacked natural rights as, rhetorical nonsense, nonsense upon stilts'. He was critical about quasi-empirical language that is used just a flat assertion that human beings have rights. His assertion was that rights can not exist outside the political society.[11] So recognition in a political society, in the form of law, is necessitated. Positive law is based on natural law. Natural law is based on the existence of certain basic assumptions. There are certain practical, as well as moral, principles which are good to pursue and practice. Both natural law and positive law are the basis for the human rights. "Natural law perspective is precisely the assertion of universal rights against local custom, it provides the basis for critique of it."[12]

However, Marx attacked both the natural rights and legal rights. According to him, these liberal bourgeoisie rights are part of "false consciousness". Human rights, as a part of civil society consider the individual as self interested, egoistic and separates the individual from the community. Marx reinterpreted the right to liberty as that of separation of the individual from the community, "the right to property as that to the arbitrary disposal of private possessions, and right to security as guaranteeing those commercial and capitalist arrangements" (See K. Marx, 1977)[13] In sum, rights represent the false nature of human being as only the self-interested one, it makes individuals one-dimensional and neglects the community living. Despite the criticism, natural law and natural rights, however, exercise a powerful influence over the development of human rights.

## Globalisation of Human Rights

It is evident that from the experience of the past two decades that the economic globalisation and the human rights are marching together. It indicates that both are interconnected. The economic basic structure of global capitalist development has been given superstructure legitimacy by the human rights language. Were no human rights existing prior to the globalisation process, which are to be called human rights? The answer is yes, there were different types of rights, recognised and promoted at the global level in the post-war period, But the cold-war politics split them into different category of rights. The globalisation process demands the agency's freedoms and liberties at the market place to buy and sell goods and services without any intervention. Therefore, it emphasises on the expanding freedom of the people to exercise greater control over their daily lives and greater access to technology and knowledge. Human rights language, in the present context, gives the least importance to the outcome of the exercise of these rights, unlike cultural and economic rights.

Advancement in productive forces unified the global community. Negatively speaking, the world was unified through colonialism and this uneven unification matured into subsequent World Wars. These developments compelled the world to evolve certain global human rights norms. These rights were thought to be used as an instrument to promote and mediate the standards at the local and global levels. This aspiration materialised in the form of Universal Declaration of Human Rights (UDHR) in the year 1948. Though this document does not enjoy the status of a treaty, it has set a global standard for the entire global community. It was a comprehensive document incorporating both first and the second generation rights. The cold war politics dichotomised both generation rights into civil and political rights and economic, social and cultural rights. Later, both got expression in two different Covenants in 1966. The third generation rights, represent the aspirations of third world countries. This right, called right to development, got universal recognition in 1986, after it was adopted in the UN General Assembly. The spirit of these documents is evident in the Indian Constitution also. Fundamental Rights (FR) and Directive Principles of State Policy (DPSP) represent the first and the second generation rights. All these documents deal with the issues of protection and promotion of human rights in order to establish a global human rights regime. There are efforts at global and national levels for promotion and protection of labour rights.

"Globalisation of human rights, by making it universally accepted to eradicating the global inequalities, is the clarion call of the current human rights movement."[14] In the present context,along with the economic globalisation, rights and rights language have been globalised. The globalisation of rights has its own politics. It has accompanied the "End of History" discourse and 'There Is No Alternative' (TINA) factor with the active promotion of civil and political rights. Paradoxically, the promotion of these rights sometimes requires the violation of some of these very same rights. In other words, liberal growth-oriented economy and liberal rights have been globalised.

The concern of human rights is human dignity. The dignity can be violated by the direct use of force by an authoritarian state through curbing the individual liberties and freedoms. Human rights impose logical limitations on the state's arbitrary power. On the other hand, lack of state's positive intervention in promoting the well-being of the people may result in the violation of all types of rights. In this situation, the state's positive intervention is necessary for the well-being of the people. The Human Rights language confines itself only to promoting the negative rights, or the first generation rights. Those rights may not suffice for reclaiming the human dignity which has been violated by non-fulfillment of positive rights by the different public agencies. The post-USSR emergence of human rights international regime was believed to have the potential to address both traditional and emerging forms of human rights violations. But the present capitalist globalised economy may complicate the situation. Rahul Rai fears that the present economic integration might result in the violations of all the rights, including the basic human rights. "Global economic relationships can produce state policies that directly violate social and labour rights and indirectly produce social conflict that leads to state violation of civil and security rights.[15] There is also an emergence of fourth generation rights asserted by the indigenous people of the world-expressed mainly in the form of right to self-determinism.

"The globalisation process has increased the tension in the domain of human rights."[16] There are conflicting claims like, on the one hand, big corporations are claiming their set of rights to set up their establishments without any hurdles. At the same time, global level institutions are aspiring for international governance over local governance. The rights of corporates are sometimes pitted against the rights of the farmers, local labour and indigenous industries. This has put pressure on democratic institutions so that accountability is flowing upward centre. Ultimately economically dominant powers are gaining the upper hand and their claims are fulfilled at the cost of others claims. The migrant labourers are the most distressed segment of the 'otherness'. Along with the economic globalisation, universalisation of human rights was also celebrated across the world. Especially, "the debate on Human Rights gained momentum in the wake of United Nations Decade of Human Rights Education (1994-2004)."[17]

## The Politics of Human Rights: Trifurcation of Rights

The labour rights become particularly important concepts to deliberate upon because of the changing balance of labour and capital all over the world in the context of globalisation of the capitalist mode of arranging production and distribution of production. Some scholars would attribute this sudden upsurge of human rights language to this changing balance. There is no problem in this upsurge, but there is the politics of prioritisation of rights by the western liberal democracies. They are very much favouring the first generation rights and promoting these as the human rights.

The first generation rights are civil and political rights which are protected by the modern constitutionalism and international law. These rights rightly can be described as the negative rights variety based on the non-interference by others for their exercise. These individual rights are the products of western liberalism. The second generation rights are social, economic and cultural rights, or positive rights. Positive rights were given legitimacy and legal sanctions through provision in the covenant on economic, social and, cultural rights. "These are subject to 'progressive realisation' and to the maximum of 'available resources."[18] These rights need an intervention for their enjoyment from the governing institutions.

The human rights movement increasingly recognises the fallacy of dividing civil and political rights from economic, social and cultural rights and the damage done to human welfare of neglecting the latter set of right entirely. 'Upendra Baxi' posits that the dichotomisations of the generation rights are resulting in lopsided implementation of *de facto* rights. There is a contradiction between basic human rights and basic human needs. It means that the basic human rights of the first generation civil and political rights variety, are not capable enough to fulfill the basic needs of all. "The neglect of these areas marks the essential difference between the human rights approach and the right to-be- human approach."[19] He points out that there is a deficiency in promoting and fulfilling these needs. These rights are necessarily freedom-oriented and incapable of providing bread to all, it is often translated to in a conflict between 'bread and freedom'; freedom usually wins with the liberal conception of rights. Freedom without bread is meaningless for many. Liberal rights are assurances to do lawful harm to others. Because it promotes individuality against the community and those rights gives him/her legitimacy to do that harm. Preservation of dignity is the cornerstone of human rights practice. Without bread, freedom cannot give dignity.

Similarly, Augustina opined that the second generation rights are a warning that human dignity does not depend solely on the existence of an acceptable degree of freedom, but also on the existence of an acceptable degree of equality in terms of living conditions.' It has to do little with political or legal equality. Rather, it cares much about material equality. Any state which cares about rights should take care of liberty base and equality base rights or else they may turn out to be contradictory. "If these rights fail it is not the failure of democracy self it and threat to the exercise of civil and political rights also."[20] The false division between political and economic rights arose partially from the political manoeuvrings of the Cold War. During that period, ideological conflict, the free-market democracies, always looking to delegitimise the communist nations, frequently charged those regimes with the human rights violations, while, at the same time, ignoring the social and economic rights abuses occurring within their own borders. The communist countries would respond that political freedoms are meaningless without social equality—never mind that a healthy and well-educated population doesn't need to be told what it can and cannot read. For decades, each side used the term "human rights" only in self-serving and limited ways.

The third generation rights, the 'rights of solidarity are the newest and most controversial category. "These are asserted by developing countries that wish to see the creation of an international legal and economic order that will guarantee the right to development, to disaster relief assistance to peace and good government."[21] Right to development, as a part of third generation rights, was adopted in UN general assembly in 1986, which was intended to promote economic security. Development implies the well-being of the entire population. It does not limit itself to the conventional notion of economic growth alone. Rather, it involves the expansion of opportunities and capabilities to get benefitted by those opportunities. This approach seeks equity and justice as the primary concerns of the development policies. Well-being is equivalent to realisation of human rights. Arjun Sengupta, elaborating on the thrust of this right, asserts "as a human right, this right pertains to every individual, irrespective of nationality, country or continent, and the obligation of a state extends beyond its boundaries to helping, through positive action, the citisens of all other states."[22] This right primarily recognises three sub-sets of rights like right to health, education, and housing. These are the successive three generation rights. These are promoted and prioritised by the different countries for different reasons. To the western liberal democracies, first generation rights are very important. The erstwhile Soviet Union and its' allies promoted the second generation rights. Developing countries take third generation rights much seriously than the former two generation rights. So there is a need to make the all generation rights interdependent and complimentary for the fulfillment of migrant's rights.

## Documental Expressions of Rights

Migrant labour consist of a major portion of the unorganised sector Rogaly, et al, advocate the political approach for the implementation of migrant labourers' rights as they enjoy their claims as being migrant labourers.' Mainly, the identified migrants' rights are as follows: Migrants have the right to be included in the welfare schemes sponsored by the state. Especially, women and children must get priority because they get very least attention at the place of origin and at the place of destination and they are more prone and vulnerable to human rights violation incidences. Inclusion in the welfare schemes like integrated child development scheme should be made compulsory. Getting shelter at the place of destination is a biggest problem faced by the migrant community. So getting shelter must be recognised as one of the basic rights. One more problem faced by the migrants is unsafe travel during the migration period. This might prove a fatal experience to many. Recognising safer travel as a right is a must. Mostly migrants' dwellings are slums in the cities. They often have to adjust with the polluted weather, water, and food etc. unhealthy environment make them sick. They have to allocate a substantial part of their earnings to health care. sometimes, it become difficult to save out of earnings because of absence of health facilities. So right to free health must be recognised. "The children of migrant labourers are deprived of education because of their parent's mobility. Right to education must be made compulsory."[23] All the above mentioned rights are inter-dependent and derivative from one another. For example, the important civil right is 'right to life'. This has been historically extended from protection against arbitrary killing. Not only that, it also means not to be killed by hunger. So without adequate food, shelter and clothing, a dignified life is impossible. To encompass it, adequate means of work and remuneration must be provided; otherwise other, human life would be sub-standard. To fulfill human expression and development work is necessary without which human life is impoverished or unrealised.[24] So migrants rights urge for integration of the three generation rights.

All three generation rights were codified into different documents and proclamations. Many provisions of the Universal Declaration of Human Rights were legally recognised by the law in different parts of the world. The very important declaration was UDHR. Carl Wellman posits, "universal declaration of human rights seems both to describe a set of fundamental moral rights and to confer a set of legal rights upon all human beings."[25] It made possibilities for full-blown global human rights regimes. It recognises a full range of civil, political, economic, social, cultural rights. It also recognised and declared that all these rights to be 'interdependent and indivisible'. Right was given priority over any other socio, political and economic goals. Universal human rights composed a concern for positive, as well as negative, rights. "One of the principal purposes of human rights in global politics is to reflect critically upon the stark contradictions between the idea of universal human rights and practice of human wrongs."[26]

In case any of the rights being violated, Article 8 of the Declaration ensures that: 'everyone has the right to an effective remedy by the competent national tribunals for acts violating the fundamental rights granted him/her by the Constitution or law'. Article 22 states, 'Every one as a member of society, has the right to social security and entitled to realisation, through national effort and international cooperation and in accordance with the organisation and the resources of each state, of the economic, social and cultural rights indispensable for his dignity and the free development of his/her personality. Article 23(1) says, "everyone has right to work, to free choice of employment, to just and favourable conditions of work and protection against unemployment. Article 23(3) says, 'Everyone who works has the right to just and favourable remuneration, ensuring for himself/herself and his/her family an existence worthy of human dignity, and supplemented, if necessary, by other means of social protection'. According to Article 24, 'Everyone has the right to rest and leisure, including reasonable limitations of working hours and periodic holidays with pay.' According to Article 25, 'everyone has the right to a standard of living adequate for the health and well-being of himself and of his family, including food, clothing, housing and medical care and necessary social services, and right to security, in the event of unemployment, sickness, disability, widowhood, and old age or other lack of livelihood in circumstances beyond his/her control.'[27]

Article 6 of the International Covenant on Civil and Political Rights says, 'every human being has the inherent right to life'. The Declaration had included both the positive and negative rights in its' content. The First World and Second World had prioritised the rights and actively promoted these. International covenants on Economic, Social, and Cultural Rights stands for the positive rights. Article 3, stands for to undertaking and to ensuring the equal right of men and women to the enjoyment of all economic, social and cultural rights set forth in the present Covenant.' Article 6(1), asserts, 'the states parties to the present covent recognise the right to work, which includes the right of everyone to the opportunity to gain his living by work which he/she freely chooses or accepts, and will take appropriate steps to safeguard this right.' Article 6(2) states, 'the steps to be taken by a state party to achieve the full realisation of this right shall include technical and vocational guidance and training programmes, policies and techniques to achieve steady economic, social and economic development and full and productive employment under conditions safeguarding fundamental political and economic freedoms to the individual.' According to Article 7(a), 'remuneration which provides all workers as a minimum with: (i) fair wages and equal remuneration for work of equal value,without distinction of any kind. In particular, women being guaranteed conditions of work not inferior to those enjoyed by men, with equal pay for equal work; (ii) a decent living for themselves and their families in accordance with the provisions of the present covenants'. Article 7(b) stands for providing 'safe and healthy conditions'.

Article 9 provides social security provision. It states, 'the state parties to the present covenant recognise the right of everyone to social security, including social insurance. Article 11, recognises the right of everyone to an adequate standard of living for himself and his/her family. "Article 11(1)&(2) enjoins on the state parties to take necessary steps, individually and through international operation to improve the production, conservation and distribution of food and recognises the right to everyone to be free from hunger.' Article 13 recognises the right to one everyone to education."[28] (*Ibid*, 11) All the articles starts from the word 'The state parties to the present covenant', indicating the role of the state as an agency of performing its duty in promoting the human rights standards.

The declaration of the Right to Development in 1986, in the UN General Assembly considered the Right to development as the basic right and provides the right approach to development. Article 8, of the declaration states specifically that realisation of Right to Development would ensure 'equality of opportunity for all in their access to basic resources, education health services, food, housing, employment and fair distribution of income', and 'that women should have an active role in the development process' as well as 'appropriate economic and social reforms', eradicating all social injustice. Article 6(3) emphasises on 'elimination of obstacles to developments resulting from failure to observe civil and political rights as well as economic, social and cultural rights.[29]

The Constitution is the document of fundamental law of the country. The enshrinement of universal human rights standards in the Indian Constitution indicates the constitutional framers' enthusiasm in universal human rights regime. Especially DPSP, "The Directive Principles of State Policy are the directives in Indian Constitution dealing with promotion of human rights through state intervention and the welfare policies." Article 15 gives direction to the state not to discriminate against any citisen on the basis of religion, race, caste, sex, place of birth and any of them. Article 16 talks of equality of opportunity to all citisens. Article 23 prohibits any kind of forced labour or *begaar*, begging, etc. Article 24 prohibits child labour.According to its definition, children below the age of 14 years, who are employed and engaged in the hazardous employment are to be considered as child labour. Article 39 directs the state to formulate policies according to the principle enshrined in the Sub Clauses of the Article: (a) that the citisens, men and women, equally have the right to an adequate means of livelihood; (b) that the ownership and control of the material resources of the community are so distributed as best to serve the common good; and (c) that the operation of the economic system does not result in the concentration of wealth and means of production to the common detriment; (d) that there is equal pay for equal work for both men and women; (e) that the health and strength of workers, men and women, and the tender age of children are not abused and that citisens are not forced by economic necessities to enter avocations unsuited to their age or strength. Article 41 talks about the right to work, to education and to public assistance in the case of unemployment. Article 42 is a directive to the state to make provisions for securing just and humane conditions of work and for maternity relief.

Article 43 is very important in terms of labour rights, It states: 'The state shall endeavour to secure, by suitable legislation or economic organisation or any other way, to all workers, agricultural, industrial, or otherwise, work, a living wage, conditions of work, ensuring a decent standard of life and full enjoyment of leisure, and social and cultural opportunities and, particularly, the state shall endeavour to promote cottage industries, on an individual or co-operative basis, in rural areas'. Article 45 talks about free and compulsory education within a period of ten years from the commencement of the constitution. Article 47 stands for raising the nutritional level of the people and the living standards.[30]All above mentioned Articles seems to faraway from realisation in the Palamur district and the labour case at the ground level.

The above-mentioned Articles were not only left to the declaration level, but sought to ensure active realisation through legal mechanisms in India. In the unorganised sector, employees are the unending reservoir of relative surplus labour. In Marxist jargon, they are the floating, latent and stagnant population. Moreover, this sector has conditions like unhygienic working conditions, and living conditions, extremely lower earnings, middlemen phenomena, harassments, and exploitative working conditions. In the unorganised sector, the migrant labour section forms the major chunk. Article 19 of the Indian Constitution recognises the right to mobility to any part of the country without any distinction or discrimination. According to Mishra, migration in itself is not a problem. "It becomes objectionable only when it leads to exploitation culminating in human misery and deprivation of the irreducible barest minimum to which every worker as a human being and as a citisen is entitled."[31] Article 43 of Indian Constitution directs the state to formulate appropriate legislations for promotion of the labour welfare. The Indian State has formulated legislations to protect and promote the rights of the migrant labour. Among these the following legislations are important: Bonded Labour System (Abolition) Act, 1976, Apprentices Act, 1961. Child Labour (Prohibition and Regulation) Act, 1986, Contract Labour (Regulation and Abolition) Act, 1970, Equal Remuneration Act, 1976. Maternity Benefit Act, 1961, Minimum Wages Act, 1948, Payment of Wages Act, 1936, Personal Injuries (Compensation Insurance) Act, 1936, Workmen's Compensation Act, 1923. Thought there are several legislations, these have not effectively addressed the ineffective in the problems of the Palamur labourers. The following cases of Palamur labour will bring out the rift between de jure rights and de facto rights.

## Palamur Labour between Globalised Rights and Localised violations

Palamur labour is the migrating segment of the population of Mahabubnagar district of Telangana State. The district lies between the North Latitudes 16° and 17° and East Longitudes 77° and 79°. The district has an area of 18,432 sq km and a population of 3.51 million (Census of India; 2001). Literacy rate is very low in the district In 1991, it was a mere 29.58 per cent, and in 2001, it increased to 44.4 per cent. The district is predominantly rural, with villages housing a population of 3.1 millions. The district has 5, 42,380 Scheduled Caste and 2, 27,405 Scheduled Tribe Population. The prime cause of the distressed migration from the district is non-availability of livelihood. Often the state attributes the cause for such mass migration to its low average rainfall, drought and other natural calamities. But the main cause of this migration could be attributed to the denial of the legitimate claim over resources. The district has a long history of out-migration. Palamur migrant labour is a result of the existing distressed socio-economic, cultural and historical structures of the district. These structures are pushing many residents of Palamur to migrate to other places for their sustenance. It is very appalling to know that, from a small place like Mahabubnagar district, people are migrating on a mass scale. Almost one third of the district population, anywhere between 10-15 lakhs, is living outside the district.[32] According to unofficial estimates, as many as 4.5 lakh people migrate from the villages every year in search of employment. Popular as "Palamur labour", their presence is common in most of the major construction sites across the country. The severity and magnitude of the large scale migration that takes place from Mahabubnagar district, indicates that the legitimate claims of these people are being ignored.

**Table 1: Percentage of Total Workers, Main Workers, Marginal Workers, and Non-Workers to the Total population of Mahabubnagar District**

| *Total* | *Total workers* | | *Main workers* | | *Marginal workers* | | *Non-workers* | |
|---|---|---|---|---|---|---|---|---|
| *years* | *1991* | *2001* | *1991* | *2001* | *1991* | *2001* | *1991* | *2001* |
| **Persons** | 50.2 | 51.8 | 48.4 | 42.1 | 1.8 | 1.8 | 49.8 | 48.2 |
| **Male** | 55.3 | 56.3 | 55.1 | 49.7 | 0.2 | 9.7 | 44.7 | 43.7 |
| **Female** | 44.9 | 47.2 | 41.4 | 34.3 | 3.5 | 6.6 | 55.1 | 52.8 |
| **Rural** | 52.6 | 54.1 | 50.6 | 43.7 | 2.0 | 10.4 | 47.4 | 45.9 |
| **Urban** | 31.3 | 32.3 | 30.7 | 28.9 | 0.6 | 3.4 | 68.7 | 67.7 |

***Source:*** *District Census Hand Book Mahabubnagar District, 2001.*

The working population during census years of 1991 and 2001 of Mahabubnagar district (Table-1) shows that the per centage of total workers to total population increased from 50.2 per cent to 51.8 per cent. At the same time, main workers decreased from 48.4 per cent to 42.2 per cent. There was no change in marginal workers' per centage, but non-workers decreased from 49.8 per cent to 48.2 per cent. Even the data analysis by Uttamkumar Deb, et al., (2002), also reveals the same thing. The working population in rural areas of the district accounted for 53 per cent of the rural population. Of these, 51 per cent obtained work for a major part of the year (more than 183 days), while the remaining (2 per cent) worked only for less than half the year.

**Table 2: Reasons for Migration from Mahabubnagar District**

| *Reason* | *Frequency* | *Percentage* |
|---|---|---|
| Low Income | 86 | 28.7 |
| Unemployment problem | 74 | 24.7 |
| Not Enough land to cultivate | 35 | 11.7 |
| Better employment | 13 | 4.3 |
| Indebtness | 4 | 1.3 |
| Drought-Famine | 78 | 26.0 |
| No demand for traditional occupations | 10 | 3.3 |
| **Total** | **300** | **100.0** |

*Source:* Koteswar (2005)[33] in Gopal Iyer.

The major cause behind the mass migration from the district is non-availability of gainful employment. One of the studies, which covered the Bijinepally Mandal of the district (Table-2), establishes this fact. A major reason for migration was non-availability of reasonable income (28.7 per cent) work at the place of origin, triggered by unemployment (24.7 per cent) situation, which was aggravated by famine and drought for 26.0 per cent people.

**Table 3: Caste and Education Background of the migrants from the selected mandals of Mahabubnagar District (In per cent)**

| *Caste* | *Bijinepally* | *Kalwakurthy* | *Makthal* | *Wanaparthy* | *Total* |
|---|---|---|---|---|---|
| **SC** | 26.7 | 14.7 | 49.4 | 38.4 | 34.4 |
| **ST** | 16.5 | 4.2 | 0.7 | 14.1 | 12.7 |
| **OBC** | 52.9 | 67.1 | 47.6 | 44.8 | 49.3 |
| **General** | 3.9 | 14.0 | 2.3 | 2.7 | 3.6 |
| **Literate** | 6.8 | 45.2 | 11.0 | 7.4 | 8.8 |
| **Illiterate** | 93.2 | 54.8 | 89.0 | 92.6 | 91.2 |

*Source:* Chakrapani and Vijay Kumar, (1994)[34]

The data collected by Chakrapani and Vijay Kumar (1994), in their study, (Table-3) on four mandals of the district, establishes that the migrants were mostly drawn from the SC (34.4 per cent) ST (12.7 per cent), OBC (49.3 per cent) communities. and general communities (3.6 per cent).

Migrating population estimates have been reported by different sources as anywhere between two and twelve lakh. "During the drought year of 2000, the district administration itself admitted to migration of six-lakh population from the district."[35] "The largest movement of people in the world who go out in search of work of these, a third are thought to be bonded labourers. This floating vulnerable population accounts for anywhere between one-fifth and one-third of the rural population and is a major determinant of the economy and politics in this district".[36] Mostly migrant labourers come from poor strata of the society. They face the problem of acute landlessness and assetlessness and, indebtness, which forces them to become migrants. Migration is the manifestation of rural poverty, distress in the agrarian sector, inequitable distribution of resources by the state, poor-implementation of government schemes for the poor strata of the society. These people's presence was documented at various construction sites. Instances includes: Bhakra Nangal Dam (circa 1951), Hirakud (circa, 1959), Nagarjunasagar Dam (circa 1961), Narmada Dam, Sardar Sarovar Project, various steel plants, railway lines, and road constructions sites.[37]

## A Few Cases of Palamur Labour Situation

Instances of violations of the rights of Palamur labourers' at the places of destination are very rampant: The female migrants are particularly more vulnerable. In this type of distressed migration,the migrants' right to life is always at stake.[38] Many newly independent governments have attributed internal or external migration to the damage inflicted by colonialism- or capitalism. "It is assumed that the newly liberated powers could end territorial inequalities and create economic homogeneity across the national territory which was supposedly the promise of nationhood."[39] But it seems that this promise is far away from being realised in Palamur labour case. In the next section, a few human rights violation cases of Palamur labour will be highlighted to illustrate the situation of Palamur labour. The section will deal with cases of rights violations at the place of origin, i.e., in Mahabubnagar district and the places of destinations.

**Case-1**: **As Drought Spreads, Migration Gains Momentum in Mahabubnagar: The Thirsty People on the Bank of Krishna River:** This wisened face of a villager speaks volumes about the plight of the drought-stricken people. This is the case of one village of Kollapur taluk in the district. The drought condition is pushing them from their villages, though the village is located on the bank of river Krishna. "Migration of people from the drought-prone Mahabubnagar district of Telangana is not new. But in Peddamaruru village on the banks of river Krishna, such a thing was not heard of till last year. The village always used to have enough water for irrigation and household consumption and the agricultural labourers had ample opportunities to make a living, but the situation has changed completely. The mighty Krishna did not flow through the parched lands this year. Severe drought and the Almatti Dam upstream in Karnataka arrested its water flow. The huge pump sets that used to lift water from the river for irrigating 10,000 acres of the village's agricultural lands remained idle. For the first time, people started migrating from the place. In the last three months, over 200 people left the land of their birth in search of livelihood. Many more are planning to leave the village in the near future. One such person is Chinna Boddanna, an agricultural labourer. Last month, he got employment just for five days. He has not been employed for a single day so far in this month. Now, he is planning to migrate to Hyderabad. As to what will he do there, he has no clue. It is not just the agricultural labourers - drought has affected the lives of everyone in the village. In case of Mr. Anjaneyulu, a tailor who used to earn at least Rs 500 per month till last year, is now not even making Rs 100 per month. He said, that "the People just don't have money to get new clothes stitched for themselves." Recently, one such migrant labourer, Laxma Reddy, was reported missing while working on the Narmada Canal Project in Gujarat. His wife,Chittamma, had to run from pillar to post to know about her husband's plight. The Palamur Contract Labour Union (PCLU) had sent a petition to the National Human Rights Commission in this regard. Consequently, the NHRC directed the Chief Secretary of Gujarat to file a detailed report. According to PCLU, which has been fighting for the cause of farm labourers in the district, there have been 560 `missing' cases in the past.[40] In this case, at the place of origin of migrants, structural causes like drought, and non-availability of irrigation water, are forcing them to migrate. Rights to adequate livelihood is being violated in the process. The non-responsive state is violating, by not providing adequate livelihood sources through utilising of water resources of the district as a part of its obligations to protect the claims of the villagers. Despite its location on the bank of Krishna River, the village gets nothing out of it. The net result has been migration and missing of a few migrants and violation of their right to life.

In this case, various rights violations could be inferred like right to food; right to be freedom from hunger, right to health, right to education, right to be included in the state-sponsored welfare schemes, right to bargain at the market places and the right to association and, above all, the right to life. The human rights protection legislations like Bonded Labour Abolition (Regulation) Act[41], 1979, has also been violated.

**Case- 3: Aged persons the Victims of Starvation Deaths:** In the given drought and search for survival situation in Mahabubnagar district, the worst hit are the aged persons. "Clouds of starvation death loom large over the poverty-stricken old in the drought-hit villages of this perennially rain- deficient district, notwithstanding the stout denial by officials. Virtually abandoned by their young ones, who migrate to far off places in search of livelihood, the old are left to fend for themselves. Take the case of the frail 75-year-old widow, Megawat Sajani, a Lambada tribal of Tellarallapally Thanda, in Pangalmandal, who is a whisker away from death. She has five sons and three daughters. Barring the eldest daughter, all of them have migrated to different places, for "*dambbarpani*," (work on re-carpeting of roads). While four of her sons left three years ago, the last one followed them, two years ago. The trickle of rice that used to come from her sons dried up, of late. The other family members — her daughter and brother-in-law- are too poor to take care of her. Too weak, she stopped working. For some time, the neighbours fed her. Not anymore. How about ration card? "Yes, she has one. But where is the money with us to buy rice," says Bhikya, her brother- in-law. Equally pathetic is the condition of another old, indigent widow, Gopia. Her only son, a physically challenged person, left for the city in search of work, along with his wife, leaving behind their five-year-old son. The old woman takes care of herself and the little one. "I can`t work anymore. I survive on alms," she says. A cot lay under a tree, has become her makeshift shelter now, the one-room tenement she owned, having caved in last year. The situation is no better in the remote Mallampalli- Kothapalli village of Ghattu, the worst drought-affected mandal in the district. Thimakka of the village is another of those old souls, solely surviving on the neighbours' munificence, having lost her two sons. She neither has a ration card nor gets old-age pension. Her grandson, Bheemanna, works in Raichur and sends a small bag of rice, "whenever he remembers me." It is matter of time, before Sajani, Gopia and Thimakka; join the list of those dying of starvation. The local editions of the vernacular press put the toll so far this year, at six. But the State Government refuses to recognise these as starvation deaths.[42] Starvations and hunger deaths are due to a combination of different types of rights violations. Firstly, the right to work and adequate livelihood rights of younger family members were violated. As a result, they were driven out of their native place in search of livelihood. Here, right to work, right to have adequate livelihood option and right to health and other moral rights have been violated.

**Case-4: A Risky Agriculture in the District:** This particular case shows that how gradually agriculture is turning into a life-risking endeavor. It is a major reason for migration and re-migration like an unending cycle. Investments in agriculture fail to get returns. Marenna, forty-two years of age, migrated to Hyderabad for almost 12 years and then returned to Thimmayyapally village of Addakalmandal of Mahabubnagar district to stay with his parents. They have 6 acres land and 2 bullocks. He invested his remittances, around Rs. 15,000, and a bank loan of Rs 40,000 for digging four bore wells in his land. He again took a loan of Rs 3,000 for fertilisers. He took this loan from a moneylender in Moosapet, a nearby village, at an interest rate of 3per cent. He spent an additional sums to buy 2 kg of castor seeds for Rs 175, and 5 kg of maise seeds for Rs 240. But with the failure of rains, there were no returns from the land. Of the four bore wells, only one has any water in it. He is burdened with the heavy loans, which have to be paid back to the bank and moneylenders with little means at his disposal to do so. Now he has to remigrate.[43] In Marenna's case, lack of assured irrigation facilities is forcing him and many other people like him in the district to investment heavily on digging bore wells. This is one of the principal reasons behind debt problems. Right to livelihood is violated in this case. It is happening on a large scale district as a whole. In Mahabubnagar district, dependency on a irrigation through Tube wells is on the rise. The total irrigated area by tube wells increased from 0.09 per cent during 1979-80 to 72.69 per cent during 2003-04.[44]

**Case-5: Government Agencies Violates the Right to Life:** The Palamur labourers are mostly distressed migration. Another widely covered rights violation Incidence of Palamur labour happened in Hyderabad city. The victims were buried alive in a pit collapse incident. All four victims belonged to Gopalpet mandal, Polkepadu and Edula villagers, the labour contractors could bear only the funeral expenses and government compensated ten thousand rupees only. The particular incident happened in Hyderabad when the labourers were digging the sewerage lines from Kundan Bagh to Shankar Makhta. That particular work belonged to the sewerage board, which is part of Municipal Corporation of Hyderabad (MCH). The work was tendered to a labour contractor. The incident happened when they were digging the new line alongside of the old one. The measured width was three feet and depth above sixteen feet. The edge of the lining was very much wet and digging in this condition was very dangerous. The contractors MCH officials knew it very well that it would be dangerous. In the unavailability of any other work opportunities Palamur labourers were compelled to do that work. On the morning of May 11th 1997 this incident happened and the victims were Jayamma (22), Laxmaiah (40), Sheelaiah (40) and Swamy (16). The right to life and safety to life was violated in this incident. The compensation that the relatives of the victim's received was reported to be very nominal. The government agency MCH had violated all the human rights norms.[45]

**Case-6: Victims of Rights Violations in Mumbai:** In wall collapse incident which happened in Navi Mumbai's Koparkerna building construction site on 25th April 2006, seven Palamur labourers died. In this incident, the victims belonged to Koilkondamandal's perkividutanda were Kishan Nayak, Chandar Nayak, Mahabubnagar Mandal Potenepally villager Telugu Sreenu[46] and Bhutpurmandal Lambadi kunta *tanda*(a tribal hamlet) villagers Somla Nayak, Bhikya Nayak and Manemma. Maharashtra government announced an ex-gratia of Rs one lakh each to the kin of the victims. The construction company gave Rs two lakh to the kins.[47] This is one of the rare cases where the victim's families were compensated. In many cases, the victims their kins are denied any compensation.

**Case-7: The Overburdened Migrant Women:** Women care more than men, Susheelamma, wife of Boya Narayana, is a migrant from Sivarampet of Mahabubnagar district. She migrated with her husband to Mumbai for construction work through a contractor. Her three children, Renuka (10), Shravani (7) and Praveen (4), accompanied her. Susheelamma's work starts at 4 am, and she works continuously till 8 or 9 pm in the evening. She has to work at home and also join her husband to do hard labour work. After returning from the work in the evening, again she has to prepare food and look after the children. Sometimes her husband helps her by fetching water, but often he sits idle smoking bidis and shouts at her if the food is not prepared on time. Sometimes she gets help from her elder daughter, Renuka, in the household chores. She laments that this is the fate of women. In the case of Rangamma who hails from Rangapur, she migrated to Mumbai along with her husband and infant child. She took her elder daughter with her to take care of the child at the destination. Pullamma from Sivarampet said that she had brought her two young children with her to Hyderabad as she had nowhere to leave them in the village. The lack of childcare facilities at their workplace caused her considerable anxiety. Moving to different places at the destination for stone-cutting work, the chances of education for these children seemed remote. As a result of their migrant life, her elder son and two daughters never went to school.[48]

**Case-8: Deprived Childhood:** The migration is badly affecting the childhood of children, especially, their fundamental rights. The impact of migration on education of children was well described by a school teacher in Thimmayyapally thanda of Addakal mandal of the district. The migration rate is very high in this thanda. Almost every family has 2 or 3 people who have migrated to Mumbai. The dropouts rates in the school are largely due to migration. Usually, in July, the enrolment rate is high in the school. The migrant children also come to school with the other children of the *thanda*, probably because of the free food and books. But after the season is over, towards October-November, they drop outs rate from the school increases. Come July, they return and rejoin the same class; soon the age gap widens and the change of place affects their lives and they lose interest in coming to school. But there are perceived changes in the behaviour and attitude of children after they complete 4-5 years of schooling. The children of classes V-VII can cope with school and do additional work in the field and house. For migrant children, school facilities should be available at the destination, so that they can continue with their education. Provision for mobile teachers or sending one teacher from the area of origin to the destination area will help in overcoming the problem of language. Incentives like clothing, monetary compensation should be provided to the (dropout) children so that they will be interested in continuing their schooling.[49] The country's future is depending upon the children of the country. The migration process has been depriving the children of Palamur labourers of their fundamental constitutional right, the right to education.

**Case-9: Exclusion from the Political Society:** Prior to the parliament and state legislative assembly elections of 2004, one issue was widely reported. The news was that some political parties were demanding exclusion of Palamur labourers from the voters list. How their names could be removed from the voter list when they had immovable properties in their native villages, besides their old parents and children were still residing in the houses. The labourers could have migrated for livelihoods for a few months in a year and returned to their native places regularly on festival days and for elections, he said. Whether their names are included or excluded from the voters list, many lakh Palamur labour miss the opportunity to exercise their right to franchise. It results in denying their citisenship and political rights. In this manner, the labourers are been excluded from the political society.[50] Not only that, the Palamur labourers are widely excluded from the state-sponsored welfare schemes also.

These are the tips of iceberg. In the vernacular media, daily, many such reports are appearing. All above cases illustrate the extent of rights violations of Palamur labour. This labour phenomenon is the outcome of the political economy of the concerned Telangana state. The state has been neglecting utilisation of legitimate natural resources for the 'sons of the soil'. The possible remedy for this type of distressed migration could be twofold. Firstly, government agency should be asked to maintain a proper data about the migrants, employment generation activities should be strengthened, dry land agriculture must be developed; labour laws should be implemented stringently and other development activities must be implemented sincerely. Secondly, irrigation projects should be constructed to tap the river water potential of the district and land reforms should be carried out. So there must be efforts to create a more enabling environment both at the place of origin, i.e., in Mahabubnagar district, and at various places of destination.

## Conclusion

The main structural causes of distressed Palamur labour migration are located in the political economy of Telangana region. At the same, time there are possibilities to overcome these constraints. In the absence of effective use of these possibilities, the region and the districts remained a victim of politically determined backwardness. For this reasons, one has to blame none than the 'state', which has a subtle dominant caste, class and regional biases in its makeup. This type of state has not been performing its duty to protect the rights of the Palamur labour. This situation further gets aggravated by the parochial emphasis of liberty based rights as the human rights by the present human rights regime. But for effective remedy of Palamur labour rights, priority must be assigned to the second and third generation rights.

# 11

# Development for Whom? Displacing People, Destroying Identity and Suppressing the Voices of the Tribals:A Human Rights Perspective

*—Sheikh RafiqUllah*

> "Our rights as the native inhabitants of this region to our land, forests and homes are being snatched away from us, as we are threatened with eviction with no options offered. What is the government's response to this?"

This paper divided into four parts. The first part is an introduction discusses at length the onset of the 'Development Debate', specifically the debate on neo-liberal and the various aspects related associated with it. The second part discusses in detail the concept and the notion of development and development induced displacement. The third part of the paper seeks to critically analyse the role of the state and more specifically in the context of development induced displacement. The fourth part of the paper highlights about the various violations of the rights of the people and the suppression of their voices. And the fifth and the final part of the paper is a conclusion.

## Introduction

Since the 1990s, with the advent of the process of globalisation and the adoption of the New Economic Policy[1], one continuous premise that has been put forward by the Government of India is that rapid 'industrialisation' can mitigate its poverty. Banking on the huge mineral resources that the various states of India possess, mining based industries can alleviate poverty.[2] Moreover, Industrialisation' will open up employment opportunities, will generate employment for the unskilled poor, the cash-strapped state will earn revenue through taxes, royalties, land-sales etc.This understanding has led to a faulty analysis of the whole situation and thus, led to a skewed process of development.[3]

The governments of the various states in India are offering exceptionally huge subsidies to investors, in the form of guarantees, tax concessions and investment subsidy. The abundance of cheap labour further makes it an investor-friendly state. As far as economic benefits of new investments and privatisation programme are concerned, the state government boasts that the new investments will spur growth which, in turn, will help in poverty alleviation.[4] And this is the message being disseminated from all quarters – the corporate media, the government, the international aid agencies, the World-bank etc. Hence, India has become the most favoured country with a long list of investment proposals, largely backed by domestic as well as foreign investors.

Majority of the new projects are solely attracted by the mineral resources of the various states of India and therefore, are located in only mineral-rich regions which are also inhabited by the tribals. And one of the first impact of all the 'developmental projects' is land being lost by the people due to acquisition.[5] Moreover, in the name of development, neo-liberalismand rapid economic growth has resulted in monopolisation and exploitation of natural resources.This process of monopolisation of resources by the state has resulted in narrowing down of natural resource base for survival of economically poor, powerless and marginalised mostly the tribal's and Dalit's population. The fate of these people is not different from other oustees who have been uprooted through large dams, mines, coal-based power projects and heavy industries, in the past, in the state they only received meagre cash compensation with no jobs and agricultural lands. The state government has not examined the extent of negative impacts on their lives.

Tribal's displaced by projects taken up in even in 1950s and 60s haven't been rehabilitated till date. Liberalisation has opened the floodgates for extractive industrialization of the tribal areas of various states, rich in minerals, water and forests, by the corporate, both Indian and Multinational. The benefit hypothesis put forward by the government becomes highly questionable when one assesses the socio-economic condition of the tribal's which is visible in their poverty, their physical and cultural displacement and their lack of rights over their livelihood resources.[6] There has been a clear and persistent bias of the state which is favorable to corporate entities at the cost of its own people.

Against such a back ground, India and its various states has been the pioneer in many of the social protest movementswhich have been aimed at the 'developmental projects' The peoples hostility against the projects is increasing which not only cause delays in the execution of the projects but, more importantly, raises the basic question- Development for whom?[7] People of India, particularly the tribal people, and dalits pitched steep resistance against the plunder and forced land-grabbing of their ancestral land. But on several occasions, these resistances of the people were suppressed brutally by State violence thereby destroying their identity and suppressing their voices of dissent. Instead of fulfilling their constitutional duty to protect the rights of the tribal people and to ensure that the tribal people land remain in the hands of the community, the respective state governments has/have been selling these lands to the highest bidder and unleashing repression on anyone who dares to protest.

Hence, against such backdrop, the paper seeks to study development induced displacement in Odisha by acquisition of (agricultural) land for setting various industries (e.g., TATA and POSCO) and the role of the state in this context. The focus of the study is how the government is taking tribal land at a low price for the public purpose use and selling it to the private industry. The study also seeks to throw light upon the establishment of private industry impact on the livelihood, socio-economic and psychological status of people, who have lost their valuable land. It also looks into the violation of rights of the indigenous tribal's community and its impact on their lives especially the social and cultural aspect.

## Concepts

Development is a many sided process.[8] Development as a concept first emerged, becoming a major theme in economic and political discourse in the post Second World War era.[9] Development is "a process which enables human beings to realise their potential, build self-confidence, and lead lives of dignity and fulfillment. It is a process which frees people from fear of want and exploitation.[10] Development in a broader sense is understood to include other important and related attributes as well, notably equal opportunities, and political freedom and civil liberties. The overall goal of development is therefore to increase the economic, political and civil rights of people across the gender, ethnicity, religion, race, region, and nation as a whole. To substantiate the above argument I would like to add the meaning of development given by International Labour Organisation (ILO). To Quote:

*"Development is defined as a process which involves improvement in the quality of life of weaker sections and greater participation and involvement of the masses in the process of decision-making in the economic, social, and political and the cultural life of society"*.[11]

Moreover, development entails a modern infrastructure (both physical and institutional), and a move away from low value added sectors such as agriculture and natural resource extraction. The purpose of development is, thus, to provide increasing opportunities to all people for a better life.[12] The term economic development is far more comprehensive. Economic development is regarded as indispensable for the progress and prosperity of any country. Economic development raises the living standards of people so that they are better off from their previous state. It involves creation of basic infrastructure like railways, roads, shipping, civil aviation, power station, irrigation facilities, means of communication, establishment of industries. Such projects are invariably required as they improve lives of people, provide employment to them and supply them better services.[13] To support the above argument I would like to cite the definition of development given by Amartya Sen. To Quote:

> *"Economic growth cannot be sensibly treated as an end in itself. Development has to be more concerned with enhancing the lives we lead and the freedoms we enjoy. Development is the process of expanding the freedoms that people enjoy. It requires removing barriers to freedom: poverty, tyranny, unaccountable government, lack of opportunities, systematic social deprivation, lack of functioning infrastructure, and repression. Development depends on people's ability to make good choices in their economic, political, and social lives."*[14]

Today, development is more and more understood as sustainable human development, addressing the human being in relation to both resource management and participation. From this perspective, economic growth has to serve human development.[15] UNICEF has a similar understanding of sustainable human development, embracing the economic, political, social, environmental, and cultural dimensions of development. Such holistic visions of development are consistent with human rights standards because human rights also refer to the whole human being.[16] Hence, one cannot make a monolithic viewpoint in defining or conceptualising development. After all, the primary aim of development is to satisfy man's spiritual and material needs. Development, then, consists of the ability to maximize resources.[17] It is for the benefit of human beings in all of their aspects, tangible and intangible. Development, from the totality of the foregoing, can be defined simply as the fulfillment of human potential.

Displacementis a ubiquitous as it is found all over the world. Wherever economic development is taking place, displacement is emerging as something that is adversely affecting the lives of affected people. At times this raises question regarding futility of economic development projects. Development and displacement reflect the relative power of various groups involved particularly the power of politically, economically and socially strong groups to impose harsh sacrifices on the weak and unprivileged groups.[18] Displacement is the project impact that necessitates resettlement of affected persons. Displacement may be either physical or economic. Physical displacement is the actual physical relocation of people resulting in loss of shelter, productive assets or access to productive assets (such as land, water and forest). Displaced persons are cut off from their homes, communities, and source of livelihood, they usually live in destitute conditions and are vulnerable to human rights abuses. Economic displacement results from an action that interrupts or eliminates access to productive assets without physically relocating the people themselves.[19] In a nutshell, displacement implies relocation of affected persons far away from their places of residence, but displacement need not always involves relocation. To make the argument more valid I would like to mention Neera Chandhoke views on displacement. To Quote:

> *"In the name of public purpose the local people have been disposed of their homes, their access to means of subsistence, disposed of their life style. Displacement means breaking up of communities, sundering their ties with their ancestral lands, dividing people who may be tied by organic links making in short people rootless. It is systematic violation of basic right i.e. the right to move and live freely in any part of India, the right to livelihood, the right to culture and community."*[20]

Thus, development induced displacement forces individual and communities to leave their homes and homesteads for the purpose of economic development. Development induced displacement involves a fundamental dilemma: economic development as a move to improve living conditions of people is desirable but displacement associated with is undesirable. Worldwide the effects of displacement are strongly felt amongst economically and socially vulnerable and politically marginalised groups and indigenous communities.[21] It has been historically associated with the construction of dams for hydroelectric power and irrigation purposes but also appears due to many other activities, such as mining and the creation of military installations, airports, industrial plants, weapon testing grounds, railways, road developments, urbanisation, conservation projects, forestry, etc. Development-induced displacement generally give rise to severe social, economic and environmental problems as it brings about widespread changes.[22] Hence, I would like to interpret theWorld Bank Group's Policy on Involuntary Resettlement (Operational Policy 4.12, approved on 23.10.2001) that clearly observes that Bank experience indicates that involuntary resettlement under development projects, if unmitigated, often give rise to severe economic, social and environmental risks. To Quote:

> *"Productive systems are dismantled; people face impoverishment when their productive assets or income sources are lost; people are relocated to environments where their productive skills may be less applicable and the competition for resources greater; community institutions and social networks are weakened; kin groups are dispersed; cultural identity, traditional authority, and the potential for mutual help are diminished or lost."*[23]

The past study indicates that the development may be boon for some but they are a curse for the rest. It is usually observed that the adverse effects of displacement are mostly due to shortcomings in rehabilitation and resettlement policies and programmes. And this lacuna in rehabilitation and resettlement policies has given rise to a number of social protest movements. These social movements take the path of protest and agitations against government policy of industrialisation that would bring more development and prosperity to the region. Sometimes these protest movements and agitations becomes a law and order issue and poses a serious threat to the democratic set-up. In such a backdrop, police and military emerge as an important state instrument to control the situation and maintain law and order. However, in course of the time, the State and its various agencies like the police becomes impatient, loses its control over itself and takes the course of violence. Instead of playing a constructive role, preserving order and preventing crime, the police with State sanction becomes more and more involved in lawlessness and disorder.

## Role of the State

In liberal theory, the origin of the state is conjectured as a product of social contract arrived at through the consent of the individuals. The contract was necessary as relations between human beings were mediated through force and it was that arbitrary force in the state of nature that was brought under the regulation of law.[24] It also maintains that every human being is endowed with reason and since reason is superior to raw emotions and uncultivated impulses it has been possible to arrive at the acceptance of supremacy of law. It is also postulated that human beings enjoyed unrestrained freedom in the state of nature. Surrendering part of the freedom was a component of the contract. This surrender was in exchange for security. Thus, guaranteeing right to security, in a way, has come to define the basic function of the state. It is precisely forthese reasons that the state has been given the power to use the force but the force can and should be used only in a way that the procedure mandates. The procedure is evolved in pursuance of the objectives for which the state came into being.[25] Therefore, the state should protect the right to life and security of every individual.

However, there have been several instances where unwanted violence has used by the state against its own people and particularly indigenous communities in the context of development and displacement. The excessive use of force by the state apparatus not only does harm to the cause of human rights but become counterproductive to the internal working of the state itself. The minute there is arbitrariness in the use of force, it has the intrinsic propensity to lead to deinstitutionalisation of behaviour. This, in the ultimate, can end up in despotic governance with no regard to any of the human rights standards-national or international.There are many reports that have discussed increasing state violence against indigenous people during land acquisition in the context of development induced development. Here, I would like to discuss one such very important report by an international non-governmental organisation.

Amnesty International[26] from time to time has pointed out about state violence. In its various reports (2007, 08, 09, 10, 11), it has pointed out that marginalised local communities, including adivasis (indigenous communities), dalits and small farmers, who protested against land acquisition (fraudulent methods of acquiring land like in the case of Kalinganagar), forced eviction, threats to their livelihood, denial of their right to participation in decision-making over development projects, and resettlement and rehabilitation (low compensation) processes went through many types of human rights abuses like unlawful killings, forced evictions, excessive use of police force and violence against women and harassment of human rights defenders campaigning for land and environmental rights of rural communities. For e.g., local communities resisted moves to acquire land for business projects and special economic zones in several states, including West Bengal, Odishsa, Jharkhand, Chhattisgarh, Madhya Pradesh, Andhra Pradesh, Karnataka, Tamil Nadu, Pondicherry, Maharashtra and Meghalaya, whose livelihoods were threatened by fast-tracked irrigation, mining, manufacturing and business projects were subjected to unlawful methods by police. [27]

Despite the scale of displacement, resettlement of those displaced by developmental projects and processes has been minimal. It would not be an exaggeration to say that veryfew resettlement programmes in the country have adequately compensated all those who are dispossessed. The low amounts of compensation and, in rare cases, land-for-land, reinforce dependency on officials and official agencies as those who face displacement hope to secure a better alternative. And yet, the state refuses to recognise this assertion, and persists in pointing fingers at civil society groups to say they are inciting the tribals.[28] Thukral, Enakshi Ganguly (1996).

A strategy under which the state allies with corporations to dispossess people of their livelihoods is nothing but developmental terrorism[29], irrespective of the political label of the political parties in office. One of the most glaring example of such kind was on January 2, 2006, the Orissa state police opened fire and killed at least 12 Adivasis who had gathered at the site of the TISCO steel plant in Kalinganagar.[30] Civil society fact-finding groups indicate that the incident was precipitated deliberately by the State and district administration to crush the resistance of Kalinganagar's displaced Adivasis.

Similarly, in June 2007, over 500 people were reported to have migrated from Jagatsinghpur, Odisha, as a result of the uncertainties surrounding the development of a large steel plant byPOSCO, which had been granted SEZ status in November 2006. Civil society groups working in the area have estimated that over 20,000 people from 15 villages in the district will be displaced by this project and be deprived of their traditional livelihood of betel leaf farming. The government does not have a uniform national policy on Resettlement & Rehabilitation (R&R) that would safeguard the interests of indigenous communities against the conflicting interests of the corporation, and the state and central governments. The R&R and Land Acquisition Bill (2007) fail to outline concrete measures to ensure the resettlement of indigenous communities and protect them from forced eviction. At the same time, the introduction of a new National Mineral Policy 2008 and the Amendment Bill to the Mines & Mineral Act, 1957, also threatens to take away whatever little the R&R and Land Acquisition Bills may ensure for indigenous communities.[31]

## Violations of the Rights of the People

India's present investment boom, as it opens its markets and "resources" to foreign companies, has a shadow side which many are not aware of. Essentially, the boom is at the expense of uprooting indigenous communities all over India, and at the cost of permanent damage to India's environment. The "mineral wealth" lying in the mountains of Orissa, Chattisgarh, Andhra Pradesh and Jharkhand States-a non-renewable resource is being opened up to an unprecedented scale of mining and metal manufacture byIndian as well as foreign companies. Extracting vast quantities of iron-ore, bauxite,chromites, coal etc. from these mountains not only affects the immediate and long-term well-being of India's environment. It also leads to mass dispossession.[32]

Development-induced displacement in the country has brought severe economic, social and environmental problems to the displaced people. The issue is not only concerned with acquisition of land but has wider and serious implications. It includes destruction of the watershed, disturbing the delicate ecological balance and distorts the surrounding environment, loss of wildlife and precious irreplaceable flora, etc. and most notorious problems of flooding, water-logging and salinity. Displacement has caused wide spread traumatic psychological and socio-cultural consequences. These include the dismantling of traditional production systems, desecration of ancestral sacred zones, graves and places of worship, scattering of kinship groups, disruptions of family system and informal social network.[33] It willsuffice to quote the UN statement in this context:

> *"Often uprootedfrom their traditional lands and ways of life andforced into prevailing national societies, indigenous people/Adivasis face discrimination, marginalisation and alienation. Despite growing political mobilisation in pursuit of their rights, they continue to lose their cultural identity along with their natural resources. Some of them are in imminent danger of extinction".*[34]

Further, development induced displacement has a gender dimension. The impact of such development hits the women hardest: evicted from their homes and surroundings, normal life in the village, however unpleasant, disrupted, their misery is much more palpable than the men's. Not getting proper compensation or land, all these people have been forced to migrate in search of work. Ignorant, illiterate, gullible, untutored in urban ways, often suffering from malnutrition and having no organised body to turn to, the women have a hard life, one of gross exploitation both sexually and work wise.[35]

## Conclusions

The development process in India has repeatedly generated self-sustaining poverty rather than self-sustaining growth. The impact of displacement by development projects in India and the rehabilitation and development of displaced people has been "difficult and unmanageable." This shows that the development planners have failed to improve the living standards for India's poor and the development policies have been "imposed from above", and devised and implemented through "top down" structures and are synonymous with large, expensive projects that are far removed from the needs and expectations of those they are intended to benefit. Moreover, industries were commonly instructed by government to provide at least one job per household to displaced families, this instruction was often ignored in practice. Although industries often had adequate financial resources to provide effective resettlement and rehabilitation, they regularly lacked the vision or interest to do so.Further,the state and national governments lack the willingness and capacity to properly resettle and rehabilitate people displaced by development projects. Even in situations where some form of legal framework to rehabilitate the displaced exists, most people among the vulnerable groups end up poorer than they were before displacement.

## References


- Baxi, Upendra (1994), '*Inhuman Wrongs and Human Rights: Unconventional Essays*',Har-Anand Publications, New-Delhi.
- Chandhoke, Neera (2006), '*Peoples Movement and the Articulation of Rights*', Indian Journal of Human Rights, Vol. 10 & 11, No.1 & 2, (Jan-Dec.) pp. 55-73.
- Gill, S.S. (1997), *'State, Democratic Movement And Human Rights In India*', Indian Journal of Human Rights, Volume-1, No-2 July-December.
- Goodland, Robert (2007), *India: Orissa, Kashipur, ' Utkal Bauxite & Alumina Project: Human Rights and Enviromental Impacts',* Library of Congress cataloging-in- Publication Data, pp-1-128.
- Hamm, B.I. (2001), *'A Human Rights Approach to Development',* Human Rights Quarterly, Vol. 23, pp. 1005-1031, The John Hopkins University Press.
- Hota, L.B. And Suar Damodar (2008), *'Involuntary Resettlement in Dan Projects Of Orissa:Risk and Reconstruction', The Eastern Anthropologist*, Vol. 61, No. 3 pp. 347-349.
- *India: Citizen's groups statement against police firing on protestors in Jaitapur, Maharashtra',* South Asia Citizens Web, 19 April, 2011 as retrieved from http:/ /www.sacw.net/article1018.html.
- Katare, P.M. and Barik, B.C. (Ed, 2002), '*Development, Deprivation and Human Rights Violations*', Rawat Publication, Jaipur.
- Kaushal, Nandita (2009), '*Displacement: An Undesirable and Unwanted Consequence of Development*', The Indian Journal of Political Science, Vol. LXX, No. 1, (Jan.-Mar.)
- Mohapatra L.K (1994), *'Tribal development in India: Myth and Reality',* New Delhi, VikashPublishing House.
- Mathur, H.M. (2006), '*Resettling People Displaced by Development Projects: Some Critical Management Issues*', Social Change, Vol. 36, No. 1, March, pp. 38.

- McCorquodale, R and Fairbrother, R (1991), *'Globalisation and Human Rights'*, Human Rights Quarterly, Vol. 21, pp. 735-766, The John Hopkins University Press.
- Mishra, Banikanta (2010), *'Agriculture, Industry and Mining In Orissa in the post liberalization Era: An Inter-District and Inter-State Panel Analysis'*, Economic and Political Weekly, Vol. XLV, No. 20 (May), pp.49-70.
- *Mining in Orissa'*, Environmental Protection Group, Orissa, Vol. I, No. 5, May-2006.
- Noorjahan Bava (Ed, 2004), Public Administration in twenty first Century, Kaniska Publishers.
- Oliver-Smith, Anthony (2010), "*Defying Displacement: Grassroots Resistance and the Critique of Development*", University of Texas Press, Texas, pp. 2-22.
- Orissa Annual Reference 2009 as retrieved from http://www.orissa.govt.in
- Orissa's new name is Odisha-The Times of India, March 24, 2011.
- Patel, M. Amrita &Jha, K. Manish (2007), *'Weapons of the Weak: Field Studies on Claims to* PUCL (People's Union for Civil Liberties) Bulletin, April 2006 as retrieved from http://www. *pucl.org/Topics/Dalits-tribal/2006.kalinganagar.htm*
- Pati, Janardhan (2006), *'A Report on the Bloodbath in Kalinga Nagar'*, Social Scientist, Vol. 34, No. 7/8 (Jul.-Aug.), pp. 86-90.
- Peet , Richard with Eline Hartwick (2005), *'Theories of Development'*, New Delhi, Rawat Publication.
- Rist, Gilbert, *'Development as a buzzword'*, Development in Practice, Routledge, Volume 17, 2007 No. 4-5, pp.485 — 491retrieved from*http://www2.dse.unibo.it/...development/Rist_Development-as-a-buzzword...*
- Sarangi, Prakash (1997), *'Notion of Rights In Rawls'*, Special Issue, Human Rights: Theoretical Perspectives, The Indian Journal of Human Rights, Vol. 1&2, Human Rights Programme, University of Hyderabad.
- Seers, Dudely (1972), *'What are We Trying to Measure? in 'Measuring Development', Journal of Development studies*, Vol. 8(3)
- Sen, Amartya (2000), "*Development as Freedom*", Oxford University Press, New Delhi, pp. 3-4.
- Udombana, N. J. (2000), *"The Third World and the Right to Development: Agenda for the Next Millennium"*, Human Rights Quarterly, Vol. 22, No. 3, Aug., pp. 753-787, The Johns Hopkins University Press.
- Update Series 13 (2007), *Charade of 'Industrialization' & 'Development', Orissa: 'Industrialization at the Gunpoint'*, Update, Kolkata.
- World Development Report (1991), *'The Challenges of Development: Published for World Bank'*, New York, Oxford University Press, pp 31.
- www.http://censusindia.net
- www.http://www.jajpur.nic.in
- www.http://www.en.Wikipedia.org/wiki/Economic_Development.com, retrieved on 18th March 2011.
- http://www.en.wikipedia.org/wiki/Kalinganagar
- http://www.en.wikipedia.org/wiki/Orissa

## Notes

1. Thorat, Sukhdeo (1997), *'The New Economic Policy and Its Impact on employment and Poverty of the Scheduled Castes'*, Published by Department of Sociology, University of Pune.
2. Patel, M. Amrita &Jha, K. Manish (2007), *'Weapons of the Weak: Field Studies on Claims to Social Justice in Bihar & Orissa'*, Report on Social Justice – I, Mahanirban Calcutta Research Group, Kolkata. (Web Source: www.mcrg.ac.in)
3. Ibid-Pg-11.
4. Update Series 13 (2007), *'Charade of Industrialization' & 'Development', Orissa: 'Industrialization at the Gunpoint'*, Update, Kolkata.
5. Mishra, Banikanta (2010), *'Agriculture, Industry and Mining In Orissa in the post liberalization Era: An Inter-District and Inter-State Panel Analysis'*, Economic and Political Weekly, Vol. XLV, No. 20 (15th May), pp. 49-70.
6. Mining and Industrialization Update (2006), *'Orissa, Environmental Information on Industries and Mining in Orissa'*, Environmental Protection Group, Orissa, Vol. I, No. 5 (May)
7. Patel, M. Amrita &Jha, K. Manish (2007), *'Weapons of the Weak: Field Studies on Claims to Social Justice in Bihar & Orissa'*, Report on Social Justice – I, Mahanirban Calcutta Research Group, Kolkata. (Web Source : www.mcrg.ac.in)
8. Udombana, N. J. (2000), *"The Third World and the Right to Development: Agenda for the Next Millennium"*, Human Rights Quarterly, Vol. 22, No. 3, Aug., pp. 753-787, The Johns Hopkins University Press.
9. Oliver-Smith, Anthony (2010), "*Defying Displacement: Grassroots Resistance and the Critique of Development*", University of Texas Press, Texas, pp. 2-22
10. Katare, P.M. and Barik, B.C. (Ed, 2002), '*Development, Deprivation and Human Rights Violations*', Rawat Publication, Jaipur.
11. Web:www.http://en.Wikipedia.org/wiki/Economic_Development.com, accessed on 18th March 2011.
12. World Development Report (1991), *'The Challenges of Development: Published for World Bank'*, New York, Oxford University Press, pp 31.
13. Kaushal, Nandita (2009), '*Displacement: An Undesirable and Unwanted Consequence of Development*', The Indian Journal of Political Science, Vol. LXX, No. 1, Jan.-Mar
14. Sen, Amartya (2000), "*Development as Freedom*", Oxford University Press, New Delhi, pp.3-4.
15. Hamm, B.I. (2001), *'A Human Rights Approach to Development'*, Human Rights Quarterly, Vol. 23, pp. 1005-1031, The John Hopkins University Press.
16. *Ibid.*
17. Udombana, N. J. (2000), *"The Third World and the Right to Development: Agenda for the Next Millennium"*, Human Rights Quarterly, Vol. 22, No. 3, Aug., pp. 753-787, The Johns Hopkins University Press.
18. Kaushal, Nandita (2009), '*Displacement: An Undesirable And Unwanted Consequence of Development*', The Indian Journal of Political Science, Vol. LXX, No. 1, Jan.-Mar.

19. Mathur, H.M. (2006), '*Resettling People Displaced by Development Projects: Some Critical Management Issues*', Social Change, Vol. 36, No. 1, March, pp. 38.
20. Chandhoke, Neera (2006-07), '*Peoples Movement and the Articulation of Rights*', Indian Journal of Human Rights, Vol.10&11, No.1&2, , Jan-Dec., pp. 55-73.
21. Kaushal, Nandita (2009), '*Displacement: An Undesirable And Unwanted Consequence of Development*', The Indian Journal of Political Science, Vol. LXX, No. 1, Jan.-Mar
22. Kothari, Smitu (1996), '*Whose Nation? The Displaced as Victims of Development*', Economic and Political Weekly, Vol. 31, No. 24, (June), pp. 1476-1485.
23. Kaushal, Nandita (2009), ' *Displacement: An Undesirable And Unwanted Consequence of Development*', The Indian Journal of Political Science, Vol. LXX, No. 1, Jan.-Mar.
24. Rousseau, Jean Jacques (1977), '*The Social Contract*', Trans Maurice Cranston, Penguin Books, London.
25. Paine, Thomas (1795), '*The Rights of Man*', Citizen Daniel Isaac Eaton Cock and Swine, London.
26. Amnesty International is a non-governmental organisation focuses on human rights with over 3 million members and supporters around the world. The objective of the organisation is "to conduct research and generate action to prevent and end grave abuses of human rights, and to demand justice for those whose rights have been violated." (Web Sources: www.en. Wikipedia.org/wiki/Amnesty_International)
26. Amnesty International Report (2007-080, '*The State of World's Human Rights*', Amnesty International Publications Limited, Peter Benenson House, 1 Eastern Street, London, United Kingdom.

    ———(2009), '*The State of World's Human Rights*', Amnesty International Publications Limited, Peter Benenson House, 1 Eastern Street, London, United Kingdom.

    ———(2010), '*The State of World's Human Rights*', Amnesty International Publications Limited, Peter Benenson House, 1 Eastern Street, London, United Kingdom.

    ———(2011), '*The State of World's Human Rights*', Amnesty International Publications Limited, Peter Benenson House, 1 Eastern Street, London, United Kingdom.
28. Thukral, EnakshiGanguly (1996), '*Development. Displacement and Rehabilitation: Locating Gender*', Economic and Political Weekly, Vol. 31, No. 24, (June), pp. 1500-1503.
29. Bhaduri, Amit (2007), '*Development or Developmental Terrorism?*', Economic and Political Weekly, Vol. 42, No. 7 (Feb.), pp. 552-553.
30. Pati, Biswamoy (2006), "*Tatas and Orissa 'Model' of Capitalist 'Development*'", Social Scientist, Vol. 34, No. 3/4 Mar.-Apr.), pp. 37-42.
31. NGO Report to The United Nations Committee on Economic, Social and Cultural Rights (2008), '*Divided Destinies and Unequal Lives: Economic, Social and*

*Cultural Rights and the Indian State'*, People's Collective for Economic, Social and Cultural Rights.

32. Padel, Felix and Das, Samarendra (2006), *'Anthropology of Genocide: Tribal Movement in Central India Against Over-Industrialisation'*, SAAG (Web Source: www.freewebs.com)
33. Pandey, Balaji and Rout, Binaya Kumar (2004), *'Development Induced Displacement in India: Impact on Women'*, National Commission for Women, New Delhi.
34. Pandey, Balaji (2008), 'The KalingaNagar Tragedy: Development Goal or Development Malaise', Social Change, December, Vol. 38, No. 4, pp. 609-626.
35. Rao, Amiya (1986), *'Cost of Development Projects: Women among the 'Willing Evacuees'*, Economic and Political Weekly, Vol. 21, No. 12 (Mar.), pp. 474-476.

# 12

# Understanding Humiliation from Double Victimisation Perspective: A Case Study of a Female Divorcee

—*Bijaya Kumar Mohanty*

## Introduction

The major objective of this paper is to advance a theoretical picture by seeing or understanding 'Humiliation' from a 'Double Victimisation' socio-cultural process. And the term humiliation is not necessarily always a socio-cultural phenomenon. Rather it has its direct or indirect resonance within the framework of certain multi-array of social/economical/cultural/legal/spatial arrangements in a given society. Since "human nature is a multi-layered affair, *and people do* acknowledge or respond to events at many levels" (Nandy 2009: 41-42 and emphasis added); keeping such multi-layered understanding of human nature in focus, at the outset, this paper will focus on certain socio-cultural or socio-psychological practices, within the domain or through which a person largely lives his/her everyday life or subjected to certain kind of humiliating practices.

The peace researcher, Johan Galtung (1996) once set a basic question - what is humiliation (?).[1] To him, humiliation is more or less a psychological phenomenon and when physical violence, directly or indirectly, constitutes the act of humiliation, it leads to a series of other socio-cultural stigmatisation or victimisation process. Putting it another way, the wound or the trauma is not always a direct outcome of physical act of violence, but sometimes or to some group or individual cases, the very act of humiliating process leaves a deeper psychic tantrum in the victim's post-traumatic life turn-outs – a sort of follow-ups[2] which, in some cases, happens to follow or taunt a victim to her or his social or professional relocating, or resettling, life world spheres.

To pursue these lines of contentions, this paper is divided into three parts. Firstly, an attempt will be made to understand the act of humiliation from the perspective of socio-cultural or psychological phenomenon and its specific meaning to women, in general, and an individual victim, in particular.

Secondly, it will attempt to paint a localness of the debate called 'divorce' in general and a female 'divorcee', in particular, and finally, an individual case study will be taken up to understand the socio-cultural and psychological web of humiliating life turn-outs and the votaries of social institutions, and traditional customs/beliefs associated in the life of an individual victim's victimisation processes. This paper will address the issue of humiliation and its effects on the victim and explore its significance of creating a traumatic experience. The word humiliation will in this paper be used in the sense of the feelings or emotions endured by a victim.

## Understanding Humiliation from a Perspective of an Individual's Feeling or Emotion

The word humiliation has an extremely complicated semantic field. In addition humiliation is a concept that connects macro, meso and micro levels, and since this paper's major concern is to understand an individual victim's humiliating process in a micro level, in order to do so, this paper will proceed in a direction, which would help us to understand how "humiliation is *directly linked to some* sort of behaviour or condition that constitutes a sound reason for a person to consider how his or her self-respect *was violated or* injured" (Margalit 1996, 9 and emphasis was not original). The word humiliation is usually used, both an act perpetrated by an actor and a feeling felt by a victim. The act of humiliation may occurr as a short-term event, or as long-term structural[3] continuation in one victim's day to day life-turnouts. So it is plausible, to understand the linkages between certain dominant structures and its, direct or indirect, receptions of one particular individual's life turnout, which are crucial to understanding the victimisation, which one victim happens to encounter or participates willingly or unwillingly in a particular event or action, which leads one individual to experience some form of humiliating life turnout.

It is within these webs of structures, one individual or a group/collective[4] happens to engage in various forms of interactions or a mode of 'doing life' or a pattern of 'living live', which, someway or other, leads to humiliating[5] experiences. In a typical Raymondian sense; "*it is these relational patterns,* which sometimes reveal unexpected identities and correspondences in hitherto separately considered activities, sometimes again reveal discontinuities of an unexpected kind, that *in some form or* other *turns out as a generalised kind of social and cultural practices* (Williams, 2009, 35 and emphasis added). In a similar vein, while describing 'societal meaning of structures', the renowned clinical psychologist Klaus Holzkamp, in 'On Doing Psychology Critically', suggests that -

> 'humans do not respond to external stimuli, but to certain meaning, *a process of participation, not necessarily always a direct result of somebody's willingness to be a volunteer in any such behavioural*

*interactive processes, rather it is those 'structures' which not only affects a person's living pattern, but such human and societal interactions also opens up the gateway for such generalised*[6] *form of social practices'* (Holzkamp, 1992, abstract, emphasis added).

While attempting to understand certain characteristics or social situations, in which someone faces or experiences humiliation, Silver, *et al.,* pointed out, that "humiliation can be treated, either as a social act or an emotion". To them, humiliation can be experienced by certain provocations, which comes through certain triviality "of everyday life; being ignored, *stalked*, slighted, patronised, or even, being pitied or helped, is sometimes humiliating". Looking at humiliation from emotional aspects, it can be viewed as 'compelling, brute, irrational, and undecorous' and 'is the sort of emotion that may overwhelm us even when we know that we have done nothing to 'deserve' it; it is often a striking example of passivity, and suffering'. It would seem more at ease with one that sees emotion as an immediate, automatic, thoughtless effect of the provoking situation. This latter view has deep roots within academic psychology, as it was rightly concluded by William James that emotions are the feeling of the bodily changes caused by the direct stimulation of an 'exciting fact'; the appraisal of the fact occurs afterwards: "If one abruptly see a dark moving form in the woods, our heart stops beating, and we catch our breath instantly and before any articulate idea of danger can arise"[7]. This citation can be linked to certain form of social behaviours, for example in a particular locality or in a neighborhood, if one individual is known for her failed social life, or due to some sort of socially susceptible disease or anything similar to that effect which usually tends to raise the eyebrows of the so-called moral sanctity of certain social institutions.

Let us discuss one particular example, which can be directly linked to this paper's concern. Consider a divorcee or a widow who decides to live single in a different location which has no direct connection with her natal-relativity or with the affinal family (with whom she had recently delinked her relationship). Even though, she tries to live her life after any such traumatised social life, there is no guarantee that she won't be subjected to some form of neighbourhood gossips, which often makes her to believe that it was she who was entirely responsible for such failed social life, or in some cases, her chastity was even questioned or even sometimes she is subjected to certain form of lecherous comments (usually these consist of slang language, bad gestures, and buyable type of proposals etc.) and even sometimes she is being stalked by some 'anonymous social institutions'[8]. These are some kind of triviality of one's social life, which can be described in Silverian sense as "*somebody's* powerlessness and not something more brute, such as revulsion through contact or *unwanted interactivity processes*, that causes humiliation rather it is *somebody's* incapacity, powerlessness, which underlie the triviality of humiliations in every-day lives". In a different context, while discussing 'emotion in social life' Derek Layder[9] has beautifully explained that it is when one individual self enters into 'social interaction',[10] s/he is subjected to certain kind of vulnerability, which can be understood in Laingan sense as "ontological insecurity". In *The Divided Self* (1960), Ronald David Laing contrasted the experience of the 'ontologically secure' person with that of a person who "cannot take the realness, aliveness, autonomy and identity of himself and others for granted" and who consequently contrives strategies to avoid 'losing his self'[11]. In other words, "the distinguishing features of this sort of insecurity are a feeling of unreality, an experience of 'deadness' rather than aliveness, a confusion around identity, a sense of estrangement from one's body and a general alienation from the self or a feeling of being inappropriate to life (Branden 1985, cited in Layder, 2004, 41)". The section to follow will review the existing literature on how divorce leads to humiliating experiences, particularly for women and its linkage with some specific factors which lead to divorce in contemporary 'Indian Hindu Family Systems'.

Marriage and Divorce in Indian Hindu Society: a Post-divorce Socio-cultural Repercussion.

Daughters and sons are one's own, but the daughter-in-law is other.—Indian proverb.

When a girl marries off, she expects to start out a new life with a possibility of having a joyful post-married life. But in some cases, certain unfavourable situational turn-out as well as societal oddities that not just shatter her dream but also push her to a world, where she is just left to succumb to a volume of uncertain sufferings and humiliations. This could lead to a situation, where such a victim silently experiences her own 'humiliation' or succumbs to the web of 'double victimisation process'. Firstly, surprisingly, through her in-laws, husband or child (in some cases it appears that even her own child not only disapproves her motherhood but also abandons her social identity, possibly, when she expects or considers them as consoling left-over). Secondly, unsurprisingly, through the form of societal disapproval regime, which often seems to be re-questioning her past social identity or failed social life-turnouts. As it has been observed in a different context "among all the dilemmas divorce poses, the power of the past is the hardest to understand and once understood, the most difficult to overcome" (Krantzler, 1973, 51-53, as cited in Usha Devi R, 2008, 82). In order to trace its socio-historical root or attempting to understand clues for such dubious relational conun-drums[12], particularly in contemporary society, the following section will discuss the existing literature on divorce in "Indian Hindu Society vis-à-vis women Divorcees".

According to the traditional Hindu view, marriage is a sacrament. For the vast majority of people, marriage is always within one's religious group, and the family also, therefore, prevails within it. Going by such a generalised view point of family, marriage, *vis-à-vis* the current social status of women in

Indian society, one dominant view of existing literature indicates that women in the Indian society mostly derive their social status from their husbands, and would need a researcher's cautious approach while delineating the women's position in current changing values of Indian family and its direct influence on early social institutions like family and marriage and even divorce. As it has been beautifully described by M. N. Srinivas: "It [the changing position of Indian women] has many facets and generalisation is well nigh impossible because of the existence of considerable variations among regions, between rural and urban areas, among classes, and finally among different religious, ethnic and caste groups" (Srinivas, 1978, 7). Keeping such a cautious approach of macro socio-cultural understanding in mind, a sort of micro perspective can be contextualised or explained for studying some specific or some individual cases. This paper will attempt to understand the various social climates which usually surround a divorce and the kind of social stigma attached to this marital-discord. To do so, it would be plausible to make an entry point from the general understandings, which are usually associated with the stages of one girl's marriage stage to her wifely transformations (which sometimes follow the successful motherhood stage, while in some other cases, it tends to end in tragic fallout called divorce).

Ideally, marriage binds the two families and two persons of these families together forever. Through the marital bond, families became affines or they enhance their affinity and persons become a complementary union of husband and wife. To Trawick (1996, 155), marriage is "a ritualised, public and formal sharing of persons and the materials of life among families." Moreover, the marriage ceremony is one of the major rituals of the life cycle that alters a person's status and position. The marriage rituals not only express these alterations but define, construct, and interpret them for the actors themselves (Fruzzetti, 1982, 9). The women's 'fluidity' and 'permeable' quality (Trawick, 1996, 133) facilitate the transformation of their personhood which is necessary in order to incorporate them into their husband's families and to become the full personalities of first as auspicious wives and later, blessed mothers (Fruzzetti 1982, 31). A process of identity alteration which starts with a solemnisation of a marriage, and this also usually viewed as the passage which usually brings a sort of gender transformation for a newly married woman from early wifehood periods to motherhood blessings. And it is also observed that, in some cases, it is the same passage which unleashes a life of uncertainty and unwanted crisis for some Indian women. A transformative process which announces their new identity is usually viewed as divorced or separated – not always such an identity allows them to live a smooth life rather it is such a turn-out that leaves them to cope with a world of susceptible social environment, which further opens up the gate-way for a host of negative life anxieties, insecurity, stress and moreover, it also negatively affects her post-separation daily-dealings or day to day daily-life world.

And to some divorced, particularly those happened to upheld the typical Smithian rational approach that is 'how dare you make me less than I am' (?), or, as it has been beautifully summarised by Singh and Uberoi (2008, 430), that it is the process of one 'woman's quest for selfhood in relation to a chosen man', she either ends up in a social picture of losing her 'selfhood *or* ironically construed' as living a happy marital life or develops towards an unending saga of conflicting situations which presupposes many negative emotional rides like '*not conforming to certain spousal overtures*/demands/criticising-withdraw/defend interactional patterns that characterise distress and predict divorce' (Johnson 2005, 96). Further, it was very clear from the arguments aptly made of Singh and Uberoi that the modus operandi of spousal conflicting situations which often leads to contradictory life-turnouts "is located in the woman's assertion of her individuality and personality, and' or in her failure to compromise when marital problems becomes manifest. This is what threatens the stability and endurance of a marriage; it can lead to marital breakdown"[13]. Since this paper's focus is to understand the infidelity factors involved in contemporary Indian couple's marital breakdowns, the plethora of literature[14] which suggests and traces its social history from classical Hindu textual prescriptive roles for women, particularly in texts like *Apastamba Dharmasutra* to *Manusmriti* did not find their recitations in this paper. In a typical hermeneutical sense[15], let us turn to some specific contentions which hold the theoretical breadth of the following section, which will unfold as a case study. To put it in another way, this paper will focus on the meaning of certain life events, from an insider's (victim) perspective, mainly going by the insights forwarded by C. K. Riessman while studying "human actors' ascriptions of meaning to actions or events and *the kind of specific structures, which set the tone for human being's living, acting, and thinking within it*". Which can be further stressed on by engaging in some meaningful questions like- "how do individuals actually go about constructing meaning for events that happen to them?, how do understandings of the same event differ?, and what are the range of constructs that underlie these understandings?"[16].

## Wifely Transformations are not always a Happy-Ending[17]

It is usually considered that one girl's marriage allows her to settle or move to the affinal home and that marks the beginning of marital life and of course, that is considered as the second stage life for an Indian woman, a process which transforms into wifehood. The affinal home is supposed to be a woman's eventual place to live with her husband, children and the husband's potential family. Patrilocal marriage contributes to the continuity of the patriline but it causes a break in the continuity of the woman's natal kin and this break is felt especially keenly by the daughter who is cut off – albeit only partially and temporarily – not only from the mother but from the entire natal family (Trawick, 1996, 167). To move from the natal home into the affinal home after the marriage is a rite of passage and an important step in order to transform a daughter into a wife. Generally, this is considered as most stressful period of a woman's life and this transformation is usually supported by regular visits to her natal home in South India (Srinivas ,1999, 142).

But in some cases, such transitional phases of a newly married woman take a drastic turn, when she realises or encounters the illusive presences of someone who is "outsider" other than her husband. Eventually, such illusive presence turns out to be none other than that of her husband's extramarital sexual partners. As it was the case with Aparna[18]; when she was just into the 3rd month of her marital life, in a very unusual manner, she was not only introduced but also asked by her husband to entertain the same suspicious character or person, whom she was suspected to be the woman who seems to be filling that extra-marital fidelity to her husband. Although, initially she tried to accept such unfaithful overtures of her husband on the basis of a disillusioned or stereotyped hope that both 'time and a child' in her later period of life-course will change her husband's womanising nature. But no such change was ever destined in her fate-cum-marital-life which spanned between the years of 1993 and 2009. In course of time, it has been confirmed by her own tryst with destiny, which forced her to keep an alert eye on her husband's outside occupational habits and the kind of places he visited on business pretexts. By the end of the first year of her marriage, she had earned a status of being a bad type woman within her affinal family members. A kind of unwanted living identity, which had not only projected herself as the route of all types of regular conflicting situations with her husband, but also with in-laws and even their relatives.

Despite these odds, she was she was counting on a social hope that her child[19], who happened to be her only child-cum-son will take care of marital ordeal in the course of time to follow. Unfortunately, by the end of her seven years of marriage, and when her son was just a five and half years old kid, she could realise that her social identity has been merely pushed to a space, where she could only recognise as that of a caretaker or a maid for that kid. In addition to that, the typical grannies pampering-cum-upbringing process that turned that kid to imbibe all sorts of patriarchal values into his life-orientations. And, it was no surprise that Aparna's repetitive attempt to culture her kid went in vain, as one typical incident substantiates this understanding. Once, on a fine evening, she found out that her son who was busy in watching some televised serials with his grannies, which he was not supposed to do, as he regularly spends those slotted time for completing his school-assignments. When she reminded that to her son, her in-laws immediately took that advice in another-way and was harshly lectured that she need not to worry about such things, as their grandchild will do well in future, as he is going to succeed his father's well-established family business, and most mockingly, they put aside her suggestion, in a questioning manner, they laughed at her and reaffirmed their traditional belief- systems, to them - what will happen if he attends or completes his homework in time?, will he become an IAS?, can you guarantee this? etc. etc. If not, then just mind your own business, as his father is there to care his future and, of course, we will be always there to nurture his future-goals.

Such regular-basis humiliating experiences[20] became very apparent or synonymous to her routinely life and the eventual process had reduced her to live a life of dead-soul type living. And it was during such course of unevenly life-odds' timely 'hide and seek' play finally and forever announced her social death, when[21] she came to know about his husband had already moved to another divorcee woman and started to stay away from home for some consecutive days or sometimes for some months altogether. This time, she felt helpless, so she has finally brought the matter to her elder brother and married elder sister's knowledge. This action from her side at least assured her some sort of temporary consolation that made her to keep-going on the basis of another social-hope that at least some sort of mutual understanding or settlement could be reached between herself and her husband, for the sake of their son's future interest. Whether that intervention-cum-negotiation was destined to fail or only a further in-depth study can shed some light on those minute-details of what exactly went into those series of negotiations/talks/ interactions[22] between her husband and her natal-family members. Unfortunately, the years between 2002 and 2009, many attempts and interventions which were attempted but nothing could actually succeed to patch-up their marital-discords. And in the later part of the 2008, finally she was summoned and asked to sign the divorce paper by her affinal family members, including her husband, which she did not sign for almost seven months and finally, she had complied with her natal-family members wish-cum-pressures[23] and walked away from that suffocated life or a life which never existed (in a more symbolical sense).

## Post-separated Divorced life vis-à-vis Societal Re-questioning Process

It was since 26th March 2010 onwards, she is staying with her lonely widow mother. And by the end of 2010, her elder sister's reference could secure herself a low-grade clerical job to start a fresh life altogether. But in some sense, it appears as if her past failed marital life stories and her coming back process to her mother's home had re-opened her mother's sorrow[24]. And it is not just the question of a burden to this elderly woman but the day, her younger daughter (Aparna) re-joined her, she seems to be living a sort of reclusive life[25]. Aprnra, seems to be taking life on a different track altogether, when I have been on my visit, she projected herself, as if she is trying to start a fresh life again, putting those marital ordeals behind. But to my surprise, it appears from her series of conversations with me that still she was finding it difficult to digest certain societal questioning process and some sort of anonymous social institutional scrutinising process, which gossips the same story for some million times, to quote her "even though I have left my in-laws family in last March, why is it the case that people still find interest in gossiping about my husband's womanising habits and his recent whereabouts". So in some way or other, these continuities[26] hardly offers her a space, where both she and her widowed mother can breathe a fresh air.

However, the societal reach not just ends within its social spheres rather in some way or other, it does plays the role of a helping-hand to spoil the party, to whichever spaces, an individual victim intends to relocate or looks to start a new journey-cum-life. As exactly, it is happening with Aparna, according to her, in the first month of her joining in a job itself, she used to bear with many vulgar staring, and from second month onwards she was constantly reminded by the receptionist of that organisation that, the director wants to meet her after the office hours etc. and even at some point of time, she was made to wait for nothing by her seniors etc. Such ordeals still continues to crop up in her way, it might be the case that over the years of such a life experiences which were full of humiliating experiences and violence makes her to live a life as it is or in other words living a life just for life sake. What these simple narratives, doesn't tell us are that the kind of backhanded processes, who plays the indirect or second fiddling roles or supposedly the kind of elements which precedes such unwanted humanly (mainly manly) overtures.

A social fact or a pattern of life-orientations not just puzzles me a lot. Rather, it invites all of us to engage in more and more in-depth studies, at least to make an entry point for such interdisciplinary social science academic engagements that can be lead to a sort of culture among Indian social science scholars. If we can proceed with such directions, I am sure that it will help us to understand what makes an individual victim or sufferer to feel why and what are the paths that pushes her at least for a certain period of time or stages, where she happens to live a temporary bare self or a process that becomes merely to live a shadow of her original self.

# 13

# Women and Right to Food: A Special Focus on the Tribal Belt of Odisha

*—Rajadarshini Patra*


## Abstract

*Women have been generally invisible in the history of human life. Women are regarded as subjugate, inferior and dominated under the patriarchal structure of the society. Life and choice are not women's subject to think about, they are just recognised as man's daughter, sister, wife and mother. The right to food is recognised in the 1948 Universal Declaration of Human Rights as part of the right to an adequate standard of living. Generally male biasness is reflected in each and every household and the tribal belt is more prone to this system since they are always not aware of the importance of food for a woman and girl and they mean to live at any cost. Women's food security has been an issue for tribal regions of India. As far as the state of Odisha is concerned, empowering women can lead to food security in tribal areas as women and food security are closely linked (Sarada Lahangir, Women's Feature service July 26, 2013). Today ensuring food security for women is one of the important aspects of women empowerment strategies and plan of action. The right of a woman to have sufficient food is a matter of discussion for all nations as both food and financial crises become a major problem everywhere. The policy and programmes made to ensure food security too need to give women a chance to access their right to live with all sorts of necessecities of life and adequate means of livelihood.*


**Keywords:** *Subjugate, patriarchal, food security, tribal, rights, livelihood*

## Introduction

Food is one of a whole range of factors that determine why the poor take decisions and spread risk and how they finally balance competing needs, in order to survive. Food security is a multifaceted concept that goes far beyond the number of people that can be sustained by the earth's limited food resources to encompass a broad range of issues, like population growth, control and mobility, resource distribution, consumption patterns, agricultural production, climate change, environmental degradation, socio-economic status, development, trade relations, land ownership rights, access to micro-finance and access to health care services. Protecting the human rights of women and girls is now an upcoming issue everywhere. A very important aspect is women's health and nutrition, which is very much neglected in almost every part of our country.

The right to food is an inclusive right. It is not simply a right to a minimum ration of calories, proteins and other specific nutrients. It is a right to all nutritional elements that a person needs to live a healthy and active life, and to the means to access. The right to food can be described as: "The right to adequate food is realised when every man, woman and child, alone or in community with others, has physical and economic access at all times to adequate food or means for its procurement" (Committee on Economic, Social and Cultural Rights). Right to food is linked with other human rights too, such as violating the right to food may impair the enjoyment of other human rights, such as the right to health, education or life, and vice versa. The right to food is a human right recognised by international human rights law. The Universal Declaration of Human Rights recognises, in the context of an adequate standard of living, that: "Everyone has the right to a standard of living adequate for the health and well-being of himself and of his family, including food." (Art. 25).

The discourse on the right to food often involves two other terms: "food security" and "food sovereignty." [1]Neither term is interchangeable with the right to food, yet they are related. Indeed, one of the most detailed international documents issued on the right to food is the FAO Right to Food Guidelines, which note that a human rights-based approach to food security "emphasises the achievement of food security as an outcome of the realisation of existing rights." This follows the 1996 Rome Declaration on World Food Security, which viewed the realisation of the right to food as a way of achieving food security. Thus, food security has been defined as existing "when all people, at all times, have physical and economic access to sufficient, safe and nutritious food to meet their dietary needs and food preferences for an active and healthy life." But there are certain elements of right to food that may determine one's food status.

***Availability*** requires, on the one hand, that food should be available from natural resources either through the production of food, by cultivating land or animal husbandry, or through other ways of obtaining food, such as fishing, hunting or gathering. On the other hand, it means that food should be available for sale in markets and shops.

***Accessibility*** requires economic and physical access to food to be guaranteed. Economic accessibility means that food must be affordable. Individuals should be able to afford food for an adequate diet without compromising on any other basic needs, such as school fees, medicines or rent. Physical accessibility means that food should be accessible to all, including to the physically vulnerable, such as children, the sick, persons with disabilities or the elderly, for whom it may be difficult to go out to get food.

***Adequacy*** means that the food must satisfy dietary needs, taking into account the individual's age, living conditions, health, occupation, sex, etc. For example, if children's food does not contain the nutrients necessary for their physical and mental development, it is not adequate. Food that is energy-dense and low-nutrient, which can contribute to obesity and other illnesses, could be another example of inadequate food. Food should be safe for human consumption and free from adverse substances, such as contaminants from industrial or agricultural processes, including residues from pesticides, hormones or veterinary drugs. Adequate food should also be culturally acceptable.

## 2. Tribes and food habits in Odisha

About half of the world's autochthonous people, comprising 635 tribal communities, including 75 primitive tribal communities, live in India. Orissa, the most picturesque state in eastern India, occupies a unique place in the tribal map of the country having the largest number of tribal communities (62 tribes including 13 primitive tribes). Most of the food habits of tribes have been determined by their history. They primarily reside in the hills, and forests. For a long time, their staple food was animal flesh, and forest products. The increased interaction among diverse ethnic groups, the process for urbanisation, various changes in the crop pattern and above all, the implementation of Five Year Plans have changed food ideology to a great extent. Food habits and food ideology of a society are the results of ecology, changing food commodities, food processing and use. Shift in food habit is also one major factor influencing the consumption pattern.

The spectre of starvation in western Orissa has its roots in the rising inequalities within the agrarian regime. The lack of purchasing power to buy food even at the public distribution system (PDS) rates and the distress sale of whatever food surpluses exist are the main reasons for the starvation deaths in the KBK region. A survey on starvation deaths in Kashipur in Koraput district showed that the poorest tribal families were declared above the poverty line even as a clique of local government and traders siphoned off the grain that was supposed to be distributed to below the poverty line (BPL) families under the TPDS scheme. This is even more shocking when one considers the fact that the number of BPL cardholders outstrips the number of registered

BPL families by 8.5 lakhs in Orissa. The lack of food supply through the TPDS is compounded by the fact that Adivasis have no rights in forest lands that used to provide them food and shelter in times of distress.

To meet the daily requirement of food, people belonging to tribal groups of Ganjam district consume cheaply available food during scarcity season. Tapioca and sweet potato, usually harvested in the months of November and December are available in the hilly areas (The scientific name of Tapioca is Manihat esculenta and Sweet Potato is Ipomoea batatas). Tribal crop patterns also determine their food consumption and the amount of food intake by each individual of the household. Croppings according to family status too important (ref. Table1).

**Table 1. Cropping Pattern in the Tribal Belt of Odisha**

| *Family type* | *Cropping* |
|---|---|
| Mariginal /small farmer families | Wage, Non-Timber Forest Produce (NTFP), share cropping |
| Large families farmer | Agriculture, Non-Timber Forest Produce (NTFP), share cropping, animal husbandry |

*Source:* Orissa Tribal Empowerment and Livelihoods Programme (2003-2013).

## 3. Tribal Women and food Security

Women play a key role in achieving food security. Yet, women are often disproportionately affected by hunger, food insecurity and poverty, largely as a result of gender inequality and denial of opportunities for enjoyment of social, economic, civil and political rights and power to them. In many countries, girls are twice as likely as boys to die from malnutrition and preventable childhood diseases, and it is estimated that almost twice as many women as men suffer from malnutrition. Women and girls may face discrimination at home. In many countries, they receive less food than the male members of the family, because of their lower status. Violence against women or other practices that violate women's rights may contribute to women's food insecurity. Women play a central role in food production. Yet, women are, in many instances, discriminated against in accessing the means for producing adequate food. Because of discrimination, women are also less likely to find and maintain a job with adequate conditions. They are active economic agents with rights, and contribute to both the productive and reproductive economy. "A gender perspective means recognising that women stand at the crossroads between production and reproduction between economic activity and the care of human beings, and therefore, between economic growth and human development."

In a separate study conducted by the Regional Medical Research Centre (RMRC), Bhubaneswar, 66 per cent of primitive tribal population (6-15 years age group) of Mayurbhanj and Sundergarh districts was found to be malnourished . Similarly, chronic energy deficiency was found to be very high among Langia Saura (89.4per cent) and Kutia Kondha (88.9per cent) primitive tribes of Rayagada district of Orissa.

Gender is significant in influencing livelihood outcomes significantly. For example, gender differences in distribution and access to assets – such as credit or technology – are crucial in ownership and management of sustainable enterprises. The UNDP's Social Development and Poverty Eradication Division (SEPED) has integrated technology into its Sustainable Livelihood framework (see UNDP, 1997) since gendered access to and use of technologies is crucial for livelihood outcomes.

## II.2 Food Consumption pattern and women

Proper food availability with distribution determines food security for all in a particular household. What the food consumption of a family tells is – 'how much food is taken by each family member'. Food consumption pattern of household is one of the criteria of ensuring food and nutrition security. It is sometimes used as a criteria for an understanding of social stratification. It varies from culture to culture, religion to religion and is sometimes also affected by food habits. Women's food consumption pattern is determined by the following these two factors:

1. Economic factors affecting food consumption pattern
2. Food habits affecting consumption pattern.

There is a basic distinction in the perception of food between tribal and other general castes. Generally, people have a very systematic method, pre planned ways of food preparations. But for tribals whatever food is gathered in a day is meant for survival. Shifting in food habits is also one of the major factors influencing the consumption pattern in general, but the tribal food habit and its consistency throughout the year does not make any difference in consumption patterns. History shows that several factors have influenced tribal food habits and their food ideology. Relative opening of their isolation, the degradation of forests, soil erosion, the land fragmentation and the implementation of various development programmes, particularly in agriculture with a dose of capitalism added to it , have influenced the tribal food habits. Women usually follow the traditional method of preserving paddy and other dry food items. Basically, they use their seasonal food as far as possible. Their daily food chart in different seasons is also characterised by availability of food items in the particular season. Though there is no such difference in seasonal food habits, food grains and production method is different. (Ref. Table 2).

**Table.2 Seasonal Food products**

| *Season* | *Food items* |
|---|---|
| Summer | Roots (Rani kanda, barada kanda), mahula, mango kernel, jack fruit, different leafs from forest, tamarind |
| Rainy | Kosala, kuiri, maka, kangu, vegetables from kitchen garden, paddy |
| Winter | Vegetables, maise |
| Autumn | Kandula, pumpkin, vegetables |

Annual rates of growth for crops in the area vary from time to time. From 1980 to 2001, there was a vast change in the production of agricultural products.(Ref. Table 3).

**Table 3. Annual rates of growth for selected crops**

| *Crop* | *1980-81 to 1989-90* | | | *1990-91 to 2000-01* | | |
|---|---|---|---|---|---|---|
| | *Area* | *Production* | *Yield* | *Area* | *Production* | *Yield* |
| Rice | 0.41 | 3.62 | 3.19 | 0.63 | 1.79 | 1.16 |
| Wheat | 0.47 | 3.57 | 3.10 | 1.21 | 3.04 | 1.81 |
| Coarse cereals | -1.34 | 0.40 | 1.62 | -1.84 | 0.06 | 1.65 |
| Pulses | -0.09 | 1.52 | 1.61 | -1.02 | -0.58 | 0.27 |
| Food grains | -0.23 | 2.85 | 2.74 | -0.20 | 1.66 | 1.34 |
| Non-food grains | 1.12 | 3.77 | 2.31 | 0.84 | 1.86 | 0.59 |
| Oilseeds | 2.81 | 5.20 | 2.43 | 0.44 | 0.66 | 0.61 |
| Sugar cane | 1.44 | 2.70 | 1.24 | 1.72 | 2.62 | 0.89 |
| Cotton | -1.25 | 2.80 | 4.10 | 2.21 | 0.92 | -1.26 |
| All crops | 0.10 | 3.19 | 2.56 | 0.08 | 1.73 | 1.02 |

*Source:* Government of India (2002)

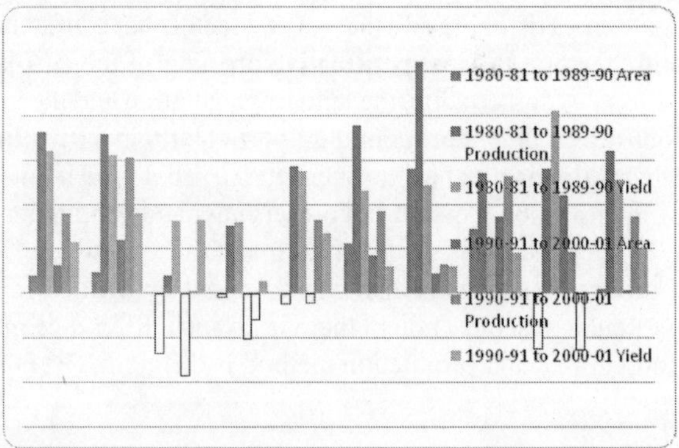

When women are involved in supply of energy giving, protective and body building foods, their empowerment for food security is very much essential. The majority problems of India's food security are related to the resources and means of having access to stock powers of good grains. Lack of food is due to the lack of the means to acquire it not due to shortfall in food grain production. It is proved that Indian rural women are responsible for every phase of the food cycle-production, post harvest activity, marketing, meal planning and preparation. So here the question arises how much is the involvement of women in food security of their families.

In tribal districts of Odisha, basically women do every type of work, for example collecting food materials, fuel, and fodder from the forest, fetching water and working in the agricultural field. Their right to food is not a matter of concern to any society. As women are pressurised under double burden of the managing the household and the outside, they need sufficient amount of food with proteins, nutrition and much calories. The tribal women gather many forest products (minor forest products or MFP) for food, drink, fodder, medicine, and house-building, as well as for agricultural or other domestic purposes, (ref. Table 4).

**Table 4. Gender analysis of work in the study area**

| *Work category/primary source of income* | *Male (per cent)* | *Female (per cent)* |
|---|---|---|
| Agriculture | 80 (80.00 per cent) | 20 (20.00 per cent) |
| Wage labour outside | 70 (70.00 per cent) | 30 (30.00 per cent) |
| Forest product collection | 10 (10.00 per cent) | 90 per cent (90.00 per cent) |
| Selling forest products in the local market | 60 (60.00 per cent) | 40 per cent (40.00 per cent) |

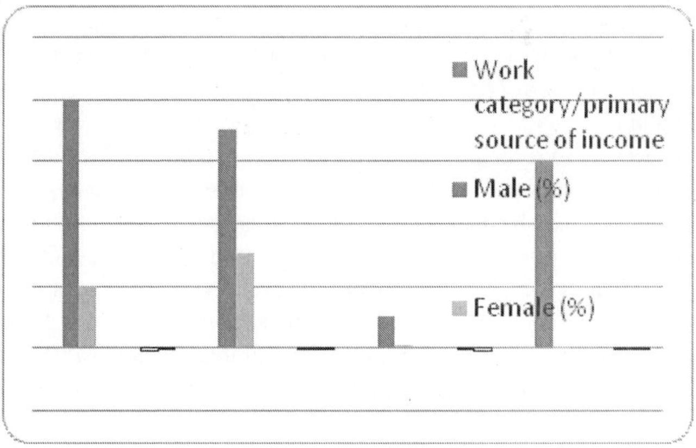

There is a seasonal variation in the availability of different products for household consumption. Women are deprived of all rights and are generally not able to get the actual benefits, despite all the hard work they do in the food gathering process.

## Conclusion

The Convention on the Elimination of All Forms of Discrimination against Women seeks to provide women equal access to work, land, credit, income and social security, which are essential to ensure women's equal enjoyment of the right to food. For example, Article 14 provides a set of concrete measures to eliminate discrimination against women in rural areas, and create an enabling environment for women to enjoy the right to food. Article 11 seeks to ensure women equal enjoyment of labour rights and Article 13(b), their access to financial resources. ILO Conventions, such as the Conventions on Eliminating Discrimination in Respect of Employment and Occupation (ILO Conventions Nos. 100 and 111) also protect women's labour rights.

Here are some basic points to cover while suggesting a few broad aspects related to women's food rights. Women as the motors of change and as central to food 'they should have access to agricultural credit and loans, marketing facilities, appropriate technology and equal treatment in land and agrarian reforms as well as in land resettlement schemes'. To protect the right to food, States have to protect individuals' enjoyment of the right to food against violations by third parties (e.g., other individuals, groups, private enterprises and other entities) and ensuring that food put on the market is safe and nutritious.

Legislative and other measures are needed to protect people, especially women and children. Instead of advertising and promotions of unhealthy food so as to support the efforts of parents and health professionals, encourage healthier patterns of eating and physical exercise. Fulfilment of the right to food is very important. People's access to and use of resources and means of ensuring their livelihoods, including food security should be taken into consideration. When adopting food policies, Governments also need to carefully balance investment in cash crops for export and support for domestic food crops. Access to food must also be guaranteed to people in remote areas and to victims of conflicts or natural disasters, as well as to prisoners. For example, to guarantee physical access to food to people living in remote areas the infrastructure could be improved, so that they can reach markets by public transport. Women play a vital role in ensuring sustainable food security in the household. They are chief manager of household food security and should get all sorts of opportunities in development programmes related to livelihood, food security, and skill development trainings.

## References

1. Action Against Hunger, 2011 .
2. Arun, Shoba, Heeks Richard, Morgan Sharon, "Researching ICT-Based Enterprise for Women in Developing Countries: A Livelihood Perspective", Women's ICT-Based Enterprise for Development project, IDPM, University of Manchester, UK, 2004.
3. Ashley, C and Carney, D (1999) Sustainable Livelihoods: Lessons from Early Experience. Department For International Development: London.
4. Bruijn de Mirjam, Gender equality and Food Security: A Development Myth, African Studies Centre, Leiden, The Netherlands, CODESRLA Bulletin, No. 1 & 2, 2006.
5. Carney, D. *et. al,* 1999, 'Livelihood Approaches Compared'. London: DFID.
6. Crises. Rome 2010.
7. FAO/WFP. 2010. The State of Food Insecurity in the World 2010: Addressing Food Insecurity in Protracted.
8. Hussein, K., 2002, 'Food security: rights, livelihoods and the World Food Summit-five years later' in Food in Social Policy – Special issue of Social Policy and Administration. Summer 2002. Edited by Catherine Finer Jones and Elizabeth Dowler.
9. Jaspars S. S.O' Callaghan and E. Stites, 2007 "Linking Livelihoods and Protection:" A Priliminary Analysis based on review of literature and agency practice, HPG Working Paper: Overseas Development Institute.
10. Lenka A., Nedunchezhiyan M., Jata Sushant Kumar, Sahoo Biswanath, "Livelihod Improvement and Nutritional Security Through Tuber Crop in Odisha", Odisha Review, 2012.
11. Long-term Food Security: Investigating in people and livelihood, International Federation of Red Cross and Red Crossent Societies.
12. Maxwell, S., 1991, Introduction in Maxwell (ed.) To cure all hunger: Food policy and food security in Sudan. IT Publications.
13. Oraon, Vijay, "Changing Patterns of Tribal Livelihoods: A Case Study in Sundergarh District, Odisha" , Thesis of Development Studies, 2012.
14. Padhee Shakti and P. Nilakantha ,Tribal Movements and Livelihoods: Recent Developments in Orissa.
15. Report on Conference Sessions XVI International AIDS Conference, "HIV/ AIDS, Food Security and Gender Equality", Toronto, Canada, 2006.
16. Saad Bne, Majda, Food Security for the Food-Insecure: new challenges and renewed commitments, Centre for Development Studies, University College Dublin, Ireland, December 1999.
17. Terminal evaluation of the GOI-UNDP food security programme in Odisha, draft report, UNDP,2006.
18. UNDP (1997) Sustainable Livelihood Approaches in Operation: A Gender Perspective. Paper Prepared by Perpetua Katepa-Kalala at the International Associates.
19. World Food Programme, 2009.

# 14

# Caste and Class: Trends and Challenges for 'Dalits' with in the compass of Indian Writing

*—Patel Heena L and Yogesh N Vansiya*

The study of colonial discourse such as Said's has however, blossomed into a garden when the marginal can speak or spoken to, even spoken for. In this way, the modern era plurality of cultures, genders and ethnicities is established with argument that no particular type should be privileged over others. There should be an equal representation for each class, caste, gender, race, and culture. Dalits and the marginalised were literary pushed for the establishment of the egalitarian society. The impact of these ideologies and to margin for the contemporary history and geography of the world's civilisation need to be established. By describing multilingual, multicultural ethos of these oppressed people, it will become a tool in social expansion of knowledge which will help in the blossoming of Dalit literature in all Indian languages. It is one of the many newly emerged literatures of the post 1950 global scenario, but with the difference that it is indigenous, home made with local and is experimental. Dalit literature empowers the marginalised, by retrieving the voices, spaces and identities silenced or suppressed by casteist powers. It examines the human condition and provides inspiration for struggle to the marginalised, because authentic shame, anger, sorrow and indomitable hope are its cardinal ingredients. The position of Dalit literature can be graphically understood in terms of the paradigms such as the colonised or coloniser, oppressed or oppressor, victimised or victimiser, dominant or dominated and subject or subjugated. Dalit Literature is simultaneously local and global. It is universal because starting from the ages to ages, from the ancient Greek Tragedy to the present Modern times, it raised the fundamental question: Why does Man suffer? The question has remained the same, but the answers might be varied such as God, Fate, Chance, Choice , Evil and Society. In the present era, Dalit writers focus on victimhood, oppression, suffering and demand for their dignity as human beings and their answers is "caste". People may not believe in such barriers of caste and creeds, or obstacles of the caste and creeds and breeds, but in reality, it seems to be ingrained in the D.N.A of Indian Society. In a way, "Caste is in the root of the Indian Society". As soon as the child is born, caste determines his or her destiny. Dalit is a word which has come from the Marathi ward 'dalan', i.e., the class which is called the exploited class. In this way, Dalit literature is pan-Indian in its scope, impact and motivation- cutting across provincial and linguistic boundaries. The indeliable impact of Mahatma Phule and Ambedkar on this literature is clearly perceptible. By the 1960s, Dalit literature saw a fresh crop of new writers like Baburao Bagul, Bandhu Madhav and Shankarao Kharat though its formal form came into being with the little magazine movement. Dalit voice, a political magazine which started publishing in 1981, become another potent force in the rise of Dalit literature in India. The living world of Dalit oppression is found in the literature of difficult languages, which blossomed out of the socio-political and cultural transformation. Dalit literature is a composite and homogenous body of massive creative corpus emerging from different regional languages like Marathi , Kannada, Hindi, Tamil, Punjabi, Gujarati and Telugu. Dalit Literature in various Indian Writing in English is " the burning charcoal of Dalit experience". However, Dalit literature can be called as the post-colonial literature. The term post-colonial, in relation to Dalit Literature is not intercultural, but intracultural because both the coloniser and the colonised were still and are within India, the one is in the centre and another is on the periphery.

The word Dalit is highly related to the Indian cosmos which has been specially used for the erstwhile so-called Untouchables or the Scheduled Castes of India to describe their political identity. Dalit literature is written for such category of people who are crushed and the downtrodden. According to Bishop A.C Lal, "The word 'Dalit' is a beautiful word because it transcends narrow national and sectarian frontiers. It is a beautiful word because it embraces the sufferings, frustrations, expectations and groaning of the entire cosmos." Human suffering, woes, inner conflict, injuring of the self , the damage of the 'self honour' by the society, deprivation is the esoteric theme of the Dalit literature. Dalit literature is the solid voice in the literature which has been represented firmly by the writers with the exactness which cannot be separated from the existence of the real sufferer. It is not a soft voice, but the solid strike with the clear words and the clear expression as the exact condition of the *'Dalit samaj'*. Dalit literature is the outcome of the society in which the equality of the humans does not exist. Dalit literature is the reason of those crushed, suppressed voice which was engraved by force by the so called authorisers of the society who got born in the upper surface of the society and called themselves superior and the real owners of the society. Mankind can bear the onslaught strikes of natural disasters which can be so harsh, which can be tolerated, but the pain and suffering caused by one man to another is much painful which is the most terrifying aspect of the human life and existence. Suffering, pain, pathos, woes, given by man to man is more intensely and painful than the suffering cause by nature.

History is witness to such human suffering , pain, pathos, revolt, the unspeakable violence caused by man to his fellow human beings. In the ancient times, the '*Varna Pratha*' was established in the society to set up better management of the society, but it damaged the human hierarchy. The society is for human, but the human and humanity both disappeared from the social understanding of humans. The entire effort was for better enhancement and establishing a better society and enhancement of the management of the society, but it brought inequality in the human world. Royal became royal and the downtrodden became much more deprived, ignored, suppressed, isolated and victims of violence physically , psychologically and socially. In the Medieval times, peasants were exploited by the feudal lords without any sense of remorse on the part of the oppressors. In the time of the British colonialism, the gap between various '*Varnas*' widened to keep divide the Indian society. Socially declared downtrodden remained the same and exploited much more like low caste peasants, chamars, Bhangis, Dhobis etc. Society did not give them a chance to rise from the social platform and the Britishers supported the same to pursue divide and rule policy in India. In the Gandhian era, efforts were made to establish total equality. However, even today, Dalits continue to face challenges. It appears that we have accepted violence as a way of our life. Where there is violence, there is suffering and violence in our times springs from so many sources. Social inequalities, on the basis of caste, class, race and gender, too breed violence. The violence of the white against black, the non- tribals against the tribal population, the upper class against the low caste people, the patriarchal violence of men against women breed counter violence as the oppressed will also rise in revolt one day against the oppresors. The vicious circle of violence goes on endlessly, engulfing the life of innocent people. In India, more than one-sixth of its population suffers from neglect and humiliation just because they born as the deprived and downtrodden class. The sufferings faced is man-made and hence more painful and unfortunate. The suffering undergone by the depressed class went unnoticed until recently as the writers and artists hardly captured the indignities and inhumanities suffered by the untouchables, or Dalits.

This paper will explore the dark corners of the trends and challenges for Dalits, with special focus on works of some very famous writers such as Munshi Prem Chand, U.R. Ananthmurthy, Raja Rao, Mulk Raj Anand, Om Prakash Valmiki, Arundhati Roy and the poet, Arjun Dangle.

All of Anand's 'Untouchables' reflect the reality of real life. Caste is the disability, which a person has to suffer as a consequence of his belonging to a low caste. The worst affected by caste consideration are the so called 'untouchables'. These untouchables are not allowed draw water from a common well, or even though they are Hindus, they cannot enter to the temple to make offerings to the God. They are allowed to talk to their cast people only. The life of the outcast untouchables is projected as of facing misery and inhuman treatment. It also highlights how an 'untouchable' leads the life meaner than that of animals and how he has to tolerate inhumane insult and abuse. Bakha , the protagonist of the novel '*Untouchable*' had been ashamed of the Indian way of performing ablutions. He remembered so well the Britishers abused them as: '*Kala admi Zamin par hagne wala*'(black man, you who relieve yourself on the ground) (page-10). The untouchables are socially isolated people who lead a deplorable and miserable life beyond imagination. According to E.M. Forster, " The sweeper is worse than a slave, for the slave may change his master and his duty even become free, but the sweeper is bound for ever, born into a state, from where he can never escape."

Truly this view shows that the cleaner of the dirt itself has been addressed as the polluted. The sweepers clean the latrines, dirt and other filth, but as the people hate the dirt and garbage, they also hate the sweepers by taking as the shape of dirt. As the garbage thrown out of the village, just the same way the untouchables too are thrown out of the village having 'outcastes' colony. As per the social designs they have to live outside the village, neither get pure drinking water, nor good and healthy food. Sometime they die like flies, due to diseases. There are not only divisions of castes, but also the watertight compartment of Indian people and culture. One should bear in his/her particular class, grow up, eat, drink, marry and die in the caste. This has become the tyranny.

In the beginning of Mulk Raj Anand's '*Untouchable*', we find the very beginning description from the colony of the untouchables.

"*The outcastes' colony was a group of mud-walled houses that clustered together in two rows.........A brook ran near the lane, once with crystal- clear water, now soiled by the dirt and filth of the public latrines .....the odour of carcases left to dry in its banks, the dung of donkeys, sheep, horses, cows and buffaloes heaped up to be made into fuel cakes and biting. Choking pungent fumes that oozed from its sides. The absences of a drainage system had through the rains of various seasons......which gave out the most offensive stink. And altogether the ramparts of human and animals refuse that lay on the outskirts of this little colony, and the ugliness, the squalor and the misery which lay within it, made it an 'uncongenial' place to live in (page-1). People also make them realise that what is their responsibilities, limitations, codes, conditions. etc....*In the novel, the old black moneylender shouting towards Bakha in his sharp southern diction that —

'There is not a latrine clean.

*You must work for the pay you receive'* (page-11)

The outcastes are exposed to the sub-human life of long-term diseases. They are underfed, weak and prone to infections and disease Lakha suffers from Asthama, Bakha's mother dies because the family fails to give her right timely treatment, Bakha also has some illness. Whenever such critical condition happens with any untouchable, none help them, that they'll be 'polluted' if they help them, see them, touch them, even enter their colony.

The novel '*Untouchable*' presents the social and the religious rigidity in such a manner that reflects the strong focus on the caste Hindus' darkest sight of the mind and motives who do not want the untouchables to upgrade but to crush them under their feet, yet who can at least fulfil their wrong need and of course the cleanliness of their day to day routine. Bakha is the centre of those untouchables who have been oppressed for thousands of years. Bakha is an 18 years old son of Lakha , the jamadar of north Indian cantonment town. He is bullied everyday by his ageing father to clean the latrines. He wakes up to the abuses of Havildar Charat Singh, a caste Hindu, a famous hockey player but suffering from piles, for not keeping a latrine clean for him. But he is puzzled by seeing that Bakha remains clean himself, he is not the filthy kind even though he belongs to the sweeper caste. He has some good impact over his mind about Bakha that he promises to give him a hockey stick. After cleaning many latrines, Bakha gets thirsty and tired, he wants to drink water but when he comes back at home, he gets neither water nor tea, for there was no water at home. Sohini goes to fetch water from the caste- well. Now the trouble of the day for Bakha and his sister begins- a series of humiliation and shocks. At the well, Sylph like Sohini confronts a humiliating circumstance typical of India, we can see over in the villages of India. The quite normal scene occurs every now and then there are scolding and insult that if the outcastes touch the well, it would become polluted. When Sohini goes to fetch the water, there were more then ten outcastes waiting for fetching water.

Gulabo is the washerwoman who claims "*a high place in the hierarchy of the castes among the low castes.*"(page25) and who had a well-known Hindu lover in her youth time, was feeling extreme jealousy towards Sohini who was looking quite beautiful in her age, but was born in low caste family. So she does not leave even a single chance to humiliate Sohini. She treats her as the biggest rival. She even tries to beat her. Om Prakash Valmiki creatively illustrates in his "Sahavayatra", the fact that there is untouchability even among the 'untouchables' too. The lower hates the lowest. He poignantly records the misery, helplessness, humiliation, insults, oppressions and brutality that the lowest castes have to suffer in a society of lower caste. *(From the Article- Politics of Pain and Suffering: A Dalit Perspective, by- Umed Singh, Book- Dalit Literature, Page-123.)* Gulabo, the washerwoman, scolds Sohini at the well as soon as she sees her. She unconsciously betrayed her feelings in the mockery and light-hearted abuse which she showered on Sohini.

*'Go back home.......There is no one to give you water here! And, at any rate, there are so many of us ahead of you!' she starts to use extremely bad words for silent innocent Sohini.. 'Bitch, why don't you speak! Prostitute, why don't you answer me ?' Gulabo insisted. 'You annoy me with your silence, you illegally begotten! You eater of dung and drinker of urine ! You bitch of*

*a sweeper woman ! I will show how to insult one old enough to be your mother.'*

(page- 16-17)

Pandit Kali Nath was fascinated by the beauty of Sohini. He had seen her before, noticed her as she came to clean the latrines in the gullies in the town- the fresh young from whose full breasts with their dark beads of nipples stood out so conspicuously under her muslin shirt, whose innocent look of wonder seemed to stir the only soft cord in his person, hardened by the congenital weakness of his body, disillusioned brazened by the authority he exercised over the faithful and the devout. And he was inclined to be kind to her. Pandit Kali Nath had wrong intentions for Bakha's sister so he gave first preference to her so he could entrap her in to the false intentions and can fulfil the carnal desire. When she refused for that he began to shout———

*'polluted ! polluted ! polluted !' 'Get off the steps, you scavenger! Off with you ! You have defiled our whole service, You have defiled our temple! Now we will have to pay for the purificatory ceremony. Get down, get away, you dog!'(page53)*

The upper caste Hindu gave them the remnant of their food left after they have taken. The untouchables had to live in a ghoulish condition where derogatory epithets, were used excessively like '*illegally begotten (page 17) 'Bitch', 'prostitute!' 'wanton!'(page28) 'son of a pig!'(page131)', 'dirty dog!' (page53) ....etc....*

Bakha couldn't even tolerate the thought that someone who holds Sohini like this and burst into anger by thinking that———

"Why didn't I go and kill that hypocrite! , I could have sacrificed myself for Sohini. Everyone will know about her. My poor sister! How can she show her face to the world after this?"(page-56)

The episode of Pandit Kali Nath trying to seduce of Sohini's, shows that the practice of untouchability is essentially a matter of pretentious religiosity and exploitation. The religious terms make the person so blind that except him he takes others as the out of existence. Feelings of humiliation frequently injured Bakha, but helpless Bakha felt just burning within himself, getting anger and almost feel like the wounded wolf, searching the reverse revolt with silent lips snarling. When Bakha goes to beg for food from the caste Hindu's house, the housewife stands to scold him more than ever and flings a bit of cake towards him which fell on the dirty pavement.

'*You eater of your masters, she shouted,*
'may the vessels of your life never float on the sea of existence!
Go! Get up, get up! May you perish and die!
you have defiled my house !

Go! Get up, get up! You eater of your masters!
*Why didn't you shout if you wanted food?*
*Is this your father's house that you come and take rest here?*
*(page-63)*

He wins the 'battle' because he has rested his fatigued body on the wooden platform of her house and defiled it. On the contrary the same house wife treated the Sadhu with utmost most respect and honour. Even though Bakha apologises, she goes on:

'Why did you sit down on my doorstep, if you had to sit down at all?
You have defiled my religion! you should have sat there
in the gulley! Now I will have to sprinkle holy water
all over the house! You spoiler of my salt! Oh ! how terrible!
You sweepers have lifted your heads to the sky, nowadays.....
(page-63)

The woman changes her behaviour when she sees the saint. Instead of giving the bread directly to Bakkha, she flings it in such a way that it falls in the same place, where her son is relieving himself. Bakkha felt disgusting. She forced him to clean the drain first then and then he will get the bread. *He picks it up quietly and wraps it in a duster with the other bread he has received. He was too disgusted to clean the drain after this, especially as the little boy sat relieving himself before him. He throws the little broom aside and goes away without saying thank-you. (page- 65)* Bakha too doesn't like the dirty, wet bread, he too feels irritated and the feeling of the disgust like anybody else in the world and especially who prefers the cleanliness.

Moreover he faces a whole lot of humiliation when an act of love involves the demon of defilement, the child in him is grievously hurt. Bakha lifts the child who falls unconscious on being hit by a stone in the melee in the midst of a game of hockey and carries him to his house. Despite the taboo against his touch, he cannot help being kind towards him. Instead of being thankful to him the mother of that child starts to scold him and cursed him alleging, that he has killed her son and defile her house. Bakha is touched to the quick and his heart-strings are disturbed by this rude accusation.

Bakha is the undefined representative of the lowly caste people who faced and tolerated the oppression by the caste Hindus from the ancient times. Bakha presents the untiring journey of oppression and humiliation from the very beginning of the day. It is in a way the symbol of the long, long years of untiring and oppressive journey of the lower castes with silent lips. Even today after 60 years of Indepencence , the Dalits continue to suffer social neglect; the Dalit women are paraded naked in the streets; Dalit colonies are set ablaze; they work as labourers and their wives are raped and they too are beaten.

'*Joothan*' is an autobiographical novel in which the author has expressed the heart agonies as an untouchablity victim. This novel begins by a detailed description of the poor living surrounding by Chuhra community, where poverty reigned supreme. The lake of civic amenities, and poor sanitation facilities were the curse of that dwelling place. Animals like pigs and human begins shared the same living place as there no other place to go. In this concern we find one of the most breathing atmosphere in the poetry of Arjun Dangle who has given the horrific picture of their wretchedness entitled as "*Chhavni Hilti Hai*" *(The Cantonment has Begun to Shake)* :

We fought with crows,
Never even giving them the snot from
our noses.
As we dragged out the Upper Lane's
dead cattle.
Skinned it neatly
And shared the meat among ourselves,
They used to love us then.
We warred with jackals-dogs-
Vultures-kites
*Because we at their share.* (Abedi)

The narrator in '*Joothan*' describes the hardship what he has faced in his life. The author faces series of various obstacles while getting the primary and the higher education. People of the upper class created problems for him at each and every steps of his life. Even some of the teachers and the head master too are against giving education which can be reflected through such words..

"What is the point of sending him to school?"
"What has a crow became a swan?"

A Dalit child passes through the physical, psychological, and social harassment by the upper class even by the inter low castes too. As we see in Mulk Raj Anand's '*Untouchable*', Sohini was subjected to a lot of constant humiliation by the washer woman Gulabo. '*Joothan*' means the left over remnants of food from wedding or at home which is relished by the Chuhras. The writer expresses the inner fury by the words that——*"What sort of a life was that? After working hard day and night the price of our sweat was just ' Joothan'"*.

The social ostracism faced by the chuhras haunted the author's mind since his childhood right up to his adulthood. Even he was deceived by the Brahmin girl in love when she learnt that he is a Valmiki and not a Brahmin, it is just by the name only he is that, actually he belongs to the Bhangi's family. It is jubalpur which gave him the healthy world of human where he could find the place for himself, and the enhancement too. A kind of healthy clean air of healthy attitude of the human world he could realise. Valmiki poured his anger through the inner conflict that—

> *"Being born is not one's contrast, then why would have I been born in Bhangi's household? Those who call themselves the standard-bearers of this country's great cultural heritage, did they decide which homes they would be born into?"*

Dalit writers like Valmiki are thus producing literary analysis and literary theory simultaneously with their literary creation. On the one hand, their work has broken the hegemony of high caste literary establishment which can no longer continue to present its choices as universal and timeless, and on the other, by producing their own literature they have created their specific corner in the literary revolution called 'Dalit Literature'.

In the short story of Om Prakash Valmiki " *The Killing of a Cow",* an element of resistance is embodied through Sukka, a Dalit, who has menial job at Mukhiyaji's home. Sukka has a beautiful wife who was observed lustfully by Mukhiyaji. Mukhiyaji wanted to satisfy his sexual desire through Sukka's wife. Sukka stopped his work there and chewing over his words that "*She will not come to your haveli*" when Mukhiyaji threatened him, he again resists that-

> "It's when I work , Mukhiyaji,
> that you give me two handfuls of rice.
> She will not come to your haveli."

Sukka received severe punishment for this revolt. This shows that in the past, the Dalits had to submitted themselves before the mad desire of the upper caste people. If they resisted, they had to face harsh treatment by them that they couldn't even exist in their own community. Dalit is a face of low caste, part of low caste but like other upper castes he/she is also a face of his/ her caste. It doesn't mean that he/she is least or degraded born person. Dalit is a combination of the realisation of the joy, experiences, sorrow and the deep feeling of humiliation and insults which has been given by the other castes people. Dalit literature is not about the stories of merely the woes, pain, pathos, or unacceptable inhuman experience which can be seen by the literary perspective only but it's a sociological, perspective which is highly related with the society and the social experience. It is the saga of the silent crushed voices, the slow but steady and stony resistance of the souls.

Society and social management is not something related to the ownership of any one. It's not something or somebody's authority to crush others considered as degenerated and low. Dalit literature is the voice of the unvoiced souls, where we have to spend a time to, peep in to. We must study the socio-economic conditions of Dalits as that will enable us to make out the real meaning and significance of Dalit literature.

"*Kanthapura*", Raja Rao's greatest novel portrays radical social changes, and marks a turning point in the history of modern India. "*Kanthapura*" is not merely a socio-political document against the Colonial power but prophesies future social changes and the saga of the unification of the castes and the low castes for the freedom movement. "*Kanthapura*" shows the deep rooted orthodoxy of the caste system, the Brahmins against pariahs. Moorthy the Brahmin is considered the saint of the village. He is the true follower of Gandhian ideals. He goes to the Pariah houses . He takes tea and food with them too. He narrates the Harikatha to them. He doesn't keep any difference between touchables and the untouchables. But his mother doesn't like this. She warns him not to enter in house except he gets bath with Ganga water. She is deeply shocked when Venkamma poison her ears about Moorthappa's living, eating and his having physical relationship with the pariah woman. She dies of shock. Moorthappa is not even allowed to perform the last ceremony of his mother.

The stories of Munshi Premchand, identified untouhability as among the worst evils of the existing Indian society. "*Shudra*" is a tale of a untouchable woman who is transported as a part of a racket involving trafficking in women. These poor underdogs of the society often become easy prey to the cunning traffickers. In another story, *"Mandir"*, there is a pathetic tale of a wretched Dalit mother who is desperate to take her sick child to the temple to pray for his recovery. But the priest does not allows her to enter the temple. *"Salvation*" gives a picture of inhuman torture by Brahmin on a poor illiterate Chamar, Dukhi who consider the priest almost as the representative of almighty God. Dukhi dies due to starvation and his body is not allowed for the last offering, instead the Dalits dragged his body outside of the village to feed on the jackals and vultures. This shows no sign of repentence for such action and no sympathy for them, even after death.

" *Samskara*" the great novel written by U.R. Ananthmurthy , also shows the trends and challenges both for the Dalits. Naranappa , the Brahmin has an illicit relationship with the low case prostitute, Chandri. The whole novel is revolving around the last offering , the last samskara of the dead body of Naranapa. The Brahmin community never accepts the revolted caste Hindu who slept with the low caste woman. They want a share in the property of Naranapa, but they don't want to give the last offering to his body. Chandri, the Dalit prostitute, offers that in the dark night with the help of Naranapa's friend, without anybody knowing.

"*The God of Small Things*" by Arundhati Roy, narrates the same shocking experience of Dalits. Velutha , the paravan and professionally a skilled carpenter, is introduced as bare-bodied- calling himself to be an untouchable and not middle-class. "the parvans were expected to crawl backwards with a broom sweeping away the foot prints so that Brahmin or Syrian Christian would not defile themselves by accidently stepping onto the parvan's foot print. Valutha's grandfather accepts Christianity but faces troubles. They become casteless and therefore, devoid of the benefits guaranteed by the Constitution. Love between Valutha and Ammu is also rejected by Mammachi. Valutha is an untouchable, so he cannot love the upper class woman. Moreover, he is accused for the death and kidnapping of Sophie Mol and her two children. Valutha is arrested and inhumanely tortured and beaten till he bleeds to death. The novelist castigates the society which denies a dignified and decent life to certain individuals, because they are born in a 'low Caste'. Though unprotected and unpatronised, Valitha tries to live a dignified life, but he becomes the victim of a degraded social system.

The analysis of certain works on the basis of trends and challenges for Dalits within the compass of Indian writing point to the fact that the creative writers, Dalit or non-Dalit writers do not have any ready made solution for evils like social degradation, untouchability, castism, classism, etc, upper and lower. But they portray the social realities in such a way that we feel shaken out of our complacency.

## References

1. Randhawa, Harbir Singh, "Dalit *Literature: Contents, Trends and Concerns*", Sarup Book Publishers, 2010. Delhi.
2. Umed Singh, Politics of Pain and Suffering: A Dalit Perspective, from the book " *Dalit Literature: Contents, Trends and Concerns*", Sarup Book Publishers, 2010. Delhi.
3. A.S.Sujatha, Dalit and Indian Literature, "*Introduction, Ch- 1*", ALP Books, New Delhi, 2013.
4. Mulk Raj Anand, '*Untouchable*'(Text), Mehta Publishing House,june-2003.
5. *'Untouchable' : A Manifesto of Indian Socio-Political Realism*, by- Gajendra Kumar, ch-3,(page-32), Vol-*9*, (From the book- Indian Writing in English, Edit.by- Manmohan K Bhatnagar).
6. A. Jagmohan Chari,*Outside the Magic Circle:A Study of Anand's Untouchable*, ch 16, (page- 148) Vol-6 (From the book- Indian Writing in English, Edit. by- Manmohan K Bhatnagar).

# 15

# Trajectory of Tribal Life: Cases of Missing Human Rights

—*Deba Ranjan Hota*

*The human rights literature often speaks about the pathetic condition of the tribals, who are almost at the receiving end of apathetic attitude of the state. The present study focuses on two cases from the Kokna and Varli tribes of south Gujarat depicting the human rights condition. Data was collected through case study over a period of two to three months in the field. The condition found to be extremely subhuman on all the dimension or aspects of human rights is viz: health, environment and education factored with vulnerabilities which are the focal point of the present research. The daily experiences and encounters of the two cases with the state and the society summarise the present development discontent and dilemmas of development in a society which are also burdened with their own history and culture.*

## Introduction

The spectrum of definitions pertaining to right is broad and illuminating in its different implications and ideological positions. While one approach sees rights as 'normative attributes' that belongs to a person – the term used for self-conscious human beings, conceiving of themselves as initiators of purposive actions (Gerwith A, 1984). Another approach regards rights as entitlements to choose (Beitz, 1989). A third school explains rights 'positively as entitlements to do, have, enjoyed or have done' (McClokey, 1976). A fourth contends that right always and necessarily concern human goods, that is, concern what it is, at least in normal circumstances, good for a person to have (MacCormick, 1982). Rights can be 'possessed, enjoyed, exercised' and 'claimed, demanded, asserted' (Feinberg, 1980).

B.K. Roy Burman (1996) has dealt lucidly with the issues on indigenous people and their problem of human rights and tries to clear the conceptual dilemma. The term indigenous was first introduced by the International Labour Organisation (ILO) in 1957. In that year the ILO has adopted convention 107 "concerning the protection and integration of indigenous and the other tribal and semi-tribal population in independent countries". In this convention tribal and semi-tribal population are considered as a broad social category and indigenous population as a sub-category of the former, who are descendents of the original population of the countries which were taken over by the colonisers by conquest. According to this convention, it only applies to: (a) members of tribal and semi-tribal population in independent countries whose social and economic conditions are at a less advanced stage than the stage reached by the other sections of the national community, and whose status is regulated wholly or partially by their own customs or traditions or by special laws or regulations; (b) members of tribal or semi-tribal populations in indepen-dent countries who are regarded as indigenous on account of their descent from the population which inhabited the country, or a geographical region to which the country belongs, at the time of conquest or colonisation and which irrespective of their colonial status live more in conformity with the social, economic and cultural institutions of that time than with the institutions of which they belong; and (c) for the purpose of this convention, the term semi-tribal includes groups and persons who, are in the process of acquiring the attributes of tribal, are not integrated into the national community.

## Conceptualisation Kokna and Varli Tribes in Gujarat

The Kokna are the tribal group of Gujarat. The etymology of the terms Kokna is by virtue of their wearing armlet i.e. 'Kokna'. The other synonyms of the tribe are 'Kukna' and 'Kokni'.

Major concentrations of the Koknas are in Dharampur and VansdaTaluka of undivided Valsad district and in Dangs district of Gujarat. According to 2011 census the total population of Kokna is 329, 496 which is 4 per cent to the total population of the state. They speak Kokni language which is a dialect of Marathi. They speak Gujarati quite well and can also converse in broken Hindi and use Gujarati script.

According to 2011 Census of India the Varli's population is 255,271 in Gujarat which is 3.4 per cent to the total tribal population of the State. Varli has recorded 0.6 per cent urban population which is the lowest among the tribes of Gujarat. Varlis are principally found in Thane District in the State of Maharashtra. They are also scattered to Nasik and Greater Bombay and who migrated to Gujarat in undivided Valsad district which includes Vansda, Dharampur and Dangs. They are also settled in good number in Dadra and Nagar Haveli. According to the Census of Maharashtra Scheduled Tribe Report (1961) most Varlis say their original home was Nagar Haveli in Daman, while some believe that Dharmapur was their original town in the State of Gujarat.

## The Aim and Method of the Study

The main aim this study is to analyse sociologically the Human Rights issues among the Kokna and Varli tribes of South Gujarat. Here, an attempt has been made to investigate the impact of human rights on the social and non-social aspects of the tribal life. Further, the study also deals with the role of the internal and external agencies/institutions/processes/ phenomena of the state vis-a vis human rights issues.

The research sample comprises of three hundred (300) respondents from both Kokna and Varli tribes were selected from various villages, talukas of Navsari and Valsad districts of South Gujarat, India. An interview schedule was administered in order to understand the socio—economic, political and legal aspects of Human Rights as well as the impact of human rights on social and non-social aspects of tribal life with reference to Health, Education and Environment.The researcher has also undertaken a few case studies in order to have in-depth understanding of the local changes that are taking place among these tribes.

The approach of researcher is basically foundational approach making vulnerability an important point of analysis. Foundationalism is any theory in epistemology (typically, theories of justification, but also of knowledge) that holds that beliefs are justified (known, etc.) based on what are called basic beliefs (also commonly called foundational beliefs). This position is intended to resolve the infinite regress problem in epistemology. Basic beliefs are beliefs that give justificatory support to other beliefs, and more derivative beliefs are based on those more basic beliefs. The basic beliefs are said to be self-justifying or self-evident, that is, they enjoy a non-inferential warrant (or justification), i.e., they are not justified by other beliefs. Typically and historically, foundationalists have held either that basic beliefs are justified by mental events or states, such as experiences, that do not constitute beliefs (these are called non-doxastic mental states), or that they simply are not the type of thing that can be (or needs to be) justified.

## The Studies on Gujarat

R. S. Negi and A. Maitra (1974) worked on the A B O Blood Groups in Kokna and Varli tribes. Godavari Parulekar (1975) in her work on Varli tribes includes the Adivasi Revolt. Pupul Jaykar (1990) in the Earth Mother described the tribal world of Varlis. Nag, N .G. (1980) worked on Kokna Tribe in Dadra Nagar and Haveli with a detailed ethnographic note. S.K. Mandal and R. Malhotra (1992) had given the profile of Varlis in Gujarat. Lancy Lobo (1994) highlighted the suppression of Valiatribals in Bharuch District and the role of state's police and other criminal justice system. K Singh (2001) had given an Anthropro-Historical perspective of the Varli tribe in 1985.

David Hardiman (1995; 2006) presented a historical account of nationalist movement and peasant struggle in tribal society and on Christians and the Adivasis of South Gujarat, exposing the links of religious freedom and rights of the group. Stany Pinto (1995) linked land alienation and assertion of Adivasis in Bharuch District of Gujarat focusing on the environmental concern. Shalini Randeria (2002) in her work focused on environmental action in the legal arena through promotion of rights of the tribals. A.M. Shah (2003) highlighted the relation of tribe and religion with economy and territory focusing on tribals of Gujarat. Satyakam Joshi (2005) focused on development, deprivation and discontent among the Dang tribals, highlighting the close links with rights. P.M. Patel (2005) has analysed and interpreted the process of mobilisation which involves the concern of lower classes including the Dalits, tribals and Other Backward classes of Gujarat.

Hardiman (2006) analysed the revolt of Koli tribe against the British during 1872 in the Konkan region. The revolt brought new form of subaltern political organisation.

## Case Study – 1

Navjibhai Chima aged 65 years residing at Kevdi village, talukaVansda, district Navsari is the elderly chief (Agevan/Kathiya) of Kokna community. He became chief in the year 2006 and commands authority over 15 villages or 'Fadiya' of their own 'Kul'. He presides over decisions related to social, cultural, religious, political, legal and economic life of the Kokna community. Being illiterate he has very little land which he got from his ancestor. This small piece of land does not earn him much and also he does not poses legal ownership (Patta) on his own. He resides with his family which includes his two wives, his ten married and unmarried children. He has final say in the marriages of boys and girls in their own community. He mediates during the engagement of boys and girls. He decides on the issues of widow remarriage and other forms of marriages. He also takes decisions related to divorce, property disputes, small thefts, and conflict and tension related to inter tribal disputes. Normally, his outlook is to see at least equal respect for the both the gender in community barring certain religious and cultural spheres. He demonstrates a strong sense of community feeling and sharing of common food during 'Nawa' which is normally celebrated after the harvest of paddy crop usually in the month of Bhadarva and Asho. 'DungarMauli', the goddess of mountain is chosen once in five years, by certain procedure under his supervision. In this process he summons two or three Bhagats from their own community. They keep fasting, worship Gram Devi, beet the drums the whole night. Copper coin is put inside the bowl of rice poured by milk. They seek for the blessings from their Gram Devi for locating a sacred place for Dungar Mauli. Next morning, they visit the nearby mountain rock and place the copper coin as per the directions given by goddess in the dream of Chima.

Navjibhai enthusiastically described various goddesses worshiped and feared by Kokna community. According to him, Kanasri Devi, the goddess of paddy is a household feature, kept very sacredly and worshiped regularly for the good production of 'Dangar' (paddy) and 'Nagli' (wild millet). Himaidev is the god for good crop worshiped during the time of Diwali. Tortoise is considered as carrier of Himai Dev as shown in the figures and because of this killing of tortoise considered as taboo among Koknas. Chima claims Bagh Dev as most important deity who protects them from natural disaster, protect their livestock from animals and diseases, protect crop from wild pests, and importantly peace and harmony among villagers. Normally, location of Bagh Dev's statue is set up near entrance of Faliya or villages close Gram Dev.

Any important decisions related to community are discussed at a elevated place situated near Gram Devi. This place is considered as sacred place. According to Navjibhai, labour contracts and annual wages are fixed and determined at this place which serves as a moral obligation to the whole community. They believe, violation of this can bring malevolent troubles to the village. In contemporary time, sarpanch and village council members utilise the same place and tactics to resolve the disputes related to marriage, divorce and property. Chima showed his unhappiness and dissatisfaction over new generation for not obeying and following the moral authority structure. As per his argument this is happening because of modern education, technology, averting their elders and traditions.

Navjibhai gave an account of Baghbaras, a unique festival being celebrated before three days of Diwali. As per the ritual of this festival, the cowherd will collect some amount of Rice Dal and take some of money from each house who have cows and buffalos and he will invite all persons to the big grazing zone. All invitees are fed before starting of celebration; the food is collectively prepared for this purpose. After having food, all cows and buffalos are made to stand in circle formation. At the centre of circle, an egg will be put up. Then, they will make the cows and buffalos run inside that circle. If the egg in circle is broken than it would be considered that the year will pass smoothly and there will be peace and prosperity in the village. If the egg remains unbroken it brings bad omen for the whole community and village. This festival is now on the verge of decline and it is not a regular affair as the private investors are showing up their interests to grab the vacant grazing grounds for their development projects.

Chima is unhappy about the displacement taken place in that area. He explained his helplessness in front of developmental agencies and said "government can print notes, not land". This shows his analytical outlook and his ability to think critically about conditions regarding land and livelihood issues prevailed in that area. His vulnerability against governmental and non-governmental forces is evident of conditions that Kokna community is facing in remote places of Navsari district. Along with his discontent about land acquisitions and non participatory development around Kevdi village he also expressed some sense of appreciation for the improvement he observed in public distribution system and election reforms.

Navjibhai Chima radically explained that the Koknas are left with no option in the health sector where they are not able to get modern health care facilities and on other side they are losing their own knowledge about herbal medicines. Along with this he is also worried about fast depletion of herbs and disinterest of new generation to grasp the traditional knowledge about medicinal plants and herbs. He is afraid that if he tries to use available herbs or other plants and animals, he may have to face legal harassments and consequences. In his concluding response he critically rejected the very notion of modern education system. He said "you'll get food if study, and even if you don't you'll get..., nature has plenty for all of us in this world....."

## Case Study– 2

Jikli Powar, a Varli female aged 28 years, residing at village Bopi, Taluka Dharmpur, District Valsad stays with her blind mother and one son aged 2 years with no land. She being a single parent, work as contract labour. She does not have any kind of support from her siblings. She studied up to fourth standard handles all family responsibilities. She shifted to Dharampur in search of work and wages where she was hired by a labour contractor. Initially, she got work at construction site in Dharampur. A non tribal labour contractor made her pregnant. And later he denied taking any responsibility of her. He also threatens her repeatedly by saying that he'll defame her and she won't be able to get any work in entire Dharampur. In 2007, he also threatened her not to complain to community and police by showing his political connections. As Jikli sorrowfully narrated "...that person told me, that you Dedh Praja (slang) is made for this only..., you are here only to entertain people like us...and it is his right to use and abuse us..,..Because we deserve that...else how will we run our family? ".

Showing some courage, Jikli went to her community 'Vadil' and explained her condition to them. Community leader refused to help her by telling that culprit is a nontribal person and community cannot fight against nontribal person. After not getting any help from community people, she approached police. Police also denied taking action by advising her to claim money from labour contractor and settle dispute with him. Police officials showed readiness to be mediate to settle the dispute unofficially. When Jikli denied settling dispute unofficially, police official explained her about political influence of contractor. Official said "...if you lodge complaint about him, he'll remove her name from BPL list...and she'll not get any other facilities from panchayat". By doing this, police denied to lodge complaint against that contractor.

For seeking treatment during pregnancy in PHC, she was asked to reveal identity of the father. As she refused to reveal the identity of the father she lost her eligibility to be beneficiary under Janani Suraksha Yojna, a programme for pregnant mother by the State government. She denied abortion and courageously taken decision to be a single parent. Fortunately, she delivered the baby in PHC itself, without getting any government benefit but with the help of a teacher of ashram sala of Bopi village. The Varli community did not deny her child but rather accepted her son as a community member.

Her mother was having difficulties in eyes. In a free eye check up camp her mother was detected with cataract. She initiated treatment for her mother as per the directions given in the camp. Being pregnant and facing other issues along with wage earning she failed to have follow ups with doctors of her mother. This resulted into permanent blindness of her mother which added a burden to her miseries. Her mother was denied old age pension given under BPL benefits. Same Contractor influenced authorities for not providing any kind of benefits to her family. With no land, and no income source, this pension was very important for her to run her family. Jikli expressed her condition to the wife of sarpanch. The wife of sarpanch went to social welfare officer and reported her exceptional difficulties and travails of her life. Due to sympathetic attitude of social welfare officer, Jikli managed to enrol her mother for old age pension scheme. Jikli understands the value of education and gives credit of her strength and decisions to her little education up to standard fourth. With this she also feels sorry for not continuing education due to poverty and family burden. She didn't force her child to go for work; instead she encourages him for getting educated. According to her, education is a weapon for women and also she abhors superstitious beliefs and rituals.

Her courageous decision of being single parent kept her away from the SHGs which she wanted to be part of. She wanted to be self employed to get financial stability but being single parent in remote village stigmatise her. She tried to get second hand sewing machine and start her own enterprise but her effort was ridiculed by people. She also faced problems in getting drinking water nearby home. Geographically, area in which she resides is at elevated locality. She wanted to extend supply of water at least up to aganwadi centre which is near to her house. But government officials failed to extend water supply in this locality. Jikli is very apprehensive towards the quack medicine men migrated mainly from entering in village and treating women for reproductive health especially for abortion. 'Jholawala Doctors' have also opened clinics in villages and are playing with the health of villagers especially of pregnant women. She expressed her disappointment towards systems of government and society for not being sympathetic towards people like her. She blames contractor for being non-tribal, because she believe that tribal community norms do not allow tribal males to do such immoral deed. She also blames new generation of tribals for not being supportive to single parents and stigmatising them. Jikli analytically expressed her view on political situation which is manipulative and supportive to the elite people. Her discontent and disrespect for people who gets influenced and also influence government policy implementing workforce is clearly observed. Her narration pointed out the lapse of government to frame mechanisms to help such destitute who are the real victims and at mercy of government schemes.

## References

*Adivasi: Legal Provisions, Languages and Locations*, (2004). BHASHA Research Centre, Baroda and Tribal Research Academy, Tejgadh, Chottaudepur.

Basu, D. D. (1994). *Human rights in constitutional law.* Prentice-Hall of India.

Baxi, U. (1986). *Towards a sociology of Indian law*, Satvahan .

Centre For Study Of Developing Societies. (1996). Conference Proceedings. *Conference on 'culture, rights and culture of rights': organised by centter for study of developing societies.* economic and political weekly.

Nag, N. G., & Sah, M. L. (1980). Kokna, a schedule tribe in Dadra and Nagar Haveli. *Office of the Registrar General, India*, 50.

Punalekar, S. P and Randive J. (1984). Tribal Education: An Extensive Study, Centre for Social Studies.

Punalekar, S. P., & Randive, J. (1984). Tribal Education: An Inter-State Study. *Sociological Bulletin, 28* (1).

General, R. (2001). *Census of India.* Census Commissioner, India.

# 16

# Unveiling the Plight of Domestic Workers in Delhi: A Hidden Workforce

—*Vibha Singh*

**Abstract**

*The present paper discusses the practice of paid domestic work in Delhi and the treatment meted out to migrant tribal domestic workers by the employers, local agents at village and placement agencies in the city. With some cases highlighted by media lately, there is little awareness about the issues the migrated domestic workers face in Delhi. These are the young girls hired from rural and tribal belts of Jharkhand, Odisha and Assam and other eastern states for domestic work. No adequate food and water, no facility of proper accommodation, less salary, long hours of work, no time for rest, inhuman conditions for work and physical and sexual exploitation are some glimpses of plights of full time tribal domestic workers in Delhi. The paper is based on the work experience and close interaction with the full time domestic workers in Delhi while interning with a Delhi based organisation and the rigorous analyses of the disorganised process of migration and of violation of human rights of the tribal and rural workers who come to Delhi in search of employment and a better life. The paper explores the process of migration of domestic workers and their experiences of work and life in Delhi.*

**Key words:** *Domestic work, Migration, Placement agency, Trafficking, Tribal women worker, Unorganised sector.*

*'Gar vale bej diye'* said MS Sunita, a live-in domestic worker, when asked about the reason of coming to Delhi from her village. They are 'the help' many cannot do without. They clean our houses, cook for us, wash our clothes and utensils, and bring semblance to what would be otherwise an untidy space. Their daily presence allows us to go along with our lives with relative comfort (Ningthoujam, 2013). Most of the full time domestic workers have migrated from tribal and rural areas of Eastern states of India. They are most vulnerable to multiple exploitative practices and are subjected to verbal,

physical and sexual harassment. Due to the lack of proper recognition and regulation of the profession, these workers hold no right as workers/laborers. They work for longs hours without proper rest and are often denied even the basic social and human rights.

The paper will explore the experiences of migrant women domestic workers and the trends of this profit making business of placement agencies which are both boon and bane for domestic workers. The paper is based on the voluntary work experience and uses data from secondary sources. Studies related to paid domestic work and migration and statistics from NSSO along with the reports of non-governmental organisations were reviewed to analyse the process and trend of this sector.

## "Work like any other, yet work like no other"

Domestic work is one of the oldest and most important occupations for many people for many years but unfortunately not in line with other respectable jobs. It is highly undervalued and considered as unskilled work. Traditionally, women have been considered as capable of doing this but paid domestic work also remains undervalued and poorly regulated. We don't have an updated statistics about domestic workers. According to NSSO (2004-2005) there were 4.75 million domestic workers. Out of which 3.05 million were women. Clearly, this is a highly gendered profession. The percentage of domestic workers in total female employment in the service sector increased from 11.8 per cent to 27.1 per cent in 2004-5–a phenomenal increase of about 2, 25 million in a short span of five years. (N, 2010). Despite being a highly grown sector it has failed to get the attention of policy makers. It is said to be grown by 222 per cent since 2000 (Sinha, 2010). According to Domestic workers (regulation of employment, condition of work, social security and welfare) bill 2010 , 'Domestic worker is any person, who engages in domestic work in the household for remuneration whether woman or man, stay-in or live out, local or migrant, on a full-time or part-time basis or as part of contracted work within an employment relationship.There are three types of domestic workers in in Delhi: the live-in domestic workers who reside at the site of employment; live outs domestic workers who return in the evening after work and part timers who work for two-three hours at a time in different houses. All domestic workers face problems to some extent but the most vulnerable are the full timers.

Full time domestic workers have to be available for 24 hours a day and their work never gets over. Most of the full time domestic workers are the young girls migrated from rural and tribal belts of Bihar, Jharkhand, Assam, Chhattisgarh etc. by placement agencies and placed in houses in the metropolitan cities like Delhi, Mumbai, and Chennai for domestic work. Seeing the role of placement agencies and the trends of recruitment, it will be more appropriate if we call it 'trafficking' instead of migration. According to UN,

Trafficking is 'the recruitment, transportation, transfer, harbouring or receipt of persons, by means of threat or use of force or other forms of coercion, of abduction, of fraud, of deception, of the abuse of power or of a position of vulnerability or of the giving or receiving of payments or benefits to achieve the consent of a person having control over another person, for the purpose of exploitation; exploitation shall include, at a minimum, the exploitation of the prostitution of others or other forms of sexual exploitation , forced labour or services, slavery or practices similar to slavery, servitude or the removal of organs." Most adult domestic workers fall into the category of voluntary economic migrant workers, but many domestic workers toiling in intolerable conditions are exploited, held in virtual captivity and physically and sexually and psychologically abused and isolated and are solely dependent upon their employers. (State of world population, 2006).

## Migration or Trafficking and the role of placement agency

According to UNDP, 20 million people (mainly women and girls) migrate for domestic work to Delhi, Mumbai and other large cities from eastern states of Bihar, Odisha, Chhattisgarh, Jharkhand, Assam and Mizoram (Alter and Deshingkar, 2009; (Shree, 2012)). In India's internal migration scenario, female migrants outnumber male migrants in several categories (Shree, 2012). Neha Wadhwan in her study discussed that the most popular urban destination for migrant work from the surveyed village is Delhi for both men and women. (Wadhwan, 2013)

In the search of better and debt free lives, these migrant workers get lured by the false promises of a decent job by placement agents. About Jharkhand, Neha Wadhwan reveal that domestic work is the largest category in the type of work available to migrant women from Jharkhand (Wadhwan, 2013). This is quite fascinating for tribal women belonging to low socio-economic background to come out from their villages and experience the life in the big city. However, it does not always give them the same pleasure as they expect. Unemployment, poverty, loss in crops, mortgaged land, siblings to be married, death, sickness, etc., are some of the reasons that force these workers to migrate to cities in search of jobs. (Menon, 2010). Collecting money for dowry, poverty and lack of work opportunities and the money-spending capacity of those who come back for holidays on clothes, make-up, and jewellery, etc., are other factors that entice women to the big city. Women also feel that this is the only way they can travel and see the world before they get married and are tied to household responsibilities. (Wadhwan, 2013)

The mediating role between the employer and employee is played by the placement agencies. These placement agencies are the private agencies which bring workers from rural and tribal areas and place them with employers in Delhi. Albeit such agencies should be registered under the Shop and establishment Act but most of them remain informal, therefore cannot be regulated. According to estimates, about 2000-2300 placement agencies operate in the national capital region (Yadav, 2012). Most of these agencies keep the name of their agency on God's name like 'Om Sai', 'Jesus and Mary' etc. to fascinate worker and their families that they are doing some kind of social service by providing them employment. To some extent it can be seen as a boon to the migrant workers as it provides them opportunity to earn living for them and to assist their families but can be turn into bane also. With the help of local agents at village level workers reach to placement agencies which places them with employers in cities. A deep-rooted nexus exists between local job contractors and unregulated placement agencies and is instrumental in the exploitation of domestic workers (Wadhwan, 2013). Until they get placed somewhere they live in the agency only, some of the workers have reported of being sexually abused by the agents. With no rights and rules to fall back on, most domestic help have become contemporary slaves in our metros. Many women and children are trafficked from backward districts and exploited financially – and even sexually – by placement agencies which operate openly without any form of restrictions and regulations (Yadav, 2012). Megha Shree (2012) purports that hazardous condition for work, lack of sanitation, malnutrition, exhaustion, separation from family, forced restrictions, lineless, physical exploitation affect the mental health of women too.

Ms X, 17 years old from Jharkhand: She was suppressed and beaten up on a regular basis by mixer jar and all other utensils available in the place. Rescued by NGO with injury mark on her face and entire body. She was asked to put linen cloths which see through and inner wears were torn into pieces.

Ms Y (33 years) from Assam: The employer and his son both were habitual in seducing her by praising her for her beauty and hair. They both enticed her always to attract her attention by touching her hair, cheeks, and neck. Somehow she escaped from the house.

A contract is signed between the employer and placement agents mentioning the duration of the job and salary. All the agencies charge a registration fee and commission from the employer ranging from 3000-10,000 rupees for a contract of 11 months. Sometimes the salary is direct given to agents not to the workers. Once they get placed, their misery starts. They are bound to live within the four wall of the house. The nature of the profession itself makes it vulnerable for the workers. Employers with the fear that they may run away, don't let them maintain contacts with the outside world. They are even restricted to visit the religious places to offer prayer if the employers are not of same religion. '*Church jane ko nahin milta hai kyoki sahib Christian nahin hai*'. Said one of the domestic workers staying at placement agency in south Delhi. She had come there on annual vacation of 10 days from employer's house. Not allowing anyone to practice their own religion is a sheer violation of human rights as well as constitutional rights. Domestic workers experience a degree of vulnerability that is unparalleled to that of other workers (state of world population UNDP 2006). In some cases reported to Delhi domestic workers' forum, both the placement agency and employers had refused to take the responsibility of their medical treatment during any casualty. They send workers back to their villages if they fall sick. They get salary of INR 1500 to 3500 per month according to the rates in that particular area. They often receive salary annually which is given to their family after cutting the commission of placement agencies and any other fine or penalty for any loss if happens by the worker. For the rich and the influential, the domestic workers are paid slaves (Menon, 2010). Throughout the procedure, workers stand weak in this whole negotiation process.

There is no accurate data available on the number of live-in workers. Accessibility to those workers is nil because they seldom come out or interact with others (Menon S. , 2010). One of the domestic workers revealed in interaction after having been rescued by an organisation that she used to keep her stuff in the cooler. Some are even not allowed to use the same bathrooms. 'The cases of rape, suspicious deaths, sexual harassment, physical and mental harassment are very common (Delhi domestic workers' forum: Record).

## The interplay of other structural barriers

The major barriers for these migrant women workers revolve around caste, race and language with gender and culture as cross cutting factors. Caste and race intersect at the very first stage of recruitment itself. Employers discriminate and deny employment on the basis of their caste, religion and race. This is an utter violation of their rights being human. Their "new Hindu names" made them more acceptable to their employers who were mostly upper-caste Hindu or Sikh families living in Delhi and nearby suburbs. (Wadhwan, 2013) The level of vulnerability increases with their inability of speaking Hindi language. They were already voiceless by the circumstances and the language barrier makes the situation more pathetic for them. The living style of the both the place from which she came and that of city is totally different. It comes to them as cultural shock sometimes. They get to use electronic devises and technology like cooking on gas stove, oven, iron etc. for the first time.

If we look at this as a whole, gender plays a huge role. Instead of their sons, seeing the growing demand of women workers, family from indigenous communities send their daughters to the city for work. They don't have many options in front of them to earn money for survival. Not enough research or data exists on gender and internal migration in India, barring few exceptions (Deshingkar et. al. 2009; Mazumdar et. al. 2013; (Wadhwan, 2013)). Their exploitation starts with their contact with placement agencies. Then they experience the treatment from employers and go back to their place after the completing the tenure of the contract of job. But their misery does not end here. After having returned back to the village they experience discriminative behaviour by their own community people. Then they are known and labelled as 'Dilli returned' or '*dilli vali'*. This tag has negative implications for them. They are seen as exploited women and believed to have lost virginity during their stay in the city (Kukreja, 2009). It sometimes hinders their marriage also. People hesitate in accepting their marriage proposals considering them as 'exploited women'. They take time in coming back to normal life. There were some cases where migrant domestic workers had not returned to the village for several years (Wadhwan, 2013).

There is a need of strong regulation of this profession. The idea of recognition of domestic work through a convention is to make sure that working out of sight does not mean being cut off from labour rights, or exclusion from the basic human rights of decent work (Seeta Sharma, 2010). Since 1950s the bill for the regulation of domestic work has been pending in the parliament. Many times it was reintroduced with some modifications in the parliament but could not be passed. This issue does not seem to be in the priority list of parliamentarians. The latest bill domestic workers (regulation of employment, condition of work, social security and welfare) bill 2010 is highly recommended to be passed soon. After much lobbying, domestic workers were brought within the ambit of the recent 2008 Unorganised Workers Social Security Act. Social security of these workers is of great concerns. Social security of live-out domestic workers can be ensured but due to the nature of employment of full time domestic work, its regulation is very difficult. India does not have any national law to regulate this profession which restricts it to become signatory to ILO 100th convention that talks about rights of domestic workers and protection from exploitation. 19 Countries have laws specifically concerning domestic work (ILO).

The right of freedom of association and the effective recognition of the right to collective bargaining seems to be a utopia when we are not able to secure even their basic rights. ILO is highly recommending and promoting 'decent work for all' which can be achieved by implementing a strong legislation only. There is also need to pay attention towards the growing demand of civil society organisations to include domestic workers under the gamut of sexual harassment bill (2012). Domestic workers are excluded from standards governing working conditions. They are excluded from the National Minimum Wages Act, 1948 implicitly, but some states have extended this to cover domestic workers on their territory through state legislation like Andhra Pradesh, Bihar, Karnataka, Rajasthan, Dadra and Nagar Haveli.

Albeit mere having a new law will also not ensure the protection of these workers as most of the influentially of the law depends on its effective implementation. Many laws still exist like to prevent violence against women, non-payment of wages and Indian Penal Code but the actors need to be questioned. How supportive is Delhi Police when they portrait domestic workers as suspicious in their advertisements. If we talk about the employers, do they allow police or any activist to enter their premises of their house to meet them to know about their conditions? There is need of proper planning for the regulation part of the law. All agencies will have to work together if the interest of domestic workers is to be protected. There is also need to think beyond the legislative advocacy and that is the awareness among the middle and upper middle class people about the rights of domestic workers. This would work more within in those four walls than any law. Unless we become sensitive about the issues of domestic workers the plights are not going to diminish. If the placement agency work properly and maintain the transparency and accountability, this profession can bring about a positive change in the lives of migrant workers along with the prosperity. And these agencies can be regulated with Placement agency (Regulation) law which is also yet to be passed in the parliament. They are workers, part of a productive economy and their identity as workers must be recognised, respected and protected (Menon G., 2010).

## Notes


JAGORI. (2004). *Rights & Vulnerabilities :A Research Study of Migrant Women Workers in the informal sector in Delhi.* New Delhi: JOGORI.

JAGORI. (2010). *Domestic workers : conditions, rights and responsiblities.* Delhi: JAGORI.

Kukreja, R. (Director). (2009). *Delhi bound for work* [Motion Picture].

Menon, G. (2010). Stree Jagriti Samiti: spreading awareness among domestic workers. *Labour File* , 56-59.

Menon, S. (2010). Anecdotes from the life of Domestic workers in Delhi and in Defense of Sumari's right. *Labour file*, 6-12.

N, N. (2010). Domestic workers: Profile and Emerging concerns. *Labour File*, 13-15.

Nagarajan, R. (2013, March 16). *All work, little pay for domestics*. Retrieved March 16, 2013, from The Times of India: http://timesofindia.indiatimes.com/city/delhi/All-work-little-pay-for-domestics/articleshow/18999239.cms

Ningthoujam, D. (2013, July 16). *Domestic work remains deeply rooted in bias, says study*. Retrieved October 15, 2013, from The Hindu: http://www.thehindu.com/news/cities/Delhi/domestic-work-remains-deeply-rooted-in-bias-says-study/article4917714.ece

Seeta Sharma, A. I. (2010). Domestic workers and Trafficking. *Labour file*, 35-37.

Shree, M. (2012). Female tribal migrants as domestic workers: A study of their compulsion and working conditions. *Man and development.*

Sinha, S. (2010). Social protection for domestic workers: Need for innovative approaches . *Labour File* , 38-40.

Wadhwan, N. (2013). Living in Domesti-city: Women and migration for domestic from Jharkhand. *Economic and Poilitical weekly.*

Yadav, S. (2012, April 7). *No balm for the helping hands*. Retrieved october 15, 2013, from Deccan Herald: http://www.deccanherald.com/content/240475/no-balm-helping-hands.html

# 17

# Political Economy of Tribal Development in Madhya Pradesh: The Case of Korku Tribe

—*Janmejaya Mishra*

The paper examines the nature of poverty and marginalisation of the Korku tribe in Khandwa district in Madhya Pradesh. It provides detailed analytical insights to the contributing factors of poverty and the processes of marginalisation of the lesser-known tribe alongside discussing the politics of tribal development through anatomy of a development project in the Khalwa block based on the author's ethnographic research over the period of last five years. Major findings are; the Korku adivasis confront chronic poverty, food insecurity, acute malnutrition, distress labour migration and cyclic indebtedness in their day-to-day lives. On the other hand, socio-economic and political marginalisation make them vulnerable day by day. This caused mostly due to the upper caste subjugation and exploitations by the political leaders leave very little scope for the tribal community to work themselves out of the poverty trap. Further, the political mass also ensures that while the state does very little for development of the Korku tribe, civil society organisations doing genuine work are not allowed which poses potential threats to their vested interests and legacy of ruling for years.

## The Korku tribe

Korku is a scheduled tribe community predominantly found in East Nimar (presently Khandwa and Burhanpur districts), Betul district of Madhya Pradesh and adjoining areas in Melghat region of Amravati district in Maharastra. The Korkus are found in highest concentration in the highland of Central India, especially in the regions surrounding the Mahadeo hill, a centrally situated peak in the Satpura mountains (Fuchs 1988). The Korkus are a branch of the great Munda tribes and are placed in the vicinity of the great tribe – the Gonds (Deogaonkar et. al. 1990). Korkus have derived their name from the combination of the word *'koru'* meaning man and *'ku'* which makes it plural meaning tribal men (Russell et. al. 1916). Korkus are believed to be a hunting gathering community dwelling in the forests of Satpura ranges on either sides of the Tapti river. They were dependent on forest based resources and practising shifting cultivation on large scale for their livelihoods in earlier times. Eventually, they started settled agriculture. Their late introduction to settled agriculture made them less skilful in comparison to their neighbouring tribesmen of Bhil and Barela tribal communities. Besides deforestation, degradation of land and water resources was also rampant in the area. Massive soil erosion made the land unsuitable for cultivation. Further, scanty and erratic rainfall made the situation more worsen leading many water bodies to dry off. As a result of the direct consequences of degradation of land and water resources, agriculture productivity has been declined substantially over the years thus affecting livelihoods of the Korku tribe and other peasant communities. Chronic poverty, food insecurity, acute under/malnutrition and distress seasonal labour migration are the primary issues that the Korko tribe faces today.

## Poverty among the Korkus

The cash flow analysis of Korku tribal households in the Khalwa block reveals many surprising features. Agriculture and manual labour work are the only sources of income for most of the households. Based on household survey data of 2008-09, average annual income of a household is estimated to be Rs 20460 (approx.), wherein the contribution of income from agriculture and labour work is estimated to be nearly Rs 14000 (70 per cent) and Rs 6300 (30 per cent) respectively. Likewise, average annual expenditure of a household is estimated to be Rs 26634 (approx). Thus, there is a net deficit of Rs 6174 per household per annum. To meet this deficit, the tribal families borrow money from informal sources i.e. local money lenders and traders at a very high rate of interest. To pay off the debt and for meeting other household expenditure, a major portion of the workforce migrates to better off areas in neighbouring state of Maharashtra and parts of Madhya Pradesh during lean seasons. Mostly engaged in agricultural labour works, they earn their livelihoods. Saving of money is found very little among the Korku families. On the other hand, expenses on social obligations like marriages, rituals and festivals are very high. Formal financial institutions like banks and credit cooperatives do not easily extend credit to them, leaving these families to depend on the mercy of money lenders and traders to fulfil their credit needs.

Average landholding size of a Korku household is 2.5 to 3 acres. Most of the farmers fall under the marginal/small holder category. Nearly, 85 per cent of the households have land and about 15 per cent are landless. Only, 12 per cent of the land owning households has access to irrigation sources mainly dug wells. Soybean, cotton, sorghum and pigeon pea are the major crops cultivated during kharif season. Wheat and gram are the major rabi crops cultivated only by those farmers who have access to irrigation. The average annual income of the households ranges from Rs 15000 to Rs 25,000/-.

## Debt, Migration and Exploitation

Significant changes have taken place in the cropping patterns in recent years. Cultivation of cash crops has been widely adopted by the tribal farmers in the region. Korku tribal farmers prefer to cultivate cash crops – soybean and cotton in particular on large scale basis and give less preference for cultivation of food crops such as sorghum, maize, pigeon pea and minor millets. The tribal farmers in the region have been historically exploited by local money lenders and traders. They depend on the private traders and local money lenders – mostly the upper castes for purchasing agriculture inputs such as seeds, fertilizers and pesticides required for the cultivation. However, due to lack of cash during agriculture season, the tribal farmers are compelled to take credits from the money lenders and purchase inputs from them who are also the traders running input supply shops in the name of krisi seva kendras in the local markets. The inputs purchased on credit from the traders and money lenders are very low in quality for which they are charged high price and exorbitant rate of interest. Further, most of the tribal farmers are also get into informal agreements with the traders that they would sell the agriculture produces to them during post-harvest season. As an obligation to repay the credit, the tribal farmers are further compelled to sell their agriculture produces to these traders at much lower price than the prevailing market price from whom they have taken credit during monsoon season. Thus, their continued dependency on the traders and money lenders make them prone to harsh economic exploitations and thus, the Korku tribal farmers are trapped in cyclic indebtedness year after year. Consequently, low crop productivity and negative income from rainfed agriculture and cumbersome debt force them to resort on distress seasonal labour migration. A significant portion of the Korku tribal population migrates to relatively better off areas like Akola, Jalgoan, Akot, Bhusawal, Nasik and Nagpur in neighbouring Maharashtra state and Harda, Hosangabad, Pithampur and Indore in Madhya Pradesh during off-seasons along with their entire family members. The family members of most of the rainfed farmers migrate out for 5-6 months in a year. Among the landless households, duration of migration ranges from 6-9 months. Mainly engaged in agriculture wage labour work in private farms, labour work in cotton, dal mills and construction sites they survive with bare minimum needs.

Mosse et. al. also found similar features of seasonal labour migration among the adivasis in the western Madhya Pradesh and mentioned that seasonal labour migration has become an irreversible part of the livelihoods of rural adivasi communities in western India. Labour migration is not just a means to cope with below subsistence agriculture and debt have become the only means by which valued agrarian lifestyles can be reproduced. For a few, migration is a route of upward social and economic mobility; but for the vast majority migration not only perpetuates debt and dependence, but exposes the poorest to extreme hardship and cruel exploitation (Mosse et. al. 2005).

## Food Insecurity

Sorghum (jowar) is the major staple food of the Korku tribal community. It meets consumption needs and is grown in nearly 20 per cent of the total area. Few farmers grow jowar in large farm lands which is confined to them only. It was also found jowar grows well in the region and gives good yield. However, the amount of jowar grown by the farmers is not enough to meet their consumption needs. Therefore, they rely on the market for purchasing jowar to meet their needs. Pigeon pea (tuar) is another important food crop grown by the tribal farmers which is grown in 14 per cent of land of the study area. It is the only food crop which gives cash income as well as kept for consumption. Tuar is cultivated with cotton as a mixed crop. The yield is around 300 to 500 kg per acre. However, it is prone to frequent pest attacks. The tribal farmers keep some amount of tuar for consumption and sell out the rest in the local markets. Cultivation of wheat is very limited to few farmers. It is cultivated only by irrigated farmers as a rabi crop.

Only 10-15 per cent of the total land is under wheat cultivation. The yield from one acre of wheat is around 738 kg. Discussions with the farmers revealed that the cultivation of wheat is very recent in the region. Farmers who have access to irrigation mainly through dug wells are the ones who cultivate wheat. It was also found that those families which are cultivating wheat have shifted their food habit from jowar to wheat. Nearly, 55 per cent of the total produce is sold in the market and the rest is kept for consumption. Those families growing wheat do not face any problem of food scarcity. Seasonality is a major factor which affects the availability of food grains of the households. Discussions with the community members revealed that food grain availability gradually decreases during the period of monsoon (July-August). The stored food grains get finished and farmers have to depend on market for their consumption needs. 40 per cent of the respondents mentioned that they faced problem of food shortage during the month of monsoon. Besides these food crops, traditional minor millets like Kodo, Kutki and Sawariya are also grown in the region. These crops serve as an important source of nutrition especially for the kids and lactating women. However, the area under cultivation the minor millets have drastically decreased over the years. The tribal farmers do not prefer to grow these crops any more.

The functioning of public distribution system (PDS) in the study villages was found to be very poor. It was found that families having good landholding have BPL cards whereas those who deserve it most are excluded. 38 per cent of the ration card holders are BPL and the rest belong to the APL category. Nearly, 18 per cent of the households which indeed deserve ration cards do not have. Black marketing of wheat, sugar and kerosene by PDS dealers came out during discussions with the villagers. Wheat and kerosene are supplied regularly to the households while sugar, rice, salt and pulses are not. Dependency on PDS for food grain was high among the poorest families. Nearly, 32 per cent of the families are completely depended on the PDS for consumption of wheat. Further, though the Integrated Child Development Services (ICDS) is running in most of the villages, only 15 per cent of the parents prefer to send their children to the anganwadi centres. A large majority, 85 per cent of the parents do not send their children to these centres. The major reasons for not enrolling the children in the anganwadi centres are frequent migration by parents to different places in search of labour works, location of anganwadi centres from their home and poor quality of food served at the centres.

## Acute under/malnutrition

Malnutrition among the children and under-nutrition among the adult members mostly women are very high in the area. Most of the children are born with underweight. Malnutrition related deceases like Kwashiorkor is seen in among the children in all the villages. Nearly, 60 per cent of the children have reddish colour hair which is due to protein deficiency. Also, 15 per cent of the children suffer from skin disease which is due to the prevailing unhygienic conditions. Night blindness caused due to deficiency of vitamin A is found among 15 per cent of the children. Nearly, 10 per cent of children suffer from polio and rickets and Kwashiorkor taken together. Further, diseases like measles and diarrhea are found to be common to most of the children. Nearly, 70 per cent of the women have expressed conditions matching to anaemia. It is not only found among women but also among the adolescent girls. Anaemia is associated with deficiency of Iron in blood. Moreover, exposure to smoke while cooking also is a known risk factor of Anaemia. About, 65 per cent of the respondents perceived that anaemia is the most prevalent disease among adolescent girls. Other common ailments are fever, vomiting and skin disease. These findings were also validated through an interview with the health workers.

Nearly, 60 per cent of the women reported that they prefer to consult traditional birth attendants rather going for institutional deliveries. The remaining 40 per cent have opted for hospitals/private doctors. It was found that the incidence of infant mortality is very high primarily owing to dependency on unqualified traditional birth attendants. Further, 50 per cent of the tribal women responded that they got married at the age between 12 to 14 years, 30 per cent of women getting married at the age of 14-16 years and 20 per cent get married at the age of 16-20 year of age. In 85 per cent of pregnancy cases, the gap between two consecutive deliveries is only one year. Because of early marriages and low gap between subsequent deliveries, the growth of both children and mothers is severely affected.

## AKRSP (I)'s Intervention

Aga Khan Rural Support Programme (India) started developmental interventions in the remote and poor districts of Khandwa, Burhanpur, Khargone and Barwani in south-western Madhya Pradesh after a systematic appraisal of the area in 2004-05. At present, it is working with more than 16,000 households of Korku, Bhil, Bhilala, Barela and Gond tribal communities over 120 villages in Khalwa and Pandhana blocks of Khandwa, Khaknar block of Burhanpur, Zirniya block of Khargone and Niwali block of Barwani districts in order to sustain their livelihoods through promotion of community based institutions which are being capacitated to manage natural resources and address the core issues of poverty through improved agriculture productivity and with locally suitable off-farm activities to improving the economic conditions of poorest tribal households. The key areas of interventions are watershed development, participatory irrigation management, saving and credit services through self help groups, alternate livelihood promotion through animal husbandry, skill development and placements of rural youth.

This author directly worked in the region for three and half a years in the capacity of monitoring and evaluation specialist with AKRSP(I) being based at its regional office in Khandwa from July, 2008 to December, 2011. Afterwards, he was moved to its central office at Ahmedabad, Gujarat in January, 2012 from where he continues to work till date.

AKRSP(I) started its interventions in Khalwa block of Khandwa district in July 2006. Participatory irrigation management, watershed development, self help groups (SHG) promotion and providing agriculture extension services including agriculture input supply were the major areas of its intervention in Khalwa block. As of now, more than 3000 households of Korku tribal communities in 30 villages of the block have been directly benefitted through these interventions. Broadly speaking, these 30 villages have been covered in three phases. From 2006 to 2009, 17 villages were covered under the European Commission (EC) funded SCALE project. Under this project, AKRSP(I) major thrust was reviving the old irrigation tanks and canals in 8 villages which were build by government's water resources department in 1980s. Remaining villages were covered through watershed development intervention. However, promotion of self help groups and providing agriculture extension services including agriculture input supply were the activities done across the 17 villages.

In the second phase, 12 villages including 2 old villages were selected for the Integrated Micro-plan Project (IMP) in 2010. The IMP was a newly conceived project by the State MGNREGA Council of the Govt of Madhya Pradesh under MGNREGS. The State MGNREGA Council, GoMP selected AKRSP(I) as its implementing partner for the newly launched IMP project in

Khalwa block of Khandwa district and Khaknar block of Burhanpur district. It must be noted that concentration of the Korku tribe is very high in both the blocks of these two districts. AKRSP(I) followed necessary guidelines provided by the State MGNREGA Council and Jila Panchayats of respective districts to implement the projects. While implementation of the IMP project in Khaknar block of Burhanpur district went on smoothly, however, it was unlikely in Khalwa block of Khandwa district. The underlying reasons for this are discussed in detail in the following section.

## Politics of Tribal Development in Khalwa Block

AKRSP(I) strictly adhered to the norms and necessary guidelines prescribed by the State MGNREGA Council and Jila Panchayat, Khandwa to implement the IMP project in Khalwa block. As the first step, it started following the set of activities for preparation of detailed project report (DPR) of the project villages. Round of meetings, discussions, PRAs, transact walks and job card verifications were held in the villages by the mid of 2011. Thus, DPRs were prepared and approved by the Gram Sabhas held in the villages. All the DPRs approved by Gram Sabhas of respective villages were submitted to Jila Panchayat, Khandwa by the mid of 2011. With this all the official formalities were completed by AKRSP(I) for sanctioning of the project and its subsequent implementation at village level and the villagers were promised of the project. However, AKRSP(I) has made several queries to concerned officials at Jila Panchayat, Khandwa for updates on sanctioning of the project since then. But, no clear responses were given to it. The concerned officials have just said that it will take time to move the files for sanctioning of the project which they are trying. Meanwhile, the IMP project in Khaknar block of Burhanpur district for which AKRSP(I) was also the implementing partner was sanctioned and its implementation was in full swing in 14 villages.

However, in Khalwa, expectation of villagers of the 12 IMP project villages was on raise and whenever any field staff of AKRSP(I) was visiting the villages, they were increasingly finding it difficult to talk on the status of the project. Instead of waiting for sanctioning of the IMP project, AKRSP(I) started mobilising resources from other sources and implemented agriculture related intervention alongside promotion of self help groups (SHGs) in these villages. On the other hand, it continued to seek updates on sanctioning of the project to concerned authorities at Jila Panchayat, Khandwa. It was in early 2012, the Jila Panchayat officials informed that they have forwarded the files to concerned officials at Bhopal and now nothing is in their hands and the fate of the project lies with the higher authorities at Bhopal. During the same time, another project submitted to National Bank for Agriculture and Rural Development (NABARD) for horticulture promotion in Khalwa and Pandhana blocks of Khandwa district got sanctioned giving much relief to the organisation. By March 2012, the concerned authorities at Bhopal informed

AKRSP(I) that now it can talk to the secretariat of the department of rural development on status of the project. Soon, AKRSP(I) made contacts with the secretariat of the rural development department. To its surprise, concerned officials at the secretariat informed that now AKRSP(I) should forget about sanctioning of the project because, the minister of tribal development who hails from the same Khalwa region does not want this project to get sanctioned at all rather he wants to meet senior officials of AKRSP(I) at his residence in Khandwa. As a follow up measure to this, two senior level officials of AKRSP(I) met the minister of tribal development at his residence in Khandwa. During the meeting, the minister was very calm and appreciated the organization's interventions among the Korku tribe in Khalwa block and stated that he has nothing personal against the organisation's working in Khalwa block; that is also his constituency of state legislative assembly which he is holding for past 15 years. He further suggested that AKRSP(I) should now forget the IMP project in Khalwa and if wants can have similar projects elsewhere but not in Khalwa for which the minister can help whatever possible. The two senior staff who went to meet the minister returned back in empty hands. It is now understood that why the sanctioning of the project was taking so much time which was almost 1.5 years in this case. After few days of this meeting, the district collector called on the two senior level staff of AKRSP (I) along with the district development manager (DDM) of NABARD, Khandwa to have discussion on the recent sanctioning of a horticulture project by NABARD in Khandwa district. Unlike the minister in the previous meeting, he was rude in his behaviour and asked them who gave permission to AKRSP (I) and the DDM to sanction the horticulture project in Khalwa and Pandhana blocks which was of worth Rs. 7.5 crore and told them categorically that such a situation should not be repeated in future without the permission of the district collector. Later on, it was learnt that he was told by the tribal development minister to do so. At present, however AKRSP (I) mobilises funding from private donors and is implanting watershed based intervention in Khalwa block.

The minister of tribal development in Madhya Pradesh belongs to Khalwa block. He is being elected to the state assembly consecutively since past 15 years. He himself belongs to the scheduled tribe community of the Gonds. His forefathers were rulers of the erstwhile princely state which was covering Khalwa block before the independence. However, now he rules the region being a democratically elected representative of the people and his wife also holds the post of mayor of the municipal corporation in Khandwa town. He has a very good support of the masses at village level and enjoys unconditional support of the people especially the Korkus and other castes in Khalwa block. He offers occasional feasts to the community members and party workers each year and captures the votes of masses by offering populist measures before elections. He has also a stronghold among the other castes especially the Yadavs who are money-lenders and traders in the region from whom the Korkus take credits and agriculture inputs during monsoon season at a very high rate of interest and sell their produces at low price and sometime sell in advance. The minister knows very well that if organisations like AKRSP (I) and others are allowed in the region, it would pose threats to his legacy of ruling the region by developing and empowering the Korku tribal community in long run. Hence, they get eliminated on the way in such humiliated manner.

## Concluding Remarks

Khalwa block in East Nimar – Khandwa district of Madhya Pradesh has been in contemporary debate over development not only in the state but also in national level for many reasons and there is no irony over the fact that Khalwa has its place in the list of most backward blocks in the country. Wide spread poverty, food insecurity, malnutrition, mass scale exploitations by money lenders, traders and political leaders and gross violation of human rights in the region are the main woes to the marginalised Korku tribe of recent times. This paper only provides a firsthand glimpse of these grim situations. It seems that the future of the Korku tribe lies in their own hands. The sooner they understand the realities the better it is for them which cannot happen on its own. Therefore, the role of organisations like AKRSP(I) should be making the community aware and empowering them socio-economically. Only then can there be an end to the present predicament of the Korku tribe in the region.

## References

Deogaonkar, S G and S S Deogaonkar (1990): *The Korku Tribals*. Concept Publishing Company: New Delhi.

Fuchs, Stephen (1988): *The Korkus of the Vindhya Hills*. Inter-India Publications: New Delhi.

Mishra, Janmejaya and Raj Kumar Gupta (2010): *"Food Insecurity among the Tribals of Madhya Pradesh: Causes and Consequences"*, paper presented at Fifth Annual International Conference on Public Policy and Management held at Indian Institute of Management (IIM), Bangalore on 9th August, 2010.

Mosse, David, Sanjeev Gupta and Vidya Shah (2005): 'On the Margins in the City: Adivasi Seasonal Labour Migration in Western India' in *Economic and Political Weekly*, July 9th, pp. 3025-38.

Russel, R V and Hiralal (1916): *Tribes and Castes of the Central Provinces of India, Vol-III, London.*

Sahoo, Bijaya Laxmi (2009): "*Mapping the Nutritional Status of Tribal Communities in Khandwa and Burhanpur Districts of Madhya Pradesh*", AKRSP(I): Khandwa.

# Index


**A**

A. Maitra 273
A.M. Shah 274
AAD 68
Abhishek 34
Abhiskeh Das 167
Achyut Yagnik 186
AD Shroff 55
Adivasis 25, 28
Afra Bay 122
AFSPA 94
AGERAC 196
Ahmedabad Merchants Association 186
Ahmed-I 179
AIMS 71
Ajay Gudavarty 89
Ajay Saini 117
Ajay's paper 32, 34
Akbar 179
AKRSP 292, 293, 294, 295
ALBA 100
ALBA 100
Almatti Dam 218
Amartya Sen 228
America 78
American Civil War 49
American War of Independence 18
Amit Choudhury 135
Ammu 269
Amnesty International 230
Anand Kaushalyaran 190
Anand Teltumbde 32, 47
Andhra Pradesh 284
Andhra Pradesh 33, 101, 145, 231, 232, 284
Andhra Pradesh 92, 101
Annihilation of Caste 42
Antyaja 178
Anup K. Karan 65
Aparna 245, 246
Apastamba Dharmasutra 244
APL 290
APRS 141
Ardeshir Dalal 55
Arjun Dangle 261, 266
Arundhati Roy 261, 268
Arvind Acharya 172
ASER 146
Asho 274
Assam 280, 281
Assam 35
Atisudra 178
Augustina 211
Augusto Pinochet 49
Avarna 178
Avinash's paper 33
Aymara 163
Ayyan Mani 169, 172

**B**

B.K. Nagla 26
B.K. Roy Burman 271
B.R. Ambedkar 18, 23, 27, 31, 39, 40, 41, 42, 44, 45, 46, 52, 55, 71, 167, 176, 177, 178, 189, 190, 198
Babri Masjid 78
Baburao Bagul 260
Bagh Dev 275
Bakha 262, 263, 265
Bandhini 179
Bandhu Madhav 260

Bangladesh 105, 109, 110, 111, 114
Barela 292
Basuto People 112
Baum's Formulation 47
Bhadarva 274
Bhaiyasahed 191
Bhakra Nangal Dam 218
Bhakti Movement 26, 27
Bhambi 181, 182
Bhangi 181, 182, 184, 187
Bharat Vijay Mill 192
Bharati 145
Bharuch 189
Bhikya 220
Bhil 292
Bhilala 292
Bihar 280, 281, 284
Bijaya Kumar Mohanty 239
Bijaya Kumar Mohanty 35
Bijinepaily Mandal 217
Bishop A.C. Lal 260
Bodo 163
Bombay Plan 55
Boudhjan Samiti 190
Boya Narayan 222
BPL 251, 252, 276, 277, 290
Brahmins 184
Brundtlard Report 98
Bruthiaux 113
Brutt-Griffler 105, 111, 113, 114
Buddha 41, 42
Buddhist Vihar 191
Budh Jayanti 190
Burkett 60

C

C.K. Riessman 244
Carothers 93
CEDAW 89
CEDAW 91
Ceylon 112
Ceylon Mahabodhi 190
Chakrapani 217
Chamars 184, 268
Chandi 120, 121
Chandola 178
Chandra Gupta Maurya 179
Chandravilash 191
Charat Singh 263
Chennai 280
Chhattisgarh 231, 232, 280
Chhotalal Mill 192
Chicago boys 49
Chima 275
China 62, 77
China 77
Chinna Boddanna 219
Chittagong 110
Chuhra 266
CIA 49
Ckakma 111
Cocacolisation 80
Communist Manifesto 48
Copra 123
Copra 123
Cranston 92

D

Dadra and Nagar Haveli 284
Dalit 17, 23-32, 35, 51, 58, 69, 82, 168, 170, 185, 188, 189, 198, 259, 260
Dalit Panthers 177
David Hardiman 273, 274
David Ricardo 59
David Rosnick 60
Dean Baker 60
Deba Ranjan Hota 271
Debrajan Hota 35
Delhi 279, 280, 281, 282
Delhi 34
Derek Layder 242
Development Debate 225
Dhana Balu 189
Dharampur 276
Dhdasahed Gayakwad 191
Dhirubhai Ambani 56
Dilli Vali 284
Directive Principles 44
Directive Principles of State Policy 27
Directive Principles of State Policy 27

Domestic Violence Act 101
Donnelly 95
Double Victimisation 239
DPEP 135
DPR 293
DPSP 208, 214
Dr Avinash Pandey 155
Dr P.G. Jyotirkar 191
Dr Venkatesh Nayak 205
Dungar Mauli 274
Durban Conference 92

**E**

E.M. Forster 262
East India Company 180
EBBs 139
Edalji 180
EFA 134, 137
English Revolution 18
Escobar 99
Even Todaro 206

**F**

Fa-Hien 172
Fakirbhai Vaghela 197
FAO 250
FDI 70
Fishman 114
French Revolution, 19
Fundamental Rights 26

**G**

G. Raja kumari 145
Gaby Weiner 135
Garoda 181, 182
GATS 68
GATT 69, 70
GD Birla 55
GDP 60, 64, 70
GDP 64, 70, 75
Ghanshyam Shah 27
Glele-Ahanhanzo 79
Globalisation 53, 54, 61, 78, 79, 80, 158, 159, 160
Godelier 171
Gonda 287, 292
Gopal Guru 21
Gopia 220
Gould 95, 96
Govind shamji parmar 192
Govindji R. Parmar 190
Gram Devi 274, 275
Grin 113
Gudavarthy 100
Gudavarthy 94
Gujarat 179, 180, 182, 183, 189, 193
Gujarat 29, 35, 175, 179, 180, 182- 187, 189, 191, 192, 193, 196, 198, 199
Gujarat High Court 194
Gulabo 263, 266
Gupta 97
Gurjar 187, 191, 192, 197, 198
Guru 177

**H**

Haribhai 188
Harijan 178
Harijan Temple Entry Law 193
Hecksher-Ohlin theory 59
Held and McGrew 48
Himai Dev 275
Hindu 190, 193
Hindutva 81, 82
Hinglish 160
Hira Bhogal 186
Hirakud 218
Hodi 126
Homo Hierchicus 167
Humayum 109, 111
Humiliation 239, 240
Hussain 114

**I**

ICCPR 89, 91, 93
ICDS 291
ICERD 89, 96, 97
ICESCR 89
ICLU 90
ICT 79
IERD 91
IESCR 91

IFRI 64
IIM 71
IIT 71
ILO 227, 256, 271, 284
IMF 32, 49, 50, 56, 74, 78, 81
IMF 49, 50, 56
IMP 292, 293
India 114
Indian Hindu Family Systems 242
Indira Gandhi 194
Indira Gandhi 50, 56
Indira R 135
Iniquitous 183
Iswar Chandra Vidya sagar 135

**J**

Jagannathan Begari, 17
Jaganntham 177
Jaisukhlal Halhi 194
Jajmani 56
Jan Morcha 197
Janmejaya Mishra 287
Janmejaya Mishra 36
Jari 179
Jayamma 221
Jean Dreze 31
Jean Dreze 39
Jeremy Bentham 207
Jesus and Mary 282
Jethabhai 188
Jharkhand 34, 35, 231, 232, 280, 281
Jholawala Doctors 277
Jikli Powar 276, 277
Joaguin 206
Johan Galtung 239
John Matthai 55
Joothan 266
Joshi 91
JRD Tata 55
Justin 117
JVC 67

**K**

K. Aswani 145
K. Manasa 144
K. Marx 208
K. Singh 273
Kadi 193
Kalol 192, 193
Kanaiyalal Munshi 188
Kanbi 184
Kant 91
Kanthapura 268
Karl Marx 18, 41, 48, 207, 208
Karl Marx 48
Karnataka 219, 231, 284
Karuna Chanana 135
Kashiya Deva 189
Kasturba Gandhi 33, 139
Kathis 184
Kaul and Dilwali 118
KBK 251
Kennedy 185
Keshavji Ranshodji Vaghela 192
Keynesianism 53, 56
KGBV 135, 139, 140, 141, 143, 145, 147, 148, 150, 151, 152
KGBV 33, 139, 140, 141, 150, 151, 152
Khasi 111
Kheda 189
Kheda 194
Klaus Holzkamp 240, 241
Kokna 271- 275
Kolis 184
Korku tribe 287, 288, 289, 292, 295
Korku Tribe 36
Kotha 192
Kothari Commission 72
Krauss 106
Krishna River 218
KRRS 74
Kshantipulo 190
Kukreja 284
Kulupur 193
Kumar Gupta-I 179
Kutia Kondha 253

**L**

Lakha 262
Lambada Tribal 220

Langhorne 47
Langia Saura 253
Laxmaiah 221
Laxmivilash Hotel 191
Lechte 47
Lesotho 111, 112
LHR 106, 108
Lokean Rights Theory 207
Louis Dumont 167
LPP 111, 114
LTTE 120

**M**

M.B. Gaijan 35
M.K. Gandhi 186
M.N. Srinivas 243
Madhya Pradesh 231, 287, 289, 292, 294
Madhya Pradesh 36, 231
Magna Karta, 18
Mahabodhi Amedkar Mission 191
Mahabub Nagar 216, 217, 218
Mahals 180
Maharashtra 157, 161
Mahasthivar Chanramani 190
Mahatma Gandhi 135, 178
Mahatma Gandhi 33, 139
Mahya 186
Mahyavansi 182, 188
Majdoor Mahajan 198
Maka Chua 123, 126
Makanji Kuber Makawana 187
Makawana 178, 187, 188, 189, 191, 192
Malwa 179
Mammachi 269
Mangoloid 118
Mani 176
Manmohan Singh 50
Manu 81
Manu Joseph 168
Manusmriti 244
Maphatiya Nana 189
Mapuche 163
Marathy 33
Marenna 220
Marginality 22, 23
Mark Martinez 61
Mark Weisbrot 60
Marma 111
Marshall McLuhan 47
Martin Hart-Landsberg 60
Martin Macwan 185
Martin Makwan 29
May 112, 113
Mc Donaldisation 80
MCH 221
Megawat Sajani 220
Megha Shree 282
Meghalaya 231
Meghval 181, 182
Mehsana 194, 195
Mehta 119
MERCOSUR 100
MERCOSUR 100
Merkist Jargan 215
MFP 255
MGNREGA 123, 124
MGNREGA 292, 293
Michael 177, 178
Michael Mann 48
MICS 134
Ministry of Human Resource Development 42
Mizoram 281
Mlechha 178
MNC 79
Mohanbhai Durgabhai Parmar 192
Mohanty 27, 28, 30, 35
Moorthy 268
Mr Drew 192
MS Sunita 279
MTM 106, 107, 108
Mughel 179
Muljibhai Vaishya 193
Mulk Raj Anand 261, 262, 266
Mumbai 280
Mumbai 80
Munda tribes 287
Mundari 111

Munshi Prem Chand 261, 268
Murli Manohar Joshi 42

**N**

NABARD 293, 294
Nadia 181, 182
Nadiya 189
Nadiyad 192
Nagaraju 33
Nagaraju Gundemeda 135
Nagarjuna Sagar Dam 218
Naran Vora 198
Naranappe 268
Narashiah Mehta 186
Narashiah Mehta 186
Narashimha Rao 50, 56
Narmada Dam 218
National Minimum Wages Act 284
Navji Bhai Chima 274, 275, 276
Navjivan Mill 192
Nawa 274
NCDHR 96
NDA 64
Neera Chandhoke 229
Neha Wadhwan 281, 282, 283
Neo-fascism 79
Neo-Nazism 79
NEP 30
Nepal 114
New Chingenh Bosti 122, 123, 126
New Economic Policy 225
NFHS 64
NGO 200
NHRC 219
Nicobar Islands 117, 122
Nicobarese 121-126, 128, 129
Nicobarese 34
Ningthoujam 279
Nishada 178
Nitin Patel 198, 199
Noam Chomsky 39
NPEGEL 139
NSS 63, 65
NSSO 280
NTFP 252
Nussbaum 95

**O**

OBCs 25, 195
Odisha 34, 231, 249, 251, 281
Okin 96
Om Prakash Valmiki 261, 263, 267
Om Sai 282
On Doing Psychology Critically 240

**P**

P. Sudharani 144
P.M. Patel 274
Padma Velaskar 135
Pakistan 114
Palamur Labour 216, 221, 223
Panchama 178
Panchaseet Triharan 190
Paraganas 180
Parekh 96
Partha Chatterjee 24
Patel Community 184
Patel Heena L. 259
Patels 180, 187
Patia 123
Patola 179
PCLU 219
PDS 251, 290
PDS 63
Pennycook 113
Periyar, 18
Petlad 193
PHC 276, 277
Phule, 18
Pigeon pea (tuar) 290
PIL 90
Pinglish 160
Pondicherry 231
Poona 189
POSCO 227, 231
POTA 94, 95
Prabhat Patnaik 57
Praveen Kachhap 35
Prithviraj Rao 188

Priya Namrata 35
PROBE 146
PSU 67
Pulo Panja 123
Pulobha 123
Puloulo 123
Punnayya Committee 66
Puritan Revolution 18

**Q**

Quechua 163

**R**

R. Malhotra 273
R.S. Negi 273
Radio Hotel 191
Rahul Rai 209
Raja Dhale 198
Raja Ram Mohan Roy 135
Raja Rao 261, 268
Rajadarshini Patra 249
Rajasthan 284
Rajiv Gandhi 31, 56
Rajiv Nagar 122, 123, 126
Rajni Kothari 30
Rajputs 179
Rajputs 184
Ram 178
Rameshchandra Parmar 198
Raoof Ahmad Lone 36
Ratna Sudershan 135
Rawat 137
Reddy and Patnaik 101
Reform Movement 26
Resettlement Rehabilitation (R&R) 231
Right to Development (RD) 98, 99, 100
Right to Development 33
Right to Development 33
Right to Employment guarantee Act 29
Right to Food Security Act 29
Right to Information Act 29
Rights of Man 207
RMRC 253
Rodrigues 22
Roland Robertson 47
RPL 198
RTE 164
RTE 72, 73, 164

**S**

S. Parasuraman 129
S. Rana 194, 195, 196
S.K. Mandal 273
S.K. Sasikumar 65
S.K. Thorat 178
S.K. Thorat 21
Sadhana Saxena 135
Sadhu Shri Muldas 190
Saini 118, 119
Sakas 179
Samata 27
Sambarda Swaman Jyoti 197
Samrasta 27
Sankarvijay hotel 191
Sarada Lahangir 249
Sarangapani Padma 135
Sardar Sarovar Project 218
Sarkars 180
Sarva Shikhya Abhiyan 138
Satpura ranges 287
Satyagraha 189
Satyakam Joshi 274
Sayajirao Gayakwad 186
Sayajirao Gayakwad 186
SCALE 292
Schirato and Webb 47
Scott 99
Scythians 179
Seeta Sharma 284
Sen 92, 99, 100
Senva 181, 182
SEPED 253
Seth 97
SEZ 74
Shakarbhai Prembhai Sonar 195
Shalini Randeria 274
Shankarao Kharat 260
Sheelaiah 221
Sheikh Rajiv Ullah 225

Shidhraj Solanki 186
Shidhraj Solanki 186
Shiv Sena 80
Shri Dharma Bandhu 190
Shri Krishna Sharma 191
Shri Premdas Sadhu 191
Shri Sanghrakshit 190
Shudra 268
Siddharaj 186
SIL 90
Silava 120
Silent Revolution 26
Silva 120
Simpson and Corbridge 119
Singh 90, 118, 121
Singh and Uberoi 244
Sinha Shanta 135
Skutnabb-kangas 105-108, 114
Social Darwinism 52, 53
Sonis 184
Sophie Mol 269
Sorghum 290
Soviet union 45
Sri Lanka 107
Sri Lanka 111
SSA 135
Stany Pinto 273
Stopler-Samuleson theory 59
Sukhdeo Thorat 169
Sukka 267
Suneetha 101
Surati Khaman house 192
Suresh Canagarajah 107
Surinder Jaswal 129
Susheelamma 222
Suthars 184
Swaminarayan Temple 193, 198
Swaminathan Committee 66
Swamy 221

**T**

TADA 94
Tamil Nadu 231
Tania Hossain 105
Tania Hossain 105
Tapan Basu 170
Tapti river 287
TATA 227
Teltumbde 98
Tenjo Waten Abe 19
TESUL 161
Thakordas 187
Thomas Paine 207
Thomas Paine 207
Thompson 93
Thorat 96, 99
TINA 50, 209
Tiruvalvur26
TISCO 231
TISS 129
TNC 50, 79
TOEFL 161
Tollefson 108, 111, 113, 114
Tollefson 114
Tomasevki 108
Tove Skutanbb-Kangas 106, 107, 108
Toward Equality 136
TPDS 251, 252
Trawick 243, 244
Tribals 17, 18, 23, 26, 36
Tuhet 126

**U**

U.P. Ananthmurthy 261, 268
U.R. Ananth Murthy 162
UDHR 208, 212
UDHR 26, 89, 90, 91, 95, 208, 212
UN General Assembly 79
UNCTAD 48
UNDP 253, 281, 283
UNESCO 134, 136, 163
UNICEF 133, 228
UNICEF 68
United Kingdom 49
United Nations 78
United States of America 49
Universal Declaration of Human Right 249, 250
Universal declaration of Human Rights 19

Unnikrishnan 72
UNO 19
Upendra Baxi 210
USA 79
Ushaben Bhalchandra 195
USSR 157, 209
USSR 55
Uttamkumar Deb 217

**V**

V.V. Giri Nation Labour Institute, 65
Vadil 276
Valands 184
Valitha 269
Vanias 184
Vankar 184, 187
Varli 271-273
Varna 178
Varna Pratha 261
Vedas 178
Velutha 268, 269
Venkatesh Nayak 35
Verma 176
Vibha Singh 279
Vibha Singh 34
Vienna Declaration, 19
Vijay Kumar 217
Vimala Ramachandran 135
Vincent 89
Vir Megh Maya 186
Vir Megh Maya 186
Viramgam 192
Vivek Nanda 190
Volmik Community 189
VRS 67

**W**

WCAR 96
WCAR 96
West Bengal 231
WHO 68
World Bank 32, 49, 56, 81, 133, 136
WTO 32, 70, 74, 78, 81
WTO 70
Yogesh N. Vansiya 259